# Fashion Public Relations

*fb*

# Fashion Public Relations

**Gerald J. Sherman and Sar S. Perlman**

Sherman & Perlman LLC, Public Relations & Integrated Marketing

**Fairchild Books**

New York

Executive Editor: Olga T. Kontzias

Assistant Acquisitions Editor: Amanda Breccia

Editorial Development Director: Jennifer Crane

Development Editor: Rob Phelps

Art Director: Erin Fitzsimmons

Production Director: Ginger Hillman

Associate Production Editor: Andrew Fargnoli

Copy Editor: Susan Hobbs

Cover and Text Designs: Tronvig Group

Cover Art: Courtesy of Fairchild Publications, Inc.

Library of Congress Catalog Card Number: 2009920408

ISBN: 978-1-56367-775-5

GST R 133004424

Printed in the United States of America

CH16, TP09

*To those I love most and who make my life worthwhile: my darling ever-loving wife Jacqueline; my three beautiful daughters Ilene Meg Appleton, Taylor Thunderhawk Whitney, and Valerie Sherman Frankel; my wonderful grandchildren Garrett, Douglas, Courtney, Brittany, and Brandon. A special thanks and note of appreciation to my friend, business partner, and coauthor, Sar S. Perlman.* —GJS

*To my wife Tamara, my parents, and my sister Shelly, for their unending love and support. And to my coauthor, Gerald J. Sherman, for his advice, patience, and encouragement.* —SSP

# Contents

# Extended Contents

XVII

# Preface

The fashion and lifestyle industries are highly influenced by public opinion. Consumer perceptions—not only of styles, colors, and designs, but also of the company, its brands, and business practices—can propel a company to the pinnacle or tumble it down into the lowest gutter. Public sentiment—what consumers think and feel—is the key to unlocking the emotional factors that shape trends and style preferences, as well as purchasing decisions, brand loyalty, and word-of-mouth recommendations. Public relations is the field that allows the company to decipher public sentiment and take proactive and effective steps toward creating a more favorable view of the company and its brands.

For a company to succeed in today's highly competitive fashion and lifestyle environments, it is essential to implement public relations campaigns that spread a positive word about its products through the media, word of mouth, and the Internet. The fast-paced and fluid realm of fashion public relations is far from theoretical. It is about being in touch with the company's audiences, creating strong relationships with them, reaching out to the media, initiating messages that project positive images of the company, assuming social responsibility, and even adjusting company policies.

In writing *Fashion Public Relations,* we've adopted a real-world, nuts-and-bolts approach to this incredibly important subject, giving students the opportunity to establish a foundation for a successful career in this field, as well as a perspective of the actual scenarios they will face in the daily operations within a public relations department.

With more than 25 years of experience, my (Gerald J. Sherman) background includes serving as vice president for several multi-million-dollar apparel corporations and owning a successful fashion apparel company. I've also been a consultant in the industry and taught seminars and classes both nationally and internationally. After working in the fashion industry and also as an adjunct professor at a number of institutions—Fashion Institute of Technology, New York; Lynn University, Boca Raton, Florida; Miami International University of Art and Design, Miami, Florida; and Johnson & Wales University, College of Business, North Miami, Florida—I've learned that students need to understand real-world, practical approaches to fashion public relations that prepare them for a successful career and minimize trial and error once they start working. Sar Perlman—my coauthor and business partner in Sherman & Perlman Public Relations LLC—and I have striven to make this textbook as realistic and functional as possible while still imparting the academic elements necessary to grasp the fundamentals of the subject. To illustrate the essential and often complex facets of successful fashion public relations, we have not only relied upon our own knowledge, experience, and success, but have also included numerous real-life case studies and interviews with high-caliber leaders in the fashion and public relations business worlds, such as the organizers of the New York Fashion Week and the president of Perry Ellis International, Inc.

Public relations executives and personnel serve many vital roles within the fashion industry. The comprehension and proper use of public relations methodology, media and community relations strategies, and management approaches are the base upon which a successful career in fashion public relations is built, and we hope this textbook will help set you on your way to achieving that success.

The objective of this book is to prepare you to become leaders in national and international fashion public relations, and to have you become major contributors to the fashion field. It provides you with a real world understanding of the day-to-day workings of public relations as it relates to the fashion industry. It is based on actual experiences with real world results. The case studies and other information will be invaluable to you as you pursue a career in the fashion industry. This book is packed with practical information.

# Acknowledgments

We would like to thank Olga T. Kontzias, executive editor, for helping us formulate the content of this book and for her encouragement and confidence in us. She shared with us her vision and advice for this textbook, and we feel fortunate for having had the opportunity to work with her.

A special thanks goes to Robert Phelps, our development editor, who has done a superb job editing our work while maintaining the integrity of our message. His guidance was instrumental to the creation of this textbook while his assistance was invaluable to its completion. He was always available for advice, and we could depend upon his sound judgment in the decisions we had to make to bring the textbook to fruition.

We would also like to extend our thanks to the publishing staff at Fairchild Books for their outstanding efforts and assistance in research, editing, production, and marketing: Jennifer Crane, editorial development director; Erin Fitzsimmons, associate art director; Andrew Fargnoli, associate production editor; Ginger Hillman, production director; Amanda Breccia, associate acquisitions editor; and Max Wastler, assistant development editor.

Many thanks as well to those who have generously given their time, experience, and wisdom to provide us with real-life information for the case studies: Edy Eliza, vice president of Pierce Mattie Public Relations; Oscar Feldenkreis, president and chief operating officer of Perry Ellis International, Inc.; Rod Stafford Hagwood, fashion columnist at the Fort Lauderdale, Florida-based *Sun-Sentinel* newspaper and The CW television affiliate; Daris Jasper, art director of Artistic Jeanius; Alison Levy, public relations manager at IMG Fashion;

Brian Q. Smith, executive vice president of eNR Services, Inc.; Carrie Englert Zimmerman, cofounder of The Zimmerman Agency; and their staff. Also we wish to thank the following reviewers for the publisher, who were very helpful in their suggestions: Deb Meyer, Kansas State University; Jan Haynes, Delta State University; Denise Wheat, IADT, Nashville; Kristen Regine, Johnson & Wales University, Providence; Elisabeth Hinckley, FIDM, Orange County; Lisa Amans, Art Institute of Washington; Phyllis Greensley, Illinois Institute of Art; Noreen Nackenson, Nassau Community College; and Amanda Lovell, Lehigh Valley College.

Finally, we would like to give our heartfelt thanks to the professors and instructors who have chosen to include this textbook in their classes, and to the students who have taken the text's concepts and principles to heart.

Gerald J. Sherman

Sar S. Perlman

# Public Relations Fundamentals

# PART I

# The Real World of Fashion Public Relations

## ONE

## Chapter Snapshot

The fashion industry is driven by wants as much as by needs. By definition, fashion always changes according to what's in vogue. What's in vogue is determined in great part by how the consumer views the fashion item. Whereas advertising and marketing techniques can create a want by portraying that item as desirable and cool, it is public relations that shapes the consumer's opinions about the fashion item and the companies that manufacture and sell it. Consumer opinion is a dominant factor in the buying process—if the consumer has never heard of the designer, or for some reason believes the designer's reputation is tarnished, then it is unlikely the consumer will purchase that item. Creating a positive consumer opinion is essential to facilitating consumer sales. Public relations is, therefore, an extremely important management tool that can drastically affect the longevity and future of the company. In this chapter, we will define what constitutes public relations in the fashion field, and why it is so crucial to the enduring success of the fashion company.

## Objectives

▶ Understand what the field of public relations encompasses.

▶ Explore the importance of public opinion for the success of any business, particularly in the world of fashion, accessories, and lifestyle designs.

▶ Discuss the various publics for a fashion company.

▶ Explore how public relations is different from yet connected to advertising.

▶ Gain an overview of the roles public relations plays in the fashion and lifestyle industries.

▶ Recognize the importance of ethical behavior in public relations and the consequences of dishonesty.

In 1996, an online rumor began to circulate via email about the designer Tommy Hilfiger (snopes.com, 2002). It claimed that Hilfiger made racist remarks on the Oprah Winfrey show and that she threw him off the show as a result.

However, according to Winfrey's statement during a 1999 show broadcast, "For the record, the rumored event that has circulated on the Internet and by word-of-mouth never happened. Mr. Hilfiger has never appeared on the show. In fact, Oprah has never even met him" (Oprah.com, 2006). Nonetheless, these rumors have continued to haunt Hilfiger; despite repeated denial statements from the Hilfiger corporate offices, and reports in the media disproving the rumor, they continued to spread to such an extent that most leading urban myths Web sites as well as about.com now list the rumor as an urban myth. In May 2007, more than a decade after the rumor began, Hilfiger finally appeared on *The Oprah Winfrey Show* for the first time to refute the rumor. See Box 1.2 for a transcript of the show.

As per Hilfiger's admission, the rumor cost the company in revenues. According to a Blacks Retail Analysis report, in 2006 the company reported profit losses of 23 percent due to a decline in orders from U.S. department stores (Blacks Retail Analysis, 2006). The company said that it was affected by its exit last year from the young men's denim business, and sluggish sales of its women's wear. What's puzzling is how long the rumor has persisted, and why it took Hilfiger's public relations team a decade to book him on Oprah's show to discredit the rumor. Had the rumor been discredited from the onset,

---

### Box 1.1 Example of the Rumor Email

*(Collected via email, Dec. 1998)*

**Subject: FWD: Tommy Hilfiger hates us . . .**

Did you see the recent Oprah Winfrey show on which Tommy Hilfiger was a guest? Oprah asked Hilfiger if his alleged statements about people of color were true. He's been accused of saying things such as "If I had known that African Americans, Hispanics, and Asians would buy my clothes, I would not have made them so nice," and "I wish those people would not buy my clothes— they were made for upper-class whites." What did he say when Oprah asked him if he said these things? He said "Yes." Oprah immediately asked Hilfiger to leave her show.

Now, let's give Hilfiger what he's asked for—let's not buy his clothes. Boycott! Please, pass this message along. (About.com)

FIGURE 1.1 Designer Tommy Hilfiger was not interviewed by Oprah in 1998 as the e-rumor alleged, but his company's image was tarnished nonetheless.

5

## Box 1.2   May 2, 2007, Transcript: The Oprah Winfrey Show Interview with Tommy Hilfiger

**Oprah:** Let's break this down. Tommy, in the 21 years that we've been on the air, have you ever been on the show before today?

**Tommy:** Unfortunately, not.

**Oprah:** And when you first heard it, Tommy, what did you think?

**Tommy:** I didn't believe it. . . . Friends of mine said they heard the rumor. I said, "That's crazy. That can't be. I was never on *The Oprah Winfrey Show.* I would never say that." And all my friends and family who know me and people who work with me and people who have grown up with me said that's crazy.

**Oprah:** Well, did you ever say anything close to that? Where do you think this originated?

**Tommy:** I have no idea. We hired FBI agents, I did an investigation, I paid investigators lots of money to go out and investigate, and they traced it back to a college campus but couldn't put their finger on it.

Tommy says his clothing company's intention has always been the exact opposite of what that rumor says. "I wanted to sell a lot of clothes to a lot of people," he says.

"It hurt my integrity, because at the end of the day, that's all you have. And if people are going to challenge my honesty and my integrity and what I am as a person, it hurts more than anything else," he says. "Forget the money that it has cost me."

Not only is he a fashion icon, Tommy is also the founder of a summer camp for inner city children and one of the driving forces behind the Martin Luther King Jr. Memorial Fund—a group dedicated to creating a monument to the slain civil rights leader in Washington, D.C. They're holding a fundraising concert on September 18, 2007, in New York City.

"The next time somebody sends you an email or somebody mentions this rumor to you, you know what you're supposed say to them?" Oprah says. "You're supposed to say, 'That's a big fat lie'" (Oprah.com, 2007).

perhaps it wouldn't have mushroomed into the headline-making myth that it has become.

Hilfiger's case is a perfect illustration of the sheer power of public opinion and word of mouth. When the **public** forms an opinion about a company—whether one based on facts or lies—this opinion can sway sentiment for or against that company not only for one individual, but also for that individual's family and friends. Such far-reaching changes in sentiment can send strong ripple effects through the marketplace that may even lead to the company's demise. **Public relations** is the field that addresses such public opinion crises and also develops positive public sentiments.

## The Real World of Fashion Public Relations

A picture is worth a thousand words; this is very evident in the fashion industry. In the real world of the fashion industry, the picture is painted in our minds by the media announcing a new collection, when we view a dynamic fashion show, through interviews with leading fashion designers, and when public figures are seen wearing well-known designers' clothing. To gain consumer acceptance, public relations plays a vital role in delivering a fashion message to sophisticated consumers.

In many cases, the fact that a famous celebrity is seen donning a specific label or styled clothing sets off a fashion trend that other people try to emulate.

FIGURE 1.2 Seeing photographs of fashion models on the catwalk is a primary step for consumer acceptance of new collections.

**Box 1.3   Real World Principle: Promoting Trends and Styles**

Unique to the fashion world, public relations has a secondary role, which is to spearhead new trends and styles. In addition to the fundamental role of improving the public image of the company's brands, which is public relations' main role for all businesses, public relations in fashion has the potential and vehicles to promote new trends in fashion design and make these trends seem desirable to consumers through positive coverage in the media.

Photos of actors, musicians, and designers at charity events make up another area where public relations gets the fashion message across. The message that public relations delivers is subtle yet quite effective; we love to identify with successful people and celebrity stories that appear in the media, whether in newspapers, magazines, television, or the Internet. All of these images shape our fashion sense consciously as well as subconsciously. Fashion is an industry dominated by image. The clothes we wear cover the majority of our body; therefore, what we slip on is an important part of the image we project to society. To be admired socially, one might wear upscale clothing that others can recognize as expensive. To look cool, one might wear hip and emerging styles. To be conservative, one sticks to classic and traditional colors and outfits.

FIGURE 1.3 When people think of style, they look to celebrities for direction.

7

Virtually every fashion publication reviews new collections before each season. Whether a new collection is reviewed and how well that collection is received by the media can have significant effects over the success of the collection for that season. For example, in July 2007, Style.com covered the runway shows for Armani Privé, Chanel, Christian Dior, Christian Lacroix, Elie Saab, Givenchy, Jean Paul Gaultier, and Valentino, and reviewed their collections on the front page of its Fall 2007 Couture story; this gave these collections extra, cost-free exposure.

Fashion forecasts are vital to the success of new collections. Through reputable media commentaries, we find that consumers are motivated to adapt the look. Whereas advertising directs the sale, public relations creates the aura.

Because the main thrust of public relations is the company's image in the minds of the public, it is vital to understand the complex, behind-the-scene factors that interact to mold public opinion. The image that the company or brand strives to build, the image that the media paints of the company, and the image that society itself thrusts upon the company, all mesh together and shape the composite image of the brand.

Public relations is the link between the fashion company and all media outlets, generating positive **publicity** with local, regional, national, and international media outlets, trade publications, and the Internet. The objective of

**FIGURE 1.4** Most fashion publications issue a season's preview with highlights and reviews of the new collections.

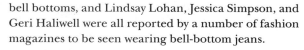

## Box 1.4   Real World Story: Celebrity Trendsetters

To illustrate the power of the media and public opinion in shaping fashion trends, let's look at some examples from fashion history. Perhaps the most memorable fashion trend set by former First Lady Jacqueline Kennedy was the pillbox hat, which got its odd name because it looked as if it was designed to hold pills. Although it has been in existence since the 1930s, it wasn't until Mrs. Kennedy was seen wearing it that the hat earned its claim to fame. Even though Mrs. Kennedy wasn't the first First Lady to wear one—the First Lady of Mexico had been wearing it for more than a year before her—the hat never caught on until Mrs. Kennedy made it look chic. But in 1963, wearing the hat became virtually a taboo following the coverage of President Kennedy's assassination. Photographs of Mrs. Kennedy cradling the President's head in her lap after he was shot, showed her wearing a pink pillbox hat, which sealed the hat's doom.

When celebrities like James Brown, Elvis Presley, and Cher were seen wearing bell-bottom pants, it soon became a trend in the early 1960s. The trend waned in the 1970s, but came back in the late 1990s following media coverage of celebrities wearing modern-day bell bottoms. In early 2007, Jennifer Lopez was seen wearing a pair of second-skin silver bell bottoms, and Lindsay Lohan, Jessica Simpson, and Geri Haliwell were all reported by a number of fashion magazines to be seen wearing bell-bottom jeans.

FIGURE BOX 1.4A

The pillbox hat became popular when Jackie Kennedy began donning it; however, the hat was virtually shunned after President John F. Kennedy was assassinated.

FIGURE BOX 1.4B AND C

The 1960s bell-bottoms trend (left) was resurrected in 2007 (right) when celebrities were seen wearing modern-day bell-bottom designs.

public relations is to establish the company's trustworthiness and brand distinctiveness. A successful public relations activity presents a steady flow of favorable stories for the media and delivers extra clout to the product. The proper public relations mix of print, television, radio, and Internet makes the story more acceptable and helps the target market retain the company's corporate message more readily. Public relations also underscores the activities of advertising and promotion because positive exposure in the media reinforces the messages broadcast in the company's advertisements. When a fashion business is aiming to enter new markets or new segments of existing markets, public relations can help gain a foothold by reproducing the published media stories in its promotional communications such as direct mail campaigns, flyers, brochures, and on the company's Web site. The use of these stories enhances credibility and helps to create name recognition.

## Box 1.5  Real World Concept: A Partnership for Success

Which comes first, public relations or advertising? In the real world, there is no chicken or egg when it comes to the two. Advertising and public relations must co-exist and coordinate in order to leverage the maximum benefits for the company's promotional efforts. If a company launches a new line, public relations must reach the media with the news while advertising reaches the various publics directly through the appropriate advertising methods. Although the two can exist without the other, an advertisement campaign without public relations will likely produce less bang for the buck, and vice versa. Ideally, the two fields should work together hand in hand to achieve the common goals, and the messages communicated by the public relations spokespeople and the messages communicated by the advertisements and commercials should be integrated and coordinated so the publics are reached with a unified positive image.

## Fundamental Terms

Before we delve into the nitty-gritty of public relations in the fashion industry, it is vital to understand some of the basic terms in this rapidly expanding field.

Who are the company's publics, for example? One sub-classification of a fashion manufacturer's consumer publics, for example, may be along household incomes, such as high-end customers, middle-income customers, and mass-market customers. Each of these subgroups requires a different type of approach from the company's public relations office. High-end customers, for instance, read high-society magazines, and so public relations efforts here may focus on getting the brand associated with a polo tournament or perhaps a fundraising gala. In contrast, efforts to entice the middle-income customers to the brand may need to focus on getting the new line featured on one of the national news channels' fashion reports, whereas for the mass-market the focus may require a celebrity endorsement. For example, Nike Inc., based in Beaverton, Oregon, is an international leading designer and marketer of authentic athletic footwear, apparel, equipment, and accessories for a wide variety of sports and fitness activities. NikeGO is the company's signature U.S. **community affairs** initiative built upon a long-term commitment to get kids to become more physically active. The project is a testament to the company's efforts to develop a stronger bond with its middle-aged, family-oriented public group, i.e., the parents who make the purchasing decisions.

A fashion company should not attempt to cater to every customer subgroup, but instead should work to clearly identify the various subgroups that comprise the company's consumer body. For a manufacturer that specializes in high-end items only, obtaining a celebrity endorsement may be a waste of valuable time and funds. Whereas a manufacturer that only produces mass-market items may not benefit from involvement in fundraisers. As you can see, the public relations strategies vary greatly depending on the company's publics, and identifying these publics is a vital pillar in a sound public relations campaign. We will discuss this topic in further detail in Chapter 3.

**FIGURE 1.5** A fashion company's public is not limited to consumers. Government regulators, board members, employees, stockholders, suppliers, and members of the media are all part of it as well.

## Public Relations vs. Advertising and Promotion

What separates public relations from advertisement or promotion? All three disciplines shape the consumer's opinion of the company or brand; however, they go about achieving that result in different ways. Public relations is primarily charged with shaping consumer opinion through the development of unpaid media exposure opportunities. In other words, public relations aims to get media coverage about the company or its brand without compensation. We all know how much money companies invest in advertising, and as a result today's average consumer becomes desensitized due to the overwhelming number of advertisements that bombard him or her daily. When the consumer wants unbiased information about the company or product, he or she turns to the media or fellow consumers—people who do not have a stake in the consumer's purchasing decision.

### Sources of Unbiased Information

In the United States, the media enjoys virtually limitless freedom of speech as guaranteed by the Constitution. Because it is not government sponsored, the media is free to report whatever it deems appropriate as long as it keeps within legal and ethical boundaries. Citizens trust the media to report the truth, or at the very least, to expose lies. Investigative reporting and exposés earn a newspaper or television station prestige and increase its audience base. When a reporter does a story on a clothing brand, the audience trusts the reporter to report objectively about that brand and provide any facts that might be of concern to the consumer. A good review by a reporter holds a tremendous amount of weight in the audience's minds.

Fellow consumers constitute an additional source of feedback (word of mouth) for the consumer. The closer these consumers are to the potential buyer, the more strongly he or she will believe their opinions about that product. If your brother or sister tells you they disliked a particular shoe brand because it was uncomfortable, you will likely be suspicious of that brand in the future. In contrast, if a friend of a friend tells you she doesn't like that shoe brand, you might or might not heed her warning because you don't know her that well and are not sure whether to trust her judgment. Such sources of unbiased information are what we are concerned with in public relations. Because these sources typically cannot be bought, advertising cannot enlist them onto the advertising campaign (otherwise advertising would do just that!) and thus these sources remain in a zone of influence that the company cannot control—without an effective public relations campaign, that is. For example, today grassroots public relations strategies can tap into this zone of word-of-mouth sources thanks to the overwhelming popularity of social networking Web sites such as Facebook, LinkedIn, Twitter, Plaxo, Blogger, and YouTube. Fashion companies are increasingly recruiting Web users to help spread their messages by rewarding spontaneous reviews and mentions of their products in blogs and online videos.

Public relations aims to control the image projected in the media and community as well. What the media says about the company and what the community at large thinks about the company are both concerns for the public relations executive. Through the development of various strategies, which we will discuss in depth later in the book, the public relations executive seeks to create a positive image for the company by repeatedly having its name and brand talked about in the media within a positive context. The end result is an overall favorable image that remains in a recess of the consumer's mind. When the consumer debates whether to purchase the company's product, this favorable impression will tend to facilitate a sale. When the consumer faces a decision between the company and its competitor, however, the consumer will likely purchase the product of the company that has the most favorable image. Therefore it is not sufficient to simply generate positive exposure in a situation where competitors are generating it as well; in this case, public relations results must be evaluated in juxtaposition with the results of competitors within the context of the marketplace.

## Image Advertisements and Calls to Action

The nonbiased approach of public relations is much different from the modus operandi of the advertising executive. He or she is looking to project—through advertisements in print, broadcast, and other media—a message that will prompt consumers to buy. Advertising efforts all lead in an unabashed and direct manner toward driving business into the store or prompting consumers to buy a specific product.

Advertisements can roughly be divided into two categories: the **image advertisement,** and the **call-to-action advertisement.** The image campaign places ads that create brand recognition. What these ads do is essentially inform the consumer of the existence of the brand and what type of fashion it stands for. Image ads are typically vague in their nature, and their aim is primarily to make the brand name known, as well as to attach a certain emotion to it. For example, if Ralph Lauren places an ad with a male model wearing a high-end wool suit standing outside a Wall Street firm headquarters, this ad reminds the viewer of Ralph Lauren as a brand and at the same time tells the viewer Ralph Lauren suits are for high-caliber executives. This type of ad is usually placed by the manufacturer and high fashion design firms. Image ads are best communicated to the consumer in *W, Vogue, Men's Vogue*, Style.com, Mens.Style.com and other prestigious fashion magazines. On the other end of the spectrum, the call-to-action advertising campaign has a message that tells the audience what we want them to do. "Buy our brand!," "Come to our store today!," and "Log on to our Web site!" are all calls to action. They lead the audience toward a specific action that is a step in the direction of a sale. This type of ad is usually placed by the retailer.

Of the two, the image campaign is closer to public relation because it is so focused on image. Still, one of its purposes is to generate sales directly from the ad. However, the consumer is aware that these messages are paid ads. Just because Ralph Lauren says his suits are for high-caliber executives doesn't mean the consumer agrees or even listens. Therefore, an image campaign is

13

FIGURE 1.6 Editorial coverage of (a) a fashion item gives it credibility with the consumer. Advertising flanks public relations by creating a want-to-purchase item. The (b) image advertisement promotes brand awareness, while (c) the call-to-action advertisement urges the consumer to come into the store and purchase the item.

14

best flanked by a public relations campaign that elicits media coverage to reinforce the ad's message. If the editor of a leading fashion magazine writes that Ralph Lauren's suits are for the high-caliber executives, many consumers will at least pay attention to it, and there's a good chance they will believe it as well because it comes from an unbiased source. Public relations and image ads work hand in hand to create the brand's image.

The marketing executive, although concerned with the public image, has increasing sales and volume as top goals. Events, fashion shows, giveaways, and other promotion tools all do their part in bringing the consumer closer to a sale. Public relations, however, is a much more subtle field of promotion.

It brings consumers to the brand in a roundabout way. Stories in the media rarely endorse a specific product, or tell people to buy a specific brand. What's much more likely to happen is that the media might mention the brand or store in a positive light. This in effect has much more significance in the consumer's mind than a paid advertisement or a special sale event. That's not to say that advertising and promotion are not necessary or effective; they are, in fact, crucial segments of marketing. However, the efficacy of advertisements and promotional strategies is highly augmented when implemented alongside public relations efforts. A favorable image develops in consumers a receptive frame of mind toward the product, and thus they are more inclined to follow the advertisement's call to action.

## Why Is Public Relations Important?

As can be seen from the example of Tommy Hilfiger, public opinion has a lot to do with a fashion company's success or failure. Specifically, public opinion can directly and subliminally affect the buying habits of the company's potential consumers. If enough consumers share an unfavorable sentiment about the company's image, that sentiment will eventually trickle down the demand chain and cause significant drops in new sales and repeat business. It would

### Box 1.6   Real World Profile: Steven Cojocaru

Celebrity insider and style maven Steven Cojocaru has served as a correspondent for *The Insider* since the television show's inception in fall 2004. Cojocaru provides exclusive interviews with the hottest celebrities while offering his unique perspective on the latest fashions worn by the most-talked-about stars on the red carpet. Cojocaru has interviewed many of the industry's biggest stars, including Oprah Winfrey, Jennifer Lopez, Britney Spears, Halle Berry, Sarah Jessica Parker, Jennifer Aniston, Debra Messing, Hugh Grant, Usher, and Sean Combs. He covers the major red carpet media events, such as the Oscars, the Emmys, the MTV Movie Awards, the Video Music Awards, and the Venice Film Festival. In 2004 Cojocaru began to co-host the CBS primetime television special *Red Carpet Confidential*, focusing on the beauty and style secrets of the stars.

Born in Montreal, Cojocaru's journalism career began covering social parties for the Canadian fashion magazine, *Flare*. In the early 1990s, he moved to Hollywood where he began writing "Hot Shots," a syndicated fashion column that ran in more than 100 newspapers across North America.

Cojocaru was a weekly contributor for four years at NBC's *Today* show and served as *People* magazine's

FIGURE BOX 1.6   Celebrity correspondent Steven Cojocaru.

West Coast Style Editor, where he authored the magazine's popular column "Behind the Seams." He has also appeared in fashion and red carpet specials for *E!* and VH1's *Behind the Music*. In 2003, Cojocaru published his first book, the best seller *Red Carpet Diaries: Confessions of a Glamour Boy*. (theinsider.com, 2008) seem then that all a company had to do was create a positive image and sales would rocket. In the real world, unfortunately, things aren't so simple.

## The Complexity of Public Opinion

First, public opinion cannot be aggregated into one single sentiment. Within the vast public of potential consumers, there may be as many as a dozen or more subgroups, each with its set of ideas of what's right and wrong. For example, a retailer of winter jackets could have, within its general public of potential consumers, one subgroup public that supports animal rights and opposes the production of leather goods, and another subgroup public that supports and demands leather production. Selling leather jackets would offend one group, and yanking leather jackets off the shelves would alienate the other.

Second, public opinion needs to be framed within its context. If a consumer hears a news report that a particular shoe company was accused of condoning sweatshop conditions in its manufacturing plants, the extent of damage to that company's brand image in that consumer's mind could range from disastrous to insignificant, depending on that consumer's interest in global human rights issues. But it would also depend on how the report was presented. If the report originates from a conservative news station, damage to the brand might not amount to much. On the other hand, if the report is broadcast from a liberal news channel, the company's image could approximate that of an evil empire.

There are many complex issues to consider when a company attempts to shape public opinion. We will explore these issues further in Chapter 2. Regardless of how we monitor, gauge, analyze, and shape public opinion, it is important to remember that mastering public opinion is a formidable challenge for any fashion company that seeks to succeed.

## No Image = Bad Image

In today's highly wired world, a fashion company cannot afford to ignore the public opinion of its potential consumers. With blogs, opinion Web sites, and consumer ratings sprouting up practically everywhere, word of mouth spreads like wildfire. If a fashion company doesn't establish and create an image, consumers will happily create one for it. That image, however, may or may not be a positive one.

Let's suppose Restart Couture is a new company just entering the competitive fashion T-shirt market. In this fictitious scenario, the target is the teenage market ages 13 to 19 years old. The company has limited funds and thus decides to spend its money for the initial launch in trade papers and trade magazines. It is not able to obtain any publicity for its product because of its limited resources. Because it feels advertising is too expensive, Restart Couture completely ignores advertising in teenage magazines, such as *Teen Vogue*, *Seventeen*, and *Cosmopolitan*. Its strategy is to sell the stores first and then the stores would reach Restart Couture's target market. The store buyers react favorably to the product because of the value, style, and great colors of the T-shirts. At the retail level, the company discovers that a great many consumers who are not teenagers are buying the product because of the value it offers. The problem is that the consumers are mostly mothers and young career women who recognize the value because similar products in the missy departments are priced much higher. Now it is evident that the manufacturer has a problem; the consumer created the image of a market that was never intended by the maker. The point is that the image is created by the consumer and not the manufacturer. With proper public relations and advertising, there would have been a greater chance of the manufacturer reaching the target market—after all, teenagers do not want to look like their mothers or older sisters. Public relations is a powerful tool that, when used properly and in conjunction with complementary advertising and promotion efforts, allows a company to proactively shape public opinion about its brand.

## Public Relations Myths

There are several myths about fashion public relations that should be explored prior to embarking on studying the subject in depth. A common misconception in public relations is that you can **spin** anything and make even the most irresponsible company or person seem like a hero. Although it may be true on a short-term basis, in most cases truth will unveil in the long run and the person's true colors will be revealed. Truth may not come out for years, or even decades in some cases, but it almost always does. And when it does, the consequences are typically devastating for that person or company. For any fashion company interested in long-term success, it is best to stick to avoiding spin by creating bona fide public relations opportunities that are meaningful in the community and promoting these stories in an accurate and professional manner.

Another concept that could qualify as myth is that "any publicity is good publicity." Although this approach may work for celebrities, who sometimes seem to depend on gossip to keep their name in the news, it doesn't work for fashion companies; perhaps the saying was invented as an excuse by a public relations firm that was unable to handle a crisis. Bad publicity is simply that: bad publicity. Sure, it increases the public's awareness of the brand, but it makes them regard the brand in a negative way. If a negative news story exposed a fashion manufacturer for conning consumers by substituting synthetic leather for real leather, it is doubtful shoppers would descend on retails stores en masse in search of that manufacturer's "leather" goods. Much more likely is that the shoppers would descend on retail stores with their previous purchases in hand for a refund. Negative publicity damages a company's image unless addressed properly. Now, if said manufacturer apologized through the media, offered full refunds to anyone who has bought these "leather" goods, replaced all "leather" with genuine leather, and gave discount coupons for future products, there is a chance consumers will forgive the manufacturer and maybe even be impressed with the company's change of heart. In this case, bad publicity could be turned into positive publicity. Could this mean then that bad publicity is desirable? Although the authors maintain that bad publicity (and especially bad publicity stunts that are created intentionally by the company to attract the media's attention) are likely to backfire with tragic ramifications, there is a school of thought within public relations that would disagree; proponents of that approach would claim that bad publicity can propel a company into the limelight where it would otherwise never have access to. Ultimately, it is up to the fashion company to set the ethical standards for its public relations efforts and define what is acceptable, keeping in mind that setting such standards too loosely could bring about severe negative consequences that the company might never be able to live down. We will discuss this and other proper crisis management strategies and techniques in Chapter 12.

## Integrity in Public Relations

The debate about the merits of bad publicity brings us to a crucial topic in public relations. **Integrity** is of particular importance in public relations because publicly stated lies, white lies, and other forms of twisted truths can potentially result in catastrophic damages to the reputation—and by extension, viability—of the company and its brands.

The top concern for the nongovernment-controlled media in a free society is to report accurately and honestly about issues of public concern. Corruption, wrongdoing, and lies to the public are of special interest to the media. A vicious media frenzy can be sparked if the public relations executive intentionally or inadvertently releases information that is blatantly false. In some cases, as is the case with shareholder reports issued by a public company, such misinformation can lead to legal prosecution and even jail time for the executives involved.

There are many facets to integrity within the realm of public relations: reporting of corporate information, dissemination of corporate information, conducting public relations events, working with community and governmental officials, and dealing with the media. We will discuss in more detail the ethical issues involved with each of these facets in the relevant chapters throughout the book, but let's look at one example now of how integrity applies to working with community officials. Suppose the fictitious well-known fashion company XYZ, which manufactures women's executive apparel, launches a joint campaign with a nonprofit foundation to benefit breast cancer research. XYZ vows to donate 2 percent of its sales proceeds during the month of October—National Breast Cancer Awareness Month—to the foundation. The campaign proves highly successful resulting in a 10 percent increase in sales nationwide. However, because the foundation is a nonprofit, its records are open to public inspection. A reporter who reviews its records discovers the proceeds donated were much less than one would expect from a company this size. The reporter digs deeper and learns XYZ gave only half a percent to the foundation. This report gets out, and the media is outraged by this blatant lie to the public. The discrepancy becomes the hot topic on the evening news and mentioned in countless newspapers around the country. The public learns about this, and a large number of clients vow to switch to XYZ's competitors for future purchases. Sales decline by 25 percent for three months following the incident, and the damage lowers the company's stock rating. The company violated its integrity by not keeping its promise to the public and the foundation. The public

FIGURE 1.7 News coverage of what well-known personalities or celebrities are wearing often results in new fashion trends being set.

19

relations executive who upholds a higher set of ethical standards is much more likely to be rewarded in the long run with meaningful, long-lasting business relationships with leaders in the community, business, and the media.

## The Benefits of Public Relations

A proper public relations program offers the fashion company numerous advantages that set it apart from the competition, as well as an opportunity to be more involved in the community within which it operates. Ultimately, public relations is what makes for a smoother interaction between the company and its publics, leading directly and indirectly to an increase in goodwill, brand awareness, and sales. It can also be a highly effective yet affordable promotional tool for the company's brand. If a public relations executive manages through his or her connections in the community to arrange for a celebrity to wear the company's product, the resultant media coverage can easily spur an overwhelming demand for the brand. The cost in this case is a small fraction of the advertising and marketing costs that would have been needed to create that same demand.

Besides the positive impact on sales, such enhanced image can also provide other important benefits. With a positive public image, the company is more likely to attract experienced, ethical personnel onto its staff roster; good personnel tend to prefer working for a company that is regarded as a pillar of

## Case Study 1.1   The Real World of Fashion Public Relations

### Word of Mouth Goes Online

The Internet is an amazing source of information. But it can also be a fantastic source of misinformation. More clearly today than in the past, Internet rumors and urban legends illustrate the sheer power of public opinion and word of mouth in the business world.

Although verbal gossip has been around for probably as long as language has existed, it is difficult to gauge or measure gossip because it is typically exchanged orally through personal conversations. Internet rumors are manifestations of gossip that are easier to monitor because they make appearances in writing through chain email, discussion forums, and people's personal Web pages. They are also harder to ignore because they reach thousands of people at a time. Whereas a rumor of yesteryear took months to spread from one person to another, a mass email can make its way into millions of inboxes across the globe within minutes.

One virtual example of the power of word of mouth is a rumor that has circulated on the Internet since the early 1990s about the international fashion designer Liz Claiborne. According to a June 30, 2007 *Los Angeles Times* piece following the designer's death, Claiborne may have been the first victim to a high-profile Internet urban legend. The vicious rumor accused the designer of being a racist and a Satanic worshipper, and has continued to circulate for years.

### Excerpt from Los Angeles Op-Ed Piece: "Liz Claiborne, First Internet Urban Legend Victim?"

"What I didn't see in last week's obituaries of clothing designer Liz Claiborne was the odd, ugly, and creepy Internet-based crusade against her as a racist and Satanist.

"First, the racist rumor: that sometime in 1990 or 1991, Claiborne had been a guest on *The Oprah Winfrey Show*, where she announced—and here's the first not-credible moment—that she doesn't design for black women because their hips are too big, or because they make her clothes look bad, or because she doesn't need the money. In the second noncredible moment, Oprah is described in these mass email as wearing a Liz Claiborne dress—hard to believe even in Oprah's pre-billionaire days. Oprah then supposedly stormed off the set, declaring that she will 'never' wear a Liz Claiborne dress, and returned wearing a bathrobe—a nice touch that, as the Mikado said, added verisimilitude to an otherwise bald and unconvincing narrative.

"This urban legend was given voice by director Spike Lee: 'It definitely happened,' he was quoted as saying in the October 1992 *Esquire*, and he was quoted as urging every black woman in America to throw out any Liz Claiborne items in her closet and never buy another Claiborne garment again." (Morrison, 2007)

Numerous online rumor debunker Web sites have labeled the rumor as a false hoax. Truthorfiction.com claims that the rumor is actually a mutation of the "infamous Procter and Gamble e-rumor except that somewhere along the way, it got attached to Liz Claiborne" (Truthorfiction.com, 2009). The Web site says that some of the rumors charged that Claiborne confessed to her Satan worship while on *Oprah*, but that Claiborne has never appeared on the show; it points out that she hasn't made these comments on any other television shows either.

the community. Suppliers might be less strict in extending credit, and might provide better turnarounds in a time bind when they know they are working with a well-regarded company. Distributors, representatives, and retailers might be more inclined to associate with a company that has a strong, positive public image because that approving image often reflects upon them as well through their association with the company. That same media exposure typically serves to develop customer loyalty. When a company gets involved in a charity drive, for example, consumers will tend to purchase the company's brands over those

---

**Case Study 1.1   The Real World of Fashion Public Relations** *(continued)*

An article by *Slate* columnist Rob Walker describes the potential effects of such rumors: "They frequently gain the most currency with a specific 'rumor public,' and serve as 'verification' for ideas that that public believes but can't quite prove, and perhaps believes traditional news sources suppress" (Walker, 2002). Walker points out that the creation and forwarding of e-rumors can be a weapon of choice for disgruntled consumers. However incredulous these rumors may seem, research cited by Walker says that consumer interviewed on the subject have admitted that although they didn't believe them, the rumors lurked in their minds. The interviewees also said the rumors affected their buying decisions, causing them to avoid the brands targeted by the rumor.

**Questions to Consider**

1.  What actions would you take if you were the public relation person for Liz Claiborne to quell the e-rumors?

2.  How would you approach Spike Lee in setting the record straight that Liz Claiborne was a victim of a malicious rumor?

3.  Do you think it would have been effective if Liz Claiborne were booked on the various talk shows to discuss this rumor? Explain the pros and cons.

---

of competitors. In this case, a consumer buying a pair of jeans will often choose the company's brand—even if it means paying more for those jeans than that of a competitor—and feel better about his or her purchase when he or she knows their purchase benefits a charity program. Moreover, well after that charity drive is over, the consumer will still remember the company's involvement in the community and will more likely remain loyal to its brands in the future.

Finally, public relations cements a strong relationship between the company and its community. This is particularly important for the long-term success of the company. A company's positive, high-profile involvement in the community can reap benefits for many years to come. Let's say a children's fashion retailer hosts a family event by inviting families to a tent outside the store. This event features carnival rides, clowns, face painting, and other activities. Such a community event shapes consumers' perception of the company as one that supports children, families, and the local community. Local city officials might pick up on this event, and perhaps the local fire department chief offers to provide fire truck rides for the children. Such an event brings the company employees and the people who shop there together in a nonformal setting, lending a more human perspective to their interactions in the future within the store. The consumers now feel they know the staff not just as cashiers and customer service personnel but also as people and neighbors, and this fosters further consumer loyalty to the store.

## Chapter Summary

▶   The fashion industry is highly influenced by the media and public opinion. Trends are set and unset according to what the public sees and hears in the media.

▶   Public relations is especially important in the fashion industry because it creates a positive public image for the company and its brands.

▶ Each fashion company, from the largest manufacturer to the smallest retailer operation, has a unique set of publics, including its consumers, employees, suppliers, and so on.

▶ All public relations efforts and strategies aim to foster and enhance relationships with the company's publics, and improve the company's public image.

▶ Whereas advertising and promotional strategies are paid for by the company, public relations primarily aims to elicit unpaid media coverage, which the public holds in high esteem as a credible source.

▶ Public relations does not direct its efforts toward creating immediate action by the public; rather, it is concerned with creating a long-lasting, positive image with the publics so as to create more confidence in the company.

▶ Gauging and improving public sentiment is a complex yet vital part of a company's public relations strategy.

▶ The proverbial "any publicity is good publicity" is a public relations myth, as is the concept that one can spin any situation—no matter how negative—into a positive one simply by manipulating the way facts are presented.

▶ Integrity is one of the most important requirements to long-term success in the public relations field.

▶ A properly run public relations program will gain the company credibility, enhance its public image, make it stand out from the competition, and develop a strong relationship with its community.

## Key Terms

▶ call-to-action advertisement

▶ community affairs

▶ image advertisement

▶ integrity

▶ public

▶ public relations

▶ publicity

▶ spin

## Chapter-End Questions and Exercises

1. Do you think that public relations plays a vital role in gaining consumer acceptance of a brand or collection? Explain.

2. Do you feel that the rumors about Tommy Hilfiger are true? Explain.

3. Think of two fashion companies you know of, and write down what kind of image you have in your mind for each of these companies?

   a. Are these fashion companies involved in community affairs? If not, what nonprofits do you feel they should be involved with? Why?

   b. If these companies are involved with community affairs, explain whether you think their community affairs involvement is effective.

4. Explain the difference between public relations and publicity.

5. How is public relations different than advertising? And how is it similar?

6. Do you feel that a report by a journalist is less biased than an advertisement? Whom do you trust more? Why?

7. What creates more buzz—advertising or public relations? Why?

8. Why is it important for a brand to try and shape the consumer's opinion about the brand? How does public relations fit within this facet of business?

9. Do you think that media coverage can change consumer opinion and buying decisions? Would a negative report about a particular brand cause you to think twice before you buy one of its items in the future?

10. What are your thoughts about the concept, "No image is a bad image"? Explain.

11. Name a fashion product that you would not purchase due to the brand's image. Explain.

12. Name a fashion product that you have recently purchased due to the brand's image. Explain.

13. In your opinion, how important is integrity in public relations? Explain your view.

14. How is freedom of speech related to public relations? Are public relations executives free to say whatever they want to make the brand look good? What would happen, in your opinion, if they did just that?

15. What do you think are the pros and cons to being an honest public relations executive and always stating the truth? What are the prospects for long-term success for the honest public relations executive versus the dishonest public relations executive?

16. Should a fashion company be involved in the community? How much involvement is sufficient? What do you think are the possible pros and cons for such involvement?

17. Have you ever participated in any type of charity drive or event by a fashion brand? If so, what did you think about the fashion brand after the drive?

18. Look online and in publications such as magazines and newspapers and find three instances where celebrities are seen wearing or endorsing specific clothing brands. For each article, answer the following questions:

23

a.  As a consumer, how did the article influence your opinion of the brand?

b.  Would you be more or less inclined to buy that brand after reading the article? Why?

c.  Did the article make you think about how you dress and how it fits within fashion trends? Explain how.

19. Look through previous issues of fashion publications and clip three previews or reviews of new collections. For each, answer the following:

a.  Do you think the preview/review is positive or negative? Why?

b.  How credible is the publication in your opinion? Do you think it's biased, truthful, objective, or not?

c.  As a consumer, how does the preview/review make you feel about the new collection?

d.  Were there one or more items you saw in the preview/review that you liked? Did you consider, even for a moment, buying that item in the future? If you saw it in the store in the future, would you buy it?

20. Clip one advertisement and one unpaid editorial article about a specific brand or collection. Analyze each article, and answer the following questions:

a.  As a consumer, which do you trust more—the advertisement or the editorial? Explain.

b.  As a consumer, did they draw you closer to the brand or item, or turn you away from the brand? Why?

c.  What, if any, could have been done for each—both the advertisement and the editorial—to create a better image of the brand or item in your mind?

21. Pair up with one or more students in your class, and exchange the clips you chose for Question 18. Answer the three questions from Question 18 again, but for the ad and article chosen by the other student. After you are done, compare the notes you and the other students took for each of the pieces and analyze for similarities and differences in your responses to the questions.

22. Look through a popular fashion magazine and find an unpaid editorial about a brand or item. Now look over the ads, if any, for that brand or item in the issue. Comparing the two, do you feel that the advertising department and public relations department coordinated the advertising and public relations efforts to maximize results? Explain why you think so.

23. Select a fashion brand that you prefer or are aware of, and research online and in your library's databases for any media coverage within the last few years. List the date, publication, and topic for each, and then answer the following:

    a. Do you remember reading or hearing about this story?

    b. If so, how did it affect your perception of the brand?

    c. If you haven't heard or read it, how would reading it change your perception of the brand?

    d. Is the story interesting enough that you would retell it to your friends? What would you say and would it be positive or negative for the brand?

24. Research and find a story that accused a company of lying to officials, clients, or both. What were the consequences of these lies in terms of client trust and sales volume?

25. Find two media stories of fashion brands that are active in the community. Answer the following for each:

    a. What did the article cover?

    b. How was the company portrayed?

    c. What do you think is the effect of the article on consumers?

26. Find a recent editorial article about a specific fashion brand and answer the following questions:

    a. What are the subgroups that will be reading the article? How will each subgroup regard the story—i.e., positive, negative, mixed? What would be their base for judging the story?

    b. What is the ideology of the publication? Does it have a bias or an agenda? Is it conservative, liberal, or perhaps independent, and how does the political view affect the story?

27. Team up with another student who is your partner in a newly formed public relations company. Your prospective client, a new retailer selling household products à la Crate & Barrel, wants you to get the word out! What would you include in your proposal that will help them to decide to use your services?

28. Team up with another student. Take turns taking a different position (pro versus con) on the topic, "Any publicity is good publicity." Write your conclusions and comments from the discussion.

29. Find a magazine article about a fashion product and find an ad about that same product. Which do you think will resonate more with the consumer, and why?

30. A *public* is a distinct group of people whose support or lack of support affects a company's success. Name the publics for the following retail stores. Then, for each public, explain why you chose it as a distinct group and why you think they would shop at that store.

    a. Tory Burch

    b. Scoop Stores

    c. Steve & Barry's

# Public Opinion and the Media

### Chapter Snapshot

n the free-market scenario where consumers have relatively free choice over what products they purchase,
which applies to most of the Western world, fashion
thrives upon public opinion of what is cool. Consumer
purchasing decisions for fashion items are often guided
more by what the consumer thinks is aesthetic rather than
whether or not these items fulfill the consumer's basic needs
for clothing. Fashion has pervaded our life to such an extent
that even underwear and socks, which are rarely if ever seen
or noticed by others, have become items that carry designer
brand labels. Public opinion of what is and isn't cool has
thus become a significant shaping force of the fashion industry, and the media has become a major influential factor
behind public opinion. The public and the media constantly
work off of each other through a complex web of information sharing patterns to define upcoming styles and change
public opinion. In this chapter we will explore what public
opinion is, how it is shaped, and what the fashion company
can do to influence public opinion to create adequate brand
recognition and increase market share.

## Objectives

▶ Understand the meaning of public opinion and its importance in the fashion industry.

▶ Discuss the effects of public opinion on a fashion company's success.

▶ Analyze the factors that shape public opinion.

▶ Explore the ways a company can improve its public image.

▶ Comprehend what comprises the media.

▶ Define the various types and categories of media, and explore the roles of each.

▶ Discuss those executives and staff who are involved in public relations and their responsibilities, functions, and duties.

Positive **public opinion** is one of the primary goals of public relations. It is also a vital key to success in the fashion industry. The way that customers, vendors, suppliers, retailers, the media, and the community at large perceive the company and its brands has tremendous effect on the success of these brands. When public opinion about the company is positive, a buzz surrounds the company in the media and through word of mouth. The results often improve relationships with existing customers, attract new customers, create stronger bonds with the community, and increase sales. As we will discuss in this chapter's case study, much of the success that the Juicy Couture label enjoyed in its early years can be attributed to the company's strategy of recruiting celebrities to wear its chic tracksuits (PR Newswire, 2003). And when public opinion turns negative, the damages can easily bring a company down to its knees—unfavorable stories in the media, bitter criticism passed on through word of mouth, and even official complaints filed with business and governmental organizations can decrease a company's sales for such long periods of time and to such an extent that the company cannot survive. Nike's ongoing battle with allegations of child labor abuse since the early 1990s, which will be discussed further in Chapter 12, shows the powerful effects of negative public opinion. Although Nike may not have violated child labor laws, human rights groups charged that Nike's suppliers did. Public sentiment against the company's association with such practices tarnished the company's reputation (Gordon, 2001). It is, therefore, extremely important for a company to identify, monitor, and proactively improve the public opinion about the company and its brands.

## What Is Public Opinion?

To succeed over the long run, the fashion company should offer products that in some way beneficially serve one or more groups of customers, as well as provide good customer service. Public opinion demands that the product must serve and satisfy the intended target customer and is delivered as promised. Imagine a fashion company that does not deliver the product that they initially sold to their buyers. The samples looked great, with lots of detail and superior workmanship. Then the product arrives at the retail level and some of the original detail is missing and there are signs of poor workmanship. How long do you think this product will survive in the marketplace? If the product gets to the consumer level and is ultimately rejected, then negative public opinion will likely result from this type of poor management and misrepresentation. The media is always alert to the positive and negative happenings to which the public is exposed, and jumps on the opportunity to report on newsworthy material—particularly of a controversial nature—that affects the public. It won't be long before such a story appears in the media. How long do you think this company will last when word of mouth spreads about this product and the company? When a product or company is seen in this negative light, it is very difficult for that product to survive, and public opinion becomes the executioner. As a corollary, when a product is superior to other products in the market, customers will likely tell their friends and family about their positive experience, significantly improving the product's brand awareness. As can be seen, public opinion has tremendous effect on a fashion product's success. But what exactly is public opinion?

In his book *Public Opinion*, influential journalist and respected political columnist Walter Lippmann analyzes the subject in depth. Lippmann likens an opinion to pictures, or perception, of a particular event or occurrence. In this scheme, any particular incident can leave a totally different impression on each witness of the incident; each witness has an opinion of what happened, which may or may not alter what actually happened, and which may or may not differ from other witnesses' opinions of what happened. In the same manner, our perceptions of any topic, from weather and sports to politics and fashion, often varies from one person to another. However, Lippmann makes the juxtaposition of our individual opinions against the overall public opinion:

> Those features of the world outside which have to do with the behavior of other human beings, in so far as that behavior crosses ours, is dependent upon us, or is interesting to us, we call roughly public affairs. The pictures inside the heads of these human beings, the pictures of themselves, of others, of their needs, purposes, and relationship, are their public opinions. Those pictures which are acted upon by groups of people, or by individuals acting in the name of groups, are Public Opinion with capital letters. The analyst of public opinion must begin, then, by recognizing the triangular relationship between the scene of action, the human picture of that scene, and the human response to that picture working itself out upon the scene of action. (Lippmann, 1922)

The triangular relationship Lippmann describes is even more pronounced in the world of fashion. Styles and trends can be likened to the waters of a river, simultaneously traveling in the direction defined by the banks while reshaping the banks and thus forming a new direction. No one drop of water can affect the river's direction, but as a collective, all of the drops become the shaper; yet, without the single drop, the collective is nothing. Similarly, people both exhibit

FIGURE 2.1 Walter Lippmann, featured on the cover of *Time* magazine, March 30, 1931.

## Box 2.1 Real World Profile: Walter Lippmann

After graduating from Harvard University, Walter Lippmann published *A Preface to Politics* (1913), a penetrating critique of popular prejudices. In 1914 he helped found the liberal *New Republic* magazine. His writings there influenced U.S. President Woodrow Wilson, who, after selecting Lippmann to help formulate his famous Fourteen Points and develop the concept of the League of Nations, sent him to the post–World War I peace negotiations for the Treaty of Versailles. Lippmann began writing columns in 1921 for the reformist *New York World*, where he served two years (1929–31) as editor. Moving to the *New York Herald-Tribune*, he began his long-running column, "Today and Tomorrow." Eventually syndicated worldwide, the column won two Pulitzer Prizes and made Lippmann one of the most respected political columnists in the world. Over the decades he contributed articles to more than 50 magazines. His numerous books included the influential *Public Opinion* (1922), *The Phantom Public* (1925), and *A Preface to Morals* (1929), all of which endorse "liberal democracy." In *The Good Society* (1937), he criticized the collectivist tendencies of the New Deal, which he had initially supported. Later works include *The Cold War* (1947) and *Essays in the Public Philosophy* (1955). Lippmann's analyses over many years earned him a special Pulitzer Prize citation in 1958 (C-SPAN American Writers).

Lippmann was a pioneer in the subject of public relations and a prominent theorist in the study of public opinion. Though his works deal mainly with politics, economics, and international affairs, their analyses of the many issues within the public relations field can also be applied to the fashion field, or any other business for that matter.

and shape style; no one person can single handedly change fashion, but as part of the collective of a group each person's style makes a difference, however small or large, on the overall direction of fashion. As illustrated in Figure 2.2, many consumers base their fashion preferences upon public opinion about style—what we can loosely call a trend—and these preferences in turn reinforce or modify the trend.

### Historical Background

Public opinion could be said to have been born with the advent of democracy in ancient Greek society, which acknowledged the power of public sentiment expressed through voting. The actual term *public opinion*, however, is generally traced back to Michel de Montaigne's 1575 *Essays*, where he coined the term *l'opinion publique* (French for public opinion) and alluded to the power of public opinion over private lives: "Whatever it be, whether art or nature, that imprints in us the condition of living by reference to others, it does us much more harm than good; we deprive ourselves of our own utilities, to accommodate appearances to the common opinion; we care not so much what our being is, as to us and in reality, as what it is to the public observation" (Montaigne, 1575). Public opinion developed as a concept and gained acceptance during

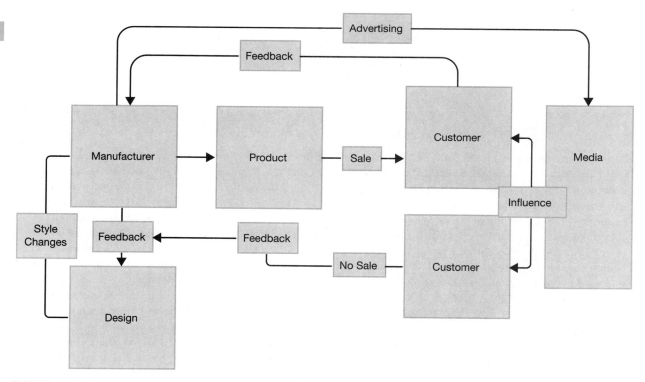

FIGURE 2.2 Fashion style and public opinion are interconnected through a reciprocal relationship. Style shapes public opinion through marketing and production of the fashion items, whereas public opinion shapes style through the purchasing decisions—items that do not sell well are discontinued.

FIGURE 2.3 One of the most important writers and greatest minds of France during the Renaissance, Michel de Montaigne pioneered the exploration of public opinion with his 1575 work, *Essays*.

31

the eighteenth century after social and economical forces reshaped the political sphere in most of the Western world following the Renaissance, French Revolution, and growing urbanization. With the rise of the media serving as the messenger of the people's voice, public opinion found an outlet that would both echo and shape it.

## Psychological Perspective

Maslow's Hierarchy of Needs is a psychology theory that Abraham Maslow proposed in his 1943 paper "A Theory of Human Motivation." Maslow's hierarchy of needs proposes that human behavior and emotions can be explained by classifying human needs into five hierarchal categories: physiological, safety, love, esteem, and self-actualization. The needs are stacked like pyramid layers one above the other (see Figure 2.4), with the lower needs having to be met first. Higher needs in this hierarchy only come into the individual's focus when the lower needs in the pyramid are satisfied. If a lower set of needs is suddenly no longer being met, the individual will temporarily reprioritize his needs and focus attention on those lower, unfulfilled needs; however, the individual will not necessarily regress to the lower level permanently (Maslow, 1943). As an example, an engineer—who is at the esteem level—has a skiing accident and breaks his leg. He will now take time off from work and concentrate on his health—his physiological needs. After the leg heals, he will go back to work and return to his previous needs level—the esteem needs.

FIGURE 2.4 Maslow's
Hierarchy of Needs.

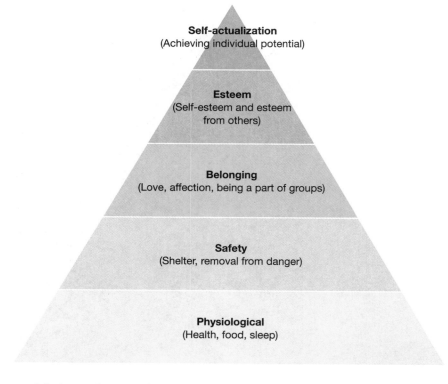

**Self-actualization**
(Achieving individual potential)

**Esteem**
(Self-esteem and esteem
from others)

**Belonging**
(Love, affection, being a part of groups)

**Safety**
(Shelter, removal from danger)

**Physiological**
(Health, food, sleep)

Maslow points out that any of the lower needs and their resulting behaviors can serve as channels for higher needs: "the person who thinks he is hungry may actually be seeking more for comfort, or dependence, than for vitamins or proteins. Conversely, it is possible to satisfy the hunger need in part by other activities such as drinking water or smoking cigarettes. In other words, relatively isolable as these physiological needs are, they are not completely so." Within

---

## Box 2.2 Real World Concept: Maslow's Hierarchy of Needs

The social psychologist Abraham Maslow's Hierarchy of Needs:

▶ Physiological—The most basic needs for survival, such as oxygen, food, water, temperature, and so on. A person who is lacking all of the needs would most probably hunger for food more strongly than for anything else.

▶ Safety—If the physiological needs are relatively well gratified, then a new set of needs emerges, focused around the safety of the individual, e.g., shelter and protection.

▶ Love—The needs for love, affection, and belonging. The individual focuses on friends,

a sweetheart or a wife, children, affectionate relations with people in general, and a place in his group.

▶ Esteem—Virtually all people in our society have a need or desire for a stable, high evaluation and respect for themselves, by themselves, and by others based upon real capacity and achievement.

▶ Self-actualization—Even if all these needs are satisfied, the individual often grows restless, unless the individual is doing what he is fitted for—a musician must make music, an artist must paint—if he is to be ultimately happy. What a person can be, he or she must be.

## Box 2.3  Real-World Concept: Hierarchy of Marketplace Needs

The hierarchy of needs is also useful in understanding the company's various markets. Some publics may share a need level that helps the company appeal to that market. For example, suppose one of the company's publics shares a passion for the environment; offering clothing made of recycled fabric might fill that public's need for self-actualization as environmentalists.

the context of public opinion, we can see that an individual may have a positive opinion of a product because it fulfills, consciously or subconsciously, another need. Thus a man who purchases a leather jacket in order to look stylish, may in fact purchase it to fulfill his love needs and feel acceptance from his group.

## Public Opinion's Effects on Business

The company's public relations department is entrusted with the function of creating a positive public opinion for the company and its products with as many publics as possible. To better understand how public opinion affects business in general, we must look at how it shapes the company's image, guides consumer buying habits, and modifies the company's relations with its business partners.

### Customer Purchasing Decisions

No fashion business can survive without a loyal customer base that buys its products and provides the company with profits in return. After all, if the company's publics do not decide to purchase its products, then the company will go bankrupt. Public opinion about the company, its brands, and its products affects consumers when it comes to their purchasing decisions. The primary considerations that most customers take into account when deciding whether to buy a particular product are: **quality, design,** price, **brand recognition,** and the reputation of the retailer and manufacturer. Other possible considerations vary from person to person; we will explore these later in this section.

The priority of these primary considerations can vary greatly from customer to customer. Some customers may care more about quality than price, whereas others may care less about quality or price as long as the item is pleasing to the eye. Still others may not venture to buy any brand that they don't trust based on their personal experience or positive experiences relayed to them by friends and family. Thus, a female customer in her mid-60s most likely may have a completely different set of criteria than a female customer in her mid-30s. Suppose Victoria, a 65-years-old retired middle-class customer, is shopping for a blouse. Her top concern is price; with social outings being limited to an occasional meeting with close friends, and with a fixed income from her retirement fund, she is first looking for a blouse that fits her budget. Her second consideration may be quality because she wants the product to last for some time so that she doesn't have to purchase another blouse soon. Colors, design, and brand may be of some or no importance. That said, not all women who are 65 and retired will share this set of criteria. Suppose Angela, another fictitious customer who

**FIGURE 2.5** The primary considerations that most customers take into account when deciding whether to buy a particular product are: quality, design, price, brand recognition, and the reputation of the retailer and manufacturer.

is 65 and well-to-do, is also shopping for a blouse. Angela attends gala dinners and such events once or twice a week, and is constantly striving to uphold her social status. She will likely look for brand recognition first. She will likely want her blouse to be recognizable as an expensive, top-quality product. In this case, price may never even enter the picture, and whether the item is priced at \$20 or \$200 will not matter to this customer.

The set of considerations and their priorities for a particular customer is what we call that customer's **buying criteria.**

Public opinion enters the scene because it can influence the customer's buying criteria, thus indirectly modifying the customer's purchasing habits. If Angela reads in her favorite gossip magazine that a particular brand has become popular with high-society celebrities, she may be much more inclined to buy that brand than if she just happened to see the brand at her local department store. Although the company's success does not hinge on just one customer or only one transaction, it certainly requires a certain number of active customers or a specific number of transactions to become profitable. Public opinion about the company and its products thus becomes quite important to the company's survival. By extension, this opinion includes that of the individual customers that constitute the company's base. Positive public opinion typically translates into more sales and an expansion of the company's operations; negative public opinion typically precedes a decline in demand for the company's products, and a decrease in sales and profits. It is, therefore, imperative for a fashion company to understand the various buying criteria of its various publics and to stay abreast of the current public opinion about its products, service, and business practices.

### Business Effects

Public opinion can also affect other facets of business that are just as important as consumer purchasing habits. The company depends on its suppliers, vendors, distributors, retailers, employees, investors, bankers, and shareholders for the smooth, uninterrupted production and delivery of its products to the consumer. A shirt manufacturer cannot make and sell its shirts if it lacks fabrics, buttons, or zippers, if it doesn't have a vendor for the stitching, printing, and finishing, or if it has no method of distributing the shirts to points of sale that are willing to sell its products. Therefore, a company's **business-to-business (B2B)** relationships—its relationships with other businesses—are vital to the success of the business.

Public opinion plays a vital role in this sphere as well because public opinion can affect these B2B relationships. Stories in the media, word of mouth, blogs, and other outlets for public opinion can affect how a supplier or vendor views the company, and in turn affect how that supplier or vendor deals with the company. Let's look at a fictitious example: a manufacturer of business shirts is in hot waters due to an employee's allegations of racial discrimination, and the details find their way into the local newspaper. The owner of a chain of retail stores that sell the manufacturer's shirts in the county reads the article; appalled at the allegations, the owner decides to stop carrying the manufacturer's products. As a result, the manufacturer suffers a substantial reduction in sales volume. Notice that the manufacturer's guilt has not been fully determined yet—the allegations have power of their own. Also, notice that even if consumer demand has not diminished as a result of the story, the fact that the retail chain does not carry the shirts is enough to disrupt sales. So this sequence of events can play out in full whether the manufacturer is indeed guilty of racial discrimination or not. In this example, a sound public relations campaign aimed at the company's B2B publics could minimize such damages to the company's supply and delivery infrastructure. Similarly, a company's success can be boosted by positive public opinion within the B2B sphere. Suppose the charge against the manufacturer of business shirts in the example are dropped, and a new design of shirts sells extremely well in the select retail stores where it has been offered. News of the success can spread like wildfire, and a manufacturer with such an asset may suddenly receive a call from a large department store inquiring about possible distribution across the nation. Needless to say, the potential for a boost in sales in such a scenario is enormous.

This aspect of public relations is often overlooked at great expense or loss of potential income to the company. News in the closely knit fashion industry travels fast. Designers talk with fashion reporters over lunch, suppliers chat with bankers on the golf links, and distributors hobnob with industry analysts, all of which are opportunities for the shaping of public opinion, or what you may call gossip. A company, therefore, is wise to keep a close watch of its B2B public opinion and proactively strive to improve it on a constant basis.

## What Shapes Public Opinion?

Public opinion is fluid and volatile. Predicting changes in public opinion may be as difficult and uncertain as forecasting the weather at times. However, understanding the forces that shape public opinion can help a company be better equipped to sense that changes are taking place, comprehend what these changes may mean, and react to these changes appropriately. Understanding what shapes public opinion also allows the company to take steps toward shaping public opinion for the better, through the implementation of sensible, ethical, public relations strategies.

35

## Hadley Cantril's Laws of Public Opinion

Hadley Cantril was a prolific 1940s sociologist and public opinion researcher. His research and writing, which identified numerous key laws about public opinion and what shapes it, have significant relevance to fashion public relations. In his 1951 book, *Public Opinion*, which he co-edited with Mildred Strunk, Cantril states that public opinion is influenced by actions and events rather than by words. It is thus highly sensitive to important public events, such as changes in politics and economics, shifts in social values and customs, or occurrences—good or bad—that affect the public at large. These events can take place overnight, or stretch over a period of years. Whereas events of sudden and unusual magnitude can make public opinion swing from one extreme to another temporarily, changes in public opinion take time to cement; public opinion requires time to stabilize, during which the public has the chance to digest the event and evaluate it with a deeper perspective. According to Cantril, public opinion does not anticipate or plan for crises and emergencies—it merely reacts to them after the fact (Cantril & Strunk, 1951).

At the center of Cantril's theory is the assumption that the core of public opinion is based on individual self-interest. Events, actions, or other stimuli are important to the public to the degree that they affect the interests of the individuals that comprise the public; an event must concern the self-interest of the individuals in order to evoke a public opinion. In other words, people in general do not care about events or actions that do not have implications on their personal life. Public opinion, therefore, does not arouse unless people feel their self-interest is at stake; people will lose interest in the event or issue after some time unless they are reminded about its effects on their self-interest. Initiatives aimed at shaping public opinion, then, should include elements that demonstrate to the public how these initiatives affect the lives of the individuals, as well as elements that create a sense of the initiative's timely relevance. As an example, let's say a local boutique launches a sale event that pledges a certain percentage of the sales to a local anti-crime charity. For maximum

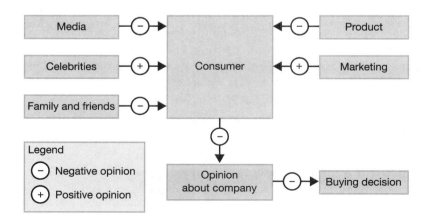

**FIGURE 2.6** The media, celebrities and community leaders, friends and family, and the product itself and how it is presented all lead to the public forming an opinion about the product. Positive public opinion occurs when the company is perceived as beneficial to the individual's well being. Conversely, negative public opinion forms when the company's image seems as harmful to the individual's well being.

impact on public opinion, it is vital for the boutique to emphasize in the advertisements and promotional mailers how exactly the donations to the charity will improve the lives of the customers in that community.

## The Media

At the forefront of shaping public opinion stands the independent media. As the pillar of free speech and primary vehicle for public sentiment, the media simultaneously shapes and echoes the public's opinions about public events and issues and offers a forum for the public to actively participate in discussions about these events and issues. Articles, editorials, letters to the editor, and investigative reports carry significant weight in the minds of the public.

## Celebrities and Community Leaders

Prominent celebrities and leaders in the community tend to set the trend when it comes to fashion. Style magazines regularly plaster photographs of celebrities, politicians, and community leaders on their covers and discuss at length their fashion preferences in their feature stories. The tabloids thrive on gossip about celebrities, where they've been spotted, and what they wear. People who read these magazines and tabloids often try to emulate these celebrities and thus public opinion about fashion is influenced.

## Family and Friends

Our family and friends have tremendous influence on our opinions. Our family customs, values, and traditions play a significant role in the shaping of our fundamental attitudes toward life. Whether our parents are conservative or liberal is a contributing factor to our own social views; although it does not mean we automatically take the same views as our parents, their views are certainly a factor in modifying the views we take. Even if the parents' ultraconservatism spur the opposite effect on the child, that force is still influential. The same goes for our friends. The attitudes and lifestyles of our closest friends have profound effects on how we think and act. We may even try to emulate a friend or family member of whom we think highly. The woman who goes clothes shopping with her girlfriends seeks approval from them as to what she think may look cool. The man who looks up to his father may adopt some of the fashion styles his father has. As far as fashion is concerned, family and friends' styles and opinions affect an individual's opinions about fashion, and thus help shape the aggregate public opinion.

## The Product

Whether the product is well designed, of good quality, and appropriately priced has a lot to do with the public's opinion about it. Consumers love to share their experiences about products, and this can be seen not only during informal conversations among friends, but also in the media and online. Fashion editors at many newspapers and magazines routinely review new collections, offering elaborate and opinionated reports about their pros and cons. Consumer Web sites, such as epinions.com and consumerreview.com, and even many of the shopping Web sites, such as amazon.com and yahoo.com, offer detailed product reviews from other consumers who have purchased the item and took the time to share their thoughts about the product. The opinions and reviews of individuals spread through the media and word of mouth thus shaping public opinion.

### The Company's Communications

These days, there is no shortage of flashy advertisements featuring supermodels wearing the latest collections from the top designers. Flip through the pages of most magazines and you will likely find many simple yet powerful full-page image advertisements, adorned by the logos of Ralph Lauren, Gucci, Armani, D&G, Donna Karan, Baby Fhat & KLS (Kimara Lee Simmons), or Hilfiger, and often not much more (see Figure 2.7). These stylish advertisements work to shape the opinions of the public as to what looks and does not look chic and hip, by showing the shirt or blouse in the best possible light, perhaps on exotic beaches or a yacht, and worn by some of the most beautiful people in the world. In addition to print advertisements, the brochures and catalogs the company sends out, the television commercials, the fashionable boutique stores on the Rodeo Drives of the world, and other promotional items originated by the company also work to shape the public's opinion about the company and its products.

## Proactive Shaping of Public Opinion

One of the chief responsibilities of the company's public relations arm—be it an in-house department or an outside agency—is to monitor public opinion and implement initiatives that will create goodwill with the company's publics

**FIGURE 2.7** Top designers invest considerable amounts of money in simple yet powerful advertisements that showcase their latest collections and make these items look chic.

> ## Box 2.4  Real World Principle: Word of Mouth
>
> In today's high-paced, globally connected digital world, word-of-mouth and media stories travel faster than ever. A fashion company that aims for a competitive edge must adopt a proactive attitude toward shaping public opinion through careful monitoring of the media and the planning and implementation of effective public relations initiatives.

and improve public opinion. When it comes to studying public opinion and formulating proactive initiatives, it is important to remember that circumstances are unique for each company. Collections differ from brand to brand and as a result the target consumers are never wholly identical; each brand image is unique, and development of the companies' relationships with the community takes different paths. Whereas it is impractical to assume a rote frame of mind when considering potential initiatives for any specific brand, the following are some of the common approaches to shaping public opinion.

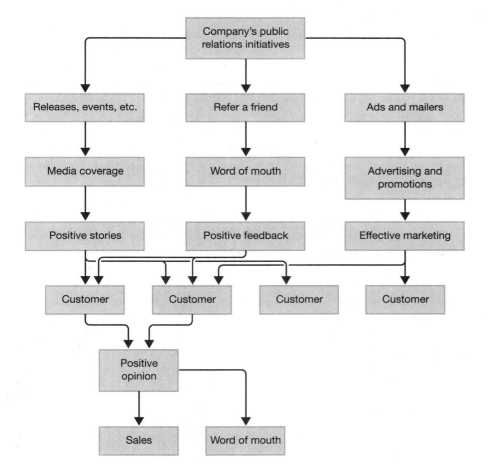

FIGURE 2.8 There are many factors that shape public opinion. Common initiatives include soliciting media coverage, encouraging word-of-mouth recommendations, and advertising, promotion, and community relations. The more positive exposure a person receives from these initiatives, the more likely he or she is to become a customer; such exposure also cements the company's relationship with existing customers and generates brand loyalty.

## Soliciting Media Exposure

Positive media coverage is a major influencer responsible for helping to shape opinion. A praising story about the company or its brands and products helps to create goodwill for the company and places the company in a positive light in the minds of its publics to think highly of the company. Soliciting media to gain exposure and shape public opinion is, therefore, a major part of public relations. Media coverage doesn't just happen by itself—a proactive approach to soliciting coverage is necessary. It would be great if we had that "magic wand" and waved it every time we wanted to get the media to do a story about our company's latest brand or one of our new collections. Unfortunately, there aren't any magic wands in the public relations business. So how does the process work? How do we reach the proper media and get results?

First we must understand the basics of successful media exposure. Soliciting media to get exposure requires R&R—no, not rest and rehabilitation but research and relationships. The work involved starts before you ever solicit the media. Like they say, "You gotta know the territory." Before sending the press release you should be able to hone in on the proper reporter who will relate the story to your target audience. This takes lots of research, reading, reading, and more reading. Public relations executives must read as many print media pieces as they have time for and watch as many of the local different TV newscasts as possible to determine who will best fit into the particular story that they are about to pitch. Read, watch, spend some time on research, and it will more than pay off. Reporters and anchors in the media repeatedly complain that they are routinely bombarded with press releases that do not relate to the type of reporting that they do. It is almost an insult to professional media folks when a company sends them a release about something they do not get involved in. Stay abreast of the news to see if the reporter has changed the type of stories he or she is writing.

After the research is completed, a press release must be written and then approved by the company's executive responsible for public relations. In Part III of this text, we will discuss in detail how to write an effective press release and how to send it out to the media. Following up on a release is one of the most important things one can do to get the story covered by the media. It takes practice, and the presentation must be short and to the point. Keep calling until you reach your source, and do not leave messages—the phone pitch is important because this will determine the reporter's interest or disinterest in the story. If he is not interested in the story but thinks it has creditability, he will invariably send it to another reporter or to the news desk. However, with a time-sensitive story, it is appropriate to call the news desk, tell them about the story, and then send the release to whomever you speak with. It is vital for the public relations executive to create business relationships with the various media contacts that cover fashion in their area. A word of caution—the relationship is vital to communicating with the media, but it will not get you a story if the material is not newsworthy. Keep your name in front of the media folks. Send them suggestions on other stories that they may be interested in that are not necessarily related to your company. Show them that you are media-conscious and are up-to-date on what's happening. Give and you shall receive.

Public opinion is best served with positive stories. What makes for a positive story? Why would the media jump on your story? Just because you think it is of interest does not make it so. What may appear to the company or the public relations agency as a definite story may not be interpreted as one by the media. It is vital that the story be considered from the reporters' perspectives to ensure it meets the criteria of a positive news story. When a story relates to a specific audience and includes information that the target group can easily see the benefit of and be able to utilize the information, you then have the recipe for a positive story. Uniqueness of information that provides a benefit to the specific publics is self-propelling and makes for a positive story that can improve public opinion. We will discuss this topic in more detail in Part III of this book.

**Word of Mouth**

Be a bee—create a **buzz**! When you hear the bees buzz, you pay attention. Public relations works in the same way. When you combine events with press releases, collaterals, community activities, and marketing other communication with the objective of getting the word out about the brand, you create excitement in the community about the brand—you start a buzz. It takes all these elements working together to start a buzz and make a buzz successful. The results of these activities give life to the buzz and most times results in a wave of informal word-of-mouth discussion about the brand, which is the most powerful communication element—more powerful than fancy ads. A buzz can be created by encouraging spread of positive word of mouth through such initiatives as one-on-one recommendations and reaching out to bloggers and social media. Getting involved in the community and its events is a great way to start the buzz and ensure success of a word-of-mouth campaign. Identifying **influencers** is vital; look for people who are highly respected in the community and who know many other people, and encourage them to talk up the brand. Another common method to spur word of mouth is to offer incentives to existing clients who help spread the word and refer friends to the brand.

**Advertising, Public Relations, and Promotion**

In Chapter 1 we discussed the value of advertising and public relations working together in the marketing effort. We know that advertising's main purpose is a call to action. Advertising is vital to get the word out—and we also know that advertising cannot be totally successful unless there is a strong public relations component. However, to fully deliver this communication message that helps form public opinion, there is a third element that completes the **marketing triangle,** and it is **promotion.** In today's fast-moving, competitive marketplace, one should not spend a disproportionate amount of time and money on only one element to attract the target market. It takes a marketing triangle to get the message across and see results (see Figure 2.9).

Active promotions amount to a large degree of street-level interaction, where the company utilizes its promotional efforts to contact potential customers directly. Community tent events, direct mail offers that are personalized for the customer, contests where the customer must come into the store to

**FIGURE 2.9** When a company's advertising, public relations, and promotional efforts are coordinated to forward a unified message, results are maximized, as each of the triangle's corners is boosted by the other two corners' support.

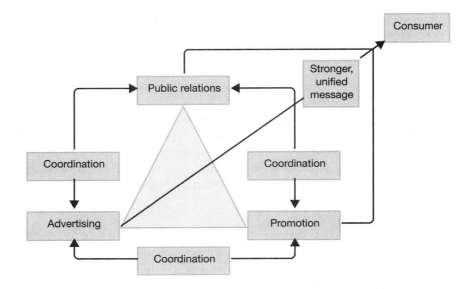

enter his or her name for a prize, and other such initiatives make a connection with the customer on a personal level. Here again, we find that one area in marketing is not sufficient to successfully market a product or service. Sales promotions such as offering special discounts, rebates, and other incentives have been and will be around for years to come. Now, with the ease and affordability of marketing online, we find running promotions to be more effective by reaching more people in real time. The trick is to coordinate the marketing triangle; we will cover this in further detail in Chapter 5.

## Ethical Issues

Engaging in initiatives that seek to proactively shape public opinion inherently carries certain caveats. Unethical dissemination of information to the company's publics is likely to have serious negative repercussions over the long run. The issue of ethics is one that holds many different meanings for many organizations and people. The culture of the company dictates the type of ethical standards and policies that the company will adopt and expect from their employees. There are degrees of ethics. What is thought to be ethical for one company may not be acceptable to another. Still, what the public or the media consider ethical

---

### Box 2.5   Real World Concept: "If It Feels Wrong, Then It Is Wrong"

Ethics in public relations is a delicate subject. Those who act ethically will succeed in the long run, whereas those who do not will falter. Along the way, there are definite temptations to exaggerate the company's reputation, embellish the product's features, and omit well-known facts that might put the company in bad light. However, these little lies come to bite one's behind. As a general rule, a public relations person can assume that "if it feels wrong, then it is wrong." The corollary, however, does not always work. Even if it feels right, one must still carefully check an initiative against established ethical standards to ensure there are no hidden issues.

is often much more important than the company's own ethical standards. The one thing that is certain is that if you want to be successful at changing public opinion, a high degree of ethical values must be evident throughout the organization. Relationships can be destroyed when one violates the rules of ethical conduct. A high degree of ethics is the catalyst for creating relationships. Public opinion can change quickly when drastic events unfold, and typically unethical conduct is behind these events. The news commentator who has not reported the news as it is and tends to put his thumb print on the news commentary to reflect his thinking and stretching the truth will not have a long career. The politician who states one thing one day and denies it in the future will lose his credibility. In public relations, the rule is not "When in Rome, do as the Romans do;" rather, it's "When in Rome, speak the truth and be consistent with it."

Although it is true that public relations' main objective is to distribute information that is positive about the company and its brands as well as manage negative situations, many ethical issues may arise. Handling both the positive and negative aspects can be an area where the true test of ethics is noticed. Within the positive aspect, we must guard against providing information that isn't accurate, or is exaggerated in order to attract readership; if this is the case, it is not ethical. In writing the press release, we must examine if all the true facts are included. In the process of trying to address a negative aspect about the company—we must make sure that the information is not tainted, leaving the reader with an untrue whole story. If the story is distorted, it will mislead both media and reader.

Ethical conduct dictates that the story be told the way it is. Just spinning it to get a positive response will end up creating more harm than expected. When the company's public relations department is perceived as unethical, it faces hard uphill battles to win back confidence. But ethics goes a long way and will bring success to those who firmly practice it. For example, in 1982 Johnson & Johnson was confronted with tainted Tylenol capsules that caused the death of several people. The company elected to immediately remove the product from the shelves all over the United States. It did not issue any claims of how it happened, nor did they give any false excuses. It just stated the facts and reported the story. But, it proceeded immediately to investigate how it could have happened and discovered that it only occurred in one specific area of the country. After an exhaustive search the company discovered that poison was inserted into the Tylenol packages at stores. Only then did Johnson & Johnson release the tampering story. Although because of the time factor its reputation was temporarily damaged, it did not succumb to an unethical practice of denial. Following the investigation, it released the information and the product Tylenol was put back on the market and remains there today because the company acted ethically.

## The Media

Now that we've covered what public opinion is and how the media shapes and reflects it, let's explore the **media** itself. Can any publication be considered media? No. According to the definition of media, it has to be a trustworthy source

43

**TABLE 2.1 Public Relations across the Board**

The media can be categorized according to medium and topic. Some examples of these categories intersect.

| | Print | Broadcast | Online |
|---|---|---|---|
| **News** | Newsweek<br>The Washington Post<br>The New York Times<br>TIME | California ApparelNews<br>abc<br>CBS<br>CNN<br>FOX<br>npr | YAHOO! NEWS<br>AP Associated Press |
| **General** | U.S.News & WORLD REPORT<br>COSMOPOLITAN<br>People<br>InStyle<br>W<br>ELLE<br>GLAMOUR<br>VOGUE<br>teen VOGUE<br>MEN'S VOGUE<br>VANITY FAIR | E! ONLINE<br>OPRAH<br>mystyle. BEFORE AND AFTER | STYLE.COM<br>It MyItThings.com<br>DAILY CANDY<br>allure<br>FN |
| **Trade** | GQ<br>WWD | N/A | WWD |

of information, and that requires the reporters and editors reporting for that publication be trained in journalism so they can properly and fairly relay the information to the public. Also, the media is expected by the public to deliver meaningful information that is based on facts; most works of literature or works of fiction, therefore, do not qualify as media. Finally, media should offer a way for the public to react to its reporting. Virtually every mainstream publication features a letters-to-the-editor column where complaints and compliments are published and responded to by the publication's editors.

It is beneficial to aim any public relations at those media outlets that will best serve the campaign's objectives and reach the intended publics. It is a waste of time to send a press release about a fashion manufacturer's corporate earnings report to a consumer glamour magazine, for example. None of the magazine readers will be interested in the figures, unless they are shareholders or thinking of buying shares, in which case they will expect to read about it in a publication focused on business. The same goes for mixing media types: it is senseless to call a reporter for a Web site that focuses on home electronics about a fashion company's latest collection.

## Media by Medium

The media can be roughly divided into three categories according to its medium, or how the content is distributed to the audience: print media, broadcast media, and online media.

### Print Media

Print media includes all independent publications that are published via print on paper. Newspapers, magazines, journals, trade publications, and reviews are all part of print media. A print publication typically has a publication term (i.e., published daily, monthly, quarterly, annually) a coverage area (i.e., nationwide, a region such as the Southeast, a state or a city) and an audience market (i.e., women, men, entrepreneurs, surfers, and so on).

### Broadcast Media

Broadcast media comprises television and radio. Such media typically airs every day, and, therefore, have a daily publication term. Many local radio and television stations are affiliates of the national news media stations such as ABC, CBS, Fox, and so on. Thus affiliates air stories about the local community that the local station produced, as well as stories about general topics produced by the syndicate national stations. Broadcast media typically targets a much wider spectrum of audiences than print publications because today basic television and radio service gives every subscriber access to virtually all of the local and even some of the national news stations.

### Online Media

It is more difficult to define media on the Web. The ease of access to publication on the Internet has made it possible for practically every person with a computer to broadcast his or her opinion about anything from the debate about global warming to the price of mushrooms. It is, therefore, vitally important when dealing with public relations online to critically analyze a Web site purporting to be online media as to its mode of operation, the qualifications of its staff, and the size of its audience, prior to contacting such a Web site with publicity information.

## Media by Type

The media can also be categorized according to the type of content it provides and the types of audiences it caters to; these include news media, general interest media, trade media, and owned media.

### News Media

The news media reports on local and world news and events that have impact on the community at large. Most daily newspapers and some weekly magazines, such as *Time* and *Newsweek*, fall into this category. The top national news networks in the United States are ABC, CBS, CNN, C-SPAN, Fox, MSNBC, and PBS. Whereas some of these networks cover news 24 hours a day, like CNN and Fox News, others such as PBS offer other programming as well. These national networks have local news affiliates in virtually every county across the nation. As can be deduced from the category name, the news media is interested first and foremost in information that is new. If your story is not new, or at least has some element in it that is new, the news media will not pick it up. Other considerations include whether the information is important for the public to know, whether the information is correct, and whether it can be reported fairly and without bias.

### General Interest Media

Under general interest, we have media that focuses on providing the reader with information and news on specific topics. Magazines, such as *Cosmopolitan*, *W*, *Vogue*, and *GQ*, that report on fashion trends, television talk shows, and radio morning shows are all examples of such media. General interest media is a prime vehicle for a fashion company's public relations initiatives aimed at consumers because this media's main audience is end users.

### Trade Media

The trade media are publications for the working professionals. Typically a trade publication focuses on a specific industry and reports on the business news, information, and events within the industry. *Women's Wear Daily*, *Apparel News*, *Footwear News*, and *Sportswear International* are all examples of trade magazines in the fashion industry.

### Owned Media

A distinction must be made here between independent media and media that is owned or published, directly or indirectly, by a company that actively participates in the fashion business. Although they constitute a valid and bona-fide form of the media as a whole, these publications cannot be considered independent because at their foundation lie pressures which by nature skew their reporting toward positive portrayals of their financial interests. If Macy's, for example, published a quarterly newsletter about retail sales, it can be hardly considered independent media because it is likely to be biased. In effect, such publications are on the borderline with paid advertisements, and are typically regarded as such by the readers; thus, they carry marginal weight on public opinion. Still, such publications have their place in a public relations campaign and can net excellent results when utilized properly. We will discuss these publications in further detail in Chapter 5.

## The Roles of the Media

It is important for anyone involved in public relations to understand the key responsibilities entrusted to the independent media. Knowing the priorities of the media is useful when forming a relationship with a reporter or an anchor, and can help orient the direction of public relations initiatives toward maximum positive media coverage.

### Informing the Public

The primary goal of the media is to provide the public with information about current affairs, social issues, and general topics. The public looks up to the media not only for the simple relay of the information, but also for the interpretation and clarification of that information. Although clarification is particularly necessary in the case of politics, economics, and law, it is also helpful in reporting on most other topics. For example, a report on a new type of stain-resistant fabric should include—in addition to the report of when and where it will be available—an explanation of the new fabric and how it repels stains. Therefore, the public relations manager is wise to include attachments that incorporate explanations of terms and other pertinent elements when sending releases to the media.

### Unbiased Reports

Independent media is expected by the public to remain objective in its reporting. Bias is not supposed to be a part of journalism; however, in the real world, every publication has inherent biases. The editor's choice of stories to be covered, the reporter's choice of sources to be interviewed, the photojournalist's portrayal of subjects in the story, all contribute to some degree of favoritism. Naturally, there isn't space in the paper or time in the news hour to allow every story to be covered, not all sources are available or are willing to talk, and photographs typically have to be taken quickly. However, with these inherent biases aside, the media should not exhibit evident signs of subjectivity or partiality, and that is achieved by always giving both sides of the story a chance to have their say. That said, some publications openly proclaim their bias. Fox News is known to be conservative, for example, whereas PBS is typically more liberal.

### Bringing the Community Together

The media works to some degree as a platform from which members of the community can make their voices heard. It allows people to express their grievances against the government and holds those in public office accountable. The media also serves as a forum where members of the community can learn about the initiatives, organizations, and events that take place in that community. In recent decades, the media has come to embrace its responsibility of spreading good news as well, and has incorporated coverage of positive stories,

## Box 2.6 Society of Professional Journalists Code of Ethics

### Preamble

Members of the Society of Professional Journalists believe that public enlightenment is the forerunner of justice and the foundation of democracy. The duty of the journalist is to further those ends by seeking truth and providing a fair and comprehensive account of events and issues. Conscientious journalists from all media and specialties strive to serve the public with thoroughness and honesty. Professional integrity is the cornerstone of a journalist's credibility. Members of the Society share a dedication to ethical behavior and adopt this code to declare the Society's principles and standards of practice.

### Seek Truth and Report It

Journalists should be honest, fair, and courageous in gathering, reporting, and interpreting information.
Journalists should:

- Test the accuracy of information from all sources and exercise care to avoid inadvertent error. Deliberate distortion is never permissible.

- Diligently seek out subjects of news stories to give them the opportunity to respond to allegations of wrongdoing.

- Identify sources whenever feasible. The public is entitled to as much information as possible on sources' reliability.

- Always question sources' motives before promising anonymity. Clarify conditions attached to any promise made in exchange for information. Keep promises.

- Make certain that headlines, news teases and promotional material, photos, video, audio, graphics, sound bites, and quotations do not misrepresent. They should not oversimplify or highlight incidents out of context.

- Never distort the content of news photos or video. Image enhancement for technical clarity is always permissible. Label montages and photo illustrations.

- Avoid misleading reenactments or staged news events. If reenactment is necessary to tell a story, label it.

- Avoid undercover or other surreptitious methods of gathering information except when traditional open methods will not yield information vital to the public. Use of such methods should be explained as part of the story.

- Never plagiarize.

- Tell the story of the diversity and magnitude of the human experience boldly, even when it is unpopular to do so.

- Examine their own cultural values and avoid imposing those values on others.

- Avoid stereotyping by race, gender, age, religion, ethnicity, geography, sexual orientation, disability, physical appearance, or social status.

- Support the open exchange of views, even views they find repugnant.

- Give voice to the voiceless; official and unofficial sources of information can be equally valid.

- Distinguish between advocacy and news reporting. Analysis and commentary should be labeled and not misrepresent fact or context.

- Distinguish news from advertising, and shun hybrids that blur the lines between the two.

- Recognize a special obligation to ensure that the public's business is conducted in the open and that government records are open to inspection.

### Minimize Harm

Ethical journalists treat sources, subjects, and colleagues as human beings deserving of respect.
Journalists should:

- Show compassion for those who may be affected adversely by news coverage. Use special sensitivity when dealing with children and inexperienced sources or subjects.

- Be sensitive when seeking or using interviews or photographs of those affected by tragedy or grief.

- Recognize that gathering and reporting information may cause harm or discomfort. Pursuit of the news is not a license for arrogance.

> **Box 2.6  Society of Professional Journalists Code of Ethics** *(continued)*

▸ Recognize that private people have a greater right to control information about themselves than do public officials and others who seek power, influence, or attention. Only an overriding public need can justify intrusion into anyone's privacy.

▸ Show good taste. Avoid pandering to lurid curiosity.

▸ Be cautious about identifying juvenile suspects or victims of sex crimes.

▸ Be judicious about naming criminal suspects before the formal filing of charges.

▸ Balance a criminal suspect's fair trial rights with the public's right to be informed.

### Act Independently

Journalists should be free of obligation to any interest other than the public's right to know.
Journalists should:

▸ Avoid conflicts of interest, real or perceived.

▸ Remain free of associations and activities that may compromise integrity or damage credibility.

▸ Refuse gifts, favors, fees, free travel, and special treatment, and shun secondary employment, political involvement, public office, and service in community organizations if they compromise journalistic integrity.

▸ Disclose unavoidable conflicts.

▸ Be vigilant and courageous about holding those with power accountable.

▸ Deny favored treatment to advertisers and special interests, and resist their pressure to influence news coverage.

▸ Be wary of sources offering information for favors or money; avoid bidding for news.

### Be Accountable

Journalists are accountable to their readers, listeners, viewers, and each other.
Journalists should:

▸ Clarify and explain news coverage and invite dialogue with the public over journalistic conduct.

▸ Encourage the public to voice grievances against the news media.

▸ Admit mistakes and correct them promptly.

▸ Expose unethical practices of journalists and the news media.

▸ Abide by the same high standards to which they hold others. (Society of Professional Journalists, 2000)

such as human-interest stories about people who help others and profiles of prominent members of the local community, into its reporting—good news for public relations directors all over.

## Those Involved in Public Relations

Upholding a positive image for the company and its brands is the responsibility of every employee. When dealing with customers, vendors, and the community at large, each employee should strive to reflect positively on the company's image. Within the company's organizational chart, there are several executives who have responsibilities, functions, and duties (RFDs) for public relations:

### Vice President for Marketing

In most organizations the vice president (VP) for marketing is involved in all aspects of the business—from research, initial product concept, and development to pricing, consumer demand, demographics, sales, and management. Typically the VP for marketing oversees advertising, sales promotions, and public relations. One of the job's biggest responsibilities is budgeting the available funds to maximize outreach to the target market. The VP for marketing is concerned with getting the word out to the company's target customer in the most cost-effective manner that will resonate most effectively with existing and potential customers. Public relations is one of the most cost-effective communication tools when executed properly, and the VP for marketing is entrusted with planning and coordinating the advertising and promotion strategies with those of public relations. The VP for marketing supplies the public relations department with direction as well as information that can be developed into positive publicity. Because the VP for marketing researches the market and determines what types of messages should be sent to their public, advertising and public relations are on the top of the list for the job's RFDs.

As we have stated previously, public relations is increasingly the venue of choice for a return on the investment. If the company uses an outside public relations agency, the VP for marketing must work closely with that agency to provide them with information and guidance on initiatives. You can compare the VP for marketing in most organizations with the conductor of a symphony. The successful results of the concert are attributed to the coordination involved in getting all the different instruments to work in harmony and result in satisfying the listening audience. The VP for marketing is most often the spokesperson for the organization and public relations is the platform for communicating a message that will impact positive public opinion. The VP for marketing spearheads the development of news stories, and is involved in the broader aspects of publicity by helping to coordinate press conferences and other media events with the rest of the organization. The VP for marketing is also the catalyst for kicking off new products, and organizing the way information about these products reaches the company's public. The VP for marketing directs the public relations department to focus in on specific types of media for a particular news event.

In his book, *Advertising, Promotion, and Supplemental Aspects of Integrated Marketing Communications*, Terence A. Shrimp refers to the marketing-oriented aspect of public relations as **marketing public relations (MPR).** Shrimp indicates how important MPR is in overall dispensing of product information and branding. MPR is involved in **proactive MPR,** which acts as a tool for product awareness that is used in concert with advertising, promotions, and selling. He also discusses **reactive MPR,** which acts as a response to negative situations that the organization may be confronted with and attempts to act as a band-aid to reduce the amount of negative public opinion. The VP for marketing is taking on more responsibility in public relations activities in today's competitive marketplace by directing the flow of information that the organization wants to disseminate (Shrimp, 2003).

### Public Relations Director

The public relations director heads the public relations department and reports to the VP for marketing in most organizations. He or she develops the public relations campaigns, oversees the implementation of publicity initiatives, arranges press conferences, in many cases originates and conducts community events, and alerts the media to positive news about the company. The public relations director is responsible and accountable for media coverage—be it print, broadcast, or online. The public relations director sees that news stories are pitched to the media and that any inquiries are properly answered. The public relations director is also responsible for the follow-through on all press releases—whether he or she does it himself or herself or delegates the job to one of the public relations department staff—and for responding to any media interests. The public relations director must be well acquainted with the company's products, target customers, and the company's competition. He or she also organizes and conducts focus groups and other research activities as directed by management. Many public relations directors create and design collateral pieces that are distributed to the target market. The public relations director has to be in communication with other company managers and personnel—always looking for items that can become the story of the day about the company. The modern-day public relations director wears many hats in the area of communications.

## Vice President for Sales

The role of the VP for sales in public relations is mostly advisory and unlike the VP for marketing who has significant control over the public relations department, the VP for sales' advisory capacity is mostly limited to providing customer feedback. The VP for sales is on the front lines and is in direct communication with the customer through their sales force. The authority of the VP for sales varies depending upon the size of the organization with some companies showing the VP for sales and VP for marketing on the same line in the table of organization. Other companies will give the VP for marketing greater authority than the VP for sales. Regardless of the organizational structure, the VP for sales is almost always in a position to receive customer reaction as an immediate response and, therefore, is a vital link to marketing and public relations. It is said that "the sales department is the company" because that segment of the company has the closest relationship with the customer. Sales thus becomes a great source of information about the product and the marketplace that is obtained virtually straight from the consumer. In addition, because of the close proximity to the customer, how the sales personnel conduct themselves reflects immensely on the company's public image. To operate efficiently the public relations department must work in close coordination with the sales people. The VP for sales and his or her sales force are involved in the day-to-day activities, and are able to supply the public relations department with the positive or negative happenings relating to the product and any news stories. The feedback and cooperation from sales is, therefore, invaluable to the public relations department.

## Company Employees

Informed employees make for goodwill ambassadors for the company. Effective press relations are based on total communication and employees, regardless of their position with the company must be knowledgeable as to what's happening. When a press release is sent to the media it is vital that the marketing, sales,

## Case Study 2.1   Public Opinion and the Media

### Juicy Couture Harnesses Celebrity Power

In 1996, with a pair of scissors, a bag of T-shirts, and $200 between them, Juicy Couture co-designers Pamela Skaist-Levy and Gela Taylor created the Juicy phenomenon. "We had originally intended to make sexy basics for our friends as presents," they say; however, they soon realized how contagious Juicy fever would become.

Having been introduced by mutual friends in 1994, the duo's first project was producing a line of maternity jeans called Travis Jeans, what would soon become Juicy Couture. Skaist-Levy, previously a milliner, had a strong background in fashion, having studied at the Fashion Institute of Design and Merchandising; Taylor was an actress who had held numerous roles in films, television, and the stage. Their common bond? "We could never find fashionable basics that were girly, flattering, and sexy!" they say. The Juicys launched their line of T-shirts that immediately flew out of every store that carried them. Based on this success, the co-founders applied their designs to revolutionizing denim wear. Juicy expanded into the jean market with the launch of Juicy Jeans in 1999. For the actual launch, Duran Duran reunited for the evening and performed at an exclusive venue for a high-profile guest list. This natural progression led the duo to later introduce a line of cashmere sweaters and scarves inspired by the styles and trends of the 1980s London punk rock scene and icons such as Johnny Rotten and the Sex Pistols. Building on this momentum, in Spring 2001, Pamela and Gela created a new Juicy twist to affordable fashion by designing the Juicy Tracksuit. "Why can't women be comfortable while still feeling sexy and chic?" asks Taylor. "As I traveled across the country last year, speaking with women about fashion, the only thing united was an obsessive interest in Juicy velours—should the tracksuit go to a dinner party? The dog run? The school cafeteria? A date? The in-laws? A cocktail party? (Answer: Yes to all of the above)," states Sally Singer, fashion features director at *Vogue* magazine.

Juicy Couture's retail success has been reinforced by the immense celebrity appeal. "We have been very

**FIGURE CASE STUDY 2.1**
Miley Cyrus wearing a Juicy cream coat. Photographs of celebrities sporting Juicy tracksuits have created tremendous appeal for the brand.

fortunate by our celebrity support," claims Skaist-Levy. Celebrities such as Madonna, Gwyneth Paltrow, Amber Valletta, Kate Moss, Amanda Peet, Liv Tyler, Sarah Jessica Parker, Cameron Diaz, Rene Zellweiger, and Courteney Cox Arquette have been often seen wearing Juicy clothing during interviews as well as in paparazzi photographs. Sarah Michelle Geller was quoted in the June 2002 issue of *InStyle* saying, "I had a Juicy weekend. My friends and I lived in our Juicy tracksuits. I love Juicy. There is nothing more luxurious than my Juicy cashmere" (PR Newswire, 2003).

### Questions to Consider

1.  What is your opinion about Juicy?

2.  Why do you think Juicy was so successful?

3.  Was public opinion a factor for the success of Juicy? Explain.

4.  How did public relations impact public opinion?

5.  How would you reach the media with Juicy's message?

6.  What type of media would you target? Why?

7.  If you were responsible for media coverage for Juicy, explain how you would go about getting celebrity support.

and administrative department personnel, as well as all other employees, be advised as to the nature of the story. (Interoffice memos or a copy of the press release is one way of getting that information to the employees.) In that way they will all communicate the same message with one voice. Many U.S. bills and coins carry the motto in Latin "e pluribus unum," which means "many uniting into one" or "out of many, one." When it comes to public relations, this phrase can serve as a motto, too—the same message should be given to the media or any interested party by all the employees. A united message—the same message from the many people involved—results in a story that is factual and consistent with its purpose. Successful corporate communication to the media comes about when all company personnel are on the same page. It is incumbent upon upper management in the company to disseminate this information and make certain that all employees know the story and are able to relay the same message. Suppose a company discovers after making deliveries to their customers that the faux metallic woven fabric that they used in their holiday dress line is flammable. A responsible company would immediately notify their customers to return the merchandise and announce that they will take this merchandise off the floor. They will also state that they will issue a credit for the dresses. They will do all in their power to replace the dresses with fabric that is nonflammable. The company will immediately send a press release to all print, TV, radio, and Internet press wires stating the information as previously described and explain the action taken. In the statement, it can explain how this happened and also if true, state that it did not know that this fabric was inferior and dangerous; it can also mention the steps it is taking now to avoid this situation in the future. Either at the same time or prior to the media and customers being advised, the company should thoroughly brief the employees on what happened. So, when the media comes knocking on the door, employees can speak with authority and integrity and with one voice.

## Chapter Summary

- Public opinion is a highly fluid and complex reflection of the aggregate opinion about a specific topic held by a large majority of a specific public.

- Creating positive public opinion is a primary goal of public relations and a vital key to a fashion company's success.

- To maximize public relations initiatives, a company must monitor public opinion about the company and its brands, and work to proactively improve it.

- Understanding human needs and how these shape public opinion can help us to undertake more meaningful public relations initiatives.

- Public opinion can have significant effects on business, as it affects customer purchasing decisions and relationships with suppliers and the community.

▶ Public opinion is shaped by the media, celebrities and community leaders, family and friends, the product, and the company's corporate communications.

▶ Proactive shaping of public opinion can be achieved in many ways, including soliciting media exposure, word-of-mouth campaigns, advertising, public relations, and promotion initiatives.

▶ Ethics plays a vital role in public relations. Those who stick to the truth are rewarded with trust from the media and long-term success.

▶ As a reliable source of information, the media has a responsibility toward the public to report about important issues clearly and objectively.

▶ The three key executives who direct and guide public relations initiatives are the VP for marketing, VP for sales, and the public relations director.

▶ Every company employee has a responsibility to uphold the most positive image possible for the company whenever dealing with the media, customers, suppliers, and the community at large.

▶ Informing the company's staff about a public relation initiative helps to create a unified voice for the company and maximize results.

## Key Terms

▶ brand recognition

▶ buying criteria

▶ buzz

▶ design

▶ influencer

▶ marketing public relations (MPR)

▶ marketing triangle

▶ media

▶ proactive MPR

▶ promotion

▶ public opinion

▶ quality

▶ reactive MPR

## Chapter-End Questions and Exercises

1. How is public opinion different than one person's opinion?

2. Do you agree that fashion is shaped by as well as shapes consumer opinion? Explain with examples.

3. How is public opinion related to democracy?

4. Do you agree with Maslow's Hierarchy of Needs? Why?

5. Do you agree with Cantril that public opinion does not anticipate or plan for crises and emergencies—it merely reacts to them after the fact? Explain.

6. What are the five main buying criteria? Which buying criteria do you consider most important when you shop for clothing?

7. Name two of your favorite retail stores and explain why they are your favorites. From your impression, what is the general public opinion about these stores?

8. Name two retail stores that are not your favorites. Why?

9. What type of store promotions (besides off-prices sales) motivate you to make a purchase?

10. Compare and contrast the five main factors which shape public opinion. Make sure to include an example for each.

11. Think of something you had heard about a particular product which later prevented you from buying it. What did you hear about it? Who told you about it? Did you check the authenticity of that opinion?

12. Which media do you use to get your news information? Why?

13. Look through style magazines and write down three examples of celebrities being featured wearing specific brands. Explain how seeing these celebrities wearing the brand affected your personal opinion of the brand.

14. Who do you listen to mostly from among your family and friends? Why? Are there any styles that you try to emulate because your family or friends subscribe to them?

15. What's the difference in your opinion between proactive and reactive shaping of public opinion? Which is better and why?

16. In your opinion, what are the ethical standards regarding the shaping of public opinion? What would constitute unethical conduct and why?

17. Research your library's news archive and find a news story involving unethical conduct in public relations. Summarize the article and identify what unethical actions took place, who was responsible, and what were the results.

18. Do you think today's media is mostly biased or unbiased? Offer specific examples to support your opinion.

19. Compare and contrast the three medium categories of media: print, broadcast, and online. Make sure to give a real-life example for each.

20. Compare and contrast the four types of media: news, general interest, trade, and owned. Make sure to give a real-life example for each.

21. Name and explain the three main roles of the media.

22. What is your favorite fashion publication? Why? Which type of media is it?

23. Name the executives responsible for public relations within a typical company and explain their RFDs relating to public relations.

24. Do you agree that it is important to inform the company employees when a public relations initiative is launched? Explain.

# Setting Up a Public Relations Campaign

# PART II

# Defining Public Relations Audiences

## THREE

## Chapter Snapshot

**B**efore a company can formulate and implement a public relations campaign, it must define the **audiences** first. Without a clear picture of the audience that the company is trying to reach, a public relations campaign becomes a hit-or-miss proposition. It is important to understand who comprises the company's audience; appreciating its geographic location, income level, family status, and other demographic information will make the campaign more focused and effective. With a clear picture of the audience's lifestyles, wants, and needs, it is easier to determine if a particular initiative is going to resonate with that group of people. Through research, **demographics,** and direct contact the company can formulate one or more **profiles** for its various publics and utilize these profiles in guiding its public relations strategies. In this chapter, we will explore the methods to identify the company's audiences, their profiles, and the ways to tailor the public relations campaign to fit these audiences.

## Objectives

- Define audience.

- Identify and explain the various classes of audiences, including consumers, businesses, and the media.

- Explore B2C audience segmentation along demographic lines.

- Be familiar with B2B audience segmentation by company types.

- Understand media segmentation according to media function.

- Be able to apply the methods for understanding an audience's motivations, needs, and values.

- Define audience profile and understand how to create such a profile for a fashion company based on demographic and psychographic data.

- Comprehend how to adjust public relations initiatives according to the company's audience profiles.

When conversing with our parents, the topics, choice of words, and tones of voice are typically quite different than when we chat with our friends. With our parents, we may speak softly and talk about topics involving the home. With our friends, we may speak more loudly and talk about the latest blockbuster movie or hit song. The difference between the two types of communication is the audience—the source of the communication has not changed, but the recipient has and that affects the entire dynamics of the conversation. Just as we adjust the way we speak and what we say according to who we are talking to, so does a company adjust its corporate communications according to the target audience. Suppose a company sends out to the consumer media a press release filled with trade specifications and focused on the technical aspects of how the clothing is made. Whereas a wholesaler may be interested in the brand of the manufacturer's machinery used to stitch the garments, the average consumer neither recognizes the brand nor cares about it. The consumer media, therefore, will never pick up the release because their audience—the consumers—will not be interested. Thus, a consumer-oriented public relations campaign that promotes manufacturing equipment is most likely destined to fail. Identifying both the intermediate and ultimate audiences and adjusting public relations communications accordingly is extremely vital to the campaign's success.

## The Public Relations Audience

The importance of identifying the target audiences prior to embarking on a public relations campaign cannot be overstated. Without knowing who the campaign will communicate to, it is difficult to establish the direction of the campaign and its initiatives. When taking into consideration the target audience's needs and values, the public relations director often finds herself or himself in a position where the entire presentation of the initiative—and sometimes even the initiative itself—must be completely reshaped. At times, the initiative's presentation must be customized for multiple audiences, necessitating a wide variety of presentation strategies, each customized to appeal to

> ## Box 3.1 Real World Principle: Focus
>
> For public relations to be effective, its message must be as focused as possible to resonate with the target audience and result in an improved public image for the company and its brands.

a different audience. If the company mixes the audiences, the message may get distorted, resulting in the audiences not receiving the message at all or even misunderstanding the message to form negative opinions of the company.

Audiences can be divided into three major categories: consumers, businesses, and the media. Beyond that, the **public relations audience** can be further sub-categorized into various unique groups of audiences within the major category. The overall approach of communicating with the audience depends on which major category they fit into.

## Business to Consumer

**Business to consumer (B2C)** is simply defined as sales made by a business to an individual consumer; the process of selling a product/service to the ultimate consumer(s), also known as the end user(s). It is differentiated from business conducted between companies; this is known as **business to business (B2B).** B2B is simply defined as "transactions that take place between fashion manufacturers, retailers, or any two business entities" (Sherman & Perlman, 2006). B2C companies sell directly to the fashion end-user whereas B2B companies sell to other fashion companies, such as manufacturers, wholesalers, and retailers. The B2C audience within the public relations context, therefore, consists of the end-user consumers and potential consumers of the company's fashion products. The public image of the product and company within the B2C sphere is extremely important because the consumer who will be purchasing the product is aware of that public image and typically consults—consciously or subconsciously—that image prior to making a purchasing decision. Thus we can see that the impact of public relations extends in the B2C sphere to direct influence over product sales. The fashion manufacturer and retailer are clearly the fashion companies that are most concerned with this audience. With positive public opinion about the company and the product exists a more conducive environment for the consumer to buy.

The long-term success of the B2C-driven company and its ability to stand out from the competition hinges upon the degree of its positive public image within the B2C audience. Suppose you were a consumer sitting at home when suddenly you get the unstoppable urge to buy a new cool T-shirt. Your decision of which brand T-shirt to buy and where to buy it is probably motivated by many factors, including which brand you think is cool, how much you are willing to pay for it, which is the nearest store that carries that brand, which other stores carry the brand, and so forth. Your decision is also likely to be affected by your opinion as well as public opinion regarding the brands or retailers that are available. For example, suppose you are an avid backpacker as well and you care whether the company from which you buy your T-shirt cares about the environment. Your choice for buying the T-shirt may go in the direction of an eco-friendly manufacturer such as REI, which has established a name for itself among outdoor fans as a green company, even if there are other retailers closer that sell T-shirts cheaper. In this case, your purchasing decision is virtually a direct result of REI's public relations efforts to create this image over the years. Besides attracting new customers, B2C public relations also aims to foster customer retention and loyalty. Through the implementation of various B2C public relations strategies, a fashion company can create and maintain a positive public image for the company and its products in the minds of its existing consumers. This positive image influences the company's existing customers to remain loyal

---

### Box 3.2  Real World Profile: Recreational Equipment, Inc. (REI)

Based in Kent, Washington, REI is a manufacturer and retailer of outdoor gear and clothing. According to Hoovers Online, the company is the nation's largest consumer cooperative with more than three million members. Through some 100 outlets in more than 25 states, REI sells high-end gear, clothing, and footwear for outdoor activities such as climbing, kayaking, skiing, hiking, bicycling, and camping (Recreational Equipment, Inc., 2008).

The section of the company's Web site "About REI" details its approach to identifying with its B2C audience. It stresses its outdoorsy, environmentally responsible commitment to making durable, quality products by including phrases such as:

▶ "Whether you're new to outdoor adventure or a seasoned pro, we gladly share our enthusiasm for our products—and the trails, slopes, and waterways where we play."

▶ "Each year, REI donates millions of dollars to support conservation efforts nationwide, and sends scores of volunteers to build trails, clean up beaches, and teach outdoor ethics to kids. Through responsible business practices, we strive to reduce our environmental footprint."

▶ "What began as a group of 23 mountain climbing buddies is now the nation's largest consumer cooperative with more than three million active members. But no matter how large we grow, our roots remain firmly planted in the outdoors.Our passion for outdoor adventure is clear, whether

you walk into one of our 80-plus stores, phone us, or visit the REI Web site."

▶ "By staying true to our roots, we've earned a place on *Fortune* magazine's list of the 100 Best Companies to Work For every year since the rankings began in 1998. We work hard to earn our reputation for quality and integrity every day. Our commitment remains the same as when we started out in 1938: to inspire, educate, and outfit for a lifetime of outdoor adventure" (www.rei.com).

FIGURE BOX 3.2  The section of the company's Web site "About REI" details its approach to identifying with its B2C audience.

to the company's brands and keep buying its products as opposed to switching to the competition. In essence, such public relations efforts demonstrate to the customers that their trust in the company is well founded and that they have made the right choice in selecting its products. With proper public relations initiatives, the company can develop a solid, long-term relationship with the community of its customers to maintain market share. Thus it can be seen that customer retention is a vital function of B2C public relations.

As we will discuss in further detail in the next section, the role that the B2C audience plays in the public relations arena extends beyond the influence it has on the manufacturer or retailer company alone; the public opinion of the consumer is the final word about whether a certain style or fashion item sells. Ultimately, all fashion companies—whether they are B2C or B2B companies—are concerned with this audience in one manner or another. Consider the role of a garment supplier in the production of the final product: the supplier buys the garments in volume and then resells them to the manufacturers. Even though the supplier never sells to or deals with the consumer, the supplier still needs to be attuned to the latest styles (B2C public opinion about design) and business news (B2C public opinion about garment production issues). A supplier that is not in touch with the final end-consumer gradually fades out of touch with the market as a whole and the company's public image deteriorates. Thus we see that although B2B companies may never implement B2C public relations efforts directly with consumers, the B2C public relations audience still affects its business throughout all of the links along the **supply chain** of the fashion industry. The supply chain can be defined as the flow of goods through all the steps involved in getting the products to the end user. Any public relations efforts by a B2B company must still consult the final public opinion of the end user if it is to succeed.

The B2C media is highly competitive and very selective as to the stories they run. The one rule in B2C media is that if the story seems commercial and is written to appear as an advertising piece, the story will rarely get published. B2C media is primarily interested in the hottest items, spectacular fashion trends, and gossip. B2C public relations has to be continuous and inspiring, geared toward urging the reader to take action and purchase the new fashion items. Although B2C stories are targeted to a general consumer base and are mostly concerned with short-term, immediate action results, repetition of positive B2C exposure strengthens the company's relationships with the end-user and develops trust in the company and its products over the long term.

## Business to Business

In defining the public relations audiences of B2B and B2C there are differences in each of these areas regarding the direction public relations must take to reach these two audiences. Understandably, B2B public relations audiences have to be reached primarily through trade media whereas B2C public relations audiences are open for all consumer media vehicles, including radio, TV, Internet, and print. However, when public relations information is published in consumer-type media, the business community will also be exposed to it; thus, an overlap between the two areas exists in the B2B area. When the *New York Times* runs a fashion story about a designer directed at the consumer market—as can be seen in the story of Marc Jacobs in Box 3.3—we see that the B2B market is also made aware of the story. Thus the B2C media typically also acts as a B2B outlet regarding recent trends and changes in fashion.

Fashion-oriented stories that run in *W, Vogue, Lucky,* and other notable consumer magazines are widely read by the business community, too; the B2B community has the advantage of being exposed to these additional channels of B2C media. On the other hand, trade publications are read by B2B readership and rarely by consumers. An industry news report about a fashion designer, fashion trend, or collection that appears in *WWD,* for example, will be read by manufacturers, retailers, designers, and other members of the trade, but not

---

## Box 3.3  How B2C Affects B2B in Fashion

Although the following excerpt from a *New York Times* article was directed at the B2C audience, B2B fashion companies and designers were able to determine if the blouson trend should be included in their future collections. Here we see an example where the B2B fashion company is able to benefit from all forms of media coverage. The following is an excerpt from "Marc Jacobs Play It Safe? Come On, Now Top of Form," by Eric Wilson, published in the *New York Times:*

FIGURE BOX 3.3 Marc Jacobs at a fashion show.

On Friday night, Mr. Jacobs closed Fashion Week with a collection that was provocative on another level. It was, as usual, a big, overwhelming production.

This time, it featured cabaret seating, buckets of Champagne on cafe tables, and a stage dominated by a video installation by Tony Oursler, which showed repeating images of crashing waves, then one blinking eye, then a woman emerging from a swim.

Before Ms. Beckham and Mr. Federline had reached their seats, there was Sonic Youth performing a rock concert on stage, with the singer Kim Gordon in a sequined tank dress, and the models walking out around them.

But against that backdrop, the clothes seemed eerily quiet and casual, with round-shouldered coats in lovely muted pastels, the color of bathrobes, and a simple waffle-knit sweater shown over roomy wide-wale cords in plain gray. The faces of some models were veiled. Was Mr. Jacobs playing it safe?

In a word, no.

Despite all the insults and abuse laid at his door for his off-the-runway antics, the only time Mr. Jacobs really seems ruffled is when critics deride him as a mere stylist of references, to Yves Saint Laurent or Comme des Garçons.

In this collection he chose one idea, the blouson, and stayed focused on it, as gutsy a move as should be expected of a real designer. He played with length, dropping the waist lower and lower until it almost reached the knees, and added volume to the back of coats with pouches of fluted fabric, giving them a 1920s shape. (New York Times, 2008)

**TABLE 3.1 The Similarities and Differences of B2B and B2C**

| Fashion B2C | Fashion B2B |
| --- | --- |
| General audience | Focused audience |
| Broad selection of media exposure | Limited selection of media exposure |
| Highly competitive media access for public relations | Less competitive media access for public relations |
| Getting media coverage is difficult | Getting media coverage is easier |
| Call for action message | Institutional message |
| Short-range objective | Long-range objectives |
| Media consumer directed | Media industry directed |
| Must be something new | Must be something new |
| Product/company oriented | Product/company oriented |

by consumers. So we see that getting the word out to the business community has more public relations opportunities than its intended path. There are distinct differences in getting public relations coverage for each of these groups, and there are notable similarities. Consumer-directed public relations must be one that is new, exciting, and informative, primarily concerning itself with new products and styles. Business-related fashion public relations directed at the B2B audience needs to be informative, primarily concerning itself with exciting and interesting information about fashion trends, the company's progress, and its impact on the marketplace. As in B2C, the B2B media is more apt to cover a story if it is newsy. The trade media want to give coverage to "what's new." Still, B2B public relations has to be consistent and geared to long-term results as well. Looking for a broader base of media coverage both national and international, B2B public relations should reflect the fact that businesses are concerned with long-term relationships with their base, and this must be included in the nature of media coverage.

### The Media

Although the media is only an **intermediate audience,** it is nonetheless a highly important link to the fashion company's other audiences. The media is a fully autonomous conduit of fashion news to other audiences. Because the media cannot be controlled by the fashion company, it has the power to disseminate the company's news or withhold it from the public as it wants; and if the media chooses to disseminate the news, it also has the power to disseminate it but focus on the positive, the negative, or both. It is thus in the company's best interests to provide the media with accurate, positive information in order to get the company's message across to the readers and viewers of the media, who are also the company's ultimate audiences.

The approach to the media is essentially, "you have got to have a story." The media is always looking for unique stories and breaking news items. Approaching the different media for B2B and B2C is relatively the same in the respect that the story must be packaged so the reporter can understand and adapt it with as little editing as possible. The more focused, researched, and compatible the story is to what the reporter has been covering, the better the chances that it will be picked up. Here again, press releases should be sent only to those in the media who are involved in the type of stories you want to see published. The public relations firm that is well informed can function in both the B2B and B2C environments. The mechanics of reaching the trade or the consumer media relatively remains the same. However, the trade media is typically more close knit with the industry than consumer media is with consumers; trade media reporters know prominent figures within the industry fairly well and speak to them often, so it becomes doubly important to ensure you do not make any claims about your product or company that other competitors can easily disprove, thus effectively destroying your credibility. It is imperative that the public relations director or firm has a complete knowledge of the product, industry, and how the different trends affect the company that is being represented. Creating unique awareness about the product will help increase recognition by the media and position the company for media coverage. It is worth pointing out that great press releases are only produced when the public relations personnel does exhaustive research regarding the story. This means that the public relations director must also be a fashion-oriented person who understands fashion trends, has a complete knowledge of fashion companies and their products, and is familiar with both well-known and up-and-coming designers. Research is vital.

## Audience Segmentation

To better understand its audience, the company must create a more specific and detailed description of the audience beyond the overall major categories previously mentioned; companies do this by segmenting their audiences into smaller groups as necessary according to demographics, and creating one or more **audience profiles.** With a clear and defined profile for the audience, the public relations director or firm can gear the public relations strategies toward appealing to the needs and value systems of that audience. In an ideal world, each public relations strategy would be geared toward just one individual, and be wholly aimed to appeal to that one individual's unique mindset. There

---

### Box 3.4 Real World Concept: B2C, B2B, and Media Audience Synergy

Whereas the B2C, B2B, and media audiences may be three different audience groups, they are intimately interconnected and interdependent. Each of the audiences affects the other two audiences while at the same time being affected by them. For example, the consumer audience affects the media audience in that consumer interests steer the direction of media reporting. Similarly, the media's opinions affect the fashion manufacturers' direction of design and consumer taste.

would thus be as many public relations strategies as there are individual audience members in the company's business environment. Centuries ago, business was closer to this model, conducted with extreme one-on-one marketing and sales interactions that developed strong personal business relationships. There were no mass mailings, advertisements, or public relations campaigns. Within today's business environment, however, this is highly impractical and unrealistic—the monetary and timely costs of truly personalizing the company's marketing efforts down to the individual level are enormous. Plus, spending resources solely on such individualized marketing efforts puts the fashion company at a disadvantage: by the time it reaches one potential client using the one-on-one method, its competitors will have reached hundreds if not thousands of potential clients using mass-media methods.

Therefore, a company must divide its audience down to the smallest group size feasible, given the company's resources. Grouping individuals with similar consumer characteristics in this manner allows the company to efficiently customize its communications for that group without sacrificing costs or results. Accordingly, there is a balance between the two extremes of macro segmentation (grouping all audiences into one group) and micro segmentation (separating the audience into its number of individuals); that balance is determined by the company's marketing budget and resources, and how varied is the spectrum of individuals who form its audience. **Audience segmentation** is necessary in order to achieve more focused and effective public relations strategies.

Love My Shoes is a chain of large women's-shoes stores in the greater Long Island area. It specializes in hip, trendy women's and girls' fashion shoes, and has six retail stores and an e-commerce Web site (lovemyshoes.com). The retailer reaches out to its public by segmenting the audience and then focusing on reaching out to the media, which targets this segment of the audience. Because the retailer sells only to women and girls, and because the shoes offered are typically trendy shoes, the segment of the audience on which the public relations campaign has focused is girls and younger women who are interested in looking chic. In 2006 and 2007, the company and its Web site were featured in trendy publications such as *People, Star, Life & Style*, as well as New York's *CW11 Morning News* (lovemyshoes.com, 2009). In this case, audience segmentation has helped the retailer narrow its public relations efforts, thus maximizing results for the segment of the B2C audience that it needs to reach with its message.

Let's see how audience segmentation applies to each of the major audience groups discussed so far.

## B2C Segmentation

In the world of marketing and advertising, creating a detailed audience profile of the company's consumer is an absolute must. The segmentation and classification of consumers has become a vital component that is typically required prior to the formulation and adoption of any marketing or advertising plan. It is important for a fashion company to know who its average consumer is, who its top consumer is, and who its potential consumer is before establishing an advertising campaign—and perhaps even before producing the actual

FIGURE 3.1 The Love My Shoes' Web site utilizes design elements, fonts, colors, and audio-visual content to make its pages appeal to the company's target audience of teenage girls and younger women who love their trendy shoes.

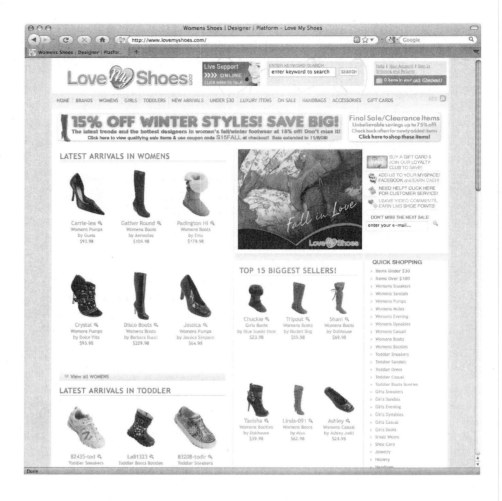

product. Although audience segmentation may be considered mandatory within the advertising field, it should be given more importance within the public relations field. Shouldn't the company know who its potential consumer is before launching a public relations campaign? If the company doesn't know its potential consumer, how could it approach the media outlets that target that potential consumer? When the fashion company studies and segments its publics, the likelihood of public relations success improves considerably. The top factors that guide proper consumer segmentation are demographic: geography, gender, age, income, profession, education, and marital status.

The major concern in segmentation is to be conscious that some of these categories in consumer segmentation are complex, constantly changing, and require constant monitoring. But when achieved, gathering information in this manner brings great rewards in gaining valuable publicity that will reach the target customers. We must be conscious of the changes in our society regarding population shifts, financial conditions, and lifestyle changes. Another concern that must be kept in mind prior to segmentation is that at times certain products are purchased by a **proxy buyer.** In this scenario, the segmented audience should be further divided so that the audience profile of the end user is consulted in parallel with that of the proxy buyer. Even though the product is designed with the end user in mind, the marketing and public relations efforts need to include the proxy buyer because the latter will be making the actual purchase. As an example, take the mother (proxy buyer) who buys board shorts for her 11-year-old son (an end user). Although the product needs to appeal to the end user's needs—the design should look cool and the fit should be comfortable in a multitude of uses—it also needs to appeal to the needs of the proxy buyer— the price should be affordable and the garment should be able to withstand the adventures of an 11-year-old boy. The fashion company that finds that most of its customers are proxy buyers must adjust its segmented audience and public relations approach accordingly.

### Geography

The consumer's geographical location and whether it is within the company's territory is one of the first factors to consider in audience segmentation; if the consumer is located outside that territory, then the company cannot even offer the consumer its products or services. Segmenting the company's public along geographical lines is done by dividing the public into the smallest possible geographical zones. The zone can be a state, a county, a town, a suburb, or even a specific neighborhood. The premise of this division is that consumers in different geographical positions have differing buying habits. Whereas consumers in the suburbs may drive to the retailer in the nearest strip mall in their neighborhood, urban consumers may window shop the various boutiques in the downtown area. Consumers who live in rural areas may have to drive to the nearest city if they want to visit a shopping mall. Each of these groups of consumers has its own set of buying habits, and thus can be deemed a segmented audience within the overall audience of consumers.

(a)

(b)

**FIGURE 3.2A AND B**
**Segmenting Audiences.** Demographics and purchasing patterns are top concerns in audience segmentation. Differences in geographical area, age, income, gender, education, profession, and other factors divide the B2C audience. The two women in the photographs have considerably different needs, tastes, budgets, purchasing habits, and value sets.

Another example of geographical segmentation is along weather patterns. In states with colder climates such as the U.S. Northeast, winter fashion is radically different than the winter fashion of Honolulu, Hawaii for example, where winter rarely brings temperatures below 40 degrees. Gloves, hats, scarves, and the like are unusual fashion items in Honolulu's department stores.

### Gender

Gender plays an important role in audience segmentation primarily because fashion has traditionally been divided into men's wear and women's wear. The majority of fashion items can be marketed only to either men or women, thus excluding the other gender from the audience. For example, it makes little sense for a manufacturer of women's underwear to embark on a public relations campaign to sponsor the local antique car club or for a manufacturer of men's ties to sponsor the national breastfeeding support group. The exception is when research shows that the proxy buyer for the product is of the opposite sex; for example, in the case of the men's ties manufacturer, it's possible that most purchases for married male clients are actually done by their wives.

### Age

Age is an extremely important factor in segmenting audiences because it typically determines, to a large degree, the customer's views, attitudes, needs, and wants. Teenagers have different sets of values and views than senior citizens. The company must determine the age brackets of its public and how to communicate with that public.

### Income

The income of the individual consumer considerably affects the type of public relations communications he or she should receive. Consumers in the higher level of income obviously have more purchasing power, but typically such consumers are more discerning and may be more costly to market to; a connoisseur consumer is much more picky about the garments, cuts, and so on, plus he or she most likely will not respond to cheap pamphlets or advertisements but instead may respond only to such pricy marketing tools as expensive full-color print catalogs, high-end advertisements, and concierge-like personalized promotions such as the one described in Box 3.5. Luxury retailers and top designers like Bergdorf Goodman and Valentino rely on their prestige and reputation to retain clientele (Boxes 3.6 and 3.7). On the other end of the spectrum, consumers of limited income are typically looking for clothing at bargain prices. This is where mass retailers such as Wal-Mart and Big Lots come in; these retailers buy in such volume that they can significantly reduce the retail price. Beyond determining product pricing and marketing, income level is an important audience segmentation factor because it also affects the approach to public relations. Consumers with high income levels read different publications than those with low incomes. Their attitudes toward a specific public relations initiative may be different than the attitudes of middle-class

## Box 3.5   The High Stakes of High-End Retail

With the big-ticket fashion items come the big-spender clients who demand luxurious style and accept nothing short of exquisite service. What's a high-end fashion company to do? Adjust its marketing and public relations strategies to raise the ante. Top designers and retailers are finding that building a relationship with their wealthy clients is more important than ever, and specialized public relations initiatives are a key to rising above the competition. The following article from MSNBC, "High-End Retailers Banking on Thanks" by Lisa Marsh, is about one such initiative:

When a large flower arrangement arrived at Joanna King's home in Ellicott City, Maryland, in mid-February, she thought she might have an admirer.

"I had no idea who was sending me a Valentine," she says. The gift turned out to be from a saleswoman at the Ethan Allen store where she had just purchased a chair for her living room.

"I went back to the same saleswoman because I liked her, but the flowers didn't hurt," says King, who soon ordered a new sofa and received another bouquet. "The arrangement was nicer the first time, but I would definitely go back."

Sending personal notes and gifts are a long-standing practice at high-end retailers, though generally for sales representatives who have relationships with individual customers. But in the face of an economic downturn—both Neiman Marcus and Nordstrom recently reported that same-store sales for February had dropped from last year—luxury retailers are stepping up the practice of thanking clients.

Spenders big and small recently received thank you notes from designer boutiques Luca Luca, Jimmy Choo, Stuart Weitzman, and Louis Vuitton. Department stores Saks Fifth Avenue, and Bergdorf Goodman (which is owned by Neiman Marcus) also sent notes, particularly to customers who bought beauty products—not surprising, as such purchases tend to be more regular.

"Personal shoppers send thank you notes as a general practice to people who spend $10,000, $15,000, or $20,000 a year," says Milton Pedraza, CEO of the Luxury Institute, a rating and research company in New York. "In a business downturn, [retailers] focus on this type of practice a bit more. Top managers at Saks Fifth Avenue in Dallas have told me, 'We'll pack their suitcases if they want us to,' to try to embed themselves in the lives of their customers, particularly in slow economic times."

A spokeswoman for Ethan Allen says gifts are sometimes sent to customers when its salespeople—designers in company parlance—"have relationships that have lasted for years." She adds, "It's a personal thing for our designers, not part of the corporate dictate." Instead, the company believes competitive pricing and perks like free design service and delivery drive sales.

Nordstrom is known for maintaining a correspondence with its best regular customers, particularly those who shop in the beauty and menswear departments. However, this reporter received a card after purchasing two moderately priced knit shirts and a jacket that was on sale.

"There is no corporate direction on this," says Michael Boyd, a Nordstrom company spokesman. "Our salespeople build relationships with their customers by calling them and sending out thank you notes."

As the economy tightens, "hopefully our salespeople—and we have a commission-based sales force—send out more thank you cards," Boyd says.

The new direction in retail is relationship management, says Tom Julian, director of trends for McCann Erickson. "From small boutiques to major department stores, retailers have had to show their shoppers how much they appreciate them in many ways. It's more than service today" (March, 2008).

consumers. In planning public relations strategies, income must be taken into account to ensure the initiatives are meaningful to the company's audiences. At times, different initiatives must be undertaken to appeal to the audiences of specific income levels.

## Box 3.6 Real World Profile: Bergdorf Goodman

Standing at the crossroads of fashion at Fifth Avenue and 58th Street in New York City, Bergdorf Goodman is known throughout the world for elegance, luxury, and superior service. The company's history traces back to 1899 when Edwin Goodman worked for Herman Bergdorf, an immigrant from Alsace, in his tailoring establishment just above Union Square in downtown Manhattan. In 1906, Goodman purchased the store from Bergdorf and moved to the site where Rockefeller Center now stands. In 1914, Goodman was the first couturier to introduce ready-to-wear, making Berg-dorf Goodman the destination for top American and French fashion. The store continued to attract New York's elite over the years, expanding its line to include fine women's apparel, handbags, jewelry, makeup, perfume, shoes, and tableware, as well as men's accessories, by designer labels such as Chloe, Giorgio Armani, and Marc Jacobs. According to Hoovers Online, Berg-dorf Goodman is owned by the upscale department store operator Neiman Marcus, and operates two stores across from each other on 58th Street in Manhattan. The smaller store is devoted exclusively to men. The elite retailer also operates a catalog and a Web site (www.hoovers.com, 2009).

FIGURE BOX 3.6 The Bergdorf Goodman store on Fifth Avenue.

## Box 3.7 Real World Profile: Valentino

The Italian designer launched his career in 1960, making a name for himself as a master of opulence, creating luxurious gowns with intricate details. Valentino has been popular with European royalty, high society, and celebrities. The fabrics Valentino uses tend to be delicate, lavish, and rich, featuring laces, chiffons, and silk crepe, along with wool, leather, and suede. His designs are often seen on the red carpet, and many collect his vintage dresses, like the black gown worn by Julia Roberts when she accepted her Oscar in 2001. His menswear collection is sharp and timeless. Valentino has been the designer behind the label since the beginning and continues to design his creations today. His gowns have been popular with the rich and famous, including Jackie Onassis, Elizabeth Taylor, Halle Berry, Jennifer Garner, Julia Roberts, Jennifer Aniston, Naomi Watts, Claire Danes, Gwen Stefani, Lindsay Lohan, and Gwenyth Paltrow (New York Magazine, 2009).

FIGURE BOX 3.7 Valentino at a fashion show.

### Profession

The consumer's profession can have a considerable effect on audience segmentation, especially, of course, when dealing with business wear. For example, a fashion manufacturer of business suits has to distinguish between its executive audience and junior staff audience; the executive relies on the suit for a certain level of quality and style that will impress clients, peers, and subordinates, whereas the junior staff may look for a basic suit that will pass the company's dress policy. The two audiences are quite different in their expectations and needs, but also in the way they react to public relations efforts. The executive may read the *Wall Street Journal* whereas the junior staff may read the local daily paper. Similarly, professionals of different vocations have varying requirements for their business attires. A salesperson who is constantly on his or her feet will look for a comfortable pair of shoes whereas a construction worker will look for shoe safety and protection against the hazards often present around a construction site. Similarly, the salesperson and construction worker are likely to favor dissimilar media and regard a public relations project differently; the salesman may appreciate a fundraiser for the local chamber of commerce; the construction worker may feel indifferent about such an initiative. It is thus helpful to segment audiences by profession, if possible. That said, however, segmenting by profession can be at times difficult if not outright impossible. If the company's products are not aimed at any specific profession, it becomes hard to identify the professions included for that audience; in these cases it can be helpful to categorize the professions for that audience in larger groups, such as management, sales, or accounting.

### Marital Status

Whether the consumer is single, married, divorced, or widowed can determine the consumer's preference of one fashion style over another. For example, a single person is more likely to consciously or subconsciously gravitate toward styles that will impress and attract a potential mate than would a married person.

### Education

The audience's education level typically indicates whether the person completed high school, attended some college, or earned a bachelor's or higher degree. It can be a segmentation factor usually in combination with the consumer's profession or income level.

### Consumption Patterns

Knowing the purchasing habits of the audience helps the company in segmenting its audience. A consumption pattern report typically indicates the types of goods the audience purchases in percentages out of their entire budget. It may also indicate the frequency of these purchases, e.g., every six months or every three months, and so on.

### Other Factors

There may be other factors that can be used to guide audience segmentation, depending on the fashion company's products; these include but are by no means limited to ethnicity, height, and weight. If the product appeals to a certain group of people, then the audience can be segmented along the defining denominator of that group. For instance, if the company manufactures jerseys for the football fan, then the overall audience of consumers can be safely reduced to those who enjoy football, and then can be further segmented along the various team lines.

## B2B Segmentation

A fashion company's B2B audience can be segmented as well to maximize public relations efforts. A B2B company, such as a manufacturer or wholesaler, depends on other businesses for its survival and thus must develop meaningful relationships with these businesses to achieve long-term success. Public relations is an essential ingredient to creating and developing these relationships in that it fosters a positive public image within the company's B2B environment. Segmenting the B2B audience is key to understanding the various subgroups within the B2B audience and adjusting the public relations efforts to fit each subgroup. Suppose a manufacturer of women's wear is seeking to enter a new market of women's shoes. In order to manufacture its designs it must first obtain suppliers as well as subcontractors for the various parts of the shoes. The company then has to distribute its shoes, so it must locate wholesalers and retailers that will sell them. The women's wear retailers with which the manufacturer is already doing business may not carry women's shoes, so the manufacturer may have to forge distribution agreements with new retailers that do carry shoes. The suppliers and retailers are both part of the B2B audience of the manufacturer. However, they are different types of audiences and a public relations initiative that aims to appeal to retailers will likely not be appealing to suppliers. Similarly, if the manufacturer aims to distribute nationwide, it may find that retailers in the Southeast react differently to public relations efforts than Northwestern retailers. Here again, adjustment in public relations strategies is called for. Let's examine the guidelines for B2B segmentation.

### B2B Industry

An important factor in segmentation within the B2B sphere is the industry of each company within the audience. A B2B fashion company typically has to deal with companies from other industries as well as those from the fashion industry. A manufacturer of shirts must get them packaged, labeled, inventoried, and shipped. If these functions are not produced in-house, the manufacturer must outsource these to outside contractors, all of which are businesses in other industries. In this instance, the shipper is likely shipping many different types of goods, not just clothing. That shipping company's executives are not reading the fashion industry publications; they subscribe to their own industry's trade magazines. Public relations efforts to reach outside contractors such as the shipping company will fail if it assumes that all of the company's suppliers follow fashion industry news simply because one of its customers is a fashion company.

### B2B Field

Within any industry, there are many fields to which a B2B company could belong. The fashion industry has knitters, fabric suppliers, accessories suppliers, manufacturers, wholesalers, retailers, and so on. Each one of these fields may be different from a public relations perspective. Thus, a wholesaler company that deals with dozens of manufacturers and scores of retailers should evaluate whether these fields should be considered as two different segments of its B2B audience, depending on the public relations campaign objectives and the company's resources.

### Business Size

The size of the business is another criterion in segmentation in the B2B sphere. Large worldwide or nationwide companies usually employ hundreds if not thousands, and the opinions of their employees about the fashion company can affect public opinion within the B2B circles. Smaller companies having fewer employees does not mean they are not as important as the large firms; word travels fast in a small company and its employees can have much influence over the local sentiment about the fashion company. Clearly, the impact of public relations differs between large corporate conglomerates and mom-and-pop boutique shops. It is in the fashion company's best interests to evaluate the size of its clients within the B2B audience. Larger companies are typically more impersonal and bureaucratic, and it is difficult to utilize public relations to get their employees' attention because they are constantly bombarded with phone calls, emails, text messages, and so on.

### Other Factors

B2B audience segmentation is not a rote procedure; each fashion company has its own unique needs, products, audiences, and approach to business. Therefore, the public relations director can find there are other factors that may affect segmentation, depending on the product, the market, and the company. The main concern is to maximize public relations efforts, and audience segmentation should lead to more focused initiatives within the B2B sphere.

## Media Segmentation

In public relations we look for the most effective media to deliver our message. Some public relations companies in their anxiety just to get something to please their clients will reach out to certain segments of the media that will not effectively deliver the client's message. The message must fit the media and the media fit the message. Media segmentation becomes paramount in getting the word out to the audience. Where to pitch the story and get the most mileage in these changing times becomes the primary challenge of public relations. Print media has been the primary source of delivering the message on fashion trends. However, as we have witnessed, the increase of television and the Internet as major media instruments is reaching more target markets effectively within budgetary boundaries. A media diversity trend is evolving whereby newspapers and magazine are now extending their marketing efforts to the global market by combining television and the Internet under one umbrella. This move extends the areas of media outreach for the public relations industry. In today's public relations environment it is vital to know where to find the right fit for the news story; this means being a communication expert—knowing where to put your efforts to get the story out. Public relations today requires the practitioners to have full knowledge of all the media outlets. Who are you trying to reach, and what section of the media will deliver the best results? Deciding who to contact to get the message across can be a very time consuming and perplexing exercise. We have to look at the client's product, understand demographics and the different media areas, and then market our information just as a merchant must market his or her products—public relations people must know where to send their stories and whom to pitch. The many varied areas of the media require public relations personnel to spend more time researching the different areas of media and deciding where they can make their mark.

### News Wire Services

Due to the complexity of getting a story out to all the different segments of the media, there is a rise in companies engaging paid wire services to help get a news release the proper coverage. The following are some of the wire services that public relations professionals use to distribute their news releases. They are all fee based, some on individual press releases and others by yearly contracts:

▶   BusinessWire—Distributes press releases nationally and internationally, and enables public relations people to target their specific area (www.businesswire.com).

▶   PR Newswire—Distributes releases (www.prnewswire.com).

▶   CisionPoint—Uses Bacon's Media Database, searches for media contacts, and measures the success of your press release (www.cisionpoint.com).

▶   VOCUS—Provides a Web platform for the public relations industry. Enables you to send releases relatively easily on the Internet (www.vocus.com).

### Consumer Media

The media that reaches out to consumers has tremendous impact on the success of a new product or line. The B2C fashion company that sells to the consumer is thus primarily concerned with consumer media; however, further segmentation can be applied to better focus public relations efforts. Consumer media publications are typically aimed at a certain readership and cater to this audience's needs. It is vital for a fashion company to research the audience profile of each publication prior to earmarking public relations efforts to reach that publication. For example, *Glamour* is one of the most influential women's magazines with more than 12.5 million modern women readers. It covers women's fashion, lifestyles, and other women's issues. Its readers' median age is 34 and the majority of its readers earn between $75,000 and $100,000. In contrast, *W* is a leading luxury fashion and lifestyle magazine that targets the world's most influential consumers—those who have the means, desire, and taste to own the very best. Its readers' median age is 48 and their median income is $146,169. Clearly, whereas the two publications both cover fashion, their readerships comprise two distinctly different audience groups. The B2C fashion company that specializes in high-end luxury fashion would achieve better results by focusing on getting exposure in *W* rather than in *Glamour*. Virtually every publication offers information to potential advertisers that outlines its readership demographics and profile, and most publications post their advertiser kits on their Web sites. The public relations staff can download these advertiser kits and get an overview of what audience they will be reaching out to through each publication.

### Trade Media

B2B fashion companies rely on trade publications that relate directly to their product and industry. Fashion trade magazine and trade papers will deliver the story directly to the target customer. A B2B company must customize its

(a)

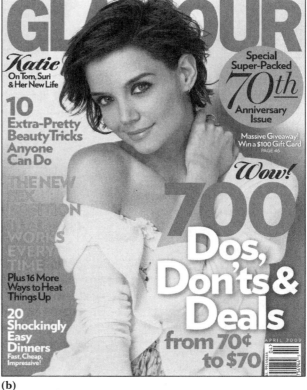

(b)

FIGURE 3.3A AND B  The B2C fashion company that specializes in high-end luxury fashion would achieve better results by focusing on getting exposure in *W* rather than in *Glamour*.

**TABLE 3.2   B2C Media Segmentation**

Consumer fashion publications typically have different groups of readerships, with unique demographic criteria. Segmenting consumer media according to their readerships helps the fashion company to focus its public relations initiatives and maximize improvement of the company's public image with the right audience. As can be seen in the following series of tables, *Glamour* and *W* have distinctly different readerships.

### 3.2A   Fashion Publication Demographics

| Publication | *Glamour* (as of May 2008) | *W* (as of January 2007) |
| --- | --- | --- |
| Subscription | 1,606,840 | 419,101 |
| Newsstand | 747,014 | 47,052 |
| **Total paid & verified circulation** | 2,353,854 | 466,152 |

Ratebase: 450,000 (ABC, 2007)

### 3.2B   *Glamour* Audience by Gender

| | |
| --- | --- |
| Total adults | 12,517,000 |
| Total women | 11,699,000 |
| Total men | 818,000 |

(ABC, 2007)

### 3.2C   *Glamour* Audience by Age

| | |
| --- | --- |
| 18–24 | 3,131,000 |
| 18–34 | 6,506,000 |
| 18–49 | 10,273,000 |
| 25–34 | 3,375,000 |
| 35–44 | 2,687,000 |
| Median age | 34 |

(ABC, 2007)

### 3.2D   *Glamour* Audience by Income

| | |
| --- | --- |
| HHI $75,000+ | 5,124,000 |
| HHI $100,000+ | 3,412,000 |

(ABC, 2007)

### 3.2E   *W* Reader Profile

| | Percentage | Index |
| --- | --- | --- |
| Female | 82% | 166 |
| Male | 18% | 35 |
| Median age | | 48 years |
| Millionaire households | 66% | 121 |
| Average value total HHI assets | — | $2,422,827 |
| Average value total real estate | — | $992,140 |
| Average value of principal home | | $608,419 |
| Income: HHI $250,000+ | 25% | 306 |
| Income: HHI $150,000+ | 48% | 161 |
| Income: median HHI | — | $146,169 |
| Attended college+ | 90% | 115 |
| Graduated college+ | 65% | 116 |
| Employed women | 58% | 155 |
| Top/middle management | 35% | 119 |
| Top management | 23% | 135 |
| Married | 76% | 87 |
| Single | 5% | 136 |
| Partnered | 5% | 189 |

(Mendelsohn, 2007)

press releases and pitches for the trade newspapers and trade magazines. The distribution is targeted to a qualified readership, and thus the message will resonate with the reader. Targeting trade magazines and newspapers assures the fashion B2B company that a quality audience will receive the message. Of course getting press coverage in *W, Vogue, Elle,* or any of the other consumer fashion magazines is a great way to reach a wide range of consumers, some of whom are their target consumers. However, B2B companies should focus their time and efforts on reaching their target customers in the trade medium while also including the targeted consumer medium. Proper media segmentation is vital in delivering the message.

### Multichannel Media

As mentioned earlier, a media trend that is having a great effect on the operational end of getting a story published is the proliferation of media houses that diversify their media outlets by combining a variety of media channels under one company. The trend of print newspapers extending their reach to the broadcast and online media to maintain and increase their audience is becoming more apparent today. In 2008, the media conglomerate Tribune, which owns 23 other television stations, put WSFL-TV and South Florida's *Sun-Sentinel* under one roof. According to a March 20, 2008, *Sun-Sentinel* article, the television station's move to the *Sun-Sentinel* offices marks the first time Tribune will combine its broadcast, print, and online operations under one roof. "We'll be able to offer our advertising customers an array of mediums to advertise that no one else can offer," says publisher Howard Greenberg, who now adds WSFL general manager to his duties. There is a possibility that *Sun-Sentinel* reporters and columnists will appear on the show, although the conceptualization of the program is in the preliminary stages, Greenberg said in the article (*Sun-Sentinel,* 2008).

### Online Publications

Today, online publications are the key to maximum exposure. Aside from the print consumer and trade magazines and newspapers that have launched online editions, a host of web-only publications now exist that comprise a substantial media segment. The rise of Internet coverage has made the relationship in the public relations community a little more complex between the reporters and public relations companies. The Internet's quick reaction to news items and the ability to disseminate information in real time has ushered in a new way of reporting. Many reporters, journalists, and public relations directors see the Internet as a way of lowering the standards of accurate reporting with the introduction of blogs and bloggers. Still, many other professional reporters use and cite the blogs on a regular basis. According to one source, half of reporters use blogs regularly and more than 25 percent of them use the blogs daily (O'Dwyer, 2005). This is clearly an indication of the importance that the Internet plays today in public relations and will play in the future. Although Internet e-zines and blogs of all different political and religious backgrounds are sprouting in increasing numbers, offering reports about news, events,

## Box 3.8   Online Trade and Consumer Publications

▶ *Allure* magazine—The "beauty expert" features articles on fashion, skincare, the latest anti-aging innovations, cosmetics, hair, diet, fitness, fashion, and more. www.allure.com

▶ *Apparel* magazine—*Apparel* magazine's Web site is a directory of apparel industry, fashion, and style magazines. In addition to providing a directory of apparel magazines, this directory provides links to apparel industry Web sites and fashion industry resources. If you enjoy reading about fashion, this Web site is a wonderful location for you to start your search for reading materials. In addition to listing apparel magazines, the *Apparel* magazine Web site also provides easy access to fashion books, fashion blogs, fashion newspapers, and more. www.apparelmag.com

▶ *Women's Wear Daily (WWD)*—Fashion, retail, beauty news, textile industries, and more. Access breaking news, trend reports, and in-depth analysis. *WWD* covers all aspects of fashion from business issues to global trends. www.wwd.com

▶ *Textiles Panamericanos*—Part of Billian Group, *Textiles Panamericanos* is the leading magazine of its kind covering the textile and apparel industries in all countries of Latin America, with special emphasis in Mexico, Brazil, Argentina, Colombia, Venezuela, Peru, and Chile. The magazine is published bimonthly in Spanish, offering up-to-date regional and global information about new technology including machinery, products, and processes as well as practical applications of new technologies and modern systems of company management. www.textilespanamericanos.com

▶ *Southern Textile News*—A 60-year-old newspaper published biweekly, it offers the latest in textile news and news that affects the industry, including trade matters; new advancements in textile equipment; developments in yarn, thread, knits, wovens, nonwovens, cotton, dyeing and finishing, and apparel; as well as updates on mill news and industry trade shows worldwide. www.textilenews.com

▶ *Style*—The online home of *Style, Vogue,* and other magazines. Detailed coverage of designer runway collections and style news with a list of job opportunities and links to other Condé Nast publications and Web sites. www.style.com

▶ *Style Canada*—Includes timely headlines, trade shows, sample sales, and designer biographies. Written for women's wear and menswear retailers, vendors, designers, and students. For more than 115 years, *Style Canada* has been Canada's fashion source. In continuing that tradition today, style keeps its readers ahead of the competition. www.Style.ca

▶ *Printwear* magazine—Part of National Business Media, *Printwear* is published monthly for the business of decorated apparel. Each issue contains a timely mix of valuable how-to articles on screen printing and embroidery, most times written by experts who have done it themselves, along with a regular look at sales, pricing, and the for-profit side of the business. NBM publishes business-to-business and specialized retail magazines, and produces trade shows in various markets around the United States. *Printwear* is their magazine that specializes in the apparel printing industry. www.nbm.com

▶ Lebhar-Friedman Inc.—A leading independent publisher and provider of information serving the retail community and its vast supplier network. For 78 years, Lebhar-Friedman has been committed to providing timely, provocative, and essential information to its over half a million subscribers. www.lf.com

▶ *The Hat Magazine*—Edited and published by Carole and Nigel Denford, who co-founded The Hat Shop in London's Covent Garden in 1983 and managed it to great International acclaim for 15 years. *The Hat Magazine* is intended to be the voice of the hat trade worldwide and is unceasing in the promotion of the making and wearing of hats. Filled with news, views, and opinion from around the world and regular articles such as: Designer's Sketchbook, which

**Box 3.8    Online Trade and Consumer Publications** *(continued)*

illustrates coming trends in design; Workroom Technique, which shows how the masters use different materials; Trade Fair and Fashion Show Previews; Reports; and other hat-related topics. www.thehatmagazine.com

▶ *Footwear News*—This Web site is owned by Fairchild Publications, a Division of Condé Nast Publications, the same company that owns *WWD*. www.footwearnews.com

▶ *Apparel* (formerly known as *Bobbin*)—Seeks to advance the competitiveness of apparel and soft goods businesses. Through their analyses of product development and design, sourcing and manufacturing, merchandising and sales, information systems, and distribution and retailing, it is their goal to facilitate key value decisions for executives and other professionals. In these pursuits, they are also committed to providing easy access to a wide range of viable resources that are relevant to the apparel, fashion, and textile industry. www.apparelsearch .com/online_news_magazines.htm

▶ Cotton Inc.—News and press releases from Cotton Incorporated. www.cottoninc.com

▶ *Drapers* magazine—A leading fashion trade magazine in the United Kingdom. Its pages provide fashion news, CMT resources, overseas contacts, EPOS systems, and almost everything else the fashion industry requires. It is unrivaled in the UK fashion industry, being the only magazine that provides up-to-the-minute trade information, great quality editorial and resources for big business, freelances, multiples, manufacturers, and other outlets. www.drapersonline.com

▶ *EMB Embroidery & Monogramming Business*— Dedicated to helping embroiderers achieve business success. Through its magazine, Web site, and face-to-face events (e.g., Imprinted Sportswear Shows), it provides professional embroiderers with the information they need to manage their business operations, source the latest products, develop their embroidery skills and market their services. www.edithroman.com

(apparelsearch.com, 2009)

81

political landscape, people, and organizations both in the private and public sectors, many of these self-proclaimed media sources do not employ trained journalists, do not follow basic reporting practices, and have personal or paid agendas. Establishing the online publication's credentials and background is extremely important before reaching out to that publication with a story. To reach out to a credible online media, the public relations professional should strive to maintain a good working relationship with one of the publication's Internet journalists by being knowledgeable as to what the reporter writes and also maintain the same high degree of integrity that is necessary to receive desired results with the print media. Fast-paced reaction, familiarity with the online medium, and thorough research are crucial skills for public relations personnel aiming to relate to the dynamic Internet media. With the advent of online media, the opportunities for immediate, mass-scale exposure are now a reality. One doesn't have to buy or read a trade or newspaper publication to keep up with current affairs. The Internet provides users with instant information, a fact that can translate into instant success for a given collection or product. Online fashion Web sites are another part of media segmentation in today's world, encompassing a whole range of products that are available with just one click of the mouse. Box 3.8 outlines some of the online trade and consumer publications that serve a dual purpose—targeting both print and online audiences.

## Understanding the Public Relations Audience

Now that audience segmentation is complete and the fashion company's public is identified—and divided into smaller sub-groups by demographics as applicable—the public relations director needs to research the audience group to better understand the **psychographics** of the audience. Such research provides the fashion company with information that allows the public relations projects to be more relevant to the audience members; the more relevant the public relations initiatives are to the audience, the more meaningful the message becomes, resulting in improved reception of the public relations initiatives and consequently improved public image of the company and its brands. Until this point in the chapter, we've discussed audience segmentation along geographical, economical, and social lines. Now, we need to delve into the company's client mental realm and understand his or her psychology to better communicate with each of the company's clients.

### Motivation and Needs

The fashion company is there to fulfill the needs of its public. Each member of that public—be it a B2C consumer or a B2B company—has certain needs, values, and motivation unique to that entity. Understanding these motivations, values, and needs gives the public relations director a good idea as to what facets of the company's products and service are important to highlight in press releases and other public relations messages. Public relations must remain relevant to the company's overall purpose of serving its clientele, and understanding the clientele's needs is a vital part of maintaining relevance. An overview of the public's needs can be obtained through discussion with the company's sales team, or directly from the public using surveys, focus groups, and questionnaires.

### Values Sets

The beliefs, social behavior, and views of the audience are all part of their set of values, which dictate how the audience will think about or react to specific topics that relate to human interaction within a social context. For example, a person with conservative leanings may react negatively to liberal projects, no matter how much good these projects may do. In that person's mind, they are simply wrong. It is generally difficult to obtain such information from the public, and the focus group is an excellent tool to achieve that.

## News Sources

Clearly, where the audience gets its news and community information is highly important in public relations research. It is essential to identify the main publications that the audience reads, the television channels or radio stations that the audience views or listens to, the news Web sites the audience visits, and any other information sources. This list will become the target media outlets list that the public relations campaign should focus on reaching.

## Focus Groups

The focus group is a powerful research tool that gives the fashion company an opportunity to interact directly with a cross section of its public in a controlled environment where the public's responses can be recorded and analyzed properly. Focus groups are a powerful means to evaluate services or test new ideas.

A focus group typically consists of 6 to 12 participants who represent a cross section of the company's segmented audience in terms of demographic characteristics. Generally, such individuals are invited to participate and are compensated for their time. There are several accepted methods to conduct focus groups, the traditional one being a discussion controlled by one moderator. Participants are asked questions about the company, its current products, upcoming products, service, advertisements, and other business topics in an attempt to better understand the audience's psychological attitudes towards the company. The focus group is an excellent tool not only for marketing research but also for public relations. The company is wise to conduct a focus group prior to planning any large public relations campaign to ensure that the campaign will resonate with the target audience. It can be used to evaluate current public relations initiatives and to test initiatives that are under consideration. Focus groups can be effective, but are not without caveats; success depends upon the participants truly representing a cross section of the audience, the applicability of the questions asked, the moderator's performance in guiding the conversation appropriately, and the analysis of the answers, among other factors.

## Audience Surveys

Another research tool that can be helpful in understanding the psychographics of the company's audience is conducting an audience survey. In a survey, the fashion company typically hires an outside company that sends out pollsters to conduct the survey by asking specific questions to individual members of the audience and then recording their answers. These can then be tabulated so as to give the public relations director an overview of the public's sentiments. The questions asked in a survey should be relevant and meaningful to the topic of the public relations initiative. Typically, surveys require dozens and even hundreds of respondents before the answers can be analyzed properly within the context of the audience-at-large.

## Questionnaires

Questionnaires are similar to surveys, but they are handed out or mailed out to members of the audience, and the responses are written and handed or mailed in. The responses are then tallied up, tabulated, and analyzed. One of the benefits of questionnaires is that there is no human interaction during the questionnaire, thus the risk of human interference or misinterpretation is eliminated from the process of gathering the information. However, because there isn't a pollster involved in the gathering process, the ratio of replies is much lower than in surveys. In addition, there is still a chance of misinterpretation during the tabulation and analysis portions of the questionnaire.

## Secondary Data Sources

Aside from questionnaires, surveys, and other raw or primary data conducted by the fashion company itself, there are several sources that can provide analyzed or secondary data about many audience groups. This information is analyzed and interpreted by an agency other than the company itself. The U.S. Census Bureau is a government agency that serves as the leading source of quality data about the nation's people and economy. The bureau collects information while protecting privacy and confidentiality, shares its expertise globally free of charge, and conducts its work openly. Information is readily available from its Web site (www.census.gov), where data is supplied about individuals, households, companies, industries, and regions. There are also commercial wholesalers of secondary data that provide information and detailed reports about consumers, companies, industries, and specific markets. A fee is required to access much of the information, but such companies do offer some valuable studies and resources for free as well. The Nielsen Company, headquartered in New York City, offers an integrated suite of market information gathered from a wide range of sources, advanced information management tools, sophisticated analytical systems, and methodologies, and dedicated professional client service to help clients find the best paths to growth. Its Web site (www.acnielsen.com) contains links to many research tools for audience segmentation, including free reports such as the Consumers and Designer Brands Global Report and the Health, Beauty & Personal Grooming Report. The Gallup company (www.gallup.com/) has studied human nature and behavior for more than 70 years. Gallup employs many of the world's leading scientists in management, economics, psychology, and sociology. Gallup consultants help organizations boost growth by increasing customer engagement and maximizing employee productivity through measurement tools, coursework, and strategic advisory services. It offers numerous studies and reports, including market research, brand engagement, as well as customer relationship management.

## Company Employees and Records

An often overlooked source of information for audience segmentation is the company itself. Employees who deal with the company's public as well as company records can yield vital data about the company's various audiences. The sales staff often instinctively or subconsciously knows who its clients are, their demographic makeup, and their purchasing preferences. Accounting records may be a gold mine of information that can give the company a breakdown of what type of audience purchases products, how much they spend annually, and in what frequency. The company can piece together a lot of information relevant for the audience profiles from these sources.

### Creating an Audience Profile

Based on all the information gathered under demographics and psychographics as previously described, the fashion company can now create an audience profile that at its most simple form lists a summary of the main characteristics that the typical members of the specific audience share. Essentially, the profile gives the company a picture of its typical customers, including their geographical location, age, gender, marital status, income level, race, education, spending preferences, and percentage of the members of the audience who are customers. If there is more than one audience, it is helpful to list the various audiences in a table form for easy comparison at a glance (for an example, see Table 3.3). Based in San Diego, California, the marketing information resources company Claritas is dedicated to helping companies engage in consumer and business-to-business marketing to maximize their profitability with marketing research and programs. PRIZM NE, Claritas's consumer segmentation research product, offers clients a detailed customer profile report

**FIGURE 3.4** Claritas is dedicated to helping companies engage in consumer and business-to-business marketing to maximize their profitability with marketing research and programs.

**TABLE 3.3   Basic Audience Profile Samples**

**3.3A   Basic Audience Profile Report Sample for Jetsetter***
*a fictitious men's suits manufacturer in metropolitan Miami

| Audience | Count | Location | Age | Marital Status | Education | Income Level | % of group that are customers |
|----------|-------|----------|-----|----------------|-----------|--------------|-------------------------------|
| Top executive | 1,259 | Beaches | 50–65 | Married | MBA | $100K+ | 25% |
| Middle executive | 5,020 | Suburbs | 40–50 | Married | MBA | $80K–$120K | 40% |
| Junior executive | 8,983 | Suburbs | 35–50 | Single | B.A. | $40K–$80K | 15% |
| Self-employed | 3,314 | Downtown | 30–50 | Divorced | B.A. | $30K–$100K | 5% |

Based on this information, the top consumers are the top and middle executives, thus more detailed audience profiles are created for these groups.

| **3.3B   Top Executives** | | **3.3C   Middle Executives** | |
|---------------------------|---|------------------------------|---|
| News source | Newspapers | News source | Newspapers and Internet |
| Publications | *Wall Street Journal, Business Journal, Miami Herald* | Publications | *Wall Street Journal,* Miami Herald.com |
| Political views | Conservative | Political views | Conservative |
| Hobbies | Golf | Hobbies | Golf, fishing |
| Who shops for their suits? | Personal assistants | Who shops for their suits? | Personally |
| $ spent a year on suits | $1,000–$2,500 | $ spent a year on suits | $500–$1,200 |

These are rather basic samples, and a company is wise to invest time into expanding upon these profiles so they are as comprehensive as possible. Utilizing these reports, the company can plan its public relations initiatives to appeal to top and middle executives, and focus on reaching them through the *Wall Street Journal*, the *Miami Herald*, and the *Business Journal*. It might want to integrate golf and fishing into its initiatives, and include the top executives' personal assistants in any of its public relations outreach programs (claritas.com, 2009).

that divides the U.S. consumer and the company's audience into 66 different unique segments, including groupings such as New Empty Nesters, Money & Brains, Suburban Sprawlers, and Multi-Culti Mosaics. Each of the groups are analyzed demographically and then ranked according to the percentage of group members who are also the company's customers (Claritas, 2009). These audience profiles help the public relations director determine which audiences are most important for the company, and what their characteristics are. In the following section, we will discuss how to utilize these reports in adjusting public relations initiatives.

## Adjusting Public Relations Strategies to Audience Profiles

Segmentation and profiling enables the company to fine-tune its public relations efforts to maximize initiative results. Taking audience profiles into account when drawing plans for and implementing the public relations campaign can prove beneficial both in terms of directing the campaign where the company needs it most (i.e., reach the company's most important customers, business partners, media outlets, and community members) and also in terms of optimizing the company's return on investment (ROI). A public relations initiative that is not adjusted to fit the audience is likely to fall on deaf ears and result in a waste of time and money; the public relations message is received louder and clearer when that message has been prepared with the needs and profiles of the audience in mind.

## Choosing a Public Relations Strategy that Appeals to the Audience and Its Needs

Now that the fashion company knows its audience's profile, demographics, and psychographics, it can begin to utilize this information to improve its public image through public relations initiatives compatible with its audience. Virtually every public relations initiative has facets that resonate with a particular type of audience, and facets that distract the audience. Ideally, a public relations initiative should completely resonate with the audience and offer little to no distractions. However, this is how things should be in a perfect world; in the real world, there are always complications even to the best laid plans. Thus even the most innocent public relations initiative can irk some member of the audience. The question to be asked then is: Will the initiative appeal to most of the audience members, and will it improve their opinion about the company and its products? To get reliable answers to these questions, the company needs to consult the value sets of the audience and determine how the audience views the topics that the public relations initiative addresses. If the audience is mostly liberal, a public relations project that is conservative will not fly. If the average age of the audience is 50 to 60, a public relations project that revolves around a marathon that raises money for surfers in the area may not fly, either. In other words, the public relations initiatives should as much as possible embody and reinforce the characteristics of the audience. It is wise to go over the customer profile characteristics one by one and evaluate whether the initiative aligns with each characteristic. The initiative that most closely matches the most audience characteristics should be considered first. In Chapter 5, we will discuss in further detail the conventional and nonconventional, innovative public relations initiatives.

## Identifying Strategy/Audience Conflicts

When issues of incompatibility between the public relations initiative and the audience are present, results in terms of improved public image and positive exposure may suffer. Identifying and attending to potential and existing strategy/audience conflicts during both planning and implementation phases of the public relations campaign can mean the difference between a successful campaign and a flop. Such conflicts typically emerge when the initiative's goals or approaches work in some way—whether real or imagined—against the values, beliefs, and lifestyles of the target audience. In such a case, the company must evaluate how negative the conflict may be for the campaign, and strive to rectify the conflict quickly and with a positive attitude. Suppose that a fashion company launches a walk to raise funds for a local charity. However, the public relations staff does not realize that the scheduled date of the walk is the same

## Case Study 3.1  Defining Public Relations Audiences

### Pierce Mattie Public Relations

Pierce Mattie Public Relations was launched in 2001 by wellness lifestyle editor and expert Pierce Mattie. Pierce Mattie Public Relations remains an industry leader in communications for fashion, luxury beauty, home, and health and fitness brands. With offices in New York and Los Angeles, Pierce Mattie Public Relations has solid relationships with the editorial world of New York and the celebrity world of Los Angeles. Pierce Mattie Public Relations has a proven track record of collaborating with its client partners to deliver consistently outstanding results. We interviewed Pierce Mattie Vice President Edy Eliza, who has worked in fashion and beauty public relations for about six years and who has received a degree in fashion merchandising from Florida State University.

**What are some of the audiences you aim to interact with in fashion public relations? Can a public relations campaign target multiple audiences simultaneously? What are some approaches or strategies you've found workable in such a scenario?**

A public relations campaign starts with an in-depth conversation with our client. The client answers a series of questions that will outline target demographic, desired retailers, design concept, brand identity, brand message, and overall media goals. We take the information and create a strategic public relations campaign that will unilaterally communicate with the target audience through press outreach. For example, a fashion company has a target demographic of 14- to 19-year-old girls who shop at Macy's. We would assess and target the key publications, blogs, Web sites, and TV programs the target demo is reading, and strive for product placement in trend stories and feature stories on the brand. Second, we would connect with different social networking communities to reach the consumer directly. Finally, we would target key influencers, i.e., celebrities, performers, and signers and gift the fashion items to be worn at a public engagement to enhance brand association and build brand awareness.

**What are the main differences between fashion public relations in a B2B setting and a B2C setting?**

The main difference in approaching B2B versus B2C is the crafting of the message or brand story. Business publications are looking for trend-driven collections and performance forecasts for the brand. As well as newsworthy angles whether that is a breakthrough fabric or a new retail chain that picks up the line to be carried at the stores.

**How do you go about defining the target media for a specific public relations project?**

The target media directly correlates with the defined demographic put forth by the client/brand. There is a core of target media and then outliers as well. The outlier media are those media that communicate indirectly to the target audience (parent or girlfriend).

**What are some of the strategies you use to reach these media?**

All forms of communication are utilized to communicate the brand message with the media, including phone calls, emails, sending look books, samples of the line for personal use, drink meetings, lunch meetings, one-on-one meetings with the designer, seasonal media events to debut the new collection, inspiration, or trend books.

---

**Case Study 3.1 Defining Public Relations Audiences** *(continued)*

**How important is the development of relationships with editors, reporters, and correspondents?**

Relationship development is what can make the difference between your client's clothing being on the page in a magazine or another brand. Developing and maintaining media relationships is what makes a public relations professional successful.

**What are the factors that help develop and maintain such relationships, and what are some factors that are detrimental to these relationships?**

The number one way to make or break a potential relationship with a member of the media is to have general and specific knowledge of their publication (TV show, Web site, etc.) and beat. Do not call and waste their time with a pitch that is not appropriate for their target audience. If you do, you will immediately hear a dial tone and will not receive a call back, ever.

*Questions to Consider*

1. List five questions you would ask a client to determine what would help outline the target demographic. Explain each.

2. If a fashion company has a target demographic of 14- to 19-year-old girls who shop at Macy's, what print media, Internet, and local radio stations would you send press releases to and pitch for a story? Why?

3. Name several celebrities that you would target for the 14- to 19-year-old female market to enhance brand association and awareness? Why?

4. What type of message would you craft for the 14- to 19-year-old girls market to B2B and B2C media. Explain.

5. What strategies would you use to reach the B2B and B2C media for the above target market? Explain.

date as the city's traditional summer parade. As flyers, advertisements, and announcement are distributed, the public relations director receives an irate call from the mayor complaining about the date conflict. She also receives a phone call from the local reporter, inquiring as to how the company plans to pull off the walk despite the date conflict. So, should the company change the date, or stick to its original plan? The public relations director investigates the circumstance and learns that if the company does not change the date, it will anger the local officials as well as the many residents who normally participate in the parade, which is a highly popular local event. On the other hand, a change in plans would mean a vast amount of time and money spent on correcting and redistributing the promotional flyers, press releases, and so on; in addition, there is a risk that regardless of the correction, people who have already marked their calendars with the walk may not see the correction and show up anyway. The executive concludes that the potential damage would be far greater in terms of bad publicity and distraction from an important community event. She embarks upon a rescheduling campaign that includes sending out new announcements as well as capitalizing upon the reporter's inquire by supplying him with the new date for his article. In such cases where the damage may not be averted totally, it should be minimized as much as possible and efforts should concentrate on pushing the revised date using the most positive perspective possible. Public relations is a highly fluid and changing part of business, and the public relations director must be prepared for crisis and able to develop creative solutions for how to avert them.

## Chapter Summary

▶ Prior to planning or implementing a public relations campaign, initiative, or project, it is important for the fashion company to identify its audiences.

▶ The B2C audience comprises the end users who will be using the product.

▶ The B2B audience comprises the companies that buy from, sell to, or offer service to the fashion company.

▶ The media audience is an intermediate audience between the fashion company and its B2C or B2B audiences.

▶ To better focus the public relations efforts, the fashion company should segment its B2C, B2B, and media audiences into smaller groups with similar characteristics.

▶ Creating a profile for each audience assists in creating public relations initiatives that resonate with that audience.

▶ The B2C audience is typically segmented along demographic lines, such as geographic location, gender, age, income, profession, education, marital status, and consumption patterns.

▶ The B2B audience is typically segmented by industry, field within the industry, company size, as well as other factors.

▶ The media audience is segmented into newswire, consumer media, trade media, and mixed-channel media.

▶ Analyzing and understanding the audience's psychographics is vital to creating public relations messages that will resonate with the audience.

▶ To properly create an audience profile, one needs to properly segment the audience and understand its psychographics.

## Key Terms

▶ audience

▶ audience profiles

▶ audience segmentation

▶ business to business (B2B)

▶ business to consumer (B2C)

▶ demographics

▶ intermediate audience

▶ profiles

▶ proxy buyer

▶ psychographics

▶ public relations audience

▶ supply chain

## Chapter-End Questions and Exercises

1. Define the public relations audience.

2. Name the three major public relations audiences, and explain each in your own words.

3. Compare and contrast the fashion company's B2C and B2B audiences. Make sure to include and cite examples.

4. If you were the public relations person for REI, who would you target in the trade medium and who would you target in the consumer medium? Explain why.

5. Why should a fashion company's corporate communication adjust from audience to audience?

6. Compare and contrast micro segmentation with macro segmentation. Explain what is the optimal balance of a manageable audience group size for a given fashion company and the factors to consider when figuring that balance.

7. In your opinion, how is public relations affected by the type of audience that the company is trying to reach?

8. How is B2C public relations different than B2B public relations?

9. Explain the concept of the proxy buyer and give an example. How does this concept affect the process of identifying audience segmentation?

10. Research a B2C fashion company online or at the local library, and write down the company's main corporate information. Include what it sells, its geographical location, and its customers. Which media outlets do you think this company should focus on for public relations? Explain.

11. Research a B2B fashion company online or at the local library. and write down the company's main corporate information including what it sells, its geographical location, and its customers. Which media outlets do you think this company should focus on for public relations? Explain.

12. Define demographics and psychographics; then explain the differences between the two sets of audience information.

13. How do the three main public relations audiences affect each other? Explain.

14. What are the five main groups within media segmentation, and how do they differ from each other?

15. Find a newswire service. Do you think the newswire is beneficial? What are its advantages or disadvantages?

16. Outline the main demographic qualities that a fashion company should utilize to identify its target audiences.

17. Pick a fashion company that you like and purchase from.

    a. Analyze your own characteristics as a customer, including all of the various demographic and psychographic elements.

    b. Create a dummy audience profile based on this information.

    c. Locate at least two advertisements, brochures, press releases, or other corporate communications from that company.

    d. Analyze these corporate communications as to their compatibility with the audience profile you have created.

18. Compare and contrast the focus group, survey, questionnaire, and secondary data source. What are the pros and cons of each?

19. How does understanding the customer's psychographics assist in adjusting the public relations' initiatives?

20. What is a strategy/audience conflict? Explain and give an example. How should a public relations director approach such a conflict in order to resolve it?

21. Fictitious scenario: You are considering opening a boutique in the town where you currently reside. Establish the fashion you will be carrying; then using the demographic and psychographic criteria, create your audience profile(s). Using secondary data resources, locate as much information as possible, and determine whether the town has sufficient members of the target audiences to support your boutique. Explain how you arrived at your conclusion.

# Setting Up Public Relations Campaigns and Goals

## FOUR

## Chapter Snapshot

A properly planned and implemented public relations campaign typically leads to significantly improved results when compared to an unplanned project that is put together at the last moment with little to no research or thought. Planning is a vital key to success when it comes to public relations because often media exposure can be obtained only if the initiative has been released in advance, and adequate provisions have been made to accommodate media coverage. Without the proper planning, the campaign can suffer setbacks that lead to reduced and perhaps even no return on investment (ROI). There are a number of crucial steps to properly plan a campaign that establishes achievable goals, sets realistic timelines, and allows for contingencies. Such a plan will provide the foundation to success with that given public relations initiative by integrating the demographic and psychographic information, audience profiles, the company's business philosophy, the company's marketing plan, the budget, and other data into a cohesive set of objectives, which results in improved public image for the company.

## Objectives

▶ Understand public relations campaigns and goals.

▶ Appreciate the importance of proper planning for the public relations campaign to ensure its success.

▶ Know the 15 steps to a properly planned public relations campaign.

▶ Comprehend the process of setting up public relations campaign goals.

▶ Examine the timeline and forethought factors within the public relations environment.

▶ Explore the topics that must be addressed to prepare for a smooth implementation.

▶ Cover the various factors to be considered in hiring a public relations firm.

Campaigns come in all different shapes and forms; they are part of the many different facets of our society. The ingredients that go into making a successful campaign, however, are consistent. We have political, military, recruiting, and **public relations campaigns**, to name a few. Let's examine whether there is a commonality under the heading of "campaigns." In the early twenty-first century, the United States of America experienced the ultimate in public relations campaigns: the political campaign to elect a president of the United States of America. This is one of the most intense, complex, and expensive campaign exercises one can experience. The political campaign has to do with public opinion and creating a positive environment for the candidates. It is obvious that enormous research, planning, and appropriating of the proper personnel is required to reach target markets and the goals, which can be a daunting affair. Reaching the goals of the campaign—election—must include not only careful planning, but also the execution of the plan. The initial strategy and measurability of the results must be put in place to determine whether the goals are reached during the activity, and also so changes can be made to adjust for the various problems that may occur. The successful presidential candidate is able to deliver the message that voting for him or her will satisfy the needs of the voting public and solve the problems of the majority of American citizens. During the campaign the political team targets many different segments of the population, analyzes their unique needs, and offers to solve their specific problems. This is not a simple exercise. The expenditures in political campaigns run in the high millions. The decisions on where to spend the advertising dollars follow the same thinking and planning that one would do in planning any type of campaign. Timing, personnel, and use of the proper form of media is essential to the campaign. Alternative plans must be included in the original plan that asks the question, "What if our campaign is not successful; what's our next step?" Proper planning should counteract any negative publicity.

The military campaign has to include the same type of ingredients that go into developing a successful political campaign. Here again, the results of careful planning and effective implementation thereof determine whether the

FIGURE 4.1 The power of a public relations campaign. In the United States, each election year heralds a slew of public relations campaigns for presidential hopefuls. Of the many candidates, only one is elected to be one of the most powerful people in the world, in no small part due to the strength and effectiveness of his or her public relations campaign.

campaign is successful. Personnel and military recruiting campaigns measure the success by the numbers recruited based on their goals.

Public relations campaigns have much in common with these other campaigns. The common denominator for all successful campaigns is in the strategy, planning, implementation, and measurement of the results. The public relations campaign, as in all the previously mentioned campaigns, must include a statement of the goals, a detailed plan, a definition of the target audiences, a determination of the public relations strategies to be used to reach them, an establishment of benchmarks to indicate how the campaign is progressing, and most importantly a resolution on how the message will be delivered so it is received and understood.

## Campaign Planning

The public relations campaign starts off with organizing a plan because planning is the key to getting the job done. This planning procedure must include the establishing goals, courses of action, funding, research, and a system of measurements as an integrated approach to the campaign. The initial overview of the campaign must be spelled out with specific goals and a plan to reach them. A clear definition of these goals is paramount to the whole procedure. The planning procedure should include the essential elements of a campaign plan; these include establishing goals and objectives; defining the target markets; setting a budget; assigning personnel and defining their **responsibilities, functions, and duties (RFDs);** scheduling; developing the message; determining the ways to deliver the message; and establishing a method to measure performance.

The planning stage comprises essentially 15 sequential steps that culminate at a completed proper campaign plan. To succeed, a public relations campaign must answer the following questions and include the following information:

Step 1. Establish the goals.

Step 2. Create an overview.

Step 3. Establish a detailed plan.

Step 4. Define the preferred results as a part of reaching the goals.

Step 5. Determine the required research for proper planning.

Step 6. Determine target markets and audiences.

Step 7. Define the timeline for implementing the campaign.

Step 8. Create the campaign's strengths, weaknesses, opportunities, and threats (SWOT) analysis.

Step 9. Consider potential positive and negative outcomes.

Step 10. Identify the **public relations message**.

Step 11. Establish the budget.

Step 12. Determine the methods for reaching the goals.

Step 13. Choose who will implement the campaign.

Step 14. Determine how to deliver the message.

Step 15. Determine how to measure the performance.

In this chapter, we will discuss each of these steps (some to be discussed in further detail in future chapters) and explore how to set up the public relations campaign and its goals in a manner that lays the foundation for a successful and effective implementation. To illustrate the sequence of development, follow the steps to formulate a fictitious public relations campaign plan in Box 4.1.

## Step 1. Establish the Goals

Establishing goals is a process conducted based on the public relations and marketing needs of the company. Whether the company aims to raise awareness of its brands, launch a new brand or collection, or become more involved in the community affects the campaign's goals. These needs change according to the circumstances in which the company is operating, and dictate the goals of the public relations campaign as well as the communication strategies to be used for reaching the objectives. Public relations goals vary in scope, complexity, and duration. For a relatively minor project, such as announcing the appointment of a new executive, there is only one public relations goal, which is plain and simple—gain publicity about the new appointment. A more complex initiative such as organizing a charity fashion show may dictate several more ambitious and complex goals. In this case, the campaign goals could be (a) forge a partnership with a nonprofit foundation to be the beneficiary of the fashion show; (b) attract a celebrity to headline the show and generate media interest; (c) plan and organize a spectacular fashion show; and (d) gain 100,000

## Box 4.1   UV-kini Collection Launch Campaign

To illustrate the 15 steps of the planning process, the following is a fictitious simulation of a scenario for a public relations campaign to launch a new fashion collection.

*Scenario:* The GoodSurf surfwear and beachwear manufacturer is to plan the launch of a new bikini collection. The "UV-kini" collection will be made of special UV-blocking fabric that repels 100 percent of the harmful UV rays of the sun. Design and production are scheduled to complete in the spring so that the collection can be unveiled and available in stores on May 1, in time for the summer season.

### Step 1. Establish the Goals

The goals of the UV-kini launch campaign are to:

▶ Unveil the new collection with maximum exposure to consumers.

▶ Promote the collection in the trade media so that wholesalers and retailers pick up the line for distribution and sale.

▶ Promote the new concept of the UV-blocking feature of the collection.

### Step 2. Create an Overview

The campaign will unveil the UV-kini collection on the consumer and trade levels by promoting the 100 percent UV-blocking feature of the garment in the media and through partnerships with the American Cancer Society and GoodBlock, a leading sun block manufacturer.

### Step 3. Establish a Detailed Plan

To get maximum exposure for the new collection, we want to create a buzz about the UV-blocking nature of the garment, and make sun safety cool again. The keystone component of the campaign will be a partnership with the American Cancer Society to fight skin cancer, and also a partnership with GoodBlock to promote the use of sun block. The plan will consist of a series of fundraiser surf events to benefit skin cancer research, and will feature surfer celebrities speaking to the media about the dangers of skin cancer and the new collection's health benefits. It will also include a partnership with GoodBlock to start a grassroots word-of-mouth

initiative at the events to promote using UV-blocking swimwear and lotions.

### Step 4. Define Preferred Results as a Part of Reaching the Goals

The preferred results would include:

▶ Positive mentions in national surf and fashion publications.

▶ Positive rating in consumer-review focused articles.

▶ Positive mentions in fashion and surf blogs.

▶ Positive feedback from distributors and retailers.

▶ Positive feedback from consumers.

### Step 5. Determine Required Research for Proper Planning

There is a need for research in the following areas to plan and implement the campaign properly:

▶ Skin cancer prevention information and statistics.

▶ UV and sun protection information and statistics.

▶ UV rating of average and competing swimwear compared to the UV-kini.

### Step 6. Determine Target Markets and Audiences

The target market is in the United States for the initial launch, focusing on the primary seaside regions, e.g., Southwest, Southeast, and Northeast with special attention to California, Florida, Texas, the Carolinas, New Jersey, and New York. We will target two audiences—teenagers and adults.

The teenager audience profile:

▶ Girls 13 to 19

▶ Enjoys the beach or pool (use bikinis or swimsuits)

▶ Stylish and pays attention to fashion

▶ Lives in homes with annual household income over $80,000

▶ Buys at least 2 to 3 swimsuits a year

The adult audience profile:

▶ Women 20 to 38

**Box 4.1 UV-kini Collection Launch Campaign** (continued)

- ▶ Single and married
- ▶ Enjoys the beach or pool (uses bikinis or swimsuits)
- ▶ Concerned with long-term health
- ▶ Annual household income over $40,000

## Step 7. Define the Timeline for Implementing the Campaign

**TABLE BOX 4.1 Timeline for Implementing Campaign: UV-kini**

| Department | Schedule | Activity |
|---|---|---|
| Legal | January | Finalize agreements with American Cancer Society and GoodBlock for campaign. |
| PR | January | Recruit professional female surfer to speak out for campaign. |
| Public Relations and Marketing | February | Plan the UV-kini tour of surf events in Florida (April), California (May), Texas (June) and New York (July). |
| Finances | February | Finalize budget and allocate funds. |
| PR | February–April | Send releases to target media and follow up with interested publications to generate. |
| PR | February–April | Send press invites to events and arrange for interviews and photo ops. |
| Advertising | February–July | Place ads promoting the initiative and events. |
| Logistics | March–May | Finalize event arrangements, staff, vendors, video streaming, and schedules. |
| Public Relations and Marketing | April–July | Implement the surf events. |
| PR | April–August | Follow up on media interests to cover the events. |
| Public Relations and Finances | September | Audit campaign and generate performance results and ROI. |

## Step 8. Create the Campaign's SWOT Analysis

Within the swimsuit market, our SWOT is as follows:

Strengths:

- ▶ The GoodSurf brand and image
- ▶ The uniqueness of the UV-kini
- ▶ The pro surfers who are on our team

Weaknesses:

- ▶ Reaching out to non-surfers
- ▶ Our bikini selection has been limited compared to other manufacturers

Opportunities:

- ▶ The 100 percent UV-blocking feature of the UV-kini
- ▶ Promoting bikinis to the health-minded individuals is practically nonexistent

Threats:

- ▶ The aggressive marketing from the leading bikini manufacturers are squeezing our market share
- ▶ The 100 percent claim could be challenged

## Step 9. Consider Potential Positive and Negative Outcomes

The positive outcomes could include thrusting Good-Surf into the publicity limelight and making the brand known among bikini consumers, as well as forging a good relationship with the American Cancer Society and involving the company in the community. The negative outcomes could include questions from the media about the 100 percent claim.

## Step 10. Identify the Public Relations Message

Our message is: "Sun safety is important, and bikini wearers should use UV-blocking bikinis as well as sun block while in the sun to protect themselves against the damaging UV rays."

98

**Box 4.1  UV-kini Collection Launch Campaign** (continued)

### Step 11. Establish the Budget

As approved by the executive team, the campaign has been allocated $100,000 to implement and carry out the project starting January and running until August. A detailed budget will be produced by the accounting department after event proposals are submitted.

### Step 12. Determine the Methods for Reaching the Goals

The methods selected for reaching the goals are:

▸ A partnership with a nonprofit organization

▸ Organizing events to promote the campaign message

▸ Using celebrities as spokespeople for the campaign

▸ Using grassroots initiatives to spread positive word of mouth

### Step 13. Choose Who Will Implement the Campaign

During the planning stages until April, public relations employee Margaret will be in charge of and implement the campaign under the VP Marketing's direction. In April, John (who is currently working on the Winter Tour project) will complete the project and join Margaret to help her with implementing the surf events.

### Step 14. Determine How to Deliver the Message

The message will be delivered through the consumer and trade media, as well as through word of mouth. The target media will include:

Consumer publications:

▸ Surf magazines

▸ Fashion magazines

▸ Teenager magazines

▸ Lifestyle sections of newspapers in target areas

Trade publications:

▸ Fashion trade journals

▸ Surf store publications

The word of mouth will travel through blogs as well as discount referral cards, which will be given out at the events.

### Step 15. Determine How to Measure the Performance

The performance will be measured by:

▸ The estimated dollar value of each published media clip utilizing the dollar value of a comparable advertising spot

▸ Number of referral coupons redeemed

▸ UV-kini sale figures

impressions from published media exposure. Public relations cannot operate independently without regard to what occurs in the rest of the company's departments. If a company is preparing to launch a new collection, getting information about the new collection and sending it out to the media and consumers should involve public relations. The public relations director must remain abreast of any new projects that are approved or being planned to allow ample time for adjusting existing **public relations campaign goals** and setting new goals that will support these new projects. Besides staying tuned in executive meetings to information on upcoming projects, the public relations director should constantly be "on the prowl" for news items within the company's other departments. It is imperative that public relations campaign goals are set in coordination with other initiatives within the company. Remaining focused solely on implementing existing initiatives while ignoring new upcoming projects that are being planned or launched by other departments can disrupt these

> ## Box 4.2   Real World Principle: Coordination Is a Two-Way Street
>
> Being coordinated with the rest of the company's various departments is not a one-way street where the public relations department simply adjusts its initiatives according to the needs of the organization. Instead, the coordination must include a flow of information and cooperation in both directions. When the public relations department launches an initiative, the rest of the company's departments must be informed of its details, and their staff should do their part to assist in the initiative's success.

projects and cause grave damage to the company. Creating a public relations campaign that is in sync with the rest of the organization is vital to success.

### Step 2. Create an Overview

An overview is a summarized statement of what needs to be done in broad terms as part of the public relations campaign. This includes the objectives of the plan for a specific period and all of the activities needed to make the plan a success. Although, as in an executive summary, it is the first item to appear on the plan, but it must be written after all the pieces of the campaign are put together. Look at the overview as a map for reaching the destination.

### Step 3. Establish a Detailed Plan

The details of the plan can be established after the overview is formed, and will list each initiative. The detailed plan outlines the steps that should be taken so that more specific directives can be implemented. The actual plan is part of the overview, including the SWOT analysis, the design of the plan, and how it will be put together to prepare it for development and implementation.

### Step 4. Define Preferred Results as a Part of Reaching the Goals

The preferred results for reaching the goal typically should be composed of positive answers to the following questions:

▶ Did the company receive the minimum amount of media coverage to gain positive ROI?

▶ Was the media coverage of the company positive?

▶ Did the media coverage of the company improve the public image?

▶ Did the company receive positive feedback from its publics as a result of the campaign?

▶ Did the company receive positive feedback from the other people of interest?

It is recommended that the public relations director explicitly identify the results that are expected from the campaign so that efforts can be directed toward achieving that end, and so that results can be measured during and after the completion of the campaign.

## Step 5. Determine Required Research for Proper Planning

To make the right decisions, it is essential to have correct and accurate information. This is particularly important when planning a public relations campaign because public relations relies heavily on research and data gathering in the background. The type and topics of research usually vary according to the circumstances and scenario surrounding the campaign; research requirements for a launch campaign of a new collection will be different than the research needed for a campaign to improve general public opinion. However, certain research requirements are universal. For example, before we can launch a campaign, we must have an inkling of what our competitors are currently doing for their public relations initiatives so that our campaign is set apart from theirs. If our campaign coincides with a competitor's existing initiative, the effect of our campaign will likely suffer and our ROI will falter. As part of that, we should also research whether our planned campaign initiatives have been done before, and if so, what were the results. If they were not successful, then it behooves us to further explore the effectiveness of the initiatives prior to implementing them. Informing ourselves about current affairs in the industry allows us to ensure our campaign is fresh and original. Additional research may have to be done in regards to the collection or design, especially if they are new, to ensure they indeed have not been done before. If they are totally new, we may need to conduct focus groups to ensure that consumers can use the new design, and that nothing has been overlooked about the product's features that could spur negative exposure.

## Step 6. Determine Target Markets and Audiences

As discussed in Chapter 3, it is essential to define the markets and audiences that the public relations campaign is supposed to reach, prior to establishing the methods and initiatives of how to reach them. Is the campaign targeting a B2B or B2C audience? What part of the market is the campaign going to reach? If there are geographical constraints on the campaign, in which cities, states, or regions will the campaign's public relations initiatives operate? As part of this section, the company should also properly identify its audience groups, their demographics, psychographics, profiles, and purchasing habits. Knowing who the audiences are and their profiles allows for proper guidance of planning toward the strategies and methods that reach the audiences with the appropriate message, and will provide the maximum results in the shortest amount of time with the least expenses. At the very least, this section should outline the public relations audience groups that the campaign is targeting as well as the profile for each audience group.

## Step 7. Define the Timeline for Implementing the Campaign

As the old adage goes, "Work will expand to the time allotted to it." When speaking with members of the media, one of the most common replies is, "I am on deadline, please send me the release." Deadlines govern media people, and they most certainly are part of the vocabulary for anyone who wants to be successful. Wasting time is more expensive than wasting money. Money comes and goes, but lost time is never recovered. The timeline for implementing the campaign must be structured and strictly adhered to for it to succeed.

### Importance of Scheduling in Public Relations

Have you ever experienced the frustration of working on an assignment and not seeing the end results? When working on an assignment, do you include a timeframe for completing it? Or do you do what most people do—just keep going, changing and adjusting the work with no end in sight unless the deadline date is near? Then you hustle to get the work completed. Think how much better it would be if you planned the amount of time you felt was needed to complete the assignment, and established a start and completion date for this assignment. Doing a simple task like that would no doubt lead to less frustration and help in completing the project on time. Time could be your friend or enemy—you make the choice. If you want it to be your friend, then manage time, set up a schedule to manage time, and remember that *work will expand to the time allotted to it.* This saying tells it all about allocating time to a project—especially a public relations campaign. Unless ground rules are established regarding starting time, duration, and completion time, a campaign or any exercise that is time sensitive has the distinct likelihood of not succeeding. In allocating time, one must include measurements as to the progress of the event. Check points must be established within the timeline to measure the progress. Without a specific timeline, *work will expand to the time allotted to it!* The results will deteriorate in the absence of mid-campaign check points that allow us to evaluate progress restructure the project or some of its tasks in order to meet deadlines.

In the UV-kini scenario discussed in Box 4.1, the company must plan ahead and schedule the release of the collection as well as the release of the event dates with ample time to spare. By knowing months in advance about the time when this new collection will make its debut and about the event information, we can be assured of getting proper coverage. The timelines will help ensure that the public relations people will have enough time and information to get adequate media coverage. Although the brand name may be well known and the collection may have brand recognition, there is a need to communicate to the media the uniqueness of this collection and do it within a specific period to receive proper media coverage. We must first determine the timeframe for the shipment of the new collection to the store and then plan for the most effective time to send out the media releases in conjunction with any advertising. If the collection is being shipped to the stores in May, our timeline for releasing public relations information for magazine coverage is at least three to four months in advance. For newspaper, television, and Internet, the timeframe will be closer to the shipment of goods to the stores. We must set up a time schedule for the release, list when it will be sent out to each of the target media outlets, when to contact editors/reporters to ensure they had received the release, when to solicit for coverage, and so on. A well-planned timeframe will help to ensure campaign success.

### Implementing the Timeline

With proper scheduling, results can be monitored and, if need be, other measures can be taken when we see that the results are not going as planned. Auditing the results in a timely manner will help us reach the target market because we will have time for readjustments. Effective timelines for future events should include a written report for all company events for a specific period of time. Some companies plan six months in advance, some a year in advance. The timeline spells out the dates of new collections and new events. In this timeline plan we must include where and to whom the press releases will be sent, what segments of the media will be targeted, and the timeframe for getting the releases to the proper media outlets. We will also be able to ask ourselves if we have the proper media contacts for these varied events to ensure that we contact media outlets that can actually utilize the specific information we are sending them. Remember, we must know who in the media industry is doing what, and we constantly may have to enlist new media contacts and update our contact lists. The timeline will give us enough time to further develop ongoing relations with members of the media and adequate time for a successful pitch. The timeline must also include what major events and types of resources to include to make the event effective. The objective is to utilize the time to execute the plan for more exposure and have it resonate with the target customer. With all this information and a timeline for each activity, the chances increase of media coverage as part of the public relations campaign. The timeline puts all available resources of the company to work in the same direction.

---

## Box 4.3   Creating a Timeline for the Public Relations Campaign

It is essential to work out the timing of the various steps of the public relations campaign to ensure a smooth implementation. Allowing for sufficient time to implement the necessary tasks is vital, especially in the public relations field because the media is highly sensitive to deadlines. One effective method to create a timeline is working backwards from the campaign's deadline. In our UV-kini scenario, the launch is scheduled for May 1. Working backwards, we know we need to have as many articles published in the April issues of the target magazines. Because the average monthly magazine takes a few weeks to print the issue and about a month to prepare the issue, we can see that if we want coverage in the April issue, we must get the release to the editor in late January or early February. This gives the editor enough time to assign the story, get a reporter to cover it and a photographer to take pictures, write the story, edit it, and send it to the art department

for layout. For a daily or weekly newspaper, the lead time is obviously much shorter; a daily newspaper will likely not want to see the release until a week or two before the launch date so it can get the latest story on the launch just in time to print it on April 30 or even on May 1.

The timelines vary from publication to publication, so it is wise to allow for extra time in the preparation and pitching.

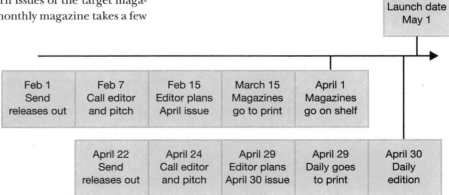

FIGURE BOX 4.3 Timeline for the UV-kini public relations campaign. Timelines vary from publication to publication, so it is wise to allow for extra time in the preparation and pitching.

### Step 8: SWOT Analysis—What Are Our Strengths, Weaknesses, Opportunities, and Threats?

We must take a leaf from marketing and look into the company, its product, culture, position in the marketplace, perception from the target customer, vulnerabilities, and opportunities. What we are talking about here is conducting a SWOT analysis before we start out. The reason a fashion company should do this is to determine the positioning of the product before it launches the public relations campaign. In determining its SWOT, the fashion company is able to plan the course of action the campaign will have to take in order to reach its objectives. By analyzing these different areas the company will be better positioned to reach the media and its publics.

Playing up its strengths and taking steps to reinforce its weaknesses will present the fashion company with opportunities. Knowing its threats can help the company maneuver in the media environment. For example, knowing that its main competitor is launching a major advertising campaign and outspending the company during the same time as the company plans to launch its own new collection will help the company decide to possibly be more aggressive with its public relations activities: i.e., doing more pitches and spending more time building relationships with the media. If the company doesn't have the funding to compete, then it must make up for it by being more creative, resourceful, and working harder to get the results.

The following are some of the considerations fashion companies can be faced with before launching a public relations campaign. A SWOT analysis is equally vital whether the company is a very small operation or a large corporation. It can be developed by members of the company in a brainstorming session or by surveys. Doing this before launching a public relations campaign will help determine the type of public relations coverage the company should strive to achieve. It's an audit in a sense. It will help determine whether it's the fast action of TV and the Internet or the credibility of the print media or a combination of both that will deliver the message effectively.

The SWOT analysis serves the purpose of doing an in-house audit to determine the extent of the company's positioning in the marketplace. It provides the tools to plan for a more productive public relations campaign. The following are some of the points to consider while doing the SWOT analysis.

#### Strengths of the Company and Its Products

What makes our company more unique than the competition? What are we best at? What are the advantages we have over competition? For example, we may be smaller than our biggest competitor, but we can move faster and are more flexible in dealing with customers' needs, on time delivery, better personal service, and value-oriented products.

#### Weaknesses of the Company and Its Products

What areas of our company need improvement (e.g., finance, marketing, distribution)? What problems do we have with our customer base? Why are we not reaching the sales goals?

### *Opportunities for the Company*

In what areas are competing companies not satisfying the public's needs where our company can? Are there changes in the competitive marketplace that afford new opportunities for us (e.g., major competitor having financial and production problems)? Opportunities can also be new products, styles, fashion trends, or approaches that the company can implement, regardless of its competitors, to better serve its customers.

### *Threats of the Company*

Threats are the areas where the company is liable to lose business, or experience a decrease in public image. A threat can be the fact that the competition has a much larger marketing budget and will react with a massive public relations and advertising campaign. It can also be that the competition has better name recognition, and they receive more media coverage. However, a threat can also exist regardless of the competition, such as when the consumer's disposable income has deteriorated due to the increase in the cost of food, gasoline, and other utilities.

## Step 9. Consider Potential Positive and Negative Outcomes

The positive outcomes of a successful public relations campaign are numerous and significant. The increased exposure, improved public image, and better community relations generated by public relations are a valuable asset to any fashion company that eyes long-term prosperity and success. Each public relations campaign aims to achieve specific positive results and ROI for the company. If the campaign results surpass these expectations, then the company's outlook and future performance may very well excel superbly. However, what if results turn out to be dismal? The top risk of any public relations campaign is that whereas the media coverage and increased public image are free publicity, the company has virtually no say on what gets printed or said in the media. Even with slander laws in place, the media can make a company seem silly, unorganized, or even ill intentioned and corrupt without directly calling it by these names. That said, it must be remembered that the media would seldom focus on the company's negative side without a good reason. Typically, one or more of the company's policies is wrong, or one of its employees is doing something wrong or unethical, which leads to bad publicity. At times, if a campaign is particularly successful, competitors may be tempted to engage in underhanded tactics and conveniently "leak" damaging information about the company to the media or start a nasty rumor about the company in an attempt to stop the company's success. Such indirect attacks cannot be wholly prevented, thus there is always a risk of a negative streak of lightning in the campaign's otherwise clear skies. On the other hand, the positive benefits of a public relations campaign are typically significant. A small mention in a prominent fashion magazine can spur an increase in sales that surpasses the results from a series of full-page advertisements costing tens of thousands of dollars. Therefore, the public relations director must weigh both the potential positive and the negative outcomes to evaluate whether the campaign is worth doing as well as to monitor its direction and progress while it is being implemented. When a public relations campaign boasts many potential positive outcomes and very few negative ones if any, then that campaign should be implemented and will likely turn out to be a home run for the company.

### Step 10. Identify the Public Relations Message—What Do We Want to Say in This Message?

The public relations campaign should have an overall message that unifies all of the public relations initiatives within the campaign. How do we determine the message? What do we want to convey to our audience? The message is based on the goals of the campaign as well as the product or event that is being promoted. If, for example, the goal of the campaign is to increase public awareness of the company and announce the opening of a new store in the neighborhood, then the message could be something along the lines of, "Our company is now your neighbor, please come check out our new store!" This message will now guide the public relations efforts so that the audience does indeed become aware of the company in a positive light and welcomes the opening of its new store.

### Step 11. Establish the Budget

In most large fashion companies, the total annual budget for public relations is typically set by the top executives of the company and is often considered part of the overall marketing budget. Unless it is set up as a special project with an independent budget, the public relations campaign is part of this annual budget and shares the fiscal pie with all other public relations campaigns for that year. Often, the scope of public relations initiatives the company will implement depends on the available funds in the budget. It pays to be realistic in the planning stage of a public relations campaign and consult the funding available; no matter how genius the plan, if there are no funds available to cover it, it will not get implemented. In an ideal world, each action in the campaign must be outlined and estimated in terms of costs, and the total costs must be managed so that the final bill for the campaign remains within the allotted budget. In the real world, this cannot and does not always happen. Some small items may pop up here and there and throw off the budget. However, the important thing is for the public relations director and staff to be aware of the budget and to try to stick to it as close as possible. We will cover this topic in more detail in Chapter 13.

### Step 12. Determine the Methods for Reaching the Goals

Choosing the right public relations method or methods to implement the campaign is an extremely important part of proper campaign planning. These are the detailed, real-world methods used to create public relations exposure. Initiatives such as sending a press release about the company's newest design team member or creating a fundraiser fashion show are the roll-up-your-sleeves type of public relations activities that actually get the campaign implemented and done. We will discuss these methods in further detail in the next chapter.

## Step 13. Choose Who Will Implement the Campaign

We must utilize many tools to get 101 percent productivity in this wonderful world of the fashion public relations business. One of the top tools brings together all of the people who help deliver and reinforce the public relations message, including the client, the public relations writer, the pitch person, and the people in the media to whom the material is aimed. The campaign is only as good as the ability to deliver the message. So we have to consider that after the creative work is accomplished, the "people work" of achieving the objectives will begin. The secret ingredient for a successful public relations campaign is the people who make it happen; at times we forget that *people* are the components that makes things work. You can have the best plan, strategy, budget, and all the elements we have been discussing—but, if you don't have the right people with the right attitudes, the right understanding of their job responsibilities, and commitment, then the campaign will be doomed for failure.

Let's look at what Peter Drucker, a leading expert of management and motivation, has said about pulling people together to do the job. It's all about "management by objectives," says Drucker in his 1954 book *The Practice of Management,* where he outlines his theory that getting people involved in the task and in the decision-making process gives the project a better chance of success (Drucker, 1954). Unless you can get the people who have signed on to understand their importance in the project and be a vital part of the job, the job will not get done; it's called commitment. To have a successful public relations campaign, the people involved must be committed to its success, and be a part of its success. Therefore, they have to have a proprietary interest in the campaign. When people are involved in the tasks and they understand their RFDs, the chances of success are greatly increased. By the very fact that they feel ownership in the project, it gives them more of an incentive to achieve the goals. It's all about getting the people who are involved in the ultimate outcome to know the objectives; Drucker calls it SMART:

- ▸ S—Specific tasks
- ▸ M—Measurable outcomes
- ▸ A—Achievable goals
- ▸ R—Realistic results
- ▸ T—Time-related projects—timelines

It is vital to discuss the objectives with the people involved in the public relations campaign, and also get them to understand the project and their role, and have them accept their responsibility to get the job done. Who are the people involved in the campaign? Everyone who touches the piece of paper called the *press release,* who helps organize the fashion show or event, or speaks to the media is a partner in the public relations campaign. Each of them must understand that being part of SMART is understanding their job, having the ability to measure the outcomes, develop, and reach achievable goals with realistic results in a set timeline.

Working out the manner in which the public relations campaign will be implemented is an important part of the campaign's planning. It is not sufficient to simply set goals in order to achieve them; it takes smart and careful planning to figure out how these goals will be carried out within the budget allotted. Questions must be asked about who will do what. Do the people involved have the resources to complete their tasks? How they will accomplish the assignment? The public relations director must evaluate the answers to these questions and then include these factors into the campaign planning phase in order to set the stage for a successful implementation. Having a proper estimation in regards to personnel requirements and time allotment is vital if the campaign is to be implemented at all. Imagine the fashion company that creates a flawless public relations campaign: the goals are set, the stories are developed, the angles are worked out, and the advertising and marketing team is ready to provide extra exposure. However, the personnel details are not worked out; the campaign is delegated to one employee who is swamped with other projects and is inexperienced in the ways of public relations. Although media interest may be sparked with the campaign's initiatives, the one employee is not able to attend the events to meet the press, and the coverage opportunities are wasted. Regardless of how perfect the campaign is planned out, it will not be implemented and the results will be dismal in such a circumstance because the proper personnel allotment had not been worked out. Thus, it can be seen that launching a public relations campaign without such an allotment is likely to be a significant waste of time and money. The public relations director has three options when it comes to campaign implementation: internal, outsourced, or a combination of the two.

### Internal Staff Only

In this implementation scenario, the campaign is executed wholly by the fashion company's staff without assistance from outside public relations agencies or companies. Depending on the company's size and the scope of the campaign, this may require one part-time employee, or a dozen or more full-time employees. To implement a campaign in-house, the public relations director should follow the company's policies and use his or her own management style to bring the campaign to fruition. In general, it is advisable to prepare a detailed breakdown of the various responsibilities and tasks needed, and determine who will implement each facet of the campaign. In a small- to medium-sized company, the public relations director may be the only person in the department, and thus all tasks and initiatives fall upon his or her shoulders. In this scenario, the executive will be the one planning and implementing—in coordination with the other departments—all facets of the campaign; he or she will be personally writing the releases, making the calls to the media, planning the events, responding to media inquires, and so on. In a larger company, the in-house public relations department may number several employees. In this case the executive should decide who will be responsible for each facet and meet with the department to review the campaign, the assigned roles, the budget, and the schedule.

The main benefit of the internal implementation option is that the campaign is wholly controlled by the fashion company. Not being dependent on an outside agency to get things done may be desirable when a campaign needs to be implemented in a hurry, or when the nature of the campaign is sensitive and involving non-employees may be impractical. An additional benefit is when the campaign is implemented in-house by the fashion company's staff, their work days are dedicated solely to the success of the campaign and nothing else; the employees at the outsourced public relations firm work on several projects at once so their workday is split among a number of clients. If the campaign calls for an intensive blitz, the company should consider doing the implementation in-house so its tasks receive the attention they require. However, if the outsourced public relations firm can promise dedicating a sufficient number of employees to the project, then the company may be better off outsourcing; the public relations director must perform a careful evaluation of the situation and the firm's ability to satisfy the campaign's personnel requirements. For example, if the campaign is urgent and calls for reaching out to more than 100 media outlets across the nation within a week's time, it may require several employees making calls and sending emails full-time until the campaign is over. Can the public relations firm do that? If the firm has the personnel and the track record of accomplishing such feats, then the public relations director may be wiser to outsource.

Finally, the benefit of in-house implementation is the assurance of confidentiality. Many of the public relations firms specialize in specific industries, and as a result they handle many clients from the same field, and the possibility for the release of sensitive information cannot be eliminated. Most public relations firms belong to some trade association and are bound by a professional code of ethics, (see Box 4.4), which prohibits them from divulging client information without permission. This safeguards against the firm divulging any of the fashion company's information to competing companies or others. However, the public relations director must keep in mind that even if no sensitive information is shared, the firm's creative employees who develop ideas for public relations initiative may serve not only the fashion company but also its competitors; thus initiatives or at least ideas for initiatives can be indirectly and inadvertently shared. This may or may not pose a problem, and the public relations director must determine whether this factor is an issue. To be fair, the same can be said about internal employees who may divulge information to competitors for a fee .

On the other hand, choosing in-house implementation may require hefty demands on personnel, which they may or may not be able to fulfill. If the campaign is large in scope or requires heavy efforts, the public relations director should ask herself or himself whether the in-house department can handle such a workload in addition to its normal activities. After all, the public relations personnel must still carry out their routine job duties in addition to implementing the campaign. Another question that must be asked before deciding on in-house implementation is whether the company's personnel have the sufficient public relations experience to implement the campaign's initiatives. If the campaign calls for advanced public relations strategies and the company's public relations staff are all relatively new to the field, it may be more beneficial to call upon a public relations firm, or hire the firm as a consultant to assist the in-house staff.

## Box 4.4    Code of Public Relations Ethics

The following is a reproduction of the Public Relations Society of America Member Code of Ethics 2000. Any society member firm agrees to abide by this code upon joining the society while a member. Among other things, this code binds the firm to remain faithful to each of their clients, and assure clients that their sensitive information will not be shared with competitors or other companies.

This Code applies to PRSA members. The Code is designed to be a useful guide for PRSA members as they carry out their ethical responsibilities. This document is designed to anticipate and accommodate, by precedent, ethical challenges that may arise. The scenarios outlined in the Code provision are actual examples of misconduct. More will be added as experience with the Code occurs.

The Public Relations Society of America (PRSA) is committed to ethical practices. The level of public trust PRSA members seek, as we serve the public good, means we have taken on a special obligation to operate ethically.

The value of member reputation depends upon the ethical conduct of everyone affiliated with the Public Relations Society of America. Each of us sets an example for each other—as well as other professionals—by our pursuit of excellence with powerful standards of performance, professionalism, and ethical conduct.

Emphasis on enforcement of the Code has been eliminated. But, the PRSA Board of Directors retains the right to bar from membership or expel from the Society any individual who has been or is sanctioned by a government agency or convicted in a court of law of an action that is in violation of this Code.

Ethical practice is the most important obligation of a PRSA member. We view the Member Code of Ethics as a model for other professions, organizations, and professionals.

### PRSA Member Statement of Professional Values

This statement presents the core values of PRSA members and, more broadly, of the public relations profession. These values provide the foundation for the Member Code of Ethics and set the industry standard for the professional practice of public relations. These values are the fundamental beliefs that guide our behaviors and decision-making process. We believe our professional values are vital to the integrity of the profession as a whole.

### ADVOCACY

We serve the public interest by acting as responsible advocates for those we represent. We provide a voice in the marketplace of ideas, facts, and viewpoints to aid informed public debate.

### HONESTY

We adhere to the highest standards of accuracy and truth in advancing the interests of those we represent and in communicating with the public.

### EXPERTISE

We acquire and responsibly use specialized knowledge and experience. We advance the profession through continued professional development, research, and education. We build mutual understanding, credibility, and relationships among a wide array of institutions and audiences.

### INDEPENDENCE

We provide objective counsel to those we represent. We are accountable for our actions.

### LOYALTY

We are faithful to those we represent, while honoring our obligation to serve the public interest.

### FAIRNESS

We deal fairly with clients, employers, competitors, peers, vendors, the media, and the general public. We respect all opinions and support the right of free expression.

### PRSA Code Provisions

### FREE FLOW OF INFORMATION

#### Core Principle

Protecting and advancing the free flow of accurate and truthful information is essential to serving the public interest and contributing to informed decision making in a democratic society.

## Box 4.4   Code of Public Relations Ethics *(continued)*

### Intent

To maintain the integrity of relationships with the media, government officials, and the public.

To aid informed decision-making.

### Guidelines

A member shall:

Preserve the integrity of the process of communication.

Be honest and accurate in all communications.

Act promptly to correct erroneous communications for which the practitioner is responsible.

Preserve the free flow of unprejudiced information when giving or receiving gifts by ensuring that gifts are nominal, legal, and infrequent.

### Examples of Improper Conduct Under this Provision

A member representing a ski manufacturer gives a pair of expensive racing skis to a sports magazine columnist, to influence the columnist to write favorable articles about the product.

A member entertains a government official beyond legal limits and/or in violation of government reporting requirements.

### COMPETITION

#### Core Principle

Promoting healthy and fair competition among professionals preserves an ethical climate while fostering a robust business environment.

### Intent

To promote respect and fair competition among public relations professionals.

To serve the public interest by providing the widest choice of practitioner options.

### Guidelines

A member shall:

Follow ethical hiring practices designed to respect free and open competition without deliberately undermining a competitor.

Preserve intellectual property rights in the marketplace.

### Examples of Improper Conduct Under This Provision

A member employed by a "client organization" shares helpful information with a counseling firm that is competing with others for the organization's business.

A member spreads malicious and unfounded rumors about a competitor in order to alienate the competitor's clients and employees in a ploy to recruit people and business.

### DISCLOSURE OF INFORMATION

#### Core Principle

Open communication fosters informed decision making in a democratic society.

### Intent

To build trust with the public by revealing all information needed for responsible decision making.

### Guidelines

A member shall:

Be honest and accurate in all communications.

Act promptly to correct erroneous communications for which the member is responsible.

Investigate the truthfulness and accuracy of information released on behalf of those represented.

Reveal the sponsors for causes and interests represented.

Disclose financial interest (such as stock ownership) in a client's organization.

Avoid deceptive practices.

### Examples of Improper Conduct Under this Provision

Front groups: A member implements "grass roots" campaigns or letter-writing campaigns to legislators on behalf of undisclosed interest groups.

Lying by omission: A practitioner for a corporation knowingly fails to release financial information, giving a misleading impression of the corporation's performance.

A member discovers inaccurate information disseminated via a Web site or media kit and does not correct the information.

**Box 4.4   Code of Public Relations Ethics** *(continued)*

A member deceives the public by employing people to pose as volunteers to speak at public hearings and participate in "grass roots" campaigns.

## SAFEGUARDING CONFIDENCES

### Core Principle

Client trust requires appropriate protection of confidential and private information.

### Intent

To protect the privacy rights of clients, organizations, and individuals by safeguarding confidential information.

### Guidelines

A member shall: Safeguard the confidences and privacy rights of present, former, and prospective clients and employees.

Protect privileged, confidential, or insider information gained from a client or organization.

Immediately advise an appropriate authority if a member discovers that confidential information is being divulged by an employee of a client company or organization.

### Examples of Improper Conduct Under This Provision

A member changes jobs, takes confidential information, and uses that information in the new position to the detriment of the former employer.

A member intentionally leaks proprietary information to the detriment of some other party.

## CONFLICTS OF INTEREST

### Core Principle

Avoiding real, potential or perceived conflicts of interest builds the trust of clients, employers, and the publics.

### Intent

To earn trust and mutual respect with clients or employers.

To build trust with the public by avoiding or ending situations that put one's personal or professional interests in conflict with society's interests.

### Guidelines

A member shall:

Act in the best interests of the client or employer, even subordinating the member's personal interests.

Avoid actions and circumstances that may appear to compromise good business judgment or create a conflict between personal and professional interests.

Disclose promptly any existing or potential conflict of interest to affected clients or organizations.

Encourage clients and customers to determine if a conflict exists after notifying all affected parties.

### Examples of Improper Conduct Under This Provision

The member fails to disclose that he or she has a strong financial interest in a client's chief competitor.

The member represents a "competitor company" or a "conflicting interest" without informing a prospective client.

## ENHANCING THE PROFESSION

### Core Principle

Public relations professionals work constantly to strengthen the public's trust in the profession.

### Intent

To build respect and credibility with the public for the profession of public relations.

To improve, adapt and expand professional practices.

### Guidelines

A member shall:

Acknowledge that there is an obligation to protect and enhance the profession.

Keep informed and educated about practices in the profession to ensure ethical conduct.

Actively pursue personal professional development.

Decline representation of clients or organizations that urge or require actions contrary to this Code.

Accurately define what public relations activities can accomplish.

**Box 4.4   Code of Public Relations Ethics** *(continued)*

Counsel subordinates in proper ethical decision making.

Require that subordinates adhere to the ethical requirements of the Code.

Report ethical violations, whether committed by PRSA members or not, to the appropriate authority.

**Examples of Improper Conduct Under This Provision**

A PRSA member declares publicly that a product the client sells is safe, without disclosing evidence to the contrary.

A member initially assigns some questionable client work to a non-member practitioner to avoid the ethical obligation of PRSA membership.

**PRSA Member Code of Ethics Pledge**

I pledge:

To conduct myself professionally, with truth, accuracy, fairness, and responsibility to the public; To improve my individual competence and advance the knowledge and proficiency of the profession through continuing research and education; And to adhere to the articles of the Member Code of Ethics 2000 for the practice of public relations as adopted by the governing Assembly of the Public Relations Society of America.

I understand and accept that there is a consequence for misconduct, up to and including membership revocation.

And, I understand that those who have been or are sanctioned by a government agency or convicted in a court of law of an action that is in violation of this Code may be barred from membership or expelled from the Society.

Signature _____

Date _____

(Public Relations Society of America, 2000).

113

### Outsourcing to an Outside Public Relations Firm

The outsourcing implementation method is a powerful approach to implementing public relations campaigns practiced by many fashion companies large and small. Working with an outside public relations firm gives the company access to the many years of experience, creativity, and media connections that the agency has to offer. The agency's business is public relations; therefore, its employees' sole purpose revolves around getting exposure for their clients. Not being a part of the fashion company's organizational hierarchy, agency personnel are not distracted by the daily demands that a company staff must deal with. Another benefit to outsourcing is that a fashion company essentially obtains access to several public relations experts when it retains an outside firm. Although the outside firm's personnel may not all dedicate their time entirely to the fashion company, having a few hours a day from a dozen people may be more desirable than one or two full-time employees; in cases where the success of the campaign relies heavily on creativity and diversity, it is better to have input and participation from a larger and experienced team. In the case of the smaller fashion company that may not be able to afford hiring additional full-time employees to staff the public relations department, outsourcing becomes a viable solution that can offer a balance between financial flexibility and sufficient workloads. Some projects—such as damage control—are better suited for outsourcing, especially if current in-house personnel do not have the necessary experience.

## Box 4.5   Hiring a Public Relations Firm

The U.S. public relations industry includes almost 7,000 companies with combined annual revenue of over $6 billion. The industry includes large companies such as Omnicom, WPP Group, and Interpublic, as well as many privately held firms. (First Research, Inc., 2008) Agencies come in many different shapes, sizes, and specialties. There are agencies that specialize solely in certain industries, such as fashion, healthcare, high-tech, real estate, and financial settings. There are small companies, privately owned companies, and large publicly traded public relations companies. Most agencies have a mixed and varied client base.

### Specialization

There are public relations agencies that cover many of the following or specialize in one of these areas:

▶ Cause branding

▶ Community relations

▶ Consumer PR

▶ Corporate branding

▶ Crisis/Issues management

▶ Diversity marketing.

▶ Domestic public relations

▶ Events management

▶ Financial relations

▶ Internal communications

▶ International PR

▶ Investor relations

▶ Media relations

▶ Product/brand communications

▶ Public affairs/lobbying, strategic consulting

Some of the giants in public relations are Omnicom, WPP Group, Interpublic, and then there is Edelman located in New York City. Edelman is the world's largest independent public relations firm, with 2,700 employees in 48 offices worldwide. The firm was named Number One Ranked Independent Public Relations Firm by O'Dwyer's, *PRWeek*'s Large Agency of the Year for 2006, and the Holmes' Group's Large Agency of the year for 2006. Coyne Public Relations is another company that specializes in diversified industries, and is one of the nation's leading independent public relations agencies, representing category leaders in automotive, beauty and grooming, entertainment, fashion, food and beverage, healthcare, household and office products, Internet and new media, pet industry, retail and restaurant, sports, technology and electronics, toys and juvenile products, and travel. Well-known independently owned Pierce Mattie Public Relations, Inc. is a leading public relations organization that specializes in the fashion, beauty, and, health and fitness industries in North America. This successful, creative company has offices in New York and California. It is far ahead of most independent companies and has the most visited public relations blog.

Like Pierce Mattie Public Relations, most agencies specialize in allied industries—like health, beauty, fashion, and fitness. Some specialize in one industry but most agencies diversify their client roster. Not concentrating on one particular business or industry is a smart way of running an agency business—by not throwing all their eggs in one basket they assure themselves of survival. By being diversified they build in a safety wedge for the company. Also, by spreading across several industries, public relations companies maintain a creative edge, constantly challenging their staff to think out of the so-called box of creativity.

### Hiring a Firm

When a fashion company hires a public relations firm, typically the firm assigns an account manager or account team to the client, depending on the client company and their needs. Major fashion companies that hire outside public relations firms usually have an account manager and a team assigned to its account. Smaller clients normally have only an account manager assigned to them who utilizes the public relations firm's other staff on a need basis; for example, when the account manager is asked to find a spokesperson for the fashion company, he may call in the firm's expert on spokespeople to help on the selection; but after that is completed, the expert will move on to another client whereas the manager continues to manage the client's public relations activities. The account manager is responsible for media results. The duties may vary from writing press releases to pitching to the media, and organizing events to developing

## Box 4.5  Hiring a Public Relations Firm (continued)

collaterals. The successful account manager has to wear many hats. It pays for a fashion company to get to know who will be their account manager prior to retaining the firm, to ensure that they can work well with the account manager.

### Compensation

Compensation to the public relations firm varies. Many companies work on an hourly compensation arrangement and the amount depending upon the size of the project, company and work involved. Small public relations firms bill anywhere from a low minimum of about $100 per hour to $300 to $400 per hour plus expenses. This can be a costly fee if the results are not as expected. From a financial perspective, the most beneficial way for a fashion company to hire a public relations firm is to sign a yearly contract for a certain dollar amount. This fee is paid monthly in 12 installments. The proposal can include a 60-day cancellation clause that can

be initiated by the client or public relations firm. The contract establishes a set monthly amount, enabling the fashion company to set aside a fixed fee each month without having to worry about surprise additional fees.

### Track Record

Performance should be on the top of the list in selecting a public relations firm. Check out the firm's record, their news clips, their dates, and the type of media response they have received. Look up the companies they worked for or are currently working with and research their public relations results. In some cases, it may be important that the public relations firm has had or is having success specifically in the client's industry. The client must check the background of the public relations firm with which they will be working. Ask to see the work that they have performed for other clients and then judge for yourself if their performance can be beneficial to your company.

Finally, at times it serves a purpose to be represented by an outside public relations firm; the outside firm may know important leaders in the media and industry to which the fashion company has no access, but could benefit tremendously from an opportunity to work together alongside these leaders. Thus, it is not only a question of whether the fashion company should retain an outside firm; if the company should outsource, the question that may be of more importance becomes, "Which firm to retain?" It is imperative for the fashion company to retain the public relations firm that is well suited for the type of the public relations campaign that the company is planning. Box 4.5 discusses hiring a public relations firm at length.

### Combined In-House and Outsourced Public Relations

Some fashion companies may find the combination of in-house implementation and outsourcing to be an effective and attractive public relations solution. Combining internal and external forces in this manner can, in some circumstances, lead to a powerful, diverse, and flexible public relations implementation force. Drawing on the experience and connections of the outside public relations firm and the commitment and dedication of the in-house staff, such an implementation solution utilizes the best of both worlds. If the two worlds can work with each other, that is. As long as the in-house staff do not feel threatened by the outside firm, and as long as the outside firm does not mind sharing its glory, such a solution can exist—and quite successfully, too. The problem arises when either the in-house staff or the outside firm personnel, or both, make it hard for the

## Case Study 4.1   Setting Up Public Relations Campaigns and Goals

### Fashion Targets Breast Cancer

Since its debut in the spring of 1994 during New York Fashion Week and its formal launch in September 1994 at a special White House reception hosted by then-First Lady Hillary Rodham Clinton, Fashion Targets Breast Cancer (FTBC) has been a prominent fashion industry charitable drive to help fight breast cancer. The program, run by the Council of Fashion Designers of America (CFDA) Foundation, enlists the support of designers, models, retailers, and other creative energies within the fashion industry to raise public awareness and funds for the breast cancer cause in the United States and around the world (FTBC, 2009).

The Fashion Targets Breast Cancer name and symbol were inspired by Ralph Lauren, launched and merchandised by Polo Ralph Lauren, and subsequently entrusted to The CFDA Foundation—the philanthropic division of the Council of Fashion Designers of America. The CFDA Foundation maintains exclusive worldwide trademark and copyright protection of the FTBC name and logo. To date, more than $40 million has been donated to breast cancer charities worldwide from FTBC's campaigns.

During the first charity drive in 1994, U.S. retailers sold 400,000 FTBC T-shirts in 16 weeks, raising and distributing $2 million that year to benefit the Nina Hyde Center for Breast Cancer Research at the Lombardi Cancer Center at Georgetown University Medical Center. The Nina Hyde Center was chosen as the beneficiary at Ralph Lauren's request in memory of his friend Nina Hyde, the former fashion editor of *The Washington Post* who died of breast cancer in 1990. Hundreds of newspaper and magazine stories have been published about FTBC, and the T-shirt has been seen on leading television soap operas, dramas, and situation comedies. Some of the world's most famous models have lent their image to FTBC, such as Naomi Campbell, Cindy Crawford, Kate Moss, and Claudia Schiffer.

The campaign is ongoing not only in the United States but also in Australia, Brazil, Canada, Cyprus, Greece, Ireland, Japan, Portugal, Turkey, and the United Kingdom. One of FTBC's beneficiaries is the London, England-based Breakthrough Breast Cancer,

FIGURE CASE STUDY 4.1
Cindy Crawford wearing the Fashion Targets Breast Cancer T-shirt.

the United Kingdom's leading breast cancer charity (Breakthrough Breast Cancer, 2009). The nonprofit organization aims to initiate and support breast cancer research; promote breast cancer education and awareness among the public, policy makers, health professionals, and the media; and campaign for policies that support breast cancer research and a pioneering approach to breast cancer services in the United Kingdom. FTBC is the flagship campaign of Breakthrough Breast Cancer and to date the campaign has raised more than £8 million since 1996. Elle MacPherson, Yasmin Le Bon, and Jodie Kidd are a few of the many super models who have promoted the cause in the United Kingdom, according to the BBC, which reports: "The money raised by the T-shirts over the last decade is proof of their success" (Browning, 2005).

### Questions to Consider

1. What do you think about FTBC as a public relations campaign? Explain.

2. How does the FTBC project reflect on Ralph Lauren as a person, as a designer, and as a businessman? Did your opinion of him change after reading this case study? How and why?

3. Do you feel the CFDA Foundation was wise to choose the sale of FTBC T-shirts for its fundraising strategy within the scheme of this public relations campaign? If not, what would have been a better choice? Explain.

other to function properly. Seemingly unintentional errors that cause the other half to look bad are not always unintentional, and the public relations director must be alert for such situations and nip these in the bud.

There are several scenarios where this option is recommended. When embarking upon new projects—especially those where the company ventures into uncharted waters by reaching out to a new and unfamiliar group of media, for example—the company may benefit from the existing relationships an outside public relations firm may already have with the target media; in this case, the knowledge of the in-house personnel about the company and its products combined with the outside firm's media relationships is likely to lead to increased exposure. Another scenario is when in-house personnel do not have the sufficient public relations experience to implement the campaign's initiatives. If advanced public relations strategies are required and the company's public relations employees are not experienced enough, it may be beneficial to bring in the outside public relations firm as a consultant. This could be a perfect time to share implementation between the in-house department and the outsourced firm, and provide the in-house staff with the opportunity to gain more hands-on experience by working alongside the more experienced staff of the public relations firm.

### Step 14. Determine How to Deliver the Message

After we establish the goals, plans, schedules, budgets, and messages for the campaign, and do the audience and media research, we need to decide on the media venues that will be most conducive for delivering the messages and providing for the most positive public exposure. The campaign's timeline has much to do with these decisions. If the campaign schedule will run for three or more months, then we have sufficient time to submit information to magazines, which are typically working on the issue that is two to three months ahead. For daily or weekly newspapers, television, and the Internet, the timeframe will be closer to the event. We must set up a time schedule for the release, listing when it will be sent out to each of the target media outlets, when to contact editors/reporters to ensure they had received the release, when to solicit for coverage, and so on. A well-planned timeframe will help to ensure campaign success.

### Step 15. Determine How to Measure the Performance

Results and ROI are among the top goals for the public relations campaign. Everyone wants the most results for the least amount of money. But how do you measure success of a public relations initiative? We will discuss the topic in further detail in Chapter 13.

## Chapter Summary

▸ Properly planning and setting up the public relations campaign and its goals leads to improved results.

▸ Careful research and coordination with the company's other marketing initiatives are key to getting the job done in the public relations environment.

▶ The planning process comprises 15 sequential steps that lead to a properly planned campaign:

1. Establish the goals.
2. Create an overview.
3. Establish a detailed plan.
4. Define preferred results as a part of reaching the goals.
5. Determine required research for proper planning.
6. Determine target markets and audiences.
7. Define the timeline for implementing the campaign.
8. Create the campaign's SWOT analysis—strengths, weaknesses, opportunities, and threats.
9. Consider potential positive and negative outcomes.
10. Identify the public relations message.
11. Establish the budget.
12. Determine the methods for reaching the goals.
13. Choose who will implement the campaign.
14. Determine how to deliver the message.
15. Determine how to measure the performance.

▶ The campaign goals are based on the public relations and marketing needs of the company, which change according to the company's position in the market, market conditions, and the company's plans for the future.

▶ Deadlines govern the field of public relations, and planning ahead is instrumental in getting results.

▶ One of the top factors that make or break a plan is the people who will be implementing it. The company must have the right number of the right people with the right attitudes to implement the initiatives. Also, they each must understand their functions within the campaign and be given the responsibility to carry these out.

▶ A campaign can be implemented by in-house staff alone, by outsourcing to an outside public relations firm, or by a combination of the two.

## Key Terms

▶ public relations campaign
▶ public relations campaign goal
▶ responsibilities, functions, and duties (RFDs)
▶ strengths, weaknesses, opportunities, and threats (SWOT) analysis
▶ public relations message

## Chapter-End Questions and Exercises

1. Define *public relations campaign* in your own words.

2. Name two steps that must be put in place to determine whether the goals are reached during the public relations campaign? Explain why they must be included.

3. Planning is the key to getting the job done in the public relations campaign. Name four areas that must be included in the planning phase to get the job done.

4. Do you think public relations goals should depend upon the company's marketing plans, market conditions, and business development plans? Explain.

5. Why is planning ahead and scheduling so important in public relations? Give an example.

6. What can we learn from a SWOT analysis when it comes to public relations? How can we benefit from this analysis when planning the public relations campaign?

7. Look through a newspaper or magazine and find a fashion story that includes a statement from one of the fashion companies at the focus of the story. What is the message behind their statement? Do you think it's the right message within the context of the story? Explain.

8. Find a fashion company that posts its press releases on its Web site. Look at one of the releases and find out if the company is using in-house staff or an outside firm to implement its campaign. After reading the release, do you think the company made a wise choice? Why?

9. You're a public relations director for a major U.S. manufacturer of business suits. Find a public relations firm that's based in the United States. Using the criteria and information in Box 4.5, determine whether you would hire that firm, and explain how you arrived at that conclusion.

10. Select any well-known fashion company. As the public relations director for this company, you are entrusted with launching a public relations campaign for a fictitious new collection for this company. Run through the campaign planning steps 1 through 15 and create a comprehensive campaign plan for this initiative, detailing the information you gathered and evaluation process for each of the steps. You may use story boards and any other visuals you feel necessary.

## FIVE

# Formulating, Modifying, and Selecting Public Relations Methods

## Chapter Snapshot

To achieve the public relations campaign goals, it is necessary to formulate and adopt one or more of the **public relations methods** in order to implement the goals in the most efficient, timely, and cost-effective manner. By assessing the various available methods and approaches to public relations, and by identifying which of these are most conducive to achieving the goals, the fashion company takes the first step toward the fulfillment of the campaign plan. There are many factors that affect which methods should be used, and these factors must be taken into account when making the final determination about implementation methods. Traditional public relations methods have stood the test of time and have proven successful when utilized appropriately. However, public relations is not a static field; it evolves constantly to adapt to new business philosophies, modern technology, and a changing media industry. In a way, traditional methods have also prepared the launching pad for contemporary, evolving methods that are quickly proving as effective in today's fast-paced and electronic business world. In this chapter, we will cover both traditional and contemporary methods, as well as the various factors that help determine which methods to use when.

## Objectives

▶ Identify and understand public relations methods.

▶ Explore the three categories of public relations methods: the media methods, the community methods, and the grassroots methods.

▶ Recognize the various typical methods used within each category.

▶ Discuss real-life examples illustrating implementation of these methods.

▶ Identify the various factors that shape public relations methods.

After the planning of the public relations campaign is completed and the big picture is drawn, we must now roll up our sleeves and get down to the details of how we are going to accomplish what we set out to do. The campaign goals can be complex or simple; however, without a well-thought-out and practical plan of how to implement the campaign, the chances that these goals will be met are slim. Many public relations campaigns break down at this stage of implementation due to lack of attention to details. To pull off the campaign successfully, the fashion company needs to divide the campaign goals into smaller, manageable steps that together lead to the fulfillment of the broad campaign goals. To the layman, public relations success may seem at first glance to be more connected to luck; however, upon closer inspection we find that the successful public relations campaign is implemented utilizing a well-planned and focused sequence of public relations methods that complement and coordinate with each other to bring about the seemingly magical results. The successful public relations director pays careful attention in formulating and selecting the public relations methods that will bring about the campaign goals. It is impossible to achieve the broad goal of raising the public awareness of a new dress shirt collection without first working out the practical methods of how to present the new collection; which media outlet would be best to communicate the message; and how to approach the media about it. The public relations director must be knowledgeable about traditional public relations methods, stay abreast of emerging contemporary methods, and be willing to explore new possibilities and create new methods as needed.

## The Public Relations Method

Suppose the public relations campaign goals call for increased exposure for the fashion company in the industry circles. Such exposure does not occur on its own, and it certainly does not occur just because the public relations director wrote it down on a piece of paper. After the planning stage is over, the implementation of one or more public relations methods is what brings about results. Certain specific and calculated actions must be taken in the field to create the exposure: We must write and distribute a clear and succinct press release; we must contact trade reporters and editors about it; and we must effectively follow up on interests from the media. This is where the public relations methods shine because they guide the way toward results. Instead of a vague and ambiguous approach that does not provide a detailed and specific path for implementation, the public relations method gives us concrete directions and actions that forward the initiative toward successful completion. Within this area we must be able to venture into different methods and find creative ways to deliver the message to different entities. The whole emphasis in today's competitive public relations market is to reach out to your audience in many different ways. We need to be able to engage the target audience and involve them in the process whether it is through an event, blog, or a sponsorship activity. We must find a method of effective communication that meets the target audience "on the street where they live." Public relations must be able to incorporate into this mix the various marketing tools to maximize media recognition.

The trend today remains and will continue in the future to find ways and means to penetrate a specific market and reach a specific customer. Expenses and overhead are ever rising, and different methods must be employed to successfully continue getting the word out, with an emphasis on reducing the high overhead of advertising and marketing and still being able to get results. We will discuss these different methods and also the need for public relations to become proficient in developing these methods. The process of improving public opinion and getting results is the major goal of any public relations method. Knowing who to contact for a specific story or event is now and will always be essential to achieve media coverage. Public relations methods can be divided into three categories: the media methods, the community methods, and the grassroots methods. We must find the right mix of these methods for the situation and determine which ones are more effective for our purpose of reaching the audience and getting media recognition. Using some of the following approaches is essential for a company to remain profitable and gain a presence with the media while reducing advertising and overhead costs. We just have to know what public relations method or methods we should pursue to resonate with the targeted audience. We will be discussing newer areas such as **Web logs (blogs),** and point out present-day tried and true methods such as celebrity involvement with charitable-cause-related events and spokespersons, fashion events, fundraisers, word-of-mouth campaigns, and partnerships with nonprofit organizations.

## Media Public Relations Methods

The media public relations methods have been with us for decades and are the fundamental methods upon which the public relations field is built. These straightforward methods focus directly on obtaining exposure in the media by distributing news items about the company or its products. The media methods are basically concerned with getting a positive message to the target audience via the media and improving the company's public image in this manner. Media public relations methods include the proper use of press releases, pitches, and follow-through.

### The Product News Method

One of the most fundamental and proven methods to getting media coverage is through releases announcing the development of a new product—in the fashion industry, it is a new collection, new look, new adaptation, and new color themes. Sending the press release and pitch with photos to the target publications has and is the standard for getting media acceptance. Product news is highly desirable by consumer media as well as trade publications because its function is to bring such news to the readership. However, product news must be what it states—something new and interesting; hollow hype will not work. Most editors and reporters know what is going on in the industry and can easily tell whether claims made about a product are true. Boasting about using the best fabrics in a press release is not going to impress anybody. That is not news, and is also a debatable fact. An experienced reporter's first question in response to such a claim would likely be, "How do you know they are *the* best fabrics? Did you test them? Were any official, impartial studies conducted to prove this?" and so on. But let's say the company is using special fabrics made from a special breed of sheep only found in a remote Pacific island, and you know for a fact that nobody has ever used this type of fabric. The fact that the company is using these fabrics that no other manufacturer has used in the past is interesting, and would likely lead to a story.

Product news is not only effective, but also cost effective. The new product or collection is being developed independently of the public relations initiative, thus the expenses to launch the new product or line will be spent regardless of the public relations actions. Faxing or mailing the release and the press kit, making long-distance follow-up phone calls, and hiring a photographer to snap a few professional photographs of the news item is about all the expenses that will be incurred with this method. On the other hand, every magazine editor today is typically swamped with emails and letters about this or that new product. It is difficult to grab an editor's attention with anything less than a spectacular press release that highlights an exciting new style, an innovative product feature, or perhaps the endorsement of a celebrity. When the Olsen twins released news of their new label Elizabeth & James in the fall of 2007, the media picked up the story and enthusiastically promoted the launch of the collection. As can be seen in Box 5.1, product news can lead to excellent media coverage.

## The Company News Method

The company news method pitches news about the company as a company, usually to the trade media. It is typically easier to get press coverage in trade media than by the consumer media, especially when it comes to stories announcing the addition of new executive personnel or designers to the company. This method also includes announcements in the local papers such as the opening of a new store within the community, or the unveiling of a new Web site for the company. Here, again, the procedure is to have substance to the news item and to know the media fit and the reporters who would be interested in this news. Box 5.2 shows an example of a press release from The Talbots, Inc. announcing company news, and a *New York Post* article that appeared as a result. It is important to note that the article was not all positive because the company had just posted lower than expected profits. The news of Chris Jackson joining the company has perhaps tempered an article that would otherwise be fully negative, but the media still reported on the company's financial woes because it is the media's duty to report all the information. So here we see another example of how independent the

## Box 5.1   Product News Translate to Media Coverage

When celebrity twins Mary-Kate and Ashley Olsen decided to expand their fashion business and launch a new line, information was released to the media. The product news, combined with the celebrity duo's fame, brought about a media buzz resulting in a host of articles as can be seen from the *USA Today* article.

### Olsen Twins Focus on Fashion Career

LOS ANGELES—Mary-Kate and Ashley Olsen might never appear together on-screen again, but the twins are still very much a team.

The 21-year-olds made a name for themselves reciting one-liners as little Michelle Tanner on *Full House.* As children, they made numerous successful home videos aimed at little girls (playing sisters pulling each other out of sticky comedic situations, of course). But they say pairing up on-screen is not in their future.

"If we did something in that sense again, it would be in terms of producing," Ashley says.

Acting aside, "we do everything together," Mary-Kate says.

That would include their new contemporary fashion line, Elizabeth & James, which they have been touting to shoppers on both coasts, first in Los Angeles, then Tuesday night in New York.

After the L.A. event, the petite power team—seated at a table in the garden of Chateau Marmont and sipping drinks (iced soy latte for Ashley, Diet Coke for Mary-Kate)—proudly chatted up their efforts.

"It was amazing, because it's something we worked so hard on, and for the first time, we actually got to see a response," says Ashley about the event at the Beverly Hills Neiman Marcus.

The pair worked on the gathering for two months, designing the invitations, décor, menu, and music and making after-hours trips to the store to style mannequins. They want to make it very clear that Elizabeth & James isn't just another celebrity-endorsed clothing line. And while their non-famous siblings are Elizabeth, 18, and James Trent, 24, they claim the line isn't named after them, as has been widely reported.

"Can you please clarify that?" Mary-Kate asks, clearly annoyed but still smiling.

It's just a coincidence, they say; they call their sister Lizzie, and their brother Trent.

FIGURE BOX 5.1  Twins Mary-Kate and Ashley Olsen at the launch of their Elizabeth & James fashion line.

"We wanted to pick a male name and a female name," Ashley says. "I remember saying Elizabeth and James, and being like, "Oh, my gosh, that's our brother and sister!''

While that might be a tough story to sell, the duo's interest in fashion is not. Their image as wide-eyed, pouty-lipped beauties in magazine spreads and clutching coffees out and about in tabloid photos shows a sense of style that, like it or not, has made a mark in fashion history. In 2005, The *New York Times* explored their bohemian bourgeois "bobo" style and called them "trendsetters for the latest hipster look."

124

**Box 5.1  Product News Translate to Media Coverage** *(continued)*

But the E&J line isn't a carbon copy of their own looks. The sisters say they wear simply what feels comfortable. "We dress a certain way, we buy a lot of vintage clothing," says Mary-Kate. "I've always been fascinated by furniture and clothes from a different time. You can change anything by the way you dress, by the way you put it together. It's almost like creating a little fantasy world for yourself, which is how I kind of look at fashion and most of the things I do."

E&J instead aims to combine two looks: a softer, feminine sophisticate (Elizabeth) and a tailored, masculine edge (James).

There are slouchy cardigans, shrunken blazers, a leopard-print coat. With most prices ranging from $145 for leggings to $775 for a leather jacket, it's more accessible pricewise than their other line, The Row, sold in Barneys New York and Harvey Nichols in London. They design both themselves, even doing their own sketches.

They also have the mary-kateandashley licensed brand, for ages 5 through 12 at Wal-Mart, for which they collaborate with an in-house designer.

**"Divide and conquer"**

To create E&J, they partnered with Jane Sisken of 'L'Koral Industries, the company behind contemporary label LaROK.

"Ashley and Mary-Kate are sticklers for detail," Sisken says. "They blow me away. They will look at something and know exactly what needs to be changed."

Because they split their time between New York and Los Angeles, where each has her own home, "we divide and conquer," Ashley says. "We design together, but for fabric selection, fittings, overseeing production . . . we always try to have one of us in each city."

They are designing for a hip, young woman who is current on trends but wants to buy quality pieces that will last more than one season, Sisken says. She and the Olsens collaborate with a design team, but every stitch must pass muster with Mary-Kate and Ashley.

"It's our name, and we wouldn't compromise that," Mary-Kate says. "We don't want things that don't represent us and what we can do."

(Clark, 2007)

media is, and that choosing the right public relations method is extremely important because of the possible repercussions, both good and bad.

## The Current News Event Method

The last media method associates with a general news story that is currently being covered by the media, which somehow relates to the fashion company, its brands, or its products. The fashion company's pitch must present the media with a new angle on the story in light of the company's products. By contacting the reporters or editors who are covering the story and giving them new information on the subject of the news story, the fashion company is likely to become part of the next report on the story. The success of this method depends upon a strong connection between the news story and the company. For example, let's say many fashion magazines are covering the surge of retro wear such as bell bottom pants, and the fashion company is manufacturing wide lapel jackets similar to those that were popular in the 1970s. The fashion company can link its jackets line to the retro wear story and pitch its product as an example of retro wear that is coming back.

## Community Public Relations Methods

As the name suggests, the community public relations methods focus on improving public opinion of the fashion company through direct community initiatives. Community methods do not merely communicate the news as the media

## Box 5.2 Company News Method: Press Release Turns into Media Exposure

In May 2008, The Talbots, Inc. announced it has named former Calvin Klein designer Chris Jackson as vice president. The following is the company's press release and the *New York Post* article that resulted.

### Talbots Names Chris Jackson SVP Apparel, Design and Development of the Talbots Brand: *Former Calvin Klein Designer to Lead Design Direction of the Talbots Brand*

Hingham, MA, May 20, 2008—The Talbots, Inc. (NYSE: TLB) today announced that it has named Chris Jackson Senior Vice President of Apparel, Design, and Development of the Talbots Brand. In this role, Mr. Jackson will be responsible for the concept and design of all apparel under the Talbots label, including its core Misses, Petites and Woman's lines.

Trudy F. Sullivan, President and Chief Executive Officer of the Talbots, Inc. commented, "Chris' appointment reinforces our strategy to become a design-led organization, focused on delivering compelling merchandise assortments that build on the classic heritage of the brand. We are delighted to welcome such a strong design talent, as Chris' extensive experience both at Calvin Klein and Donna Karan will be invaluable as we continue to strengthen the Talbots product and reinvigorate the brand image."

Mr. Jackson, 40, joins Talbots with 18 years of product design and development expertise, most recently serving as Senior Vice President of Design for the Calvin Klein Bridge and Better Sportswear collections. Mr. Jackson previously spent nine years as Design Director for DKNY's women's collections. In these roles, Mr. Jackson had the opportunity to work directly with Mr. Klein and Ms. Karan on the development of design strategies. Mr. Jackson also held design positions at Anne Klein, French Connection and Nautica. In his new role, Mr. Jackson will be based in Talbots New York Creative Studio and will report to Michael Smaldone, Chief Creative Officer of the Talbots brand.

Mr. Jackson commented, "I have long admired Talbots strong classic brand, and am excited to be joining Michael's creative and talented team in refreshing this great brand."

Mr. Jackson holds a bachelor of arts degree in Fashion design from the Kingston School of Fashion in London. He resides in Brooklyn, NY.

The Talbots, Inc. is a leading specialty retailer and direct marketer of women's apparel, shoes and accessories. The Company currently operates stores in 867 locations in 47 states, the District of Columbia, and Canada, with 595 locations under the Talbots brand name and 272 locations under the J. Jill brand name. Both brands target the age 35 plus customer population. Talbots brand on-line shopping site is located at www.talbots.com and the J. Jill brand on-line shopping site is located at www.jjill.com (The Talbots, Inc., 2008).

And the ensuing media exposure included a *New York Post* article by James Covert two days later. Although the article, "Talbots In '08: Outlook's Dim," mostly focused on the company's bleak financial news, it also mentioned the appointment and added some positive angle to the otherwise negative story:

> While keeping inventory lean to protect profits, Talbots aims to freshen up its fashions, which CEO Trudy Sullivan admits have become a monotonous "dowdy" flow of sweaters, skirts, and pantsuits. Sullivan, who was president of Liz Claiborne before joining Talbots last summer, this week hired Chris Jackson, a veteran of Calvin Klein and Donna Karan, to head design and apparel development" (Covert, 2008).

methods do; community methods create the news through proactive implementation of community initiatives.

### Partnerships with Nonprofit Organizations Method

Partnerships with nonprofit organizations provide excellent opportunities to help the community and attract media attention. Nonprofit organizations are not dissimilar to private businesses in that they are constantly on the lookout to improve their brand image, gain recognition from their public by having the ability to reach their audience, and have a well-balanced financial environment. The need to get the word out to their community is a top priority of any nonprofit organization, no matter the size. Nonprofit organizations are always looking for entities or individuals to support their services. Partnering with a nonprofit organization has many advantages; providing the nonprofit organization puts its resources to work for the common good of both parties. Public relations is the main source of recognition for the nonprofit organization—budgeting is usually not allocated to public relations for the average nonprofit organization. Most of that work is performed in-house by a member or volunteer of the nonprofit organization. The nonprofit organization is aware that in most cases, only by getting the word out to their audience will it survive. One of the most important considerations for any commercial company that wants to partner with a nonprofit organization is whether or not the company will be influential regarding the decision making of how the funds are dispersed.

Many nonprofit organizations do not have ample financial support to sustain a public relations program. If they do have the financial funding, it will invariably go to satisfy the needs of their customers. Public relations is the gateway to raising awareness of the nonprofit organization. However, most of the smaller nonprofit organizations look for "freebies" (getting public relations exposure without expending any of their funds). Obviously the United Way, Red Cross, and other large nonprofit organizations do employ public relations personnel, but for the most part, nonprofit organizations look to form relationships with companies that are able to support their media needs. Many small nonprofit organizations' executives feel that they don't have to allocate a budget for public relations because they can get it for free. So we see where there are always opportunities available for companies that want to partner with nonprofit organizations in order to serve the community and receive recognition for their contributions. Partnering with local nonprofit organizations is a great way for a company to be involved and receive recognition for its services.

## Box 5.3  Fundraising Celebrities

Although the use of celebrities for putting a positive twist on a product or cause-related activity in not new, let's consider how this method has been updated and review its effectiveness. Fashion columnist Rod Stafford Hagwood of the *Sun-Sentinel* in South Florida covered this celebrity story, (see the following story) and wrote the following in the article "Timely help from celebs" in *The Sun-Sentinel*:

Eric Dane, Russel Simmons, and Mary J. Blige have all designed limited-edition ErnstBenz watches that will benefit Chrysalis, the nonprofit helping people transition from poverty. The story was headlined as, "Time for Change." The collection of 24 styles per designer pays homage to the 24th anniversary of the charity. The prices have a wide range: Simmons' is $3,500; Dane's is $7,500; Blige's is $19,500. The article goes on to say—Look for the watches in Saks Fifth Avenue stores this fall with half the proceeds going to Chrysalis (Hagwood, 2008).

## Box 5.4   The Gap and (Product)RED

In the fall of 2006, the Gap launched the RED collection in the United States as a CRA initiative. The following is the company's statement about why the company joined the initiative. However, following that is an excerpt from a *New York Times* article questioning how much good is the initiative is really doing, which illustrates the risk that a company is exposed to when undertaking such an initiative.

From the Gap's Web site:

**How Gap will make a meaningful investment in Africa through (RED)™. Can something as simple as buying a product make a difference for Africa?**

That's the hope of Gap, Bono, Bobby Shriver, and Dr. Richard Feachem, executive director of the Global Fund to Fight HIV/AIDS, Malaria and Tuberculosis. They're some of the founding forces behind (Product)RED, a new global business initiative that raises awareness and money for the Global Fund by teaming with iconic brands to create (Product)RED branded products. Gap (Product)RED T-shirts are currently available in Gap stores in the U.K.; an expanded collection will launch in the U.S. and U.K. this fall. Half the profits from Gap (Product)RED products will go to supporting the Global Fund's HIV/AIDS programs in Africa (The Gap, 2006).

From The *New York Times*:

**Bottom Line for (Red), by Ron Nixon**

KIGALI, Rwanda — A year ago, staff members at the Treatment and Research AIDS Center could barely cope. Patients, unable to find care elsewhere, flowed in from every corner of the country. And if one of them was fortunate enough to find a bed here, she often had to share it.

Today, a dozen patients, mostly women, sit in neat waiting rooms, laughing and talking as children play around them. Doctors greet one another as they make their rounds, and take all the time they need to explain the complicated schedule HIV drugs require.

According to the center's managing director, Dr. Anita Asiimwe, doctors spend less time on crises and more time researching how to slow H.I.V. transmission in this tiny African nation, still recovering from genocide in 1994.

Dr. Asiimwe thanks an unlikely benefactor for all these improvements: the American shopper.

Just over a year ago, the rock star Bono started Red, a campaign that combined consumerism and altruism. Since then, consumers have generated more than $22 million to fight H.I.V. and AIDS in Rwanda by buying iPods, T-shirts, watches, cologne and most recently—as anyone who watched the Super Bowl knows—laptops, with all of them branded "(Product)RED."

According to Rwandan officials, Red contributions have built 33 testing and treatment centers, supplied medicine for more than 6,000 women to keep them from transmitting H.I.V. to their babies, and financed counseling and testing for thousands more patients.

Yet detractors say Red has fallen short. They criticize a lack of transparency at the company and its partners over how much they make from Red products, and whether they spend more money on Africa or advertising.

"Look at all the promotions they've put out," said Inger L. Stole, a communications professor at the University of Illinois. "The ads seem to be more about promoting the companies and how good they are than the issue of AIDS."

In the Super Bowl ad Sunday, which promoted Dell's recent Red debut, a man buys a Red laptop and finds himself cheered in the street by strangers and kissed by a beautiful woman. At the end of the commercial, three screens flash in rapid succession: "Buy Dell. Join (RED). Save Lives."

In its March 2007 issue, *Advertising Age* magazine reported that Red companies had collectively spent as much as $100 million in advertising and raised only $18 million. Officials of the campaign said then that the companies had spent $50 million on advertising and that the amount raised was $25 million. *Advertising Age* stood by its article.

**Box 5.4  The Gap and (Product)RED** (continued)

The Red campaign itself does not advertise, said Susan Smith Ellis, the chief executive. Instead, companies pay Red a licensing fee to label one or more of their products "(RED)." Then, they pay a portion of sales from those products to the Global Fund, a public-private charity set up six years ago to fight AIDS, malaria and tuberculosis in Africa. The fund sends the money to three countries—Rwanda, Ghana and Swaziland—to help women and children infected with HIV and to educate those who are uninfected in how to stay that way.

The percentage of profit that goes to the fund depends on the item and the company. For instance, 1 percent of all spending on American Express's Red cards goes to the fund, as do 50 percent of net profits from the sale of Gap Red items and $8.50 from each sale of a Motorola Red Motorazr.

In return, the companies can market themselves as socially conscious and, ideally, increase sales. (Neither Red nor the companies would disclose revenue or total contributions by company or product.)

According to a 2006 poll by Cone Inc., a marketing agency in Boston, 89 percent of Americans between 13 and 25 would switch from one brand to another associated with a "good cause," if products and prices were comparable.

Over all, more than $59 million has been contributed by Red and its corporate partners to the Global Fund. Red-financed projects have helped put more than 30,000 people on antiretroviral treatment and provided more than 300,000 HIV-positive pregnant women with counseling and treatment, according to data from Red and the fund.

Red and its donors have contributed nearly all the corporate money that has gone to the fund, which had $2.4 billion in 2007. This made Red the 15th-largest donor—more than Russia has given so far, and more than China, Saudi Arabia, and Switzerland have pledged.

Officials at Gap and Hallmark Cards say the two companies financed African HIV programs even before joining Red.

All told, Red's contributions make up less than 2 percent of the Global Fund's total. And the

**FIGURE BOX 5.4**  The Gap utilizes the RED campaign to convey to its customers that it cares about the local community as well as humanitarian global issues.

money from Red does not increase funding for the Global Fund programs it is directed to; instead, it allows the fund to shift money to other programs. Red's contributions also do not necessarily go to the countries hardest hit by HIV and AIDS; they go only to programs with proven success records.

Christoph Benn, an official at the Global Fund, said Red contributions allowed the fund to divert money to programs in 136 other countries and to increase its visibility.

Marketing centered on social causes is not new. American Express began the first "cause marketing" campaign in 1983, for the Statue of Liberty restoration project. Donating a penny to the project

**Box 5.4   The Gap and (Product)RED** *(continued)*

for every cardholder purchase, the company raised $1.7 million. American Express card use increased 27 percent, and card applications rose 45 percent.

Other companies were quick to follow suit.

But Red has taken the merger of marketing and philanthropy to new levels, becoming one of the largest consumer-based income-generating initiatives by the private sector for an international humanitarian cause.

The Red co-founder Bobby Shriver, a nephew of John F. Kennedy, said Red was an extension of his efforts to address financial and health problems in Africa. Bono and Mr. Shriver also founded Debt AIDS Trade Africa, known as DATA, an organization that lobbies for debt relief as well as AIDS funds.

When the two men decided to tackle HIV and AIDS and the dearth of access to antiretroviral drugs, they wanted to take a different approach to raising funds.

"I hate begging for money," Mr. Shriver said. "In most cases when you go and ask for a corporate donation, they'll cut you a check and that's it. We wanted something that was more sustainable."

But that argument has not impressed some activists and bloggers, who say the primary beneficiaries of cause-marketing campaigns are businesses.

Ben Davis of San Francisco, who created a Red parody online that says "Buy(Less)," is encouraging consumers to give more directly to nonprofits that support AIDS programs in Africa.

"I just think that increased consumption in America can't be the only way to solve Africa's problem," Mr. Davis said.

Mark H. Rosenman, a professor of public service at Union Institute and University in Cincinnati, noted a more basic objection to Red and cause marketing.

"There is a broadening concern that business marketing is taking on the patina of philanthropy and crowding out philanthropic activity and even substituting for it," he said.

Indeed, according to a survey by the Conference Board, a business research organization, business leaders are increasingly aligning their giving with business needs. In a 2007 survey of companies, 77 percent said that this was the most critical factor affecting their giving.

Brook K. Baker, a Northeastern University professor and chairman of Health GAP, a network of nonprofit groups seeking greater HIV and AIDS funding, says that is the problem. "Do we really want something as important as HIV-AIDS to be funded by holiday shoppers?" he asked.

In an interview in Rwanda, Tamsin Smith, president of Red, said such criticism missed the point. "We're not encouraging people to buy more, but if they're going to buy a pair of Armani sunglasses, we're trying to get a cut of that for a good cause," she said.

Ms. Smith, who formerly led Gap's government affairs department, also takes issue with those who criticize Red advertising.

"Red is not a charity; it's a business," she said.

At the Treatment and Research AIDS Center in Kigali, Dr. Asiimwe said that whatever the motivations of the Red companies, the spillover of American spending has made a real difference.

"When I was going to medical school a few years back, we would see patients and send them home knowing they were going to die without medication," she said. "I don't feel that way now. The money we get from Red through the Global Fund is helping to save lives. That's the important thing" (Nixon, 2008).

## Cause-Related Activity (CRA) and Celebrities Method

**Cause-related activity** involves the company's contribution to a worthy cause tied into a consumer purchase of the product, with proceeds from the purchase donated to that cause. Cause-related activities are an effective means of serving the community. Participating in cause-related activities is fast becoming a prominent community public relations method. It should also be noted that in this setting the company contributes to the charitable cause only if the target audience takes action and buys the company's products. Adding the involvement of celebrities has made this activity more meaningful and has created more interest from the media. More business establishments are interested in this type of activity due to the many public relations opportunities it provides for both the cause and the company. Cause-related public relations (CRPR) combines public relations, promotions, and philanthropic activity. However, within this framework the company's charitable contribution is dependent upon the consumer buying the product that will benefit the cause. The example in Box 5.5 includes product, celebrities, and a benefit for the cause, whereas Case Study 5.1 illustrates how coverage can become negative if the company does not ensure that its CRA is well managed.

Here's a win-win situation for public relations: incorporating celebrities, a product, a retail store, and a charity. The use of all these different factors in the example in Box 5.3 got the interest of Mr. Hagwood to write the story and thus another winner for the client. This was not just a testimonial from a celebrity, but actually having celebrities participate in the creative efforts in addition to contributing their names to serve a cause-related activity. Asked why he wrote the story, Mr. Hagwood said, "The 'formula' for why I talk to one public relations representative and not the other is extremely complicated and convoluted. It has a lot to do with: what projects I am working on; what stories are 'coming down the pike;' as well as does the pitch really speak to a trend or is it an isolated case." (Refer to Case Study 6.1 in which fashion columnist Rod Stafford Hagwood shares his thoughts about fashion coverage.)

### The Special Event Method

Sponsorships of special events and charitable causes enable a fashion company to reach its target audience in a specific geographical area. Corporate sponsorships have different goals and offer many public relations opportunities. There is no shortage in the sponsorship offerings; it is just a matter of the company deciding which venue can reach its audience and is compatible with its products. Many companies find this cost effective due to fewer expenses involved in advertising and marketing the event. The charitable cause does the advertising and marketing with the participating company's logo that is identified with the charitable cause in all the advertisements, mailers, and brochures. One of the best ways to capture the attention of your audience is to bring the company's products to the attention of their audience as a sponsor. Fashion companies are finding that by sponsoring events they can reach their target audience quicker and are more cost efficient. The fashion company sponsoring a fashion show or band concert is assured of an audience that will relate to their target market. The golf-wear manufacturer sponsoring the golf tournament similarly assures that its audience will take notice of its brand and products.

## Grassroots Public Relations Methods

The world is constantly concerned about *change*—political, economic, and social change. As the world goes, so does public relations methods, which constantly change to adapt to the changing business environments. Although we will continue to use traditional methods in reaching the media, we are now putting a new face in this highly competitive market with regard to what areas are available to us. Traditionally, public relations has aimed at raising awareness of the company through the mainstream media; today, however, using grassroots methods such as through local weekly community newspapers, the Internet, social media, email, and newsletters, public relations has been able to improve the company's public image by communicating directly with consumers. These public relations methods have their focus on alternative ways of reaching the audience besides through the media. Blogs, for example, speak directly to the audience without any traditional media intervention. They provide an immediate response from the target audience and create immediate "talk" about the products. Blogs are inexpensive to manage and are fast becoming a major component of disseminating information and achieving audience involvement. We will discuss the pros and cons of blogs later on in this chapter. We also find that to penetrate the target audience, a grassroots activity takes on a new meaning due to fact that it is directed at specific audiences with specific areas of interest. Reaching the audience through grassroots public relations is getting more popular because of the public's need to voice their opinions and thoughts, thus creating a new area of public relations—with a high return on investment (ROI), grassroots public relations has proven to be an innovative, low-cost, effective way for a company to reach their markets.

**Grassroots public relations** is about getting the average person on the street to spread the word about the company, its brands, or products. When you think grassroots, think, "local, local, local!" This type of public relations regards consumers and their friends and family as influencers. Any time you have the common people acting as influencers behind a project, charitable cause, or product, you have a grassroots setting. So grassroots public relations occurs when influencers are involved, pushing the public relations campaign forward through their active participation; such a method is also commonly referred to as "creating a buzz" or **viral public relations,** or just plain street public relations. All of these tags describe grassroots public relations. People create the buzz, then it becomes viral and spreads through word of mouth (WOM.) We also refer to this grassroots situation as something that is happening in the neighborhood or on the "street." It's all about people interacting with other people and spreading the word. Although grassroots originated in the political world, it is quite applicable to the fashion industry. The fashion company that is able to get the people in the street behind its brands and products is more likely to be the winner.

Perhaps the most significant benefit of grassroots public relations is its independence from the media. It is becoming increasingly hard to capture the media's attention, and coverage can sometimes seem capricious. Even though the company may offer amazingly unique collections, the target media may choose not to cover its new items or may not have space in the publication to cover them. Because it is implemented on the street level, grassroots public relations is not filtered through the news desk editor at the local paper. Instead, news of the company's items travels from person to person unrestricted. For

132

this to occur, however, the company must be able to stimulate people's interests and somehow motivate them to pass the word around, so here too the company must be creative in the way it implements the grassroots methods.

Grassroots public relations can be compared to guerrilla marketing in that it essentially serves the same purpose. As Robert P. Vitale and Joseph J. Giglierano, authors of *Business to Business Marketing, Analysis & Practice in a Dynamic Environment,* state, "Guerrilla marketing is the use of attention-getting small events intended to get the company noticed, to build small pockets of sales, and to obtain word-or-mouth diffusion of a message. It might involve passing free samples, or promotional merchandise in public places or engaging in small bits of 'street' theater to attract attention. The idea is to generate grassroots-level excitement while spending a minimum amount of money. Small companies or start-ups often rely on guerrilla marketing" (2002). The authors go on to say, "public relations (PR) activities include special events, press tours, public appearances, and any number of other activities intended to obtain public recognition." Grassroots public relations has the very same objective as guerrilla marketing with the sole objective of getting the target audience involved in word of mouth activities. Look for further discussion about grassroots public relations in Case Study 5.1.

## The Word-of-Mouth (WOM) Method

With the WOM method, the positive comments about the company and its products are spread from one person to another verbally, thus improving its public image. The WOM method successfully communicates to the target audiences in a personal way, and is best described as a hands-on approach. By making people aware of the company in creative ways and by encouraging them to share their positive views of its products, the fashion company can reach out directly to its audiences using a credible source of information—the audience itself.

To implement the WOM method we need to develop a smaller group of influencers who can help getting the word out to the larger-sized group of target audience and potential consumers. Grassroots public relations sets off a spark and lets the WOM spread like wildfire, spurring the people to act on their own volition as the ones who will spread the news of the collection, the product, and the company. A true grassroots public relations situation must be created by the people and not by spin. When spin is involved, it dilutes the very essence of true word-of-mouth, grassroots public relations and tends to lose its audience acceptance. This artificially created grassroots public relations is understandably known as **astroturfing** and is an ethically unsound practice (Anderson, 1996).

The very nature of grassroots public relations will help a company gain acceptance with a dramatic ROI because the same people who buy its products are delivering the message thus reducing advertising costs considerably. When a public relations company is able to get a testimonial from a client about the product in a local paper it becomes a powerful way of getting the message across. We witness this public relations grassroots activity among the younger generation. There will always be a new trend that will be picked up by the influencers of a particular group. All it takes is a few influencers to wear the item and then the flock will follow. When this activity takes hold we see a grassroots endorsement of the item and the start of a fashion trend. When the company observes the excitement they can then start a more aggressive campaign among their audience by donating items to various groups, organizing public events, partnering with local groups and letting the momentum of the item spread the word. The media will soon notice the excitement and report on it to their readerships. When the people take hold of the situation it has the effect of a snowball rolling down a hill—it just gets bigger and bigger. Fashion trends begin and end with the consumer. Consumers can be described as a flock of birds aloft in the sky, flying in formation—one bird is the leader and all the others follow along. Similarly, when the style leader or influencer in the group wears a new fashion, it soon becomes an item with other people in the group. There is always a person in any group who is the influencer; usually such people are the ones who are fashion leaders due to their taste level and ability to spot fashion trends. Grassroots public relations starts with the leader who organizes the groups through their own doing or others just following. Again, a word of caution must be noted: If the fashion company artificially starts a grassroots public relations trend, it will soon be discovered and the company will be admonished for this action—creating *astroturf* can be highly destructive to the product and the company.

### The Web Logs (Blogs) Method

Web logs, or blogs for short, are the latest and most dramatic and productive avenues for disseminating public relations information and reaching the audience. This method is so new, in fact, that at the time of writing, many word-processing spell-checkers still did not recognize the word. A blog's publisher, or **blogger,** can influence public opinion quite a bit if he or she has a large base of readers. As the interview in Box 5.5 outlines, there are many advantages for using blogs as a public relations vehicle, but there are also disadvantages; the understanding of the blog and the management of this powerful instrument of communication is vital for it to be effective. Public relations professionals are just beginning to explore this open forum and highly cost-effective way of creating word-of-mouth news. Getting the involvement of unknown persons who participate in the blogs creates excitement and controversy.

### The Corporate Sponsorship Method

The trend in corporate sponsorships has become a great marketing and public relations tool. Getting media coverage is more apparent when corporations become involved in community events, whether they are charitable or commercial endeavors. Although it primarily focuses on getting the word out about the company's good image directly to the general public through billboards, signs, and brochures, this method usually also yields extensive television, Internet, and print media coverage. Corporate sponsorships involve a monetary investment by the company for an event or a charitable cause with the objective of

## Box 5.5 Real World Profile: Shannon Nelson, Publicist and Chief Blogger

Shannon Nelson is the publicist and chief blogger for Pierce Mattie Public Relations, New York and Los Angeles. Pierce Mattie Public Relations was launched in 2001 by editor and lifestyle guru Pierce Mattie. As an innovator in his field, Pierce created a first-in-industry, Internet-based digital communication system. He continues to lead the industry in creative and strategic ways to leverage new and emerging media. He was brought on in October of 2006, as an already established blogger, to bring daily content to their main blog. Eventually the firm branched out into niche blogs that would cover the different aspects of industries the firm handles public relations for: beauty, fashion, jewelry, and fitness. He then became the chief blogger, overseeing all content, maintenance, and search engine optimization (SEO); managing the firm's reputation online; and handling all social media aspects for the firm.

FIGURE BOX 5.5 Shannon Nelson, publicist and chief blogger, Pierce Mattie Public Relations.

**What are your responsibilities, functions, and duties?**

As Chief Blogger I'm responsible for writing the content for the blogs, editing content submitted by our team, researching the latest trends and industry news across the niches we cover to keep our readers up-to-date, as well as maintaining the blogs to keep them running smoothly. I work on SEO, through our blog posts and interviewing key players in the fashion industry. I stay abreast of social media and create profiles on networking sites that would best reach our targeted audience.

**How can blogs help you to reach your target market?**

More consumers are heading online to research the latest buzz on products, as well as learning more in depth information about a product or company than would be given in a print magazine. Consumers are looking for unbiased opinions and are more often turning to blogs for that information. If a blogger writes a post that begins to get picked up by other bloggers and the media, it can generate more free press at a quicker rate than could be accomplished with paid advertising. This is considered a way of going viral. While the immediate benefits are fleeting, search engines soon index what has been written and this lives online for the life of your blog.

If your blog is of a particular niche and very content focused, your readers are your target market. You can influence them by educating them on the uses and benefits of your products. Blogging allows you to communicate

with your target market in a way that traditional public relations approaches cannot. It engages your client's consumers in dialogue and can help provide valuable feedback that you may have not gotten otherwise.

**How else can they contribute to your public relations activities?**

Your blog becomes your megaphone. It's where people come to learn more about your company, its practices, its level of customer service, its knowledge base and products. Your blog becomes an extension of your branding efforts and through an online presence creates an image that, for the most part, you can control. It's a place where you can communicate with the public in a way not possible through print media.

Just as I mentioned earlier, it is also a useful tool to gather feedback for your client. You can post surveys to your blog, an "open thread" which is an open-ended question that your readers answer—in a sense it can also become an indirect focus group.

Through a fashion public relations blog you can help create brand awareness for a client, garner the interest of a potential client and become a launching point for a viral campaign.

**What are the advantages of having a blog component for a public relations company?**

It is cost effective way to engage in conversation that spans across many different communities—the public relations community, the fashion consumer, the fashion industry (designers/brands), and the fashion editors. It is also one of the best ways to achieve search engine optimization and keyword domination for your firm.

### Why should a public relations company run a blog?

There are several reasons—B2B awareness, B2C awareness, building and solidifying relationships and search engine optimization.

### Have blogs become a way of life for public relations companies? Please explain.

Not yet. There are still many public relations firms that still rely on old media to spread the word about their firm and their clients. Pierce Mattie Public Relations was the first public relations firm to create a blog and had the insight to foresee the blogging platform as one with a potential for growth. We've been blogging since 2001 and it is only in the last year or so that we have seen other public relations firms launch a blog as well.

### Explain word-of-mouth PR and blogs.

In blogging it is considered influencer marketing. You can use your conversations online to seed word of mouth by targeting a key group or audience who have further important connections. More so, compared to verbal WOM, word of mouth online can be tracked and its ROI measured and understood. Online WOM is looked at as viral marketing or viral public relations. One way you can use your blog and the social networking sites you have profiles on is to launch a viral campaign through the use of multimedia. Create a video for a client, upload it to YouTube, then write about it on your blog and embed the video; promote it on the social networks you are a part of linking back to the original post on your blog. Through You Tube you can share the video by making the embed code available for others. You Tube tracks video views, allows comments, and shows who else is linking/using the video. Through your own blog tracking software, you can analyze who is clicking through to the video, if there are any incoming links from other sources to your original post. Your client can also cross reference any increase in traffic to their website, phone calls or media coverage pick-up to the timeframe you began the viral campaign.

### How does a blog reinforce the public relations message?

The blog you are writing yourself is one where the message can be controlled. You can construct a post in a way that targets specific readers with a carefully thought out message. Your comment section allows for interaction between you and your readers. You can certainly moderate the comments of your blog and chose to not publish anything negative. However, I think that stifles the conversation, and completely believe that reader's comments, regardless if they are positive or negative, should be published. You'll be respected for that and it also allows you to hear the sincerity and truth from a reader, which can be especially important if you find that a client's brand message is not being perceived in the way they had hoped. When your post gets syndicated on other blogs, your message spreads and is likely to capture attention by journalists. This actually happened to us before where an editor for *Glamour* magazine's blog loved something I wrote about and then in turn wrote her own take on the topic and posted a link back to my original post. When you post something of value and not something self-serving, the community responds and draws attention back to your product/service/client/firm.

### Explain the difference between a blog and splog?

A blog is authored by a person with valuable content that contributes to the good of the community. A splog is set up to autogenerate RSS feeds without mention or proper attribution to the original author solely for monetary gain. Splogs are riddled with Google Adsense and other pay-per-click advertisements. The goal is to make money off your stolen content. Now another blogger may also choose to aggregate or syndicate your content for monetary gain, however the difference is in the proper attribution and link back to the original post. By many bloggers this is still considered a borderline splog; however, many do not seek legal action because these particular blogs abide by fair use.

We can now understand the need for public relations to organize and managing a blog. The blog becomes a major communication method, another dimension in reaching the market place. Although blogs can't be guaranteed in reaching 100 percent of the target audience, experience has indicated that the targeted audience reach will be substantial and attained with a relatively low cost and achieve a dramatic ROI.

improving awareness of their consumer audience. The goal is to gain public relations coverage of the brand, improve the image of the company, and most of all increase future sales of the company's brand. It also enhances the reputation of the company. That's why so many companies are quick to hop on the corporate sponsorship bandwagon. As an example, Ralph Lauren was a sponsor of the 2008 Olympic Games in China.

---

### Box 5.6   Sponsorships Create Press Coverage

Quite a bit of quality press coverage can be achieved through corporate sponsorships of major events. Ralph Lauren's decision to sponsor the U.S. Olympic team in Beijing earned the company much positive coverage, as well as created a superlative public image for the brand through association with the top athletes in the country. One article, which appeared in *Fashion Week Daily,* covered the sponsorship in great detail and in positive light. After giving all of the information about the announcement and the contract, it included the following statement from the fashion company:

FIGURE BOX 5.6  A Polo outfit worn by U.S. Olympic Team members in the Olympic village for the 2008 games in China.

> We are both thrilled and honored to join with the U.S. Olympic Committee and the U.S. Olympic and Paralympic Teams to contribute to the most esteemed sporting event in history," said David Lauren, senior vice president of advertising, marketing, and corporate communications for Polo Ralph Lauren. "As our athletes take to this world stage they are representing the best of America and we are proud to be a part of that.

The piece also included a positive comment from the U.S. Olympic committee:

> As we discussed ideas about who could best outfit our athletes in a manner representative of the Olympic movement and what it stands for today, we believe Ralph Lauren is uniquely suited to deliver an outstanding product," said U.S. Olympic committee chief operating officer Norman Bellingham. "Polo Ralph Lauren is a quintessential American brand that represents a timeless and classic look which we believe our athletes will be excited to wear" (Shi, 2008).

### Public Relations Flanked by Promotional Marketing Method

This grassroots public relations method crosses paths with another method from the field of marketing, which is promotional marketing. Some public relations campaigns can benefit tremendously by having promotions implemented alongside with the public relations initiative. Promotional marketing methods, such as the giveaway and the refer-a-friend, reach out directly to consumers and complement the public relations campaign on a grassroots level. This method is optional and can be added to flank another public relations method. For example, to launch the unveiling of its new collection, a fashion company hires models to walk around the shopping malls and hand out the announcement of the company's new collection. It can be called *meet and greet*. This sort of guerilla promotion and marketing makes people think of the fashion company and its products in a positive way.

### Out-of-the-Box Methods

"They always say time changes things, but you actually have to change them yourself" (Warhol, 1977).

American artist Andy Warhol's famous quote is true in public relations as well. In these rapidly changing times, public relations has to adapt to changes to reach the target audience. Public relations methodology cannot be restricted only to the methods described previously in this chapter; because it is a creative field, public relations requires constant innovation, and new solutions and methods to tackle the various challenges the fashion company is facing. The buzzword *change* has many different meanings. We can change our personal habits, change our routine, change our jobs, but change itself has to come from within. Time may dictate a change, but as Andy Warhol said it, the bottom line is that "you have to make the change." Routines must change and you have to change with them.

With the advent of the new age of communications, including cell phones, iPods, Bluetooth, text messaging, and the other communication miracles that we are experiencing, it is apparent that the methods of public relations communication must change, too. These changes involve placing a higher priority of time on newer and different approaches to gain public relations coverage. In preparation for the 2008 Olympics, Nike launched a massive advertising campaign highlighting the human race's courage and featuring more than 30 athletes from around the world, and linked the television spots to a Web site where consumers can read narratives from the athletes and write their own comments. Box 5.7 discusses how the campaign created a new way to use a blog of sorts in conjunction with advertising to create word of mouth campaign. In recent years, there has been talk of the demise of print media, which may or may not happen for many years. However, regardless of the conversation about the demise of print media, public relations professionals are looking for additional methods or updating their present methods to reach their audiences. How does this word *change* apply to public relations methods? To understand this we must realize that the whole world of communication has changed so dramatically in the last decade that what we were accustomed to doing yesterday has changed

## Box 5.7 Out-of-the-Box Methods

Nike's recent campaign to promote the brand in the 2008 Olympics linked advertising and a hybrid format of the blog to get consumers involved in the spreading the campaign message of courage. The following is an excerpt from the online article "Nike Prepares Global Effort: Based around Beijing Olympics, the campaign includes a new worldwide spot and an event called 'Human Race,'" by Kenneth Hein, which ran in *Adweek* about this out-of-the-box public relations method:

> NEW YORK—This week Nike pushes forth with what it is calling the largest campaign in the brand's history. Based around the Olympics in Beijing, Nike will debut a new global spot called "Courage," continue to promote the Nike Hyperdunk shoe and launch the "Human Race" event.
>
> The new TV spot breaks first in Asia and Latin America. It will air in the U.S. on Aug. 8. The ad celebrates the 20th anniversary of the "Just do it" campaign by showing a collage of inspirational sports imagery. Michael Jordan kissing his National Basketball Association championship trophy and

FIGURE BOX 5.7
One of Nike's Courage TV commercials, which aired during the 2008 Summer Olympics in Beijing. The commercials harnessed the engaging power of the Internet by directing viewers to go online and add their comments to the Nike blog.

> Lance Armstrong defeating cancer are among the 30-plus different athletes from 17 different countries that appear. The Killers' "All These Things That I've Done" serves as the soundtrack.
>
> Consumers can then go to Nike.com/courage to freeze the many moments in the spot, read narrative about why they were important and add their own comments (Hein, 2008).

dramatically today. Traditionally, working up an interesting press release and pitching it to the media sufficed. Although this method is still a top method of reaching our audience, we find the need to look for and develop new and different ways of reaching this mass audience. Knowing where to go and how to get there will be the deciding factor in successfully getting the information out to the vast audience you are trying to reach. Dramatic changes in technology and lifestyles today are offering public relations professionals with opportunities to get the word out through these communication channels.

## Factors that Shape Public Relations Methods

Although the public relations method gives us a sense of direction for implementation, it is not meant to be a totally rigid procedure. Public relations is a highly fluid field with ever-changing circumstances; therefore, there is a great need for flexibility in implementation, and methods may have to be modified or replaced with more applicable methods as the circumstances change. Suppose that in the process of soliciting a partnership with a nonprofit organization, the public relations director discovers that the organization works with a well-known local celebrity. This poses the potential for the possibility of partnering with the celebrity as well. The director is wise to explore adding the celebrity endorsement method to the already-planned nonprofit collaboration method.

## Case Study 5.1 Formulating, Modifying, and Selecting Public Relations Methods

### eNR's Grassroots Public Relations Program

Brian Q. Smith is executive vice president of eNR Services, Inc., and general manager of the company's grassroots public relations business. He has 25 years' experience in communications, marketing, public relations, and information services. Smith was instrumental in developing eNR's grassroots public relations program and has implemented successful public relations programs for more than 100 corporations. Smith's clients include companies such as Avon Products, Ben & Jerry's, Century 21, MassMutual, and The Dress Barn. He holds a MSA in marketing from Western Connecticut State University and a BA in English from Saint Michael's College. eNR Services, Inc., headquartered in Norwalk, Connecticut, delivers technology solutions and programs to aid professionals during every phase of the public relations and corporate communications cycle. More than 1,000 companies subscribe to eNR's integrated product set to research public relations and marketing opportunities, build media lists, manage and distribute press releases, and monitor news coverage encompassing print, broadcast, and online media outlets worldwide. The company's hallmark service, the eNR grassroots public relations program, establishes a local news presence for businesses with multiple locations and has made the company the largest provider of community-centric public relations services in the United States.

### Lia Sophia Press Release

Lia Sophia is one eNR Services, Inc.'s clients and the public relations company has helped Lia Sophia launch a grassroots public relations campaign. The following is eNR's commentary on Lia Sophia's program:

### About Lia Sophia

Lia Sophia is a high quality fashion jewelry company that takes pride in its commitment to connect women to their dreams with an unparalleled business opportunity. Its 25,000-plus advisors and hostesses are able to offer customers an extensive line of exclusive one-of-a-kind pieces, and a Red Carpet Collection that's worn by leading celebrities and tastemakers around the world—all with a lifetime, replacement guarantee.

Founded in 1986, the company is still rooted in family and run by the second generation of the Kiam family of Remington Razor fame.

### Nonprofit Connection

Lia Sophia has also forged a successful relationship with its nonprofit partner, Dress for Success. The company annually donates a portion of its profits to Dress for Success, an international organization that promotes the economic independence of disadvantaged women by providing professional attire, a network of support and the career development tools to help women thrive in work and in life. Founded in 1997, Dress for Success has expanded to more than 80 cities in the United States, Canada, New Zealand, the Netherlands, and the United Kingdom. To date, Dress for Success has helped more than 350,000 women work toward self-sufficiency.

### Program

An early adapter of the grassroots public relations program, Lia Sophia began its public relations recognition program in March, 2004 for just 45 of its top advisors. Since then, it has expanded its recognition program to include 1,000 of its advisors, plus an additional 127 feature releases for announcements, special events and its commitment to the Dress for Success organization. Now one of the most active users of the grassroots public relations program, Lia Sophia sends monthly recognition releases for their high-achieving advisors to its local media, and up to six customized feature press kits annually.

### Results

From 173 distribution projects to date, Lia Sophia has used the grassroots public relations program to send more than 35,000 releases to local media. More importantly, these releases generated media recognizing 643 of the company's top advisors, enabling Lia Sophia to really boost sales and double their number of advisors each year over the last three years. As the company continues to grow, it will be increasing its recognition press center to include multiple levels of achievement and additional press kits.

In total, Lia Sophia's grassroots public relations program has generated more than 2,000 media clips that translated to more than 320 million impressions (enR Services, Inc., n.d.).

Brian Q. Smith, executive vice president, eNR Services, Inc.

### How would you define grassroots?

We define "grassroots" as the local media, including all media with an editorial focus on the people, businesses and events in a local area, or community. This includes daily papers with a circulation less than 50,000, weekly papers, local TV, and radio, as well as regional business magazines and Chamber of Commerce publications.

### What is grassroots public relations?

Grassroots public relations is a system for generating local news for the local media, which often requires developing customized press release content for media outlets located in specific, targeted geographic markets.

### What makes grassroots campaigns different than regular public relations campaigns?

Public relations professionals typically focus their attention on the major news organizations. Grassroots PR, on the other hand, focuses on the local, grassroots media. To put this in perspective, there are currently slightly more than 200 daily newspapers with a circulation more than 50,000—a typical focus of a regular public relations campaign. However, there are more than 1,500 dailies (grassroots) with circulation below 50,000 and more than 9,000 weeklies (grassroots) with circulation below 7,500. Adding local broadcast to the mix increases the reach of a grassroots campaign by more than 10,000. Accordingly, a regular campaign (including only 200+ outlets) is far more limited than a grassroots campaign that would include 100x as many media outlets. Also, a regular campaign typically employs a single, largely undifferentiated message. All outlets are approached as a media block. A grassroots campaign, however, entails customized messaging that respects each local media outlet's need for local news. One size does not fit all in a grassroots public relations campaign. Finally, a regular public relations campaign must often compete with all the news of the day. It is a truism in public relations that coverage is determined by "all the news that fits," meaning worthy stories are

often pushed aside during a busy news day. A grassroots campaign, however, competes in a far less competitive news market in which the media actually need, and want, local news.

### Can you provide us with examples of grassroots public relations in the fashion industry?

In the fashion industry, we have provided services for retail clothiers such as Coldwater Creek, Plato's Closet, and Dress Barn. These clients use grassroots public relations to recognize employees, localize cause-marketing promotions, and provide feature stories for local media.

### How does one create a "buzz" for grassroots public relations campaign?

Buzz is the natural outgrowth of a grassroots public relations program (or campaign). Our clients refer to it as the Halo effect. The resultant media pickup clearly creates an interest and source of conversation in local communities and allows a company's branded content to work overtime. A company's message reaches the media, but also outlet/store managers, employees, stakeholders, and others.

### Kindly add any other comments you may have.

Over the past 10 years, the media as we know it has been under severe stress—not surprisingly, much of this has been prompted by news consumers moving online. Subscribers have deserted major daily newspapers and network news shows; and, advertisers have followed. During this same period, however, grassroots media have enjoyed substantial increases in circulation. Since 2000, national media has experienced year-over-year declines in circulation approximating 5 percent. Grassroots media, however, have experienced increases of 10 percent or more. The *New York Times* (July 14, 2008) reported that Roger Ailes purchased *The Putnam County News and Recorder,* circulation 3,000. Why did he buy it? Because he liked it! Grassroots public relations touches people where they live and work. The local media are looking for news that affects their community, and grassroots public relations appears to be just what the doctor ordered.

## *Questions to Consider*

1. Do you agree with Smith's definition of grassroots? Explain.

2. Do you think grassroots public relations requires customized content? How well do you think generic information would work in this environment?

3. Based on Smith's comments, what do you see as the pros and cons of grassroots public relations?

141

## Case Study 5.2 Formulating, Modifying, and Selecting Public Relations Methods

### Perry Ellis International, Inc.

Oscar Feldenkreis is the vice chairman, president, and chief operating officer at Perry Ellis International, Inc. (PEI). Feldenkreis grew up inspired by his father's entrepreneurial vision, and in partnership with his father he runs and operates one of today's leading companies in men's and women's apparel. Since 1980, when he joined Supreme International—the company's name until it acquired Perry Ellis the brand—Oscar's keen fashion sense coupled with his aggressive sales and marketing vision, and instinct for branded business, has been the key driver in the transformation of the company from a private label resource into a fashion apparel powerhouse, with 29 national and international brands, nearly $1 billion in revenues, 32 offices worldwide and over 2,200 associates. Oscar has been recognized by multiple nonprofit and community organizations and has recently received the Entrepreneur of the Year award by the Wharton School of Business, South Florida chapter, and the Human Relations Award by the American Jewish Committee.

FIGURE CASE STUDY 5.2
Oscar Feldenkreis, vice chairman, president, and chief operating officer, Perry Ellis International, Inc.

**What are some of the public relations methods/ strategies you've found to be successful?**

At Perry Ellis International, we see public relations as nothing more than communicating the right message, to the right audience through the right channel at the right time. As a conglomerate of brands, PEI needs to have a clear and consistent set of rules to deliver a unified message as a corporation, without having to dilute the identity of each individual brand. In terms of strategies, at PEI we believe in taking control of our message, rather than allowing others to do it for us. We believe in addressing the issues up front, having clarity on the topics addressed, and making ourselves available for any follow-up.

**What factors do you consider in order to decide upon which methods/strategy to use?**

Each message has to be carefully tailored to the target audience and delivered through the right channels to maximize impact. We always start by asking the question—is the message clearly conveyed? Is the message delivered to the right audience? Is the message delivered through the ideal media? Are we optimizing

the distribution channels? Is the timing right for this message? And most importantly—are we going to have the impact we expect out of this message?

**Do you ever join public relations with advertising and/ or promotional marketing?**

In the case of brand launches, fashion shows or major marketing efforts, we do join PR and marketing. For example, during MAGIC and Fashion Week we like to hold not only the main event (fashion related), but we like to make it jointly with an investor presentation, breakfast, or meeting.

**If so, what are the benefits of using this method/strategy?**

It mainly strengthens the message being delivered, by addressing with individually crafted messages, the different audiences that should be aware of it.

**Do you feel a PR strategy can backfire if used in the wrong time or place?**

Any PR activity can backfire if not carefully managed. The right message at the wrong time can be as destructive as the wrong message at the right time.

**Do you use celebrities or spokespeople to promote any of your brands? If so, what are the benefits and caveats? Recent examples.**

We have used this strategy in several occasions and for multiple brands. The most recent and consistent example was a couple of years ago, when we relaunched our Jantzen brand with supermodel Carolyn Murphy as the spokeswoman. We have used also local celebrities (e.g., actor, singer, sports person) at geographically specific areas, to drive traffic to one of our retail partners

142

**Case Study 5.2  Formulating, Modifying, and Selecting Public Relations Methods** *(continued)*

and increase sales. For example, after the 2006 Super Bowl, we arranged that two key players of each team (Steelers and Seahawks) would appear signing autographs for our Perry Ellis brand, drawing the largest crowds ever both in Pittsburgh and Seattle.

The major risk with this strategy is also its major strength. A celebrity is susceptible to making mistakes like everybody else, with the difference that their mistakes (as well as their success) are magnified by all the public attention they receive. Your brand can be tarnished if it is too closely identified with one specific person who may run into trouble in the future.

**If a particular PR method/strategy is successful once, do you try to repeat it again or do you feel repetition wears out its efficiency?**

It depends on the circumstances. If the circumstances are correct, we repeat it.

**Do you participate in cause-related sponsorships? If so, please explain.**

PEI has a long history of social responsibility and giving back to the community. We sponsor all types of events (golf tournaments, parades, dinners, etc.) for different audiences.

**We have a chapter devoted to PR opportunities. Could you discuss some of the PR opportunities you have received from your events, donations, and celebrity endorsements?**

PR opportunities are all about reading and staying abreast of news in general especially within your industry. Many ideas are born by networking and the opportunity to co-brand with other companies, personalities, and contacts that will enable you to leverage both parties' assets. There is truth in the expression "Power in numbers."

**Anything else you'd like to add in regard to public relations methods/strategies?**

PR is about creating the buzz. In today's world, it can be more effective than investing in a national marketing campaign. From product placement to creating unique retail events are all viable mediums to create the brand exposure and build your brand equity and retail relationships.

### Questions to Consider

1. According to Feldenkreis, how does the public relations message relate to the strategies or methods selected by the company?

2. When he says, "The right message at the wrong time can be as destructive as the wrong message at the right time," what do you think Feldenkreis means? Give an example to illustrate your interpretation.

3. Do you feel the pros of a celebrity spokesperson outweigh the cons, or vice versa? Explain.

4. Why should someone involved in public relations stay abreast of the news? How could that help the public relations efforts? Explain.

143

Another example where flexibility may be needed is the method itself; methods are not set in stone and can be adjusted as needed to fit the circumstances. If there is a way to implement an event effectively but differently than most events are done, then why not? Let's say the public relations director finds a way to host an event on the company's Web site—an online fashion show, for example. The event methods can still be used but adapted to this new type of event. Let's look at some of the top factors that shape public relations methods.

## Potential for Media Exposure

Before selecting or formulating a specific public relations method, its potential for generating exposure with the target media should be evaluated and compared to other methods' potentials. The method selected should be able to produce the amount of publicity for which the campaign calls within the target media. Sometimes, a method needs to be adjusted to capture an opportunity for additional media exposure. For example, let's say the fashion company determines the product news method will be effective for unveiling the new collection; however, as the campaign starts, the company realizes one of the largest trade publications is a sister publication of the consumer magazine at which the campaign aimed. In this case, the potential for exposure will increase tremendously, thus it makes business sense to add that trade media publication to our methodology.

### Return on Investment (ROI)

Whether a specific public relations method can provide sufficient ROI is highly important. Without adequate ROI, that method should be ignored and other methods with better ROI should be sought. An alternative would also be to modify the method to increase ROI. Either way, ROI is an important part of public relations and thus it shapes the direction that future methods will take.

Estimating ROI can be done in various ways. The primary process involves first figuring out the investment by listing the expenses involved in implementing the method; then one can figure out an estimate for the return by surveying the various target media outlets and using their advertisement pricelist to work out how much getting an article in each publication is worth. Another way to estimate ROI is to look at a previous public relations initiative that's similar to the one you are about to implement, if possible, and utilize the figures from this past campaign to estimate the current project. Measuring ROI is discussed in further detail in Chapter 11.

### Resources

The public relations director must ascertain that the company has enough resources to implement the specific method. Resources include the obvious ones such as funds, time, and personnel. An event method is typically much more expensive than a simple press release, but both methods may be cheaper than corporate sponsorship. The campaign budget plays a vital part in determining funds availability. If all existing personnel are working on other projects, the method may have to be replaced with one that requires as little personnel as possible. In addition to money, time, and personnel, resources also include those that are not so obvious, such as whether the company has sufficient research information or access to clients who are willing to be interviewed about their experience with the company.

## Chapter Summary

▸ To achieve the public relations campaign goals, we must formulate, modify, and select the public relations implementation methods.

▸ The public relations method provides a set of guidelines and practical steps for implementing the campaign.

▶ Public relations methods can be divided into three categories: the media methods, the community methods, and the grassroots methods.

▶ Media methods work directly to obtain media exposure. They include the product news method, the company news method, and the current news event method.

▶ Community methods aim to create goodwill through work in the community. These efforts include the partnership with nonprofit organizations method, the cause-related activity method, and the special event method.

▶ The grassroots methods strive to create positive public image by encouraging the clients and audiences of the company to talk positively about the company. These include the word of mouth method, the blog method, the corporate sponsorship method, public relations flanked by promotional marketing method, and the out-of-the-box method.

▶ There are several factors that help shape public relations methods and create changes in these methods so as to keep up with the ever-changing business environment.

▶ The top factors that affect these methods are potential for media exposure, return on investment, and resources.

## Key Terms

▶ astroturf

▶ blogger

▶ cause-related activity (CRA)

▶ grassroots public relations

▶ public relations method

▶ viral/street public relations

▶ Web logs (blogs)

## Chapter-End Questions and Exercises

1. Define the term *public relations method.*

2. How do public relations methods help to implement the campaign goals?

3. Define the three categories of public relations methods; then compare and contrast each category with the others.

4. Online and in print, find and research an example of a fashion company using the product news method. What kind of results was received? Do you think they were satisfactory?

5. Look through trade magazines and publications and find a company news item that has been published in the last month.

6. What is the current news event and how can we associate with such an event to gain more exposure for our product?

7. How does the cause-related activity method function? Give a real-life example that is not mentioned in this text. Did you ever buy from such a campaign? Did you believe that all your money was going to charity?

8. Online and in print, find and research an example of a fashion company that is involved in a special event. What are your thoughts about this special event if you were a consumer?

9. Have you ever passed a positive review about a specific fashion company or brand to your friends or family? What did you tell about the company and who did you tell it to? What effects do you think this had on your friends/family?

10. What makes grassroots campaigns different from regular public relations campaigns? Explain why.

11. Find a blog about fashion on the Internet. What's the name of the blog and in which state is the blogger located?

12. What are the three factors that shape public relations methods? Explain and give an example for each.

13. Choose a well-known fashion brand and:

   a. Create a simulation of a public relations campaign for that brand and establish the goals.

   b. Formulate, modify, or select the public relations method(s) that would be appropriate to utilize to implement the campaign. Explain how you arrived at these conclusions.

   c. Evaluate the potential for media exposure, resources, and ROI for each of the methods you selected.

14. Your public relations company is organizing a blog. Select a three-person team and start a fashion blog. Assign responsibilities and duties to each member. Explain how this blog can reach your target market. Be creative!

15. Your public relations company is called upon to establish a theme and create a cause-related sponsorship event for your fashion client. The event will include the charity, celebrities, and product. Name the media segment you are targeting and discuss why you have chosen them.

16. Your public relations firm has been called upon by the U.S. Olympic committee to select a fashion company and celebrity to represent them for the 2008 Olympics. Name the celebrity, fashion company, and fashion item that you feel best represent the United States. Explain your reasons for the selection. Submit visuals of your selections.

# Developing Public Relations Stories

# PART III

# Implementing the Public Relations Method and Creating a Media Angle

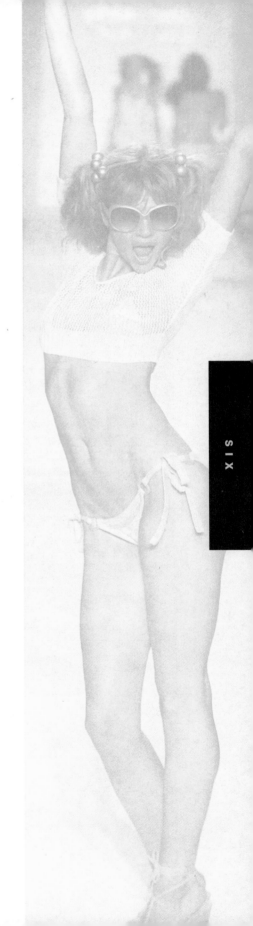

## SIX

## Chapter Snapshot

The success of the public relations campaign lies ultimately in how effective we are in improving the company's public image, whether through media exposure, community relations, or grassroots initiatives. How we implement the method or methods we have formulated and selected to achieve the campaign goals therefore become vitally important to the overall success of the campaign. It is essential to plan in advance how we will implement the public relations method in the most effective and cost-efficient manner that will achieve maximum media exposure and public image improvement. Such an implementation depends mainly upon our ability to successfully broadcast the public relations message and our skills in creating positive interest in the media circles and among the public audiences. In this chapter we will discuss the various factors that contribute to a successful implementation, as well as explore the concept of the media angle and how creating a media angle can help improve the campaign's success.

## Objectives

▶ Understand the importance of a detailed and well-organized approach to implementing the public relations methods.

▶ Discuss how scheduling affects the implementation process.

▶ Explore the timing of the release and its effects on the campaign's success.

▶ Recognize the personnel-related factors that make the implementation possible.

▶ Understand how budgeting affects the success of the implementation.

▶ Comprehend the concept of the media angle.

▶ Discuss how to study the target media in order to make the angle more relevant.

When we reach the media and our publics with a positive message that they can agree with, the company's public image will improve. The degree that it improves and the investment required to achieve that determine the success of the campaign as measured by the return on investment (ROI). We may improve the public image, but at what cost? The invested time and money should be less than what the company will earn as a result of the public relations campaign; to accomplish that, we need to implement the public relations method or methods in the most effective manner possible. A large part of the campaign's success consists of whether we are able to reach the audiences—either through the media or directly—with our public relations message and improve their opinion of the company and its products. If we can achieve that, then the ROI is likely to be quite positive. Let's discuss the various steps we need to take to implement the public relations method and generate media exposure.

## Implementing the Public Relations Method

Now that we have determined which public relations method we should use to achieve the campaign goals, we can now get to the business of implementing it. Although the method may seem simple and its implementation may seem almost self-evident, it is doomed to fail if a detailed implementation approach is not worked out in advance. The implementation of the product news method, for example, may seem fairly straightforward: We draw up a press release about the new collection, send it out to the media, follow up on it, and get as much media exposure as possible. However, many details remain undeveloped. What facts should the press release contain? Which company employees should comment about the product in the release? When should we get the release sent out in relation to the official product release date? Developing these details can spell the difference between success and failure, and the public relations director should have the specifications worked out before embarking on the implementation. The main factors that affect the implementation are scheduling, personnel assignment, and budgeting.

## Scheduling

Timing is a factor of incredible significance in the world of public relations. The media lives and runs on deadlines. When a magazine issue is sent to print, for example, there is no way to add anything to it; it will be another month or longer before the next issue comes out and if the company missed the deadline, it also missed out on a potential article. Neither the media nor the public audiences are concerned with old news and, therefore, proper scheduling is of paramount importance in getting media coverage.

### *Best Time for Implementation*

Figuring out the ideal time for implementation can sometimes determine success and failure, especially in the case of planning events. Scheduling the event is crucial to its success for many reasons, the primary one being that it must be scheduled for a time that is suitable for the purpose of the event. A fundraiser fashion show that is scheduled around Christmas, for example, when most people have many family and business commitments already, can set the event up for dismal attendance, media coverage, and public image improvement. Scheduling the event the day after another prominent community event could also have the same effect on attendance and results. On the other hand, timing the event properly can translate into excellent attendance and media coverage, as well as lead to additional public relations opportunities.

In the fashion world, news revolves around the seasons. It is crucial to take the seasons into consideration when scheduling the implementation because it is much more difficult—if not downright impossible—to get media coverage about a winter collection in June or July. The implementation must schedule the release so it coincides with the season in which it fits. In fashion, we are concerned with three major seasons: spring into summer; fall; and winter, which incorporated the year-end holiday season of Christmas and New Year's. The spring into summer season is where fashion, fitness, and keeping in shape is important to the consumer. During the spring/summer season, sleeveless and short-sleeved items, shorts, bikinis, swimsuits, and other body-revealing pieces of apparel are typically featured in stores. Fashion shows at country clubs, seaside resorts, as well as golf and tennis tournaments are in the news. Designers love this time of year so that they can create bold colors—lots of white, yellow, orange, turquoise, hot pink, bright green, and an assortment of pastel colors that are featured in most collections. The fall season features darker colors, with lots of black, burgundy, purple, dark green, gold, royal blues, and other deep colors; collections typically feature heavier, long-sleeved garments. During the winter season, people are occupied with the holidays and then with winter. The rich and famous move to their second homes in Southern destinations where winter is milder, such as Florida, California, Arizona, Texas, the Caribbean Islands, Spain, Portugal, Greece, and Italy. This season typically introduces yachting clothing, nautical colors, red/white/blue, and a palette of bright colors and black/white combinations.

Another consideration in timing the implementation is the day of the week and time of day. In the case of a community event, it is imperative to determine who is supposed to attend and then figure out which is the convenient day and time for them. If the public relations personnel have access to a handful people who comprise the target audience with which they are already acquainted and would not be offended by the inquiries, it is a good idea to consult with them about the day and time under consideration; if there is a flagrant scheduling conflict, we will hear about it and adjust the schedule accordingly. At the very least, the schedule should be checked with other managers from other departments prior to finalizing the schedule. For example, suppose the fashion show is scheduled for a holiday observed by a certain religious or ethnic group. A cursory check with some people is likely to bring attention to this conflict and give the public relations director the opportunity to choose another date for the event. In the case of a press conference or a similar press opportunity, it is conducive to schedule the event for a day and time during the work week and within normal business hours so that editors and reporters can easily attend without having to give up one of their evenings or weekends.

In general, avoid scheduling public relations events on Monday mornings or Friday afternoons when both audiences and the media are catching up after returning from the weekend or wrapping things up in preparation for the weekend. The weeks from early December leading to the first week of January are also difficult times for people to make arrangements to attend a function. The months of July and August are typically busy for people with families because children are out of school and many schedule their annual vacations. In Europe, when people routinely take a month off for summer vacation, it is not unusual to see the entire office disappear for a month during June, July, or August with only one or two employees on duty answering calls and attending only to urgent matters. The public relations director should ensure that the calendar he or she is using is annotated with all of the national holidays, religious holidays, and other important annual events so that no public relations initiatives get scheduled for these dates. Many of the computerized email and calendar computer programs such as Outlook and Eudora display reminders of these holidays.

### Editorial Calendars

Most weekly and monthly publications offer an **editorial calendar** for the year, which typically offers the main topics that will be reviewed in each issue. The publication's editorial calendar provides public relations professionals with guidance as to what the editors are looking for in each issue, and is helpful in scheduling public relations initiatives. Suppose the fashion company is looking to promote its collection of scarves in one of the top national fashion magazines such as *W, Elle, Vogue,* and *Cosmopolitan.* The public relations director can review the editorial calendars and determine which issues will cover accessories, a topic for which the collection might be most appropriate. Box 6.1 shows editorial calendars for two fashion publications that detail the topics that are tentatively set for each issue.

## Box 6.1   Editorial Calendars

Editorial calendars are excellent resources for information about which stories would best fit in which issues as well as data on each issue's deadlines. As can be seen in the *Vanity Fair* editorial calendar below, there are several special issues published throughout the year that focus on broad specific topics. In terms of deadlines, *Vanity Fair* magazine closes the issue about five weeks prior to the on-sale date.

**TABLE 6.1   *Vanity Fair*'s Editorial Calendar as of July 2008***

| Issue | Space/Material Closing Date | On-Sale Date |
|---|---|---|
| January | 11/1/07 | 12/11/07 |
| February | 11/30/07 | 1/8/08 |
| March/**Hollywood Issue** | 1/2/08 | 2/12/08 |
| April | 2/1/08 | 3/11/08 |
| May/**Green Issue** | 2/29/08 | 4/8/08 |
| June | 4/1/08 | 5/6/08 |
| July/**Digital Revolution** | 5/1/08 | 6/10/08 |
| August | 6/2/08 | 7/8/08 |
| September/**Style Issue** | 7/1/08 | 8/5/08 |
| October/**25th Anniversary Issue** | 8/1/08 | 9/9/08 |
| November | 9/2/08 | 10/7/08 |
| December | 10/1/08 | 11/11/08 |

*Editorial Calendar Subject to Change

153

### *Allowing Advance Time for Media Coverage*

Even if the press release is extraordinarily superlative and the public relations initiative is out of this world, not a word will be printed about an event if the deadline for the issue covering the event's date has already come and gone. To obtain news coverage, the fashion company must first of all work within the **advance time** framework in order to allow the media sufficient time to report about it. That could mean a few days in the case of a daily newspaper or a blog, but could also mean a month or two in the case of the monthly magazine. The main thing that should be evaluated is which of the target media we want most to attract, and cater to its deadlines. If the goal is to get the brand name into the glossy monthlies in time for the summer season preview issues—May in the Northern Hemisphere, and about November in the Southern Hemisphere—then we should be first and foremost concerned with getting the story to the magazine editors well before their deadline for the issue is due, which could be anywhere from a month to two months before the publication date, depending on the magazine. When the national daily newspapers are at the top of our target media, the advance time could be as short as two to three days prior to actual publication. Most editorial calendars offer the scheduling deadlines for each issue, which is helpful in planning ahead. Keep in mind that these deadlines indicate when the copy must be turned in; thus, to that deadline we must add the time it takes the reporter to gather the facts, conduct interviews, and write the story. If the publication does not offer an editorial calendar, it pays to make a few calls and get in touch with the fashion editors of these publications to find out their deadlines for the next few issues.

When it comes to time-sensitive stories, it is advisable to take particular care to ensure that the timing is right for the story. Releasing information too early might take the edge off the event and turn the media's interest off; releasing it too late might cut it too close to the deadline and timely coverage becomes impossible. There is no alternative to researching and adjusting to the guidelines of each individual target media publication. When the public relations director does her or his homework on the publication, then she or he can figure out an approximate advance time that is fairly close to reality. It might become clear after studying a particular daily newspaper that the only section where fashion is covered is in the weekly lifestyle section. That means that the advance time is not a few days before publication, as is the case with most daily newspapers, but a week to two weeks before publication—closer to the advance time of a weekly magazine. If the company hopes to get the media to attend an event, then it must send out invitations and press passes early enough to give reporters and editors sufficient advance notice so they can arrange their schedules accordingly. Sending passes too close to the event can be a recipe for disaster.

### Avoiding Conflicts with Other Events

Trying to implement the public relations method during the same day and time that another significant community event is taking place nearby can cause poor attendance by the public as well as the media. This stands for events organized by competitors as well, if they are well publicized and have a history of good attendance, because members of the community are likely to choose a proven event over a new event. In addition, typically local reporters are squeezed for time and cannot afford to attend one event after another, so if the other event is more known in the community, the reporter is more likely to be out covering that event than ours; with the short staff in most newsrooms, it is quite possible that the newsroom will not be able to send out two reporters to cover both events. It is essential, therefore, to remain informed of community events in the area, as well as search for conflicting events prior to finalizing our event date.

Let's say the fashion company decides to give a donation to a local charity and the public relations director is organizing a media opportunity where the company's president hands the check to the head of the charity. There are probably only a few days when both the heads of the company and the charity are available simultaneously for this photograph opportunity; still, the public relations director should verify each of these dates and make sure they are not coinciding with any public holidays, important dates in local history, or dates saved for other events. In our example, the two chiefs finally agree on a date, and the public relations director does her job and researches for conflicting events. Let's say she discovers that the local fire department's annual fund-raising barbeque will take place on the same day. The check handing will not be attended by anybody other than staff from the company and the charity,

## Box 6.2  Advance Release in Action

Fashion Fights Poverty is one of Washington, DC's largest fundraiser fashion shows. It features national and international designers who employ ethical means and practices in their design and manufacturing processes to produce products that promote economic development to support communities. As a forum for dialogue and awareness building, it showcases how fashion, textiles, and design can alleviate poverty and empower communities.

The following is one of the official press releases for the annual fundraiser announcing the benefactor of the 2008 event. Note that although the show is scheduled for September, the release is dated April 29, allowing plenty of time for arranging for media coverage:

FOR IMMEDIATE RELEASE
Contact: Kadrieka Maiden (202-387-1845)
April 29, 2008.

**Fashion Fights Poverty's 2008 Benefactor & Presenting Sponsor:** *FFP's 4th annual fashion event partners with the Historic St. Regis benefiting Nest*

WASHINGTON, DC (April 29, 2008)—Fashion Fights Poverty (FFP) announced today their 2008 beneficiary is NEST, a non-profit organization that supports women artists and artisans in the developing world by helping them create sustainable entrepreneurial businesses. Scheduled for Friday, September 26, 2008, this year's event takes place at the historic and newly renovated St. Regis Washington, DC, FFP's 2008 presenting sponsor. "Fashion Fights Poverty has been fortunate from the very beginning to have increasing numbers of individuals, organizations, and businesses involved in our annual benefit. The addition of the St. Regis Washington, DC, as our presenting sponsor and NEST as the 2008 beneficiary truly enhances our ability to bring more of these groups together," said Christopher Belisle, President of Fashion Fights Poverty.

Like all its events, this year's FFP fashion presentation addresses issues of poverty by showcasing designers that adhere to such principles as fair trade, equitable compensation, and the use of environmentally sustainable materials.

With the event being held at the St. Regis, supporters can look forward to a vast change in production, a more exclusive and intimate catwalk presentation, a VIP reception, and after party hosted by The Michael Romeo Group at Lotus Lounge.

As one of "the largest fashion fundraisers in Washington, DC" according to the *Washington Post*, the always anticipated fashion presentation continues to exceed standards of excellence set by the previous year. "The St. Regis Washington, DC, is delighted to be partnering with Fashion Fights Poverty in 2008 and to be the selected hotel for this very high profile and important social event," said André Jacques, St Regis Director of Sales and Marketing.

Founded in 2005 by the Style & Image Network (SIN) and in partnership with The United Nations Association, this annual fashion benefit is the only one of its kind. The promotional and financial effort of each year's chosen benefactor also continues to propel from FFP initiatives. NEST, this year's chosen beneficiary will undoubtedly experience that same success. Like past benefactors, NEST is a nonprofit organization advocating socially conscious practices in the fashion and textile industries. However unlike past benefactors, NEST produces its own line of merchandise, sold at boutiques and online (www.buildanest.com), whose sales directly benefit the organization. NEST provides women with micro credit loans for their art- or craft-based businesses and enables them to begin or maintain income-generating businesses (Sin PR, 2008).

155

and hopefully the media as well, and would not really interfere with the fire department event. However, the public relations director knows that each of the local media newsrooms heavily covers the firefighter's event. She correctly deduces that the event conflict will make it difficult for the media to cover the company's donation event, and moves the donation event a few days later.

### *Coordinating the Scheduling Internally with Other Departments*

In many cases, public relations initiatives involve other departments and the public relations department relies on these personnel to do their part for the successful implementation of the initiative. Coordinating the schedule with the managers and staff of these departments is essential for smooth implementation. From the onset, the public relations director should coordinate any parts of the campaign that involve other departments, ensure that the managers are in agreement with their involvement, and settle the scheduling. Suppose a fashion manufacturer is set to release a new fall collection, and the public relations department is planning for the unveiling event a special community jazz concert in the park. The public relations director has to ensure that the production manager approves the event date; otherwise, the collection might not be ready to debut at the event, thus jeopardizing the entire initiative. When the production manager agrees to the event date in writing, not only does it make for better teamwork but also it puts the pressure on the production manager to stick to the deadline. The public relations director should not be content with the preliminary approval only, but should check with production occasionally as time nears the deadline, to ensure that everything is going according to schedule. If production is progressively lagging behind and it appears that the deadline will not be met, then the director has time to react proactively—e.g., delay the concert—and avert a public relations disaster.

### *Scheduling Media Interviews*

Interviews of company executives, staff, and clients by the media can be extremely important for positive news coverage. When a company employee, such as the president or the vice president, or a satisfied client is interviewed, he or she will be providing the media with comments that will give the company's public image a tremendous boost. As long as the comments are not too commercial, there is a good chance that one of the comments will be included in the article, and direct quotes create a high degree of trust, especially when it is other customers who are being interviewed. These interviews, therefore, should be facilitated as a top priority, and the public relations director must plan for and schedule such interviews when formulating the campaign. Suppose the fashion company is launching a new and innovative fashion item, and the public relations department is arranging for a media interview with a high-profile customer; the public relations department depends on the customer to show up for the media interview. The public relations director should ideally have a backup interview just for that reason. He or she should also ensure scheduling the interviews is done conveniently for both the client and the media, and then he or she should follow up the day before the interview to ensure that all is well. In scheduling media interviews, the fashion company must keep in mind that the reporter's time is very valuable and in short supply. Thus, every effort should be made to facilitate the preparation of a prompt and to-the-point interview with minimal distraction so that the reporter can do the interview and leave as quickly as possible. When a reporter's time is maximized and not abused, the reporter will be grateful and be more willing to conduct interviews in the

## Box 6.3   Real World in Action: A Public Relations Repeating Event

The Victoria's Secret annual fashion show began in 1995 and has since become a fantastic public relations vehicle for the company, with the media and prime-time television talking up the event well in advance. As the following excerpt illustrates from the Dec 3, 2007 Associated Press story, "What's Victoria's Secret? Creating 'lingerie fantasy,'" the fashion show has become an awaited-for repeating event.

FIGURE BOX 6.3 Victoria's Secret model Heidi Klum gets her makeup done backstage in preparation for the Victoria's Secret fashion show in Los Angeles on November 15, 2007. (UPI Photo/Jim Ruymen)

LOS ANGELES, California (AP)—It might be too much to devote an hour of prime-time television to long legs, taut tummies, and half-bare bottoms and bosoms. So the Victoria's Secret fashion show incorporates elaborate staging and musical performances.

Among the performers at the Victoria's Secret fashion show: the recently reunited Spice Girls.

The annual hour-long flesh fest, featuring songs by will.i.am, Seal, and the Spice Girls, airs 10 p.m. EST Tuesday on CBS.

"This is really an event that's anchored in a fashion show," said CBS executive Jack Sussman.

But isn't it essentially an hour-long commercial?

"To a degree," he said.

Still, with top talent and a $10 million budget, the Victoria's Secret fashion show is more interesting than most everyday advertisements. This year's show spotlights 61 skimpy outfits worn by more than two dozen of the world's most beautiful women (Associated Press, 2007).

157

future. On the other hand, when a reporter arrives and has to wait for the interviewee to show up, then has to sit and listen to the interviewee chatter on and on about irrelevant information, the reporter may be reluctant to return for another interview in the future. It is vital to properly schedule media interviews so that the reporter can include these comments in the story.

### Single or Repeating Event

Some public relations methods lend themselves to repetition, especially if the inaugural implementation proves successful. So instead of just one **single event,** the fashion company implements the **repeating event,** a periodic repetition of that same event or a series of variations on the original event to maximize exposure. A local fashion show can become a quarterly or semi-annual event, for example, whereas a company-sponsored walk to raise funds for the homeless can become an annual event. The repetition saves the company money and time on planning because the first event just needs to be duplicated with minor adjustments to keep it fresh; the repetition also creates an exponential improvement of the public image because subsequent events in the series build upon the success of the previous events and considerably strengthen the public image and brand awareness. Community events are a particularly good method to implement as a series because fashion shows, classes, and seminars can be easily repeated, and the next show, class, or seminar can be announced and promoted at the current show or class. The public relations director does have to watch against stagnation, however. Simply repeating the event exactly and without a change can cause the community to become bored with the whole series. It is vital to keep reinventing the event by focusing on other topics or features, or by adding new twists to the event so that the public will want to come back and visit the next event.

## Personnel

Assigning to the campaign a sufficient number of employees who are experienced and qualified for the tasks is vital to the success of each public relations initiative. With enough personnel who possess the right mindset, the campaign can truly be properly implemented and results maximized. It is thus important to not only establish the number of people it will take to carry out the initiative, but also determine the experience necessary to get the job done.

### Identifying Tasks

After analyzing each initiative, the fashion company can create a comprehensive list of tasks that will be required to implement the campaign. Each public relations method calls for different classes of action. By breaking down the initiative to its constitutive tasks, we can begin to assess what detailed steps will be needed to complete the implementation. The number of tasks and their complexity depends upon the public relations method selected and the circumstances within which that method is implemented. A routine product news method may require only a few basic steps, such as writing the press release, sending it out to the target media, and following up with the media to obtain coverage. An online word-of-mouth initiative that targets males in their late teen years might require a longer and more complex list of tasks. It likely requires setting up an exciting blog that caters to the target audience's tastes, promoting the blog on a grassroots level using guerilla tactics such as circulating postcards about the blog in high schools, at music concerts, and outside movie theaters, as well as spreading the word about the blog online by soliciting exchanges of hyperlinks on informal Web sites such as Facebook and MySpace (see Box 6.4). Remember that public relations operates in a highly fluid environment and plans almost always change in response to changes in that environment. Therefore, the list of tasks should be updated periodically before and during the implementation, whereas tasks should be modified, added, or deleted whenever any changes are made to the plan. For example, if we plan a fashion show and a few days before the show we learn that a national television fashion news channel will be sending a team to cover the event, we might want to invest more money in upgrading the show's stage, lighting, and backdrops so that the show looks more professional and fit for national TV coverage. This will require quick response from the public relations team and the addition of several new and urgent tasks will be necessary to achieve this facelift. As we can see, identifying the tasks is pivotal to a smooth implementation.

**Box 6.4   Real World Profile: MySpace**

MySpace is an online community that allows members to stay in touch with their network of mutual friends by sharing photos, journals, and interests. According to Hoover's, Inc. (an online service that provides insight and analysis into businesses), the social networking site was created in the fall of 2003 by Tom Anderson and Chris DeWolfe (CEO), as a looser, music-driven version of Friendster (Hoover's, 2009). MySpace.com quickly surpassed Friendster—its membership of mostly teens and 20- and 30-somethings has grown to some 185 million users, making it one of the Internet's most popular Web sites and is rapidly expanding beyond that age group. In 2005 News Corp. paid $580 million to buy Intermix Media, MySpace.com's former parent company, and folded it into Fox Interactive Media (FIM). Demand Media purchased the non-MySpace.com assets of Intermix Media (www.Grab.com, www.soyouwanna. com, www.gamerival.com) from FIM in 2006. As the site develops its content channels about music, fashion, entertainment and other topics, it is blurring the line between an online community site and a media outlet.

MySpace's fashion channel, www.myspace.com/ fashion, is a place where visitors can catch up on the latest information about upcoming designers and collections, as well as watch fashion videos and designer interviews.

FIGURE BOX 6.4 MySpace's fashion portal (www .myspace.com/fashion) utilizes social networking to create a buzz about fashion trends by letting MySpace users access features such as blogging, sharing comments, and becoming friends with up-and-coming designers.

### Assigning Staff to the Tasks

When the tasks have been identified and listed, the public relations director can then assign personnel to each of the tasks. As the first step of this process, the director should figure out the amount of work and the degree of experience and expertise that will each task on the list requires. For example, writing a simple press release about a new store opening may only take 5 to 10 hours and does not require much public relations experience; in contrast, writing a press release about a partnership between the fashion company and a local nonprofit organization may take two or three times the time due to the need for researching information about the nonprofit organization, interviewing the top executives for both the fashion company and the nonprofit organization, and submitting the release to the nonprofit organization for review and corrections. There is also more intricacy and diplomacy involved in writing the latter release because the release has to balance the weight between the fashion company and the nonprofit organization while at the same time deliver the company's public relations message in an unobtrusive way. The second step of the process is to evaluate which employee is able to carry out the task and determine their workload. The public relations director should be familiar with the background and expertise of every person who works in the department; in a large public relations department, periodically brushing up on staff resumes is a good practice.

Keep in mind that most fashion companies cannot afford to maintain a large public relations staff, and typically the public relations department consists of the director alone or the director and one to two additional employees. Some larger companies may have six to eight employees, and some of these may be part-time. Nonetheless, the assignment of the tasks is vital for a structured implementation. Ultimately, the public relations director must call the shot on who would best be responsible for which task. It is recommended to get the employee's willing cooperation for the task rather than simply delegating the task to the employee without consultation. The director could discuss the tasks with the employee and motivate him or her to become excited about doing the best they can do for their part in the campaign. This would help morale and create an internal buzz about the campaign. At the very least, the director should discuss the tasks with the employee and ensure the employee is able to take on these tasks in terms of workload. Often, employees are already busy with a number of ongoing projects and time has to be freed up for these tasks. Typically, the employee should be able to shuffle the schedule to accommodate the new tasks. However, the director might have to get involved and help the employee prioritize the ongoing tasks so the new tasks can also be done on schedule without hindering the other ongoing tasks.

When a task belongs to another department within the fashion company outside the authority of the public relations director, he or she should consult first with the manager of that department and discuss who within that department could be assigned to the task. The managers of other departments should know that just as good customer service is the responsibility of all company employees, so is the case with public relations. The public image of the company is projected onto the community through the actions of any company employee and thus public relations initiatives can often require tasks implemented by other departments. For example, the unveiling of a new collection cannot be completed without samples that production must create and deliver to the public relations department by the unveiling date.

If the fashion company is outsourcing the initiative to an outside public relations firm, the public relations director must discuss the scope of the initiative with the firm to ensure they understand what the fashion company needs. The agreement between the companies should outline in as much detail as possible what services the firm will provide and their responsibilities within the campaign. The public relations director is still overall responsible for the implementation and should remain constantly involved in all aspects of the initiative. Ideally, the firm should provide the public relations director with routine progress reports. These reports should be provided on a monthly, weekly, and even daily basis depending on the project scope and scheduling— if the initiative is urgent and lasts only a few days, then daily briefings are in order while with a year-long initiative monthly reports might do. Either way, the public relations director should stipulate in advance the reports he or she feels are necessary to keep on top of the project.

### Coordinating Tasks and Keeping Staff Informed

To maximize the implementation efforts, the public relations director has to continuously and proactively coordinate the tasks among all personnel and outside firms that are involved in the project. He or she needs to stay attuned to the initiative's progress, keep a vigilant eye out for developing conflicts between tasks, and address the issue at once to resolve such conflicts before they develop into costly discrepancies which can hinder or even halt the initiative's implementation. If the fashion company is outsourcing the initiative, then the public relations director is entrusted with coordinating the initiative's tasks between the firm and any employees in the fashion company. As part of coordination, the director should institute a routine process for sharing information about the initiative's progress. Weekly meetings or email briefings can go a long way to make for a smoother implementation. By keeping the staff informed on a routine basis about what the others are doing, the foundation for coordination is cemented. Upon this foundation of information, cooperation among personnel entrusted to different tasks is encouraged and facilitated so that implementation is more effective. When no information is shared, the employees are working in seclusion and do their tasks without relating it to the tasks of other employees and the chance of repetition of work as well as conflicting tasks becomes significantly higher. As the saying goes, "the left hand needs to know what the right one is doing." When this happens, both hands can work together in harmony and increase productivity and results.

## Budget

Proper funding is crucial for the implementation of the initiative because it allows the various tasks to be completed on schedule so as to achieve the overall goals of the campaign. Without appropriate funding, employees cannot get their jobs done and the tasks go unfulfilled, resulting in loss of valuable time and resources. When we talk of appropriate funding, it does not necessarily imply an abundance of funds but merely a sufficient amount of funds to cover the expenses needed to accomplish the tasks. Such a budget utilizes ROI as a guideline to ensure that the investment in the public relations initiative is returned with dividends. Preparing an appropriate budget requires estimating costs by task, shopping for the best prices, and creating a budget report. The public relations director is wise to consult the accounting department about the costs and budgeting; accounting might also have the resources to reduce these costs through discount and preferred vendor programs.

### Estimating Costs of Tasks

Using the comprehensive list of tasks compiled in the "Identifying Tasks" section earlier in this chapter, the public relations director can review the list task by task, determine if it requires funding, and, if so, estimate its costs. The task of sending a press kit out to the media, for example, has few if any costs associated—color copies, fancy presentation folders, and mailing fees, which are normally part of the office supplies fund. On the other hand, the task of renting a sound system for a fashion show event requires a whole other class of costs. Rental fees for speakers, sound mixers, and so on can run in the tens of thousands of dollars.

### Shopping for the Best Price

The fashion company can benefit from competitive vendor bidding for the more expensive tasks. This is accomplished by sending a detailed description of the item or service purchased to three or four vendors, and requesting a competitive estimate. The lowest price is not necessarily the best price, though. As the saying goes, "you get what you pay for," and the public relations director must be vigilant against low-balled or bait-and-switch estimates. The bid that gives the cheapest price may not include certain vital items that must be done to complete the task, and latest date that these items must be paid for before an additional cost is incurred. The best price could be considered as the ideal combination of the product's or service's quality, price, and delivery time. For example, if the item is needed by a certain date and only one vendor can deliver it by that time, then the public relations director has little choice but to use that vendor. As mentioned before, accounting might have preferred vendor arrangements with vendors who have delivered good service at a good price in the past.

### Preliminary Budget Reports

After all of the costs for the various tasks have been listed and priced, the public relations director can create a **preliminary budget report** that estimates the overall cost of the campaign. Projecting the report onto a calendar according to the schedule of costs gives us a good picture of how much money will be spent in each week of the campaign's duration. Breaking down the costs according to categories of costs is also helpful for planning and reviewing the budget to ensure it is balanced. The budget report should also compare the investment against the expected ROI to demonstrate whether the initiative is sensible from a business standpoint. Although these reports are useful for planning the implementation, they are also needed to get budgetary approval prior to embarking on the initiative. Whether done verbally in casual conversation, through a detailed presentation, or with a written proposal, the budget typically has to be approved by the company's chief executive officer or another executive. The budget report allows the public relations director to submit a detailed and tangible proposal to the company's chief that shows how much of an investment the company will be making, and what are the expected returns. Often, company policy grants executives the discretion of approving projects under a certain dollar amount, in which case the public relations director can exercise this policy and forego submitting the budgetary report to the company chief; still, it is recommended to complete the budget report nonetheless because it will assist the public relations director in planning the campaign and will help safeguard against the initiative exceeding the budget upon implementation.

## Box 6.5 Implementing a Public Relations Method

The following fictitious example illustrates the process of planning the implementation of a public relations method. Let's suppose that the fictitious luxury necktie manufacturer Y Knot is sponsoring a walk for the cure of cancer in New York City, run by the also-fictitious Q Cancer Research Institute. This will be the first annual walk and it will take place April 2, during the national cancer awareness month. Let's see how the company plans to implement this corporate sponsorship method.

### Best Time for Implementation

The walk is scheduled for April 2, so in terms of the actual walk date, Y Knot is already locked into the Q Institute's implementation schedule. The sponsorship will be released February 1, two full months ahead to allow plenty of time to obtain news coverage. A special award will also be given to the Y Knot staff from the Q Institute during the ceremony following the walk on April 2, something that might attract additional coverage.

### Allowing Advance Time for Media Coverage

The company is targeting New York City newspapers, television news channels, and luxury magazines. The February 1 announcement date allows for ample advance time, which is at least six weeks in order to allow magazines to schedule the story.

### Avoiding Conflicts with Other Events

Both the February 1 and the April 2 dates do not conflict with other events in the area, and April 2 falls on a Saturday so most people are available to participate in the walk.

### Coordinating the Scheduling Internally with Other Departments

The legal department will have enough time to review all agreements with the Q Institute by the February 1 date.

### Scheduling Media Interviews

The Y Knot CEO will be available for media interviews the week starting on February 1, and will also be attending the April 2 walk where she will speak and accept the award on behalf of Y Knot employees. The Q Institute's president will also be available for media interviews on these dates.

### Single or Repeating Event

If the walk is a success, the Q Institute will be hosting a repeating walk next year, and is ready to extend Y Knot an invitation to sponsor that walk as well.

### Identifying Tasks

The following tasks will be needed to implement the initiative:

1. Sponsorship announcement—February 1.
   a. Finalize agreement with Q Institute on sponsorship details.
   b. Write press release announcing walk sponsorship.
   c. Send release to target media.
   d. Attach press passes for walk.
   e. Follow up with calls/emails to media contacts.

2. Walk event—April 2
   a. Coordinate with Q Institute on award presentation.
   b. Prepare speech notes for Y Knot CEO.
   c. Write press release to be handed out at the walk.
   d. Hand out release and answer any inquiries.
   e. Follow up with media contacts after event.

### Assigning Staff to the Tasks

Starting March, the public relations department will already be stretched in terms of resources due to the upcoming wholesaler banquet in May. But in January they will have an intern onboard part-time, who will help draft the releases and send them out under the direction of the public relations director, who will be handling the rest of the tasks.

### Coordinating Tasks and Keeping Staff Informed

There will be coordination meetings with all involved both on the Y Knot and the Q Institute staffs every other Monday at 2 p.m. in the Y Knot cafeteria to discuss progress and coordinate tasks.

163

## Box 6.5 Implementing a Public Relations Method (continued)

**Estimating Costs of Tasks**

Lawyer review of agreements—$1,250

Sponsorship costs—$10,000

Production of press kits and passes—$100

Photographer and lighting—$450

Total—$11,800

### Shopping for the Best Price

We will be using the company's long-standing law firm under the agreed-upon fee structure. A member of the accounting department recommended the photographer, who has given us good service and a discounted rate in the past.

**Preliminary Budget Reports**

Total costs—$11,800

Broken down by month:

▶ February—$1,350

▶ March—$10,000

▶ April—$450

Projected return: We project an article in the local daily paper, one local TV news stations, as well as two luxury magazines. Total expected impressions around 150,000 with estimated advertising value of $65,000.

Approval: The budget falls under the $15,000 mark so the public relations director can approve the project internally.

## Creating the Media Angle

Creating interest from the media is an invaluable skill for anyone working in public relations; it is the first step to getting a story printed, which leads to improved public image for the fashion company and brand—the ultimate goal of public relations. So how do we go about piquing an editor's interest? We need to understand how the editor determines which story should be covered and develop a **media angle** to the story. We must keep in mind that interacting with the media is not and can never become a rote procedure—it is a living and breathing process. Every reporter, editor, anchor, and other members of the media has different ideals, principles, interests, and personalities. The public relations staff must know how to develop a relationship with the media and we will discuss business relationship development in further detail in Chapter 9. To fully implement the public relations method, we need to study the target media for the approaches that might create interest and establish the media angle.

### What Is a Media Angle?

According to Webster's dictionary, angle is defined as "a certain way in which something appears or may be regarded" (Webster's, 2003). So what's the media angle? In the public relations world, the *media angle* is associated with the approach that invokes media reaction. But unlike Webster's definition, the media angle not only has to appear newsy but also must be regarded as a story that contains substance, uniqueness, and information that will create interest for the media's audiences. It can't be considered spin or have the appearance of an advertisement; it must be a substantial news item that is currently happening or something that will be happening at a near-future date that will be of interest to the media's audience. Let's not misinterpret *angle* as something underhanded or mysterious. The angle is the creative vehicle through which

### Box 6.6   Creating an Oscar-Worthy Angle

Using the Academy Awards event as the angle for gaining public relations exposure for the celebrity and designers is a good example of a creative angle. At the 71st Annual Academy Awards, Gloria Estefan was seen wearing a Richard Taylor design—a regal red gown with full-button exaggerated sleeves, sculpted neckline, and corset bodice. Estefan's matching nineteenth-century ruby-and-diamond necklace was courtesy of Fred Leighton.

FIGURE BOX 6.6 Gloria Estefan shows off her regal gown designed by Richard Tyler at the 71st Annual Academy Awards.

news stories are relayed to the public. In essence, it is the spark that sets off the story. Box 6.6 provides an example of a media angle by using an event to gain publicity for a celebrity and fashion designer.

In Chapter 5, we discussed the different public relations methods in great detail. So, at this point you should have an idea of which methods are appropriate for a particular story. Spending time researching and reading what the media covers is an investment that will yield a big payoff in the future. For example, let's suppose you are working for a public relations firm and you have a client who is releasing a creative flexible fashion group of clothing and accessories called "AM/PM." The apparel was designed to be worn both during the day for business and by adding the designer's accessories, can be suitable for evening social activities. The media angle of the story can be, "invest in clothing that can serve more than one purpose." Let's say you did your homework research and found that a reporter on the staff of *W* is writing a series of articles entitled, "Stretching the Working Woman's Clothing Budget." Bingo! Your angle for the story and the pitch can then be directed to the reporter, and the chances of publication are greatly increased.

Remain alert for stories and news items that relate to your brand or product, and check out the media coverage for your competition. Learning what type of stories are being covered and who is doing these stories can be the pathway to obtaining media exposure. For example, if your client's competition has obtained a story regarding its fashion swimwear and its participation in a fashion show, it would be prudent for you to contact the reporter who wrote the story. Chances are there will be other stories of this nature covered by the same reporter. Become an expert, study the different stories and who is writing them, and you will be able to say, "Oh, this is a story for so and so reporter because he is doing a series about fashion swimwear."

## Box 6.7 "The Hot New Swimsuits Are Bright And Luxe," by Rod Stafford Hagwood, Fashion Columnist

We project a lot onto our swimwear.

A swimsuit has to: look cool and hip; reflect our personality; redirect the eye from the sins of winter; feel like you have nothing on; completely dry in seconds; and maintain the social mores of modesty.

That's a lot . . . for a couple inches of Lycra.

And now designers are desperate to distinguish their oh-so-luxe bikinis, tankinis, monokinis, and maillots from the basic styles sold in discount stores.

For the fourth year, swimsuit stylists at the Mercedes Benz Fashion Week Swim shows staged catwalk extravaganzas around the pool at the Raleigh Hotel in South Beach with a smattering of celebrities (Billy Zane, Dennis Rodman, and Anna Kournikova) in the front rows.

For 2009, the fashion-driven swim labels are pulling out all the stops to justify their $120 to $300 price tags in tony boutiques and department stores, as opposed to $20 at Wal-Mart or Target.

Directional labels sent a tidal wave of enhanced prints, vibrant jewel tones or citrusy color (replacing this year's earthier palette) and textured fabrics down the often sand-covered runways. Many labels hope for ancillary sales through coordinated beach bags, huge floppy sombrero hats, tunic cover-ups, and ship-to-shore sundresses.

"I think we put a lot more glamour into the line," said Lynne Koplin, president of women's design at

FIGURE BOX 6.7 A model wears a swimsuit designed by Ashley Paige for the Girls Gone Wild swimwear line at Mercedes-Benz Fashion Week Miami in Miami Beach, Fla., Friday, July 13, 2007. (AP Photo/ Lynne Sladky)

Tommy Bahama. "Our customer loves quality product, but they really want a lot of glamour in their lives. You know, you have to have an escape. There's a lot of really bad news out there and people really want an escape."

So now add escapism to the list of things swimwear has to accomplish . . . by February when most of these styles hit store shelves (Hagwood, 2008).

At the risk of sounding corny, we'll mention that you don't have to reinvent the wheel to find the right angle that will interest the media. The name of the game in finding out what the media is interested in is doing your research and staying on top of the current news. Read what the reporters that you aim to interest are writing about and covering. Look at this research as an assignment that you must complete before finding the right media angle. While you are researching these stories, look for voids—things your competition is not doing to gain media attention, things that can make your story unique and different, and things that are "out of the box."

Box 6.7 gives an example of a public relations firm representing Mercedes Benz Fashion Week getting a story published. Note how the Tommy Bahama brand name and quote by Lynne Koplin, president of design, was woven into the story by that brand's public relations firm. That's great public relations, using the angle of the Mercedes Benz Fashion Week swim show, associating

## Case Study 6.1   Implementing the Public Relations Method and Creating a Media Angle

### Sun-Sentinel and CW Television Fashion Columnist Rod Stafford Hagwood

Rod Stafford Hagwood is the Fashion Columnist at the Fort Lauderdale, Florida-based *Sun-Sentinel* newspaper and The CW television affiliate. After interning at the *Arkansas Gazette* newspaper in Little Rock, Arkansas (and subsequently working there for a year), Rod wrote a syndicated men's wear column for Gannett Newspapers (*USA Today*) before accepting an offer to revamp the fashion page at the *Sun-Sentinel* newspaper in South Florida in 1990. Rod has reported fashion and beauty stories for all the *Sun-Sentinel's* media including partnerships with WPLG (ABC), WTVF (NBC), and WFOR (CBS). He has been a frequent guest on Y-100 WHYI-FM radio, CNN, MSNBC, Fashion File, Fashion Television, The Style Channel, and Black Entertainment Television (BET). He also writes a Q&A column for *City & Shore* magazine, which is published by the *Sun-Sentinel.* Currently he produces irreverent and gossipy Web casts called "The Fabulous Report" for the *Sun-Sentinel* Web site, www.sun-sentinel.com. These Web casts are also broadcast on The CW affiliate in South Florida. Rod has staged charity fashion events for the Broward House, United Negro College Fund, and AIDS awareness programs. He takes very seriously his unique opportunity to encourage local design talent in Broward, Palm Beach, and Dade counties. He has received several major awards for fashion journalism: the Aldo in 1996 and 1998, as well as the Atrium Award in 1997.

FIGURE CASE STUDY 6.1
Rod Stafford Hagwood, fashion columnist.

**What are the top elements you feel make for an interesting fashion story?**

For our purposes, an interesting fashion story can be something that affects a large number of our readership (such as discount back-to-school clothes) or emphasizes local style (like south Floridian Esteban Cortazar takes over the house of Emanuel Ungaro in Paris) or helpful (for example, tips on buying a swimsuit or lingerie) or just plain ol' fabulous (Chanel staging a resort-wear show in South Beach).

**Can you share with our students a brief overview of the proceedings at a typical editorial meeting? Who makes the decisions? How do stories get assigned?**

For fashion coverage, the editorial meetings are a little different. First of all, I usually run the meeting as opposed to my supervising editor because I—hopefully—know more about my beat than anyone else in the room. And my experience is helpful when deciding how best to get the story with the least amount of fuss (and cost). Beforehand I have usually chatted with my editor to make sure that she wants the story and has room in the newspaper for it. Then she and I decide whether the package should include video, graphics, or some online-only content (such as a dermatologist's comments on locally produced skincare products, which is too long and detailed for the broadsheet). After we make those decisions, then we schedule an editorial meeting with others needed to produce the story package. This could include multi-media (for video), photography, the page designers, and our online liaison.

**If a fashion company has a story they think is newsworthy, what is the best approach you would recommend their public relations person to take in terms of informing and contacting the media about that story?**

A pitch from a public relations account executive should be tailored to the media being sought after. If it is broadcast, then you want to emphasize the engaging and arresting images. If it is print, you may want to emphasize the helpful information for the reader. Regardless it is always a good idea to focus on the local angle of the story. Media outlets now have a much smaller "piece of the pie" than ever before, so the new mantra in newsrooms is local, local, local. It is also a

167

## Case Study 6.1 Implementing the Public Relations Method and Creating a Media Angle *(continued)*

good idea to hone your story down to specifics; not grand sweeping generalities. Don't make the journalist work too hard defining the story. It should be clear, simple, and obvious.

**How often are you contacted by public relations people? What makes you decide to talk to or answer one over another?**

I am constantly in contact with PR representatives. They call and email around the clock (especially since I deal a lot with the west coast and Europe). The "formula" for why I talk to one and not the other is extremely complicated and convoluted. It has a lot to do with what projects I am working on; what stories are coming down the pike; as well as does the pitch really speak to a trend or is it an isolated case. For example, are women really just dying to try out a "smoky eye" with their makeup, or is that just something actresses do on the red carpet?

**What do you feel makes a story too commercial?**

A story is too commercial when there aren't other examples of it from other manufacturers or retailers. If only one jewelry company is doing rings for same-sex commitment ceremonies, that may be too commercial. But if you can find three, then you may have a story.

**What advice would you give to students who are pursuing a career in Fashion PR?**

My best advice for public relation students is: do research. With the Internet, information has been democratized (much like fashion actually). So now there is no excuse for misspellings or factual errors.

Also, you should know exactly who you are pitching to and what they respond to. Again, you need to research the media outlet you are trying to work with. Read some of their previous articles or download some of the previous video. Make sure you spell the subject's name correctly or that you're not sending a press kit to someone who left the job months ago. Don't make promises you're not sure you can keep. For example, if you say you have high-resolution jpegs, then make sure you have them ready to go. No journalist wants to hear that you need to call the photographer who's on vacation on the other side of the globe in order to get images to illustrate a story . . . and yet it happens all the time. Make sure that if you have offered a subject for interviews that you have prepared that subject. Don't just throw them into an interview and expect them to know what to do (how to talk in sound bytes, how to focus an answer, how to imagine the words in print rather than just hearing them, etc.).

### Questions to Consider

1. According to Hagwood, what makes for an interesting fashion story?

2. What are the two points Hagwood checks before starting to work on a story? How do you think these two points would affect a pitch for a potential story?

3. Why do you think Hagwood avoids a story if it seems too commercial?

4. Based on Hagwood's advice, what research would you conduct prior to contacting a specific publication with a story? Explain.

their product with the glamour of the event, and knowing who and where to pitch the story.

### The Target Media

Most stories released to the media are never acknowledged nor published, and some are not even read beyond the headline. To get **picked up,** our release must first catch that specific reporter's or editor's attention. Remember, the media's time is highly valuable and an editor will not waste time reading a five-page press release, no matter how eloquent the writing may be. Reaching the media requires work—and we mean hard work. Getting to know who your *players* are in the media, knowing what type of stories they are interested in and the type of stories they are running is similar to baseball fans who know the batting average of baseball players, runs batted in, games won and lost by pitchers, and generally being an expert on their performance. When you know your players, you can more easily figure out the approach on how to talk to them—i.e., the media angle.

**Keeping It Real**

The biggest turnoff for the media staff is when they receive hype instead of facts. Stories that make the media grade must be accurate and presented with backup facts regarding the information the media receives. The rule is, "Tell it the way it is, not the way you want to make it." This applies to creating the media angle as well. The media angle needs to be creative, but it still must be factual and true. The ethics factor is one that separates the professionals from the amateurs. When a public relations release is found to be exaggerated and not substantiated by facts, it will not reach the expected results; instead, will backfire upon the source of the release. From then on, that source will not be trusted and chances for future news coverage will be slim. The chain of communication will be severed after the media receives inaccurate information or spin. Disseminating inaccurate information, hiding crucial facts, twisting the facts to give the story a more favorable look than it really is—these are all unethical ways to create an interest in a story. As the adage by William Shakespeare in *Hamlet* goes, "to thine own self be true." This couldn't be truer in the world of fashion public relations; anyone involved in public relations should be true to the facts he or she is providing to the media.

## Chapter Summary

▸ A detailed and effective plan for implementing the public relations method is crucial to the campaign's success.

▸ In the deadline-driven media industry, scheduling becomes a very important part of the implementation.

▸ Timing the release of the news when it would have the most impact and accounting for deadlines and advance times allows the media to more easily pick up the story.

▸ Editorial calendars provide information about topics and deadlines for the year's upcoming issues, and can be used to improve timing.

▸ Identifying the tasks involved in implementing the method, and assigning the tasks to employees who are qualified and able to carry them out, is vital to executing the implementation plan.

▸ Budgeting is important in public relations, and submitting a detailed budget report is often required to dispense funds for the implementation.

▸ The media angle helps us present the story in the most interesting way to the media so that it has a better chance of getting picked up.

▸ Upholding high ethical standards while formulating and representing the story's media angle is imperative to sustaining positive relations with the media and the public.

▶ Being familiar with the target media and what their reporters and editors write about can help to better tailor the media angle to the target media needs.

## Key Terms

▶ advance time
▶ editorial calendar
▶ media angle
▶ picked up
▶ preliminary budget report
▶ repeating event
▶ single event

## Chapter-End Questions and Exercises

1. In your opinion, what are the benefits, if any, of a detailed implementation plan for the public relations method? Explain.

2. Why does timing have such incredible significance in public relations?

3. What are the factors that one must determine prior to establishing the implementation schedule? Explain how each factor affects the success of the initiative.

4. Find a fashion publication not mentioned in this chapter that has an editorial calendar posted on its Web site. What is the time difference between the final deadline and the on-stand deadline? If you want to submit a release to this publication, explain how much of advance time you would allow for.

5. What day and time of the week would be best to have the family-friendly petting zoo event that the company will be sponsoring? Explain.

6. Find two fashion events—one that is a single event and the other that is a repeating event. Provide a summary of the information for each event citing your sources; then compare and contrast the two. Why do you think the former was established as a one-time only event? Why is the latter repeating?

7. How should public relations tasks be assigned to the personnel?

8. Develop a fictitious public relations initiative and identify the tasks as well as the estimated costs for the campaign. Explain.

9. Do you think it is good practice for the public relations director to consult with a departmental staffer and get his or her agreement when assigning a task? Explain your views.

10. Develop a fictitious public relations initiative and create a preliminary budget report as outlined in the text. (You may use the scenario from Question 8.)

11. What is a media angle? Why is it called an *angle*?

12. What is the importance of establishing an appropriate media angle to obtaining press coverage? Explain.

13. Locate a current fashion story in the media. Summarize the story and the coverage it received.

    a. In your opinion, what was the media angle used to get the story picked up?

    b. Analyze this angle for effectiveness. Was it appropriate for the publication, audience, and current events?

    c. What would have been an ineffective angle for this story? Why wouldn't it gain publicity?

14. Find a well-known fashion media correspondent, and learn their biography, which media outlet they are currently working for, and what topics they normally touch upon in their media coverage.

15. What are the consequences for sending out a release that knowingly contains a few inaccuracies? Do you think the media will deal with you again? Explain.

# Strategic Public Relations Tools

## SEVEN

**Chapter Snapshot**

The highly visual aspect of the fashion field lends itself to exposure in the media, and in particular the visual media such as television, online fashion sites, and glossy magazines. The fashion media thrives on glamour and pizzazz, and so the fashion company must aim to make its outreach initiatives as exciting and alluring as possible. There are a number of strategic tools in fashion public relations that can be utilized to implement the public relations method and improve the fashion company's public image. The press release and the photo opportunity are strategic tools that have proven effective and reliable in obtaining media coverage and are included in virtually every media publicity campaign. Other strategic tools such as partnerships with nonprofit organizations, participation and sponsorship of charity events, as well as cause-related activities are steadfast vehicles on the road to community involvement. Customer referrals and word-of-mouth campaigns are emerging tools that can be utilized to generate goodwill on a grassroots level. The public relations director has all of these tools and more at his or her disposal to achieve a successful campaign. In this chapter, we will cover these key strategic tools and explore how they can be employed to create positive public exposure for the fashion company, its brands, and its products.

## Objectives

- ▶ Understand the top strategic public relations tools.

- ▶ Explore how the press release is used to gain media coverage.

- ▶ Discuss the need for adequate research in a press release.

- ▶ Identify the principles of interviewing.

- ▶ Recognize the formatting and components of a press release.

- ▶ Discuss the photo opportunity and its various types.

- ▶ Explore how a fashion company can partner with a nonprofit organization.

- ▶ Understand the grassroots public relations tools used to directly improve public opinion.

Strategic public relations tools provide us with traditional and contemporary ways to achieve specific objectives within the public relations campaign. Each tool was devised with a particular purpose in mind and has proven successful in getting consistent results. Although traditional roles are still the predominant usage for most strategic tools today, the lines between the various tools blur more frequently as fashion companies are getting creative and mix and match these tools in order to stand out from the crowd and attract the public's attention. Whereas blogs have been utilized mostly to directly create a grassroots buzz among consumers, they are sometimes used by public relations firms as vehicles to get media coverage. First we will explore the key strategic tools and their traditional uses, and then we will cover their emerging nontraditional applications.

## Media-Related Strategic Tools

The **press release** and photo opportunity are the pivotal tools employed to achieve media coverage. The press release provides in a factual yet appealing manner all the information that the company wishes the media to cover. There is a delicate balance between form and function here—the release must report on the news with a journalistic perspective while at the same time lending the news some sense of excitement. How can the press release and the photo opportunity communicate the media angle in order to create media interest in covering the company's news? What makes a release capture the media's attention? The press release and photo opportunity serve as the key to the media gateway; the sleeker the key is, the better the chance of gaining coverage. With a well-researched and -written release that offers factual information promoting the media angle, backed by a photo opportunity that provides fashionable and trendy visuals, the message has a much better chance of gaining exposure in the target publications. In this section, we will discuss what the fashion company can do to better communicate the media angle and create interest in covering the company's **news story.** Later, we will discuss the main elements that make the release more engaging to the media. We will also cover the common parts of the press release and the formatting that make the release more effective.

## The Press Release

The majority of media public relations methods require a press release for implementation because it is the current standard avenue for disseminating information about potential news stories to the media. Because reporters and editors have very limited time, they prefer to receive such information in writing, which allows them to peruse the release at their convenience and quickly determine if it is an interesting story. The release has evolved over the years as the main acceptable data interchange vehicle between the fashion industry and the fashion media. That does not mean that no other ways of pitching a story to the media exist—the pitch in person and the pitch by referral are valid techniques that can get results just as effectively and that we will cover in the next chapter; however, the release is the most common avenue of dissemination and even with a personal referral, the media often wants to see the release. The reason is that the written release offers the editor a chance to review the facts carefully and objectively, and without the bias that a personal pitch may carry. In addition, a written release serves as the official statement of the fashion company, and the reporter can use the release as a valid backup **source** for the information in his or her story. Because it is understood that any **quotes** from a company official in a press release has been uttered or approved by that official, the reporter can easily include such quotes in the story, thus eliminating the need for the reporter to interview that official in person. The release becomes a crucial tool for gaining interest from the media.

## The Purpose of the Press Release

From the public relations director's perspective, the primary reason for the press release is to get the public relations message to the media and obtain coverage for the story. The written release is a proven tool that can relay the news story as well as get that message to the media in a clear and succinct way with the media angle in mind. It is an opportunity to alert the media, "Here is our company's story and it is exciting news! Shouldn't your audience know about this?" and create interest in running the company's story. With a well-written press release, the fashion company can inform the media of its news and receive coverage about it. With such a press release, the company can receive media exposure without paying for the advertisement costs. So upon a cursory look, it may seem that the press release works solely for the benefit of the fashion company; however, assuming such an attitude is a big mistake. Above all, the press release must be of value to the media; otherwise, it is not of any value at all. Box 7.1 lists some of the standards that journalists adhere to while reporting; these standards shed light on what information is of value to an editor and how a press release can aim to appeal to these values. Certainly, a press release must steer clear of sounding too commercial. The fashion company can extol the beauty and features of its new collection until the cows come home, but unless the release somehow demonstrates to the media that this new collection is of value to the readers and the general public, it will not result in any media coverage. Some public relations directors forget that the media exists for the readers, not the fashion company; the media's ultimate interest is in informing

## Box 7.1  Values in Journalism

When preparing a press release, it is vital to keep in mind the values that journalists look for in news. Understanding the criteria of the editor or reporter for determining what is news can assist tremendously in maximizing the results from the press release. The following is an excerpt from the nonprofit organization Project for Excellence in Journalism (PEJ) Web site, which outlines some of these values:

In 1997, an organization then administered by PEJ, the Committee of Concerned Journalists, began a national conversation among citizens and news people to identify and clarify the principles that underlie journalism. After four years of research, including 20 public forums around the country, a reading of journalism history, a national survey of journalists, and more, the group released its Statement of Shared Purpose that identified nine principles. These became the basis for *The Elements of Journalism,* a book by PEJ Director Tom Rosenstiel and CCJ Chairman and PEJ Senior Counselor Bill Kovach. Here are those principles, as outlined in the original Statement of Shared Purpose.

### A Statement of Purpose

After extended examination by journalists themselves of the character of journalism at the end of the twentieth century, we offer this common understanding of what defines our work. The central purpose of journalism is to provide citizens with accurate and reliable information they need to function in a free society.

This encompasses myriad roles—helping define community, creating common language and common knowledge, identifying a community's goals, heroes and villains, and pushing people beyond complacency. This purpose also involves other requirements such as being entertaining, serving as watchdog, and offering voice to the voiceless.

Over time journalists have developed nine core principles to meet the task. They comprise what might be described as the theory of journalism:

### 1. Journalism's First Obligation Is to the Truth

Democracy depends on citizens having reliable, accurate facts put in a meaningful context. Journalism does not pursue truth in an absolute or philosophical sense, but it can—and must—pursue it in a practical sense. This "journalistic truth" is a process that begins with the professional discipline of assembling and verifying facts. Then journalists try to convey a fair and reliable account of their meaning, valid for now, subject to further investigation. Journalists should be as transparent as possible about sources and methods so audiences can make their own assessment of the information. Even in a world of expanding voices, accuracy is the foundation upon which everything else is built—context, interpretation, comment, criticism, analysis, and debate. The truth, over time, emerges from this forum. As citizens encounter an ever greater flow of data, they have more need—not less—for identifiable sources dedicated to verifying that information and putting it in context.

### 2. Its First Loyalty Is to Citizens

While news organizations answer to many constituencies, including advertisers and shareholders, the journalists in those organizations must maintain allegiance to citizens and the larger public interest above any other if they are to provide the news without fear or favor. This commitment to citizens first is the basis of a news organization's credibility, the implied covenant that tells the audience the coverage is not slanted for friends or advertisers. Commitment to citizens also means journalism should present a representative picture of all constituent groups in society. Ignoring certain citizens has the effect of disenfranchising them. The theory underlying the modern news industry has been the belief that credibility builds a broad and loyal audience, and that economic success follows in turn. In that regard, the business people in a news organization also must nurture—not exploit—their allegiance to the audience ahead of other considerations.

### 3. Its Essence Is a Discipline of Verification

Journalists rely on a professional discipline for verifying information. When the concept of objectivity originally evolved, it did not imply that journalists are free of bias. It called, rather, for a consistent method of testing information—a transparent approach to evidence—precisely so that personal and cultural biases would not undermine the accuracy of their work. The method is objective, not the

**Box 7.1   Values in Journalism** (continued)

journalist. Seeking out multiple witnesses, disclosing as much as possible about sources, or asking various sides for comment, all signal such standards. This discipline of verification is what separates journalism from other modes of communication, such as propaganda, fiction or entertainment. But the need for professional method is not always fully recognized or refined. While journalism has developed various techniques for determining facts, for instance, it has done less to develop a system for testing the reliability of journalistic interpretation.

### 4. Its Practitioners Must Maintain an Independence from Those They Cover

Independence is an underlying requirement of journalism, a cornerstone of its reliability. Independence of spirit and mind, rather than neutrality, is the principle journalists must keep in focus. While editorialists and commentators are not neutral, the source of their credibility is still their accuracy, intellectual fairness and ability to inform—not their devotion to a certain group or outcome. In our independence, however, we must avoid any tendency to stray into arrogance, elitism, isolation or nihilism.

### 5. It Must Serve as an Independent Monitor of Power

Journalism has an unusual capacity to serve as watchdog over those whose power and position most affect citizens. The Founders recognized this to be a rampart against despotism when they ensured an independent press; courts have affirmed it; citizens rely on it. As journalists, we have an obligation to protect this watchdog freedom by not demeaning it in frivolous use or exploiting it for commercial gain.

### 6. It Must Provide a Forum for Public Criticism and Compromise

The news media are the common carriers of public discussion, and this responsibility forms a basis for our special privileges. This discussion serves society best when it is informed by facts rather than prejudice and supposition. It also should strive to fairly represent the varied viewpoints and interests in society, and to place them in context rather than highlight only the conflicting fringes of debate. Accuracy and truthfulness require that as framers of the public discussion we not neglect the points of common ground where problem solving occurs.

### 7. It Must Strive to Make the Significant Interesting and Relevant

Journalism is storytelling with a purpose. It should do more than gather an audience or catalogue the important. For its own survival, it must balance what readers know they want with what they cannot anticipate but need. In short, it must strive to make the significant interesting and relevant. The effectiveness of a piece of journalism is measured both by how much a work engages its audience and enlightens it. This means journalists must continually ask what information has most value to citizens and in what form. While journalism should reach beyond such topics as government and public safety, a journalism overwhelmed by trivia and false significance ultimately engenders a trivial society.

### 8. It Must Keep the News Comprehensive and Proportional

Keeping news in proportion and not leaving important things out are also cornerstones of truthfulness. Journalism is a form of cartography: it creates a map for citizens to navigate society. Inflating events for sensation, neglecting others, stereotyping or being disproportionately negative all make a less reliable map. The map also should include news of all our communities, not just those with attractive demographics. This is best achieved by newsrooms with a diversity of backgrounds and perspectives. The map is only an analogy; proportion and comprehensiveness are subjective, yet their elusiveness does not lessen their significance.

### 9. Its Practitioners Must Be Allowed to Exercise Their Personal Conscience

Every journalist must have a personal sense of ethics and responsibility—a moral compass. Each of us must be willing, if fairness and accuracy require, to voice differences with our colleagues, whether in the newsroom or the executive suite. News organizations do well to nurture this independence by encouraging individuals to speak their minds. This stimulates the intellectual diversity necessary to understand and accurately cover an increasingly diverse society. It is this diversity of minds and voices—not just numbers—that matters. (Project for Excellence in Journalism, 2006) its public of valid and important news. Therefore, the press release must focus on the media's readership and how the news will benefit these readers, rather than on the fashion company and how the news will benefit the company. We will discuss the ways the release can achieve that later on in this chapter.

## Use of the Press Release

The release is highly beneficial to the media: It alerts the editor to news, saves him or her time, facilitates the reporter's work, and serves as an acceptable source for the story. The fashion industry is driven by the capricious nature of trends and each publication wants to be the first to report about it. The release typically offers information about the collection before the collection is unveiled to the public and thus it is a tool for the editor to keep up on what is going on in the industry. When the release contains news that is significant to the editor's audience, then the editor is more likely to include it in the **editorial meeting** and add the story to the **editorial agenda.** The release serves as a flag that points to potential news. If the editor ignores the flag, the publication may miss out on covering a fashion story that made the news. Editors at leading fashion publications can receive several hundred press releases a week. If they had to listen to the public relations pitch over the phone or in person for each story, they would be so occupied with pitches that they would never have time to do their job of supervising and directing the **newsroom.** Being able to read the headline and top paragraph of a release and evaluate its merit as a news story without much discussion saves the editor time. In addition, the release also saves the reporter time by providing the reporter with some ready-to-print information. Quotes from the fashion company officials about the news, spare the reporter making phone calls and conducting interviews with these officials in order to get their comments. It also provides the reporter with other information on the news story, such as the time and place of an event, or facts about the new collection; such information is vital to the story and having the data right there in the release means the reporter can simply copy it from the release into the story. The public relations director must remember that journalists treat press releases as sources and assume that anything written in the release is fully approved by the issuer of the release—in this case the fashion company. When the release says, for example, that the new collection will be issued in a month, the reporter utilizes this data in the release as official information from the company. In many cases, journalists will not even call to confirm the information or quotes from press releases, but will simply run with it. Therefore, the public relations director must be extra cautious about the accuracy of all facts in the release. He or she should ensure all quotes are approved by the company's top executives, and that all facts are backed by credible research or other sources, which the reporter is likely to ask for.

## Research

The press release that is well researched has a better chance of gaining exposure because it is based on facts rather than opinion. Journalists are expected not only to report the facts but also to support and **attribute** each fact. As the third section in Box 7.1 points out, "Seeking out multiple witnesses, disclosing as much as possible about sources, or asking various sides for comment, all signal such standards. This discipline of verification is what separates journalism from other modes of communication, such as propaganda, fiction or entertainment."

Responsible journalists practice verification of all facts in a press release prior to printing it. Therefore, it is folly to include any information in a press release that one cannot easily and quickly substantiate. If the editor decides to run the story, the reporter who will cover it will likely call around to verify the facts; if the reporter discovers one of the facts to be false or unsubstantiated, he or she will likely suspect the entire release to be false and will most likely **kill the story.** When researching a press release, one should locate and cite a source for each fact that appears in the release. If the fact cannot be supported, then it should be omitted from the release. For example, if the release claims that the fashion company is the largest manufacturer of belts in the United States, the company should be prepared to supply the reporter with an unbiased and recent study that shows the financial numbers for the company and its competitors, proving that it is indeed the number one manufacturer. Sloppy or inadequate research can result in negative publicity as well. Suppose the company's CEO informs the public relations director that the company just signed a sponsorship agreement with a well-known national nonprofit organization and tells the director to get the release out immediately. The public relations director quickly drafts the release and sends it out without verifying the facts first. The reporter calls the nonprofit organization to verify the sponsorship and learns that the nonprofit organization has not yet approved the sponsorship agreement and will likely turn it down. The resulting story might be a scathing report about the company's false and reckless claims of sponsorship in a possible desperate search for free publicity.

When researching a press release, we should ask ourselves four questions to make sure that proper research has been done:

▸ What is the story about and what are its details?

▸ Which organizations are involved in the story and what are their backgrounds?

▸ Which people are involved in the story and what are their backgrounds?

▸ What statistics, information, or other data are needed to support the story?

Gathering the information to answer these questions provides us with the rudimentary research needed to make the release media-worthy.

### Researching the News Story

The first order of business when it comes to research is to examine the news story itself. This segment of the research process concerns what the story is about, why it is a news story, and the details about the story. Before drafting a press release, it is important to identify what exactly the story is about. Let's say the fashion company is announcing a company news release about a new store opening. The story then is about the new store, where it is located, its hours, and what merchandise will be available. To make it more newsy, the fashion company invites a local celebrity model to sign autographs at the new store on opening day. Now the story also includes the information about the celebrity autograph session and what time she will be at the store. We now need to research all of these topics to ensure the release is correct. To find out the information on the new store, we contact the new store's manager, who informs us that the new store will specialize in the women's wear portion of the company's collection, and will only carry products for women. The manager also tells us the new location is one of the biggest in the United States, a fact we check by consulting the company's human resources department records and comparing the number of employees in the new store against the staff lists of the other top existing stores. We also obtain the details from the marketing department staff who booked the celebrity autograph session, that she will be in the store on opening day from 4 p.m. to 8 p.m. and that this will be ongoing in the shoe department of the store.

### Researching the Organizations Involved

In this segment of the research process we cover the various entities that are involved in the story. To be sure, the fashion company that is publishing the release is certainly involved, so we should research our own company first. Ideally, the public relations director should formulate a universal **About paragraph,** which can be used for all press releases. Although this paragraph should be included in the release, it is likely that additional information about the company is needed for each particular release. Suppose an accessories manufacturer releases a new jeans line, which constitutes a new market for the company; it is worth mentioning that this is the first time the company has ventured beyond accessories into the jeans market. This fact is something we should research first and ensure that in the company's history it has indeed never produced any non-accessory items.

Next, we should research any other companies or entities that are involved in the story. The release should include each involved organization in the story, describe its relations to the fashion company, and include a short description of the organization. Suppose the story is about a fundraising event for a local nonprofit organization. We should research the nonprofit organization and include information about it in the release. Without a doubt, the company should discreetly verify the organization's nonprofit status, and that it has not been involved in any recent investigations or media scandals because this could reflect badly upon the fashion company. It is beneficial as part of this segment to research the fashion company's competitors as well in relation to the story. Have any of our competitors published a story similar to ours already? If so, we should find out how recent their story was to ensure that our story's timing is not going to collide with theirs. If our competitor just completed a walk-a-thon to raise funds for a local nonprofit organization, our walk-a-thon might suffer in terms of coverage if we launch it too soon. We should know when the last walk-a-thon took place and that it was long enough ago to allow for coverage.

Similarly, if our competitor recently launched a new jeans collection, we should be aware of it and ensure that our release points out the unique features of our jeans collection to set it apart from the competition.

### Researching the People Involved

In addition to the companies involved, we should also research the people who are part of the story, including anyone who issues comments about the story. In our previous example of the store opening event featuring the local celebrity model autograph session, we should research the celebrity's biography and recent media coverage to check if this celebrity is involved in any recent media scandals, and, if so, be prepared to answer questions. If an employee from our company or an independent expert is being quoted in the story, we should have their full name, title, and a brief background.

### Related Statistics and Facts

This last segment of research focuses on other information relevant to the story, such as statistics, results of surveys or studies, figures, and historical background. Such research should be conducted to support any facts that we state within the release. It is helpful and appreciated by the media if the release also includes a citation for each source at the end of the release. This allows the reporter to save time by checking the citation directly rather than having to spend time researching that fact. For example, if the release says that 2 million pairs of jeans were sold in the United States during the previous year, that fact should be backed up by a credible source. Suppose this statistic came from a study published by a business research institute. We cite this institute and the study as the source, and if it is available online add the Web address of the document. When the reporter looks over the release, he or she can quickly go to that Web address and verify the fact. Such a release makes the reporter's job easier and gives the release more of a chance of being covered; if the story revolves around this statistic yet the source of it is not cited in the release, the reporter will try to find the source of the information. If that takes too long, however, she or he will likely kill the story.

## Interviews

The interview is an essential part of preparing a press release and is a vital means to obtain information and quotes for the story. The fashion company is wise to include as part of the release several quotes about the story; such quotes give breadth and depth to the story and make it more appealing to the media. As can be seen in the release and media clip in Box 7.2, these quotes represent the official comment of each individual quoted, and the reporter can use them when she writes the story, just as if she had done the interview herself. We will cover the use of quotes in more detail later on in this section. The release should contain a minimum of two different quotes, which say completely different things from each other. We should not include too many quotes, either; if a quote does not contribute an important piece of information to the release, it should not be there.

## Box 7.2    Quotes and Interviews

When H&M sent out a release about its organic line, it contained a quote by H&M Head of Design Ann-Sofie Johansson, as can be seen in the highlighted portion of the press release below.

KUNDENSERVICE   NEWSLETTER   IMPRESSUM   KONTAKT   SITEMAP   ANDERES LAND / CHANGE COUNTRY
Österreich

FASHION
SHOP ONLINE
FILIALFINDER
ARBEITEN BEI H&M
PRESSE

Pressemitteilungen

Mode
Corporate
Archiv

Presse- und Infomaterial
Presse- und Telefonkonferen
Fotoarchiv
Mailingliste
Financial reports
Financial Calendar

INVESTOR RELATIONS
UNTERNEHMERISCHE VERAN
ÜBER H&M

04.06.2008

### H&M CONTINUES TO GO ORGANIC

H&M is continuing its big venture into organic cotton in all departments this Autumn. The season also heralds the start of other conscious choices of materials such as organic wool and recycled wool and recycled polyester.

"We are now using organic cotton in all departments. We're proud that we're able to meet increased interest from our customers and at the same time contribute to the increased demand for organically grown cotton. Garments made from organic cotton include both fashion items and updated basics," says H&M Head of Design Ann-Sofie Johansson.

The clothes will hang in their respective departments in H&M stores and be labelled with special hangtags.

**Women**
Tops, dresses and bodysuits are in solid colours or feature patterns from nature inspired by art. Garments made from organic and recycled wool include a coat with dolman sleeves and a funnel neck, a kimono jacket, Jodhpur style trousers, a tulip skirt and knitted jumpers. Wide jeans in organic denim, a patterned dress and a blouse also feature. There's outerwear too, such as a couture-inspired anorak, and an anorak made from recycled polyester. Underwear and sleepwear made in organic cotton feature floral patterns, checks or stripes, as well as pretty lace or embroidery.

**Men**
In the Menswear department, it's mostly basics that are made from organic cotton, including boxer shorts, socks and scarves as well as T-shirts in several colours.

**Divided**
For the girls there are T-shirts in several colours, plain or with prints, a romantic blouse and a waistcoat, as well as dungaree shorts and cargo pants. For the guys there are T-shirts with prints or stripes, a hooded cardigan, a waistcoat, a uniform-inspired shirt, a granddad shirt, a uniform-inspired jacket, and khaki jeans in different shades. All are made of organic cotton.

**Baby, Children and Young**
For babies there are bodies, trousers, pants and little hats for the very small. There are also hooded tops sporting stripes or fun messages, such as "I might not be as big as you but I can be louder". All are made in organic cotton.

For children there are long-sleeved T-shirts featuring patterns or prints, a dress, a nightdress and underwear in cute animal prints. There are also rugby shirts and hooded tops with prints as well as vests and boxer shorts. A shopping bag completes the collection. All are made from organic cotton.

The Young concept for children between 9 and 14 contains a complete collection of tops, blouses, shirts and a cardigan. There's also a reefer jacket along with jeans, and a skirt with matching knitted accessories for girls. For boys there are T-shirts, a shirt, cardigan, hooded top, lumberjack jacket, jeans, hat and scarf. All garments are made from organic cotton.

The prices of these pieces are in line with other H&M collections.

For further information, please contact:

Camilla Emilsson Falk
Telephone: +46 70 796 96 15
E-mail: camilla.emilsson-falk@hm.com

© H & M HENNES & MAURITZ AB 2009

**More information about
Jimmy Choo for H&M**

www.jcforhm.com/press

**Jimmy Choo for H&M**

Click on the picture to view and download the EPK from the fashion event in Los Angeles.

Fotoarchiv

**Abonnements**

Tragen Sie sich in unsere Mailing-Liste ein, damit wir Ihnen unsere Pressemitteilungen direkt per E-Mail zuschicken können.

Zur Abonnements

**Pressemitteilungen Mode**

16.11.2009
FASHION MEDIA UPDATE - WINTER EXCLUSIVES AT H&M

03.11.2009
STAR-STUDDED PARTY WITH H&M AND JIMMY CHOO IN HOLLYWOOD

22.10.2009
THE ULTIMATE PARTY WARDROBE FROM JIMMY CHOO AT H&M

28.09.2009
SONIA RYKIEL HEATS UP THE 2009 HOLIDAY SEASON FOR H&M, AND UNVEILS COLOURFUL KNITS FOR SPRING 2010

02.09.2009
FASHION MEDIA UPDATE - AUTUMN EXCLUSIVES AT H&M

Pressemitteilungsarchiv

FIGURE BOX 7.2A

Box 7.2    Quotes and Interviews (continued)

This same exact quote was repeated in a *Vogue UK* story as if the reporter interviewed Ms. Johansson herself, which can be seen in the resulting media clip:

**FIGURE BOX 7.2B**

### Whom to Interview

For most press releases, the typical interviews are of top company executives, industry experts, and other people who the company wants to be featured in the story, such as designers and celebrities. In the field of public relations where the public image is king, there are two highly sensitive topics called **media compatibility** and **positivism.** We must remember that whoever is quoted in a release could potentially be called by the reporter for a more in-depth interview, or simply to verify the quote that is in the release. Thus, a person who gets embarrassingly nervous around television cameras should not be the first-choice interview for a release that will be sent to the local news channels. Although being careful not to discriminate in any way, public relations personnel should strive to interview people who are knowledgeable and positive about the topic, and whose personalities are compatible—or at the very least are comfortable—with the media. It would not make any business sense to interview an expert who is on the payroll of our chief competitor, for example, about our new collection; his or her comments will likely not be objective. There is an ethical fine line that the public relations director must not cross, which separates positivism and spin. Suppose the fashion company is unveiling a new collection of coats made of special experimental fabric. With such a technical story, the public relations director interviews the director of production to get the information on the product. Then the director can interview the CEO or director of marketing from a sales perspective about the benefits of the coats to consumers. Finally, the director can also interview an impartial expert on coats about what effect this new fabric will have on the coat market.

### How to Interview

Conducting the interview in a professional manner and being thorough in questioning and writing down the answers is essential. Even though the interview is for the purpose of composing a press release, it still requires us to obtain all the needed information. It helps to write down a plan for the interview beforehand, with an outline of the questions to ask and the topics to address. This plan ensures that we do not forget to ask anything during the interview. In many cases, where the subject we will interview is extremely busy, we may only get one or two chances of interviewing. During the interview the public relations director asks the subject the questions and notes down the answers. The director might have to steer the conversation back in the direction of the press release news because some people tend to be very wordy—the release should not have long-winded quotes; rather, the quotes should be short, straight, and to-the-point. Also, this is a good time to test the subject's media compatibility and positivism; if all the subject does is complain about the company, then he likely is not a candidate for quoting in the story.

### Signed Waivers

When the release quotes as sources people who are not hired employees, obtaining signed waivers for the subjects to highly recommended. Such waivers are composed of legal text that protects the fashion company from getting sued. Typical waivers state that the source gives the fashion company permission to utilize their words—and likeness if a photograph or footage is included—in the press release to the media. It is important to use a waiver that is approved by the fashion company's legal team. The public relations director should keep each waiver in the file of the release for as many years as legally necessary; these legal documents can serve as evidence in the future, should a past source decide to threaten the company with a lawsuit.

### Writing the Press Release

How the press release is written can make a difference on whether the story gets covered. A well-written, informative, and concise release appeals to the reporter because it speaks his or her language. After all, the journalist surely appreciates a professional, interesting, and thorough style of presenting information. Now that we have all of the information, quotes, and sources, we can roll up our sleeves and get to the business of writing the release.

#### *Format*

The press release should be formatted with clear black type and average font size so that it is simple to follow and easy to read. While it is not common, using fancy or ornate formatting, such as bold or colored type, can sometimes be useful to make the release stand out. Each company typically develops its own formatting guidelines, so that all of its releases appear uniform in style. However, as illustrated in Case Study 7.1, it is an accepted general rule that the press release should contain the following:

**1. The Company's Logo.**   Usually the release includes the logo of the fashion company at the very top of the release. This allows the reporter to tell in one glance which company originated the release. If it is a joint release by the fashion company and a nonprofit organization, it is beneficial to include both logos at the top with the nonprofit organization's logo at the left corner and the fashion company's at the right.

**2. The Words Press Release.**   This indicates that the document is an official press release from the fashion company. It also means that it is acceptable for the media to use any of the information in the release for their story, that the information released by the company is accurate and true, and that all quotes included in the story are the approved statements of the attributed sources.

**A Headline.**   The headline is an extremely important part of the press release because it is the first sentence read by the editor. The headline sets the tone for the release, and should be a strong and appealing synopsis of what the release is about. Often, the editor will read the headline only, and if it sounds interesting then he or she will read the rest of the release. The headline should be in bold letters, be no longer than two lines of text, and should include clearly what the main news is. An ideal headline should be based on the media angle and state the benefit of the news story to the media's audience. Keep in mind that the considerations of the editor or reporter in choosing stories revolve solely around the readers and the publication's needs. Unlike the public relations director, the editor's job does not depend on whether the fashion company receives media coverage; his or her job depends solely on whether he or she can engage readers, inform them accurately about current fashion news, meet deadlines, and maintain the size of the readership. The fashion company could be the best company in the world and its collections could be the most stunning collections in the world, but if the company's story is not new and does not affect readers, it will simply not be printed. Assuming the perspective of an editor on deadline, take a cold look at the headline and check if it would grab your attention; if not, modify the headline until it does!

**A Sub-Headline.**　The sub-headline is an addition to the headline and is also a vital part of the release. It provides additional important information about the news story that helps to entice the editor to read further. It should be in regular or italic type, slightly larger than the rest of the release, and should not be longer than two lines of text.

**A Dateline and Release Date.**　The **dateline** is a news term describing the beginning text of a news report that indicates where and when the story was written. Newsprint datelines are traditionally placed on the first line of the text of the article, before the first sentence, followed by two dashes, i.e., "TOKYO, Japan, Jan. 1, 2008—" The press release can include a dateline to facilitate coverage. It can indicate where the news is happening if it is a local story, or omit the geographical reference if it is a national story.

Including a date in a release has significant functions. A date on a release is tantamount to the release date, and means that the news is effective as of that date. A delayed release (which we will discuss in the following chapter in more detail) should be clearly indicated on the release by including a future date for when the release will be effective. With a standard release, it helps to emphasize the fact that the release is effective immediately by including the phrase "For Immediate Release" at the top of the release or immediately before the dateline.

**A Lede.**　The **lede,** or lead paragraph, is the first paragraph in a story and, like the headline, has to be a strong and informative paragraph that indicates the importance of the story and stresses its newsy nature. The lede should give an overview of the story and include the most important facts that readers would be interested in. Again, we must forget our bias toward our own company and products in formulating and evaluating the lede. If we were an editor on deadline who knew nothing about our company or collections, would we read the rest of the release or move on to the next release? The lede must grab our attention and show us how the story is news. It must elaborate on the way the story affects the readers and focus on the facts that make the story newsworthy.

**The Copy, or Main Text.**　The main text in the release, also called **copy,** is the material for the news story. It gives all the facts, quotes, and other information about the story. We will discuss what the copy should include in further detail in the next segment. As stated before, sentences should be simple and direct so that the editor/reporter can digest them in a single bite. Use strong verbs (e.g., "galvanized" versus "was"). Use active voice (e.g., "President Obama galvanized everyone" versus "Everyone was galvanized by President Obama"). Strictly limit your adjectives and adverbs (i.e., "President Obama galvanized the crowd" versus "The galvanizing aura of authority ever-surrounding President Obama was viscerally experienced by all"). Nouns should be specific: "the Committee on Foreign Relations" versus "all," or "everyone." But don't be afraid to break any of these rules to get the idea across more effectively (i.e., use *being* verbs for expediency and avoid chewy phrases like "the Committee on Foreign Relations" instead of "they" or "all" after you've established who your "they" are, and so on. When it comes to writing style, most journalists follow *The Associated Press Stylebook*, a style manual published and annually updated by the Associated Press that provides fundamental journalism guidelines for preferred spelling, grammar, punctuation, and usage, with special sections on reporting business and sports. It is highly recommended for any public relations department staff who works on the company's press releases to be thoroughly familiar with this essential reference book.

**About Paragraph.** The About paragraph should be included at the very end of the copy and usually is preceded by an italicized headline, "About [the fashion company's name]." If it is a joint story with a nonprofit organization, an About paragraph for the nonprofit organization should be included above the fashion company's.

**Contact Information.** This segment provides the people that the media should contact if they have any inquiries about the story. It should include the contact's first and last names; the name of the public relations firm handling inquiries, if applicable; the fashion company's name; and the contact's direct telephone, mobile number if any, and email address. It can also include the fashion company's address and Web site address. If the story comes jointly with a nonprofit organization, then include a contact for that nonprofit organization if available.

**Photo.** In such a visual world as the fashion world, providing a number of photographs to accompany the story is quite helpful in securing coverage. The fashion company should always own the rights for photos provided or have an agreement with the owner of the rights to use them, in which case a photo credit listing the name of the owner should be included next to the photo. We will discuss photos in more detail later in this chapter.

**Cutline.** The **cutline** is the newsroom jargon for a photo caption. The cutline is a sentence or two placed directly underneath or next to a photo, describing what happened in the photo, which usually relates to the story and identifies the people in it. If there are several people in the photo, they are always identified from left to right. Identifying the models in photos featuring fashion items (as opposed to celebrity photos that focus on the celebrity) is at the discretion of the fashion company, but the publication is not obliged to include it.

## What the Copy Should Contain

The main text of the release should at the very least contain the following important elements to provide as thorough of a story as possible. The public relations department should add other information that they deem necessary according to the specific story being released. In Box 7.3, a Coach, Inc., press release illustrates how these elements can be incorporated into a release.

## Box 7.3   The Elements of a Press Release

A release should include several elements in order to give
a complete picture to the media about the news story.

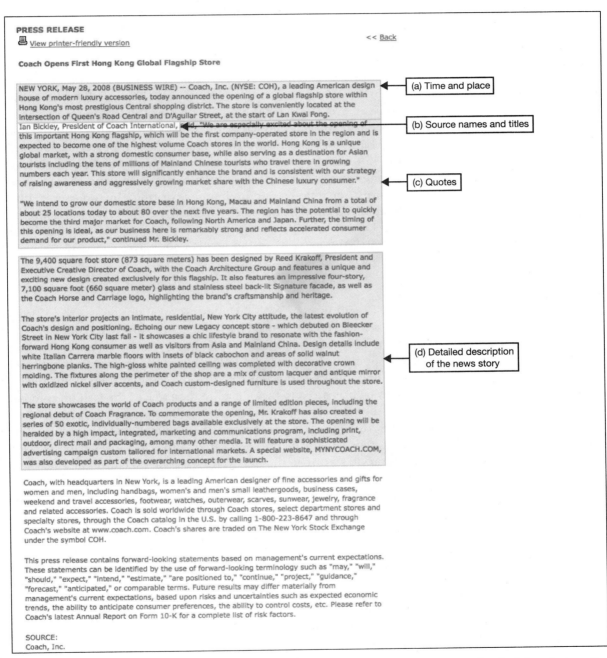

FIGURE BOX 7.3 Labels: (a) time and place, (b) source names and titles, (c) quotes, (d) detailed description of
the news story.

### *Detailed Description of the News Story*

Beyond the concise information expressed in the headline, sub-headline, and lede, the release should include a more detailed description of the news story. Naturally, if the editor reads the headline and lede and finds the topic of the story interesting, he or she will want to know more. The release's copy must convey to the media the full details of the story so they can determine whether it should be covered. If the editor adds the story to the schedule, he or she will hand the release to the reporter. Our aim in writing the release is that when the reporter receives the release, he or she could write the whole story using only the data in the release and a few phone calls to verify facts. The question can be asked: Aren't we doing the reporter's job for him or her? To a degree, we are. Consider the public relations staff as a researcher and assistant to the reporter, conducting the necessary research and interviews that the reporter might use. Ultimately, however, the reporter decides which facts to use in the story, which quotes to include, and whether other sources should be interviewed. All the public relations staff can and should do is to provide information, quotes, and preliminary writing; the reporter is still the one who actually writes the final story. The acid test of the release is whether a layman who knows nothing about the company, its products, or the news story (in other words, the majority of the media's audience) can read the release and easily understand the news story.

### *Quotes*

The successful press release includes two or more quotes from two different sources. The quotes should be significantly different from each other and should not repeat or paraphrase other quotes in the story; in other words, each quote should be unique and should address important facets of the story not commented upon by other sources already. Although the public relations director may be pressured to include more than one of the fashion company's directors in the release regardless of what they have to say, he or she should not simply follow these suggestions. Instead, the public relations directors should get creative on how to divide the topics among the executives who the fashion company wants to feature in the story. This way, one executive can speak about the market conditions while another executive covers the fashion company's excitement about the news, and so on. The point is not to have overlapping comments that are too close to each other. Otherwise, who will be interested in reading such superfluous comments? Nobody. That is why each quote must be distinctive and exciting, and add some significant bit of information to the story. A quote can be direct—reproduced exactly word-to-word within quotation marks, followed by the source of the quote; for example, "'This textbook is extremely interesting to read,' said John Doe, Acme vice president for marketing." It could also be indirect—paraphrased without quotation marks and be attributed to the source; for example, "Acme Vice President for Marketing John Doe said that the textbook is extremely interesting to read."

### Names and Titles

Following journalistic style, each quote and bit of information in a release should be attributed to its source, and each source should be identified with a full name, title, and company or organization that source is associated with. To ensure accuracy, it is good practice to double-check the names and titles with all sources prior to sending a release out.

### Logistical Information

The release should include all logistical information for the story, particularly when the story is about an event or community program. Such information includes the date and time of the event, the place where it will happen or has happened, and, if the public is invited, admission price if any, the address and directions of the venue, as well as a phone number or an email address people can contact for more information.

### Research Information

The release should cite relevant studies, surveys, statistics, and other hard facts as often as possible. Such information helps to support the release message and makes the story more relevant to the media's audience. If, for example, the fashion company is sponsoring a local food drive for the homeless, the release should include the estimated number of homeless people in the area and cite the study or source for this information. In this example, the fashion company could consult with the local nonprofit organization that assists the homeless or the local county administration, and find out if it has this type of statistical information. Incorporating the number of homeless into the release can immediately add a human perspective to the urgency and importance of the food drive. Research information such as this could make the difference between the story getting picked up or ignored.

### Length

The length of the press release should be as short as possible while still conveying all the information that pertains to the story. It is good practice to aim and fit the release into one printed page, and it is recommended never to exceed two printed pages. An overly elaborate release that blabbers on and on will be ignored and pitched into the circular file, i.e., the recycling bin.

## The Photo Opportunity

Photographs and video footage are extremely important in the field of fashion where new styles and trends can often be best communicated visually. Providing a photo opportunity to accompany a press release increases the chances of the story getting picked up. The fashion company should set up a **photo opportunity** whenever possible to go along with every press release. The media relies on the **artwork** to draw the reader into reading the publication; it is a journalist principle that people read the headline first, look at the photo next, read the

189

---

**Box 7.4   Writing an Effective Press Release at a Glance**

▷ Keep the release short—ideally one page—and to the point.

▷ State clearly and succinctly early on in the release what the news story is about and why it is of interest to the audience.

▷ Answer the basic content questions: what, who, where, when, why, and how.

▷ Include two different quotes from two sources.

▷ Clearly identify every source and organization mentioned.

▷ Provide detailed information about logistics and costs.

▷ Fact-check and cite all information and figures.

▷ Include at least one press contact name and his or her phone number(s).

▷ Think creatively how to present the release so it relates to the media publication's audience.

▷ Don't bury the information about the story's essence later in the release.

▷ Avoid slang or jargon that the average reader is not familiar with unless necessary and in this case explain what it means.

---

cutline after that, and then read the story. Although many stories are printed without artwork, having artwork available makes it easier for the media to print the artwork as well. Stories with artwork receive more attention by readers and thus are displayed more prominently on the page. As we can see, having a photo with the story is crucial.

## What Comprises a Photo Opportunity?

The photo opportunity can be any photo or video that gives a visual enhancement to the news story. If, for example, the fashion company is releasing a new collection, then the release should be accompanied by several photos of some of the items in the new collection. Whether the photos feature the items themselves shot simply against a white backdrop in a studio, or models wearing the items while running through a field of pumpkins, the bottom line about a photo op is its ability to add depth to the story using the graphic dimension. The six main photo opportunities are the mug shot, execution at dawn, grip and grin, the product shot, the action shot, and the video op.

### The Mug Shot

The **mug shot,** or head shot, is a smaller photo of the person's face, typically a front portrait measuring from the chest or the bottom of the neck to the top of the head. The name is borrowed from police terminology, where the mug shot describes the front and side profile photos taken when someone is arrested. Whenever the story includes a quote from someone, we have the chance to submit a mug. The media typically utilizes the mug shot when attributing the quote to the source by adding the mug next to the quote, usually the first quote by that person in the story. Typically, the last name of the person serves as the cutline for the mug shot.

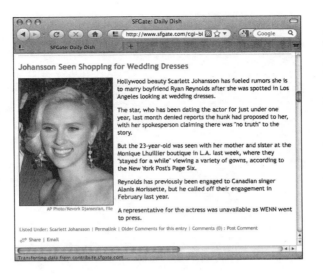

FIGURE 7.1 This Scarlett Johansson mug shot was used to go along with a February 2008 story about the celebrity shopping for a wedding dress. Even though the settings of the photo had nothing to do with the story, Johansson's mug adds flair to the story (Daily Dish, 2008). Source: The Daily Dish.

### Execution at Dawn

The **execution-at-dawn** shot is a facetious media jargon term for the type of photo op where a group of people who are involved in the new story are lined up against a wall to be shot—with a camera, of course! These photo ops are popular in events and happenings where people in attendance pose together, and the cutline is usually a long list of their names.

### Grip and Grin

The **grip-and-grin** photos typically feature people receiving awards, cutting ribbons, or passing out fundraising checks. In such a photo, the person usually poses shaking hands with the person who presents them with the award and smiles at the camera.

FIGURE 7.2 The execution-at-dawn shot features two or more people mentioned in the story, posing, typically lined up in a row, for the camera.

FIGURE 7.3 The grip-and-grin shot, such as this one featuring Richard Woolcott accepting his award at the LA Fashion Awards ceremony in 2005, features people holding awards, ribbons, plaques, and so on, and smiling at the camera.

### Product Shot

The **product shot** is a photo of a fashion item by itself or with other items. This shot does not include people; solely objects and sceneries.

### Action Shot

The **action shot** is a photo of a fashion item in action (i.e., being worn) or something happening in real time. All shots which focus on the fashion items as they look when worn by people fall into this category, including models

FIGURE 7.4 The product shot, as seen in this Adidas release of the limited edition Hellboy sneakers, features the fashion item alone or in a specific setting without any people.

FIGURE 7.5 As can be seen in the artwork for the Summer Camp story in the August 2008 *W* issue, the action shot features fashion items being worn by models.

193

walking the catwalk during a fashion show. Some publications oppose staging action shots and only want the real-time shots when the story is actually happening; other publications encourage staging of shots to get the best photo for the story. Into this category also fall the event shots, such as photos from walk-a-thons, fundraisers, and so on.

### The Video Op

The relatively new category of photo op is the **video opportunity,** where the news story is captured on digital video. This type of opportunity is audio-visual in nature and is tailor-made for news stations to incorporate into their snazzy style reports. If the fashion company is organizing a fundraising fashion show, it can invite the television news media to cover it on video. The footage from the show is then used to create a television news report or a special fashion segment.

## Photo Ops Interesting for the Media

As with the press release, the main concern in organizing a photo op is how to attract the media. In planning the photo op, we must again think like the media and consider the needs and wants of the publication's audience. What photo would be interesting and appealing for the audience? What photo or video would make the audience want to read or watch the story? Whereas the executives of the fashion company may favor the execution at dawn, we must realize that a group of executives in business attire posing and smiling for the camera is quite boring for the average reader. The world of fashion opens a wide door of creative photography for the photojournalist, who is typically bound to strict hard-news guidelines. The photo op should complement the news story and contribute to its appeal. Naturally, the photo op should be relevant to the story—a news story about the company's donation to a nonprofit organization best be accompanied by a grip-and-grin shot of the CEO giving the organization's representatives a large poster of the check with the amount donated large enough to read. However, within that scheme, the public relations department should take advantage of the artistic license that fashion offers and invest the time in creating a plethora of unique and trendy photo opportunities. Instead of the cliché shot of the executives dressed in conservative business suits against a background with the company's logo, how about dressing the executives up with the new collection for the shot? Such creative public relations efforts will be rewarded more easily with the coveted media coverage.

## Arranging for the Photo Op

There are two types of photo op arrangements: the **supplied photo op,** and the **attended photo op.** Each type has its own circumstances and requires different logistical arrangements.

### Supplied Photo Op

Artwork supplied along with the story should first and foremost be owned by the fashion company or under contract for that purpose. The rights to the artwork must be the property of the company or licensed to the company for the purpose of distributing it to the media. If a company employee who is on the company's payroll creates the artwork as part of their job, then generally the rights belongs to the company; however, the local and applicable laws should still be consulted. If a professional photographer or illustrator is hired on a free-lance basis, then a contract or agreement should be signed to establish the use of rights. The legal department or the company's law firm should advise on these matters. Either way, the artwork must be credited to the company or the creator of the artwork when submitted to the media. Additionally, all photos, charts, illustrations, and other artwork should contain a cutline naming the people in the photos or explaining the chart or illustration. A story that is pitched to television stations and online channels can benefit greatly by providing **B-roll** footage. The B-roll gives the media complimentary footage which saves the news team work while enticing them to cover the story in more detail. Not having to shoot the B-roll makes it easier and faster to put together the news package and turn it in; when deadlines are looming and there are only a handful of stories available, the ones with the B-roll will be the top contenders.

### Attended Photo Op

It is vital to properly prepare for the photo op by arranging for a convenient date and time as well as by structuring the photo op for a smooth interaction with the media. Try to schedule photo ops during the regular weekday and normal business hours, i.e., Monday through Friday, 8:30 a.m. to 5:00 p.m. If you already have an interest from a specific publication, find out the best time for the photojournalist and schedule the photo op for that day and time. Plan ahead and rehearse the photo op either on paper or in practice with an employee standing in for the photographer, so everyone involved knows what they have to do. This helps to ensure that when the photo op begins, the process goes smoothly and professionally. If possible ahead of time, it is helpful to hand the photographer a typed sheet with the exact names, titles, and descriptions of the people who will take part in the photo op. It is important to remember that photos or video footage taken by the media is copyrighted and belongs to the publication or television station. Therefore, it is a good idea for the fashion company to assign an employee or hire a freelancer to take additional photos or video footage of the news story independently of the media; these photos and video footage can then be distributed to other publications with the aim of gaining additional coverage.

## Community-Related Strategic Tools

There are a number of key strategic public relations tools that can help a fashion company become more involved in its community, and thus improve its public image in the eyes of its neighbors, customers, vendors, and partners. Participating in community initiatives to help other members of the community can make the company's reputation improve by leaps and bounds. Such involvement creates a more direct link between the company employees and the customers, fosters trust in the company and its brands, and obtains media coverage for both the fashion company and the nonprofit organization that is involved. Meaningful and caring community events, educational initiatives, community improvement projects, fundraising campaigns, and direct sponsorships all play a vital role in developing a positive community image for the fashion company. We will discuss these tools in great detail in Chapter 10.

## Grassroots Strategic Tools

The need for a fashion company to exert direct influence on its public image without having to rely on the media is more pronounced in today's highly competitive business environment. It is increasingly difficult to get the media's attention due to the growing number of fashion companies and designers and the sheer number of news stories sent in to the media daily. The grassroots strategic tools allow the fashion company to reach out to its customer base directly and develop street-level public image enhancement opportunities. Grassroots

195

tools are certainly not limited to a specific number because the main elements of grassroots are authenticity and buzz, and both can't be confined to a restrictive bundle of rules and guidelines. Instead, the public relations director should keep an open mind when approaching grassroots initiative planning to allow creativity and spontaneity to lead to better results. Some of these tools could even be arguably considered as part of sales promotion—in many cases of grassroots initiatives, the separation between public relations and promotions is not distinct. Let's review some of the top grassroots tools that have become instrumental and proven successful again and again.

### Recommend a Friend Program

This program encourages customers to bring a friend or family member to the store and receive a credit or discount applied to their next purchase. Although the incentive is important, it is essentially a nudge to help the customer get over the hump of spreading word of mouth (WOM); if the customer is not genuinely happy with the product he or she will rarely recommend it to friends just for monetary gain. In other words, this public relations tool capitalizes upon the human natural tendency to tell others about one's experience and simply adds the credit or discount as a way to enhance this effect. Offering credit or discounts is more economical for a fashion company as opposed to providing cash rewards or other prizes because the reward here is tied squarely to the condition of other purchases being made first. Thus, the referring customer only gets the reward after the friend has made a purchase and money has been accepted by the company.

### Ambassadors and Fans

The fashion company can enlist the help of loyal customers who avidly shop for its products to spread the word—although caution should be taken not to overformalize such an initiative to a degree that it turns interest off. It is recommended to design the program so it is fun, exciting, and allows these steadfast supporters of the company to help it expand in their own creative ways. This, in fact, could be likened to an informal ambassador circle or fan club for the company and its brands. This program harnesses the enthusiasm of these satisfied customers and utilizes it to spread the positive word about the company.

### Blogs and Internet Word of Mouth (WOM)

Getting the company's news repeated in independent popular blogs can have a tremendous positive effect on the company's public image. Because blogs are often written by consumers and self-appointed reviewers, they can be seen as even more credible than the media. Blog subscribers are also influenced by the blogger's personality as much as by his or her impartiality. Therefore, top informal blogs that draw considerable number of subscribers can and should be approached with the company's latest collection. Exposure in these informal forums can lend the company's brand WOM credibility. Because these informal blogs are independent of the constraints of most mainstream media, it is often easier to obtain coverage. Internet WOM begins with the understanding

## Case Study 7.1  Strategic Public Relations Tools

When Giorgio Armani unveiled his Autumn/Winter 2008–09 underwear collection in August 2008, the release revolved not so much around the collection as it focused on the model featured in the advertising campaign—world-famous soccer player David Beckham. To launch the campaign, the image of the athlete scantily clad in Armani briefs was plastered on a huge billboard in San Francisco and made headlines around the country, including CBS, the *Telegraph*, *New York Magazine*, *Us Weekly*, and others. The press release behind the campaign can be seen in the following figure. Although the format of the release is mostly traditional, it still breaks away from the mundane; note that it is designed to resemble a newspaper edition in order to give the release some flair and flavor. As can be seen, the release contains all of the 11 elements as discussed in the chapter:

1. Company's logo
2. The words "press release"
3. Headline
4. Sub-headline
5. Dateline and release date
6. Lede
7. Copy
8. About paragraph
9. Contact information
10. Photo
11. Cutline

From the start, the racy photo captures attention, supported by strong headline and sub-headline wording that lets us know right away what the story is about—the unveiling of an unusual ad campaign featuring Beckham.

The lede immediately delves into the most important details, creating a strong link to Beckham's celebrity status, specifying which collection will be advertised, and where the billboard will be placed. The release is

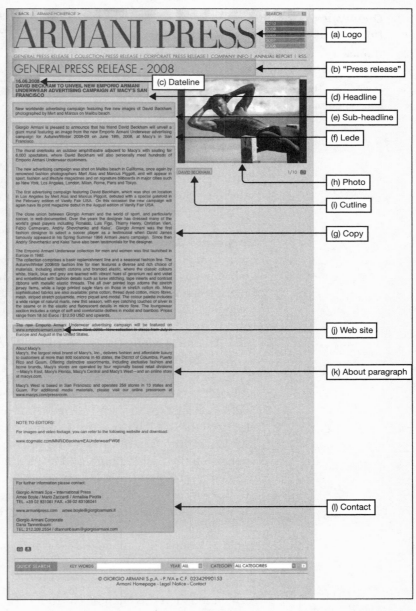

FIGURE CASE STUDY 7.1 Labels: (a) logo, (b) "Press Release," (c) dateline, (d) headline, (e) sub-headline, (f) lede, (g) copy, (h) photo, (i) cutline, (j) Web site, (k), About paragraph, and (l) contact.

197

---

**Case Study 7.1   Strategic Public Relations Tools** *(continued)*

effective not only because of its intriguing design and format, but also because of the content: the strong use of celebrity hype combined with a respected label and a new collection.

### Questions to Consider

1. Do you think the release is effective? Why?

2. If you were Armani's public relations director, what would you change in this release, and why?

3. If you were the editor for a leading fashion consumer magazine, would you:

   a.   Read the release, and why?

   b.   Add it to the editorial agenda, and why?

   c.   Place it in the publication? If so, where and how much space would you allot it?

4. Do you feel the release is too traditional? Too unconventional? Explain.

5. Analyze each of the 11 elements in the release and give your thoughts on whether each element has been properly utilized, and why.

---

that the seemingly invisible visitors to the company's Web site in fact form a virtual public that is accessible through various Internet WOM tools, such as offering visitors free registration for a free online monthly newsletter or providing online coupons.

### Corporate Sponsorship

Supporting the local little league baseball team or the town's scouts troop can go a long way in generating grassroots goodwill for the fashion company. Naturally, a company that sells nationwide will have to sponsor a cause with a wider, national influence. When you look more carefully around your community, you will start to notice just how many sponsorships exist right in your backyard. The local high school football field most likely displays a host of signs announcing the sponsoring companies that helped build or maintain the field. If the company wants to step up to the next step, then the stadium of the local NFL, MLB, or NBA teams typically offers sponsorship opportunities as well. Such sponsorships are solely a monetary contribution and demand nothing else from the fashion company; so, won't such a sponsorship qualify as advertising? Yes and no. There's a slight difference between the company whose logo appears on the flashing billboard inside the stadium, which is clearly an advertisement venue, and the company after which the stadium itself is named. The public views the sponsor in a slightly different light than the advertiser because the sponsor's dollars are obviously helping the community first and advertising the company's name second. This tool is thus a blend of image advertising and public relations with an emphasis on improving the company's public image.

### Innovative Strategic Tools

As mentioned in this chapter's introduction, new and innovative strategic tools keep being introduced into the public relations field as the industry evolves, and companies find unique and unconventional ways to achieve public relations objectives. From donations of clothing products to disadvantaged working families, to organizing fashion shows in the local malls, fashion companies are increasing efforts to utilize innovative venues where goodwill can be generated for the company while setting the company apart from the competition. Such new tools will continue to mark the fashion public relations landscape in the future. The public relations director and staff should keep abreast of these changes in the industry, as well as keep an open mind to try new things rather than rely solely on traditional public relations tools. Only by keeping ahead of the competition within the public relations arena will the fashion company be able to make its mark on its public and achieve its public relations goals.

## Chapter Summary

▷ There are many strategic public relations tools that enable the fashion company to improve its public image.

▷ Whereas traditional strategic tools are tested and proven, new and innovative tools are vital to the evolution of public relations; the fashion company should be aware of new emerging tools to stay ahead of competition.

▷ The press release and photo opportunity are key media-related strategic tools crucial to gaining publicity in the fashion world.

▷ The press release is the common vehicle used to carry news from the fashion company to the fashion media, and on to the consumer.

▷ Although the release serves the fashion company by spreading its news, it also serves the media by alerting them to news, saving the reporter valuable time, and serving as a source for the story.

▷ For best coverage results, all facts and quotes in a press release must be substantiated and attributed; this makes the reporter's job much easier.

▷ The interview is the main tool for obtaining information and quotes for the news story.

▷ The typical press release contains the following formatting elements: the company's logo, the words *Press Release*, a headline, a sub-headline, a dateline and release date, a lede, the copy, or main text, an About paragraph, contact information, photo, and cutline.

▷ Emphasizing the media angle, providing all of the information in an easy-to-read format, and including appropriate quotes and artwork can maximize results for the press release.

▷ The photo opportunity provides artwork to accompany the news story. The types of photo ops are: the mug shot, execution-at-dawn shot, grip-and-grin shot, product shot, action shot, and the video op.

▷ The photo op can be provided by the fashion company, or it can invite the media to send a photographer to cover the news story directly.

▷ The community-related strategic tools, such as partnerships with nonprofit organizations, are important to community involvement and the long-term success of the fashion company.

▶ Grassroots strategic tools, such as blogs and corporate sponsorships, allow the fashion company to reach out to its audience directly and improve its public image independent of media publicity.

## Key Terms

▶ About paragraph

▶ action shot

▶ artwork

▶ attended photo opportunity

▶ attribute

▶ B-roll

▶ copy

▶ cutline

▶ dateline

▶ editorial

▶ editorial agenda

▶ editorial meeting

▶ execution-at-dawn shot

▶ grip-and-grin shot

▶ kill the story

▶ lede

▶ media compatibility

▶ mug shot

▶ news story

▶ newsroom

▶ photo opportunity

▶ positivism

▶ press release

▶ product shot

▶ quote

▶ source

▶ supplied photo opportunity

▶ video opportunity

## Chapter-End Questions and Exercises

1. What are strategic public relations tools, and how do these benefit the fashion company in its public relations efforts?

2. Explain what makes a press release capture media attention?

3. What are the two purposes of the press release, and how does it fulfill them?

4. Is a journalist obliged to call the fashion company to verify comments or facts in a press release, or can he or she assume that it is the official company statement? Explain.

5. What are the 11 main elements in a press release? Explain and give an example for each.

6. What are the six elements that the release's copy should contain? Explain and give an example for each.

7. Why should a release include two quotes, and why should they be different from each other?

8. Select five of the values as cited in PEJ. Explain each.

9. Explain the following:

   a. Objective of the editorial meeting

   b. Editorial agenda

10. What aspects in a press release will kill a story? Explain.

11. Is research needed to write a press release? Why? What are the possible consequences of writing a release without research verification?

12. Why does the writer of a release need to support and attribute facts and comments in press releases?

13. Compare and contrast the four facets of researching a press release.

14. What is a photo op and what is its importance?

15. Compare and contrast the six types of photo ops. Go through newspapers, magazines and Web sites, and clip a fashion-related example for each type (for the video op, you may include a still shot of it and a link to where it can be viewed).

16. What is the supplied photo op, what is the attended photo op, and how do they differ? Give an example of an instance when each would be used.

17. What is the main tool for obtaining information and quotes for the news story?

18. Who are the people that should be interviewed for a particular press release? Explain the concepts of media compatibility and positivism and how these factors could affect the selection of interviewees.

19. Locate a company that uses the recommend a friend tool, and explain how it is utilized to improve public image.

20. What is the ambassador/fan tool, and how can a fashion company use it to enhance public opinion about its brands?

21. Locate a fashion blog online and:

   a. Research what is the blog about

   b. Determine who the person is behind the blog and what his or her qualifications are

   c. Determine if it promote certain fashion values

22. Find an example of a corporate sponsorship by a fashion company. How do you think does it help the company's image in the community?

23. Locate an established fashion company that maintains a press center online. Select one of its press releases and analyze whether the release answers all of these questions. Then, for each of the facts and quotes, write down what is the fact/quote, whether it was attributed or researched, and whether you think it will make it easier or more difficult for the reporter to use the release.

    a. What is the story about and what are its details?

    b. Which organizations are involved in the story and what are their backgrounds?

    c. Which people are involved in the story and what are their backgrounds?

    d. What statistics, information, or other data are needed to support the story?

24. Create a fictitious scenario whereby you are the public relations director developing a press release for a fashion company of your choice about a specific news story.

    a. Who in the company would you interview and why?

    b. What questions would you ask each?

25. Pair up with another student and run through a simulated scenario where you are the public relations director and your partner is an executive within the fashion company. You are to interview him or her about a new collection or other news story.

    a. Prepare questions ahead of the interview applicable to the news story.

    b. Conduct the interview while keeping notes of the answers for your records.

    c. Pick the best quote to include in the story, write it verbatim or paraphrase it, and then give it to the other student for approval.

    d. After changes are made (if needed), finalize the quote and explain why you picked that one.

    e. Summarize the interaction and hand it in along with your interview notes.

    f. Switch roles and repeat the exercise so you both interview and get interviewed.

26. Choose a well-known fashion company and write a fictitious press release for an event or news story for that company. Make sure to include all of the eleven formatting items discussed in this chapter.

# Obtaining and Handling
# Media Coverage

## EIGHT

## Chapter Snapshot

To obtain positive media coverage, it is important to know how to properly submit the story
to the media and how to conduct conversations
and correspondence with the media in order to
receive the most positive coverage possible; otherwise, the
story may never be inked, or worse—may be inked with negative exposure. Often, simply emailing the press release is not
enough—in today's fast paced world, pitching the release is an
involved process that requires personal contact and follow-up
in order to capture the media's attention. In this chapter, we
will discuss the various ways to pitch the story, follow up on
the pitch, and obtain media coverage. Also, after the media
has agreed to cover the story, it is essential to prepare for the
story and the reporter's interviews. Such preparations will set
the foundation for a smooth interaction with the media and
for a better story; mishandling the media's coverage of the
story, on the other hand, can bring about disastrous results.
As we will see in this chapter, the proper pitching of the news
story and the correct handling of media inquiries are vital
parts of fashion public relations, which can improve both the
quality and scope of media coverage.

## Objectives

▸ Understand the concept of the pitch and how to pitch a news story in a professional manner.

▸ Explore the segments and elements of the verbal and written pitch.

▸ Understand the concept of the objection and how to use it to secure a coverage commitment.

▸ Cover the basics of the pitch follow-up.

▸ Understand the media inquiry and know how to respond to it properly.

▸ Discuss the ways to turn media interest or inquiry into coverage.

▸ Grasp the tasks involved in wrapping up the news story after coverage.

Pitching a news story can appear to be a highly elusive skill of fashion public relations. It seems that some public relations directors and firms can work magic and get stories covered left and right, whereas others receive virtually no coverage. Beyond how newsworthy and exciting the story is and how well the release is written, if the pitching is done incorrectly, the story is likely to go unnoticed; if the story does get picked up but the fashion company commits serious errors while dealing with the media as they cover the story, the fashion company could be featured in the story in a negative light. In such a case, all of our efforts made so far to identify our audiences, create a campaign, plan its implementation, define its parameters, and develop the news story, press release and photo op would have been in vain. Therefore, it is important to fully explore and understand the processes of pitching the story and handling media coverage.

## The Pitch

The word **pitch** has a variety of meanings. In baseball, it means throwing the ball at the batter to strike him or her out; in music, it refers to the different levels of sound (pitch of a sound); and in conversation it can refer to a low- or high-pitched voice. In the sales field, it refers to the verbal presentation or talking points that a salesman uses in a sales meeting. Fashion public relations borrows that meaning from sales and applies it to the world of media relations. In fashion public relations, the *pitch* means the talking points that are voiced or written to the media in order to solicit publicity. It can be in the form of a pitch letter or email that includes all the information needed to encourage the reporter to publish the material, or a casual phone conversation in which the topic of the story—among other topics—is discussed with the reporter.

Unfortunately, many people may look at the word *pitch* as an expression used by a fast-talking salesperson trying to push a sale. However, this false impression is far from the truth, and pitching as we use the term in public relations is truly an act of professional selling. It basically refers to the professional sales presentation of the news story to the media. We stress that selling is a professional endeavor and not "a dirty word" (Sherman & Perlman, 2006). We define **sales** as, "An exchange of goods and services designed to deliver a

---

**Box 8.1  Real World Principle: Pitching the News Story**

Pitching a news story is essentially a sales presentation of the news story, where the public relations director aims to sell the reporter on covering the story by highlighting the story's benefits to the readers.

---

mutual benefit for both buyer and seller, resulting in a continual and positive relationship." The key here is that the sale delivers a benefit both to the buyer and the seller. For a salesperson to succeed, he or she has to sell a product or service that is needed by the customer; selling the right product or service is ethical whereas selling a product or service that is wrong for the customer constitutes a breach of the salesperson-customer relationship and eventually leads to trouble. Thus we see that salespeople who are professionals and sell properly provide a service to their customers and succeed in the long run; fast-talking salespeople who care only about making a commission fail in the long run. With this in mind, we can extend the definition of sales to pitching a news story, where the public relations director is actually looking to sell the reporter on the content of the story and to indicate how it will be beneficial to both the media and its audience.

While we compare pitching to professional selling, it is important to understand that pitching a release is significantly different than selling products or services. When we sell a high-end suit, for example, we must consult the **needs** of the consumer who is buying the suit. The concept of the buyer's needs is extremely important in sales because the product or service being sold must fill

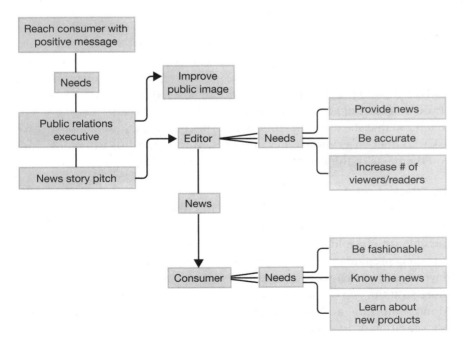

FIGURE 8.1 The pitch works as long as the news story benefits all parties—the fashion company, the media outlet, and the audience—and these benefits are clearly communicated to the editor.

those needs if the sale were to be successful. The fashion media's audience has a need to keep up-to-date on the latest trends and style and the fashion media in turn has a need to be at the forefront of reporting on such trends and style. The news story and its release must fill these needs to a degree if the story is to be picked up.

An example of a pitch to a reporter can start with something like, "Hi Miss Whitney, we have just received the exclusive endorsement from the Olympic committee authorizing the American swim team to model our latest swimwear collection at the New York Fashion Week. The merchandise will be featured in all XYZ Department stores, and 20 percent of the gross sales will be donated to support the future American Olympic swimming teams. Team members will be available for interviews and photo op." Such an opening gives the reporter the synopsis of the news story right away in an exciting way. It then goes on to add important details about the percentage of proceeds that will support the Olympic teams and about the team members' availability for interviews and photos—details that could encourage the reporter to cover the story. It also showcases the newsworthy features of the story right in the first sentence, highlighting the facts that the collection is new, that the company just received the exclusive permission for the Olympic Swim Team to model the new collection, and that it will be modeled at New York Fashion Week—a pivotal show that everyone both on consumer and trade levels is interested in.

## Whom to Pitch

Knowing whom to call is basic to anyone in the public relations industry. Just as you have to know the facts and figures of the story you are pitching, you must know if your story is the kind that will resonate with the specific journalist or publication you are calling to pitch. We are constantly mentioning the importance of knowing who to call, when to call, and when not call as the most basic of all preparations in performing the pitch. In the real world it may be next to impossible to contact some of the journalists by phone. If the story is **breaking news** and needs immediate attention, contacting the newsroom or news desk and asking who to contact for the story can be a way of making a viable contact. If you do get a hold of a reporter and start to pitch the story but she interrupts to tell you that she does not cover these types of stories, your response can be to ask who does cover these types of stories. Most journalists will oblige and give you the name of the person to contact, especially if the story is of merit.

## The Verbal Pitch

The verbal pitch is typically done over the phone, but occasionally it can be done in person. It is good practice to try and schedule the pitch for the best possible time. Avoid calling first thing in the morning when the editors and reporters prepare for the day. Avoid also calling close to the end of the business day; remember that reporters are almost always working on some deadline, and more so at the end of the day when they are busy wrapping up their story. Early Monday morning and late Friday afternoon are also not good times, unless it is a sensational time-sensitive story. The opening remarks of the verbal pitch

## Box 8.2   Real World Profile: The New York Fashion Week

Set against the backdrop of midtown Manhattan, the historic Bryant Park Tents host one of the most prominent fashion events in the world: the semi-annual New York Fashion Week. Over the course of eight days, the event hosts more than 100,000 industry insiders, professionals, and guests attending runway shows, conducting interviews, reviewing and buying collections, and re-affirming the importance and economic impact of the city's prestigious fashion industry. The 2009 Fashion Week featured a long list of world-famous labels and designers, including Michael Angel, Perry Ellis, Duckie Brown, Rubin Singer, Nicole Miller, Erin Fetherston, Venexiana, Lacoste, Charlotte Ronson, Tony Maticevski, Abaeté, Andy & Debb, Rosa Chá, Verrier, Alexandre Herchcovitch, Rock & Republic, Macqua, Lela Rose, DKNY, Tracy Reese, Terexov, Hervé Léger by Max Azria, Diane Von Furstenberg, Y-3, Akiko Ogawa, Tibi, Miss Sixty, Thuy Diep, Twinkle by Wenlan, Carolina Herrera, Peter Som, Jill Stuart, Sergio Davila, Diesel Black Gold, Luca Luca, Yeohlee, Tony Cohen, Ports 1961, Gottex, Cynthia Steffe, Badgley Mischka, Monique Lhuillier, Iódice, Betsey Johnson, Dennis Basso, Joanna Mastroianni, MAX AZRIA, Vivienne Tam, Brian Reyes, Michael Kors, Nanette Lepore, Richard Chai, 3.1 Phillip Lim, Carlos Miele, Pamella Roland, Milly by Michelle Smith, Anna Sui, Mara Hoffman, Malan Breton, Vera Wang, Naeem Khan, Rebecca Taylor, Reem Acra, Calvin Klein, Leifsdottir, Chris Han, Custo Barcelona, Zac Posen, Aurelio Costarella, Project Runway, Ralph Lauren, Tadashi Shoji, Sabyasachi, Carmen Marc Valvo, Donna Karan Collection, and OmniaLuo by Zheng Luo (Mercedes-Benz Fashion Week, 2008).

The event's history and importance is illustrated in the following news article:

### How the Runway Took Off: A Brief History of the Fashion Show

**Amanda Fortini**

Fashion scholars have penned histories of the high heel, the corset, and the little black dress, but no one has yet written a definitive history of the fashion show. The omission is curious: The fashion show is not only the promotional linchpin of a multibillion-dollar industry, it was also central to the development of the American department store—and thus to the rise of American consumer culture. The problem may be that the fashion show, like any performative enterprise, is by nature ephemeral. Or perhaps it's that the fashion crowd, always in pursuit of the next thing, lacks the archival impulse: Why hash over yesterday's clothes? Whatever the reason, as Valerie Steele, chief curator and director of the Museum at the Fashion Institute of Technology, told me: "The topic of fashion shows remains to find its historian."

It is, however, possible to stitch together the tale of New York's semiannual Fashion Week, which commenced once again last Friday in the tents at Manhattan's Bryant Park. Fashion Week in its earliest incarnation was, in some sense, a bid to overthrow the sartorial tyranny of the French. According to Steele, the event got its start in 1943, when a well-known fashion publicist named Eleanor Lambert organized something called Press Week. Lambert was a canny PR maven who recognized that it was a propitious moment for American fashion. Before World War II, American designers were thought to be reliant on French couture for inspiration. When the Germans occupied France in 1940, one of the ensuing calamities was that buyers, editors, and designers were unable to travel to Paris to see the few remaining shows, and the fashion world fretted—would American fashion founder without the influence of French couture?

With Press Week, Lambert hoped to give editors a chance to see—and more important, write about—the work of American designers, who, freed up to create without the anxiety of French influence, were quietly making innovative strides with indigenous materials and techniques, writes Caroline Rennolds Milbank in *New York Fashion: The Evolution of American Style*. Ruth Finley, publisher of the *Fashion Calendar* (a pink-and-red schedule that the industry finds indispensable) was present at those early shows. As she tells it, Press Week was held alternately at the Pierre and Plaza Hotels. Journalists and editors stayed on-site, which meant there was none of the modern dashing between tents and taxiing around. (Buyers, a key constituent at today's shows, were in those days forced to visit the designers' showrooms for a look, Finley says.)

207

**Box 8.2    Real World Profile: The New York Fashion Week** (continued)

Lambert's plan worked. As Milbank writes, magazines like *Vogue* and *Harper's Bazaar,* whose editors were besotted with French fashion, began to feature more work by American designers and, most crucially, to credit them by name. (Many supposedly "unknown" American designers had been working for years, but their clothing usually bore the label of the retailer for which they created.) American styles were praised as modern, streamlined, and flattering, and American ready-to-wear designers were finally garnering the respect previously reserved for European couturiers. Press Week, which continued through the late '50s, eventually featured work by designers like Bill Blass, Oscar de la Renta, Mollie Parnis, and Pauline Trigere.

Long before Lambert entered the picture, however, there were fashion shows in America. William Leach writes in *Land of Desire,* his excellent study of the rise of capitalism, that in 1903, a New York City specialty store called Ehrich Brothers put on what was likely this country's first fashion show, in an effort to lure middle-class female customers into the store. By 1910, many big department stores, including Wanamaker's in Philadelphia and New York, were holding shows of their own. (American retailers had likely witnessed what were called "fashion parades" in Paris couture salons and decided to import the idea.) The events were an effective way to promote merchandise, and they improved a store's status in the eyes of its clientele: Showing couture gowns bought in Paris, or, more frequently, the store's own copies or adaptations of these garments was evidence of connoisseurship and good taste. The irony, of course, was that the stores emphasized the exclusivity of French couture, even as they made it—or some approximation thereof—available to a mass-market audience.

By the 1920s, the fashion show had gone mainstream. Retailers throughout the country staged shows, often in a store's restaurant during lunch or teatime. These early shows were often more theatrical than those of today. They were frequently organized around themes—there were Parisian, Persian, Chinese, Russian, and Mexican shows, Leach notes—and often presented with narrative commentary.

**FIGURE BOX 8.2** Over the course of eight days the event hosts more than 100,000 industry insiders, professionals, and guests attending runway shows, conducting interviews, reviewing and buying collections, and reaffirming the importance and economic impact of the city's prestigious fashion industry.

Wanamaker's 1908 show, Leach writes, was a tableau vivant styled to resemble the court of Napoleon and Josephine, and the models were escorted by a child done up as one of Napoleon's pages.

The department-store shows were wildly popular, drawing crowds in the thousands. According to Leach, the throngs were so disruptive to city life that merchants in New York City and elsewhere were eventually required to obtain a license for shows using live models. In New York, police threatened to put an end to the shows altogether. Indeed, the phenomenon became so widespread that in 1950 Fairchild published a book titled *How To Give a Fashion Show,* which begins with an appeal to the executive assistant: "Have you ever been called into the boss's office at the end of a hectic day to be greeted with, 'Miss Gordon, I've been going over the figures of the ready-to-wear division today, and I've decided that what we need to pep them up is a fashion show. I'd like you to go to work on one immediately'?" And in 1954, Edna Woodman Chase—former editor of *Vogue* and organizer of the 1914 Fashion Fete, an event to benefit the war-relief effort that is often (apocryphally) called the first fashion show—complained in her memoir about the ubiquity of the phenomenon: "Now that fashion shows have become a way of life . . . a lady is hard put to it to lunch, or sip a cocktail, in any smart hotel or store front from New York to Dallas to San Francisco without having lissome young things . . . swaying down a runway six inches above her nose."

**Box 8.2   Real World Profile: The New York Fashion Week** *(continued)*

When, then, did the shows make their way to Bryant Park? During the '70s and '80s, American designers began to stage their own shows in lofts, clubs, and restaurants. According to Fern Mallis, vice president of IMG, the company that houses 7th on Sixth—the organization that produces New York's Olympus Fashion Week, as well as several other shows—the impetus for the event we are familiar with today was literally an accident. It was 1990 and Mallis, then executive director of the Council of Fashion Designers of America, was attending a Michael Kors show in a loft space in downtown Manhattan. When the bass started thumping, a piece of plaster came loose from the ceiling and fell onto the models as they went down the runway. As Mallis remembers it, the girls strutted on, but plaster also landed in the laps of writers Suzy Menkes and Carrie Donovan, while the rest of the crowd nervously searched for fire escapes. During another show in the early '90s, this one in a Soho loft space that was "packed to the rafters," a generator blew, leaving the crowd of editors and buyers in the dark. The audience waited for 30 minutes, holding cigarette lighters aloft as though swaying through a power ballad, until the generators were restored. It was then, Mallis says, that the fashion set said enough with small, unsafe spaces. "The general sentiment was, 'We love fashion but we don't want to die for it.'"

As head of the CFDA, Mallis took up the cause and sought out a venue where all the shows could be held in a single space. Designers, she says, were reluctant to sign on; they worried that showing in a group setting would hamper their creativity. But they also realized it would allow their work greater visibility. After an experimental first run at the Macklow (now the Millennium) Hotel on 44th Street, the concept took off. Mallis then worked out a plan with Bryant Park to put up tents in the East and West Plazas. A year later, the Spring 1994 collections were sent down the runway, and Fashion Week as we know it began. The CFDA also created 7th on Sixth, a separate company with its own board, and this organization formalized a schedule, drew up a press list (which is harder to infiltrate than the Vanity Fair Oscar party), and sold sponsorship to various companies. Finally, Mallis says, the shows were "organized, centralized, modernized." (Of course, as anyone who has braved the suffocating crush at Bryant Park knows, "hectic, chaotic, and frantic" seem more appropriate designations.)

Fashion Week—like Press Week before it—helped American designers reach a more international audience, as it allowed editors, writers, and buyers from abroad to see the country's best work at a single time, in a single place. But even though it can feel these days like it's always Fashion Week, the average American woman is now more removed from the fashion show than ever. Of course, department stores still host shows on occasion, but they no longer draw throngs—most of us can now safely lunch without lissome models undulating past us (if we take lunch at all). Now, the fashion show belongs to Manhattan the way the movies belong to Hollywood; the spectacle exists elsewhere, apart from our everyday lives.

*Thanks to Ruth Finley, Valerie Steele, Caroline Evans, and Fern Mallis. (Slate, 2006)*

should be timed initially to about 30 to 45 seconds. So planning what you are about to say in this limited time frame will dictate the outcome of the pitch. The pitch can make or break the story. Proper planning of the pitch is essential; however, few people actually spend sufficient time in planning the pitch. The verbal pitch is the bell ringer when it is constructed and organized for the specific media person. The number one requirement in planning the pitch is to have complete knowledge of the story including all the facts and figures before proceeding with the pitch. Before making the pitch it is important to develop a checklist of "what if" questions that may be asked by the reporter. For example, what if they ask a question about the last financial statement the client sent to its stockholders. The public relations director must be involved in the day-to-day happenings of the fashion company, both in kicking off a new collection as well as the financial situation. In pitching the media we must be prepared for questions that concern areas of the business other than fashion releases or executive changes. We must know the inner workings of the organization or the pitch to be successful.

Let's say the fashion company you represent is a public company that is having financial difficulties. You can bet your bottom dollar that when you pitch the media on the new collection that they will question you about the financials. Being prepared can be your best friend so you must be able to think like the media, by putting yourself in their shoes and able to anticipate what questions they will ask. Be empathetic and this will help you communicate with the "tough press" and answer tough questions. Knowing the facts and figures of the profit and loss statement will definitely make a positive impression on the journalist when the questions are asked about the financials. Knowing how to communicate this information is as important as knowing about the fashion details in the next collection. The ability to answer the reporter's questions satisfactorily is a major area that one must be in control of when making a pitch. The public relations director must anticipate questions and objections that will arise during the pitch.

## The Written Pitch

When introducing ourselves to the media so we can present the pitch or follow up on a pitch, our best friend can be email (and, more rare these days, letter or fax). Although many reporters receive dozens and even hundreds of emails a day, it is still a highly effective way to communicate. Attracting attention and getting people to read the email is becoming increasingly more difficult; the way the email itself is structured and written can be instrumental in reaching the person. The subject line is the key. It must attract the reader, create interest, and must not contain false information. To attract attention it must be short, sweet, and deliverable. It should tell the reporter whether the email contains a new release or a follow-up for a release that has already been sent before. It should also contain the topic of the news story in no more than six to eight words. For example, the following is an acceptable wording: "Subject: Press release: Fashion First Charity Show—Follow-up." This tells the reporter in one glance what to expect from the email and, therefore, does not waste the reporter's time. The body of the email should introduce the news story in two to three sentences, for example:

"Hi _____, or Dear _____,

Our company has just released its plan to host Fashion First, a charity fashion show to benefit the local humane society chapter. The show will feature the local celebrity model who was on a *Project Runway* episode.

She will be modeling our latest collection of women's wear. Below is the press release and the full details.

Respectfully,

First and Last Name

Company name

Phone number

Email address Web site

*Cut and Paste the press release."

Due to the large number of Internet viruses, many emails containing attachments are automatically deleted. Cutting and pasting the release on to the main body of the email can be a more effective way of getting the information delivered to and read by the recipient. This is particularly effective when the public relations person does not have a relationship with the reporter; if the reporter knows the public relations person, sending the follow-up as an attachment may not be a problem.

## Questions and Objections

Journalists are not running a popularity contest—they are only concerned with getting an accurate story that is meaningful to their audience. Their names are always on the line when they do a story; therefore, they may appear negative, suspicious, and will constantly challenge some of the statements. What they are really doing is looking to poke holes during your pitch to make certain that the information is accurate and will be of interest to their audience. During the pitch one should look for the journalist's reaction: when they voice questions or **objections,** these normally indicate that they need more information to decide if the story is newsworthy.

Questions or objections are quite different than a final negative response; they are questions or comments that the public relations director can utilize to focus the pitch on what concerns the reporter. But if the reporter says boldly that he or she is not interested in the story, or that the publication does not cover this type of stories—i.e., a final negative response—this is a clear indication of the reporter's polite desire to end the pitch. Carrying on with more information about the news story will in most cases irritate the reporter and could possibly even cause the reporter never to take the company's calls again. Instead, in this scenario the public relations director should politely thank the reporter for their time and end by saying that she will call the reporter at a future time when another more appropriate story is available. A polite goodbye is always in order.

The first step in answering questions and objections properly is to refrain from taking them personally or being defensive. Armed with the understanding that objections actually move the pitch toward a commitment of coverage, the public relations person accepts the fact that objections are an integral part of pitching, and regard answering them as one of the job's challenges. During the pitch, objections should be welcomed. Again, remember that the objection is one way that a reporter asks for more information. This phase of the pitch allows the public relations director to provide answers that can solidify the relationship with the reporter and increase trust.

The second step is to provide an honest and positive answer to the questions or objections. This is where the aforementioned familiarity with the company's current business affairs comes in handy. In all instances the public relations director should refrain from arguing with the editor and remain open to objections and other forms of editor participation. Understanding the editor's objections and offering truthful responses can be the best pitching tool a public relations person has at his or her disposal. Let's assume you are presenting a release about a new collection and the editor asks, "Why are the prices so high?" The best response is not to fight the editor about his or her question, but to answer it honestly and emphasize the positive aspects of the story. "Yes, the prices may seem too high at first, but not if you take into consideration the fact that we are the first to come out with this style concept. We have made substantial investment into research and manufacturing in order to implement the unique features of the collection, like the hand-made buttons and zippers. According to the research, consumers were excited about these features and did not consider the prices out of range for the quality they are receiving." Such a reply addresses the editor's concerns that if the prices are too high, then covering the collection might upset some of the readers who would feel that the publication is promoting an overpriced line. By emphasizing the unique design and hand-made production of the extra features, the public relations director can effectively justify the costs and show the editor that the collection is not as pricy as it seemed at first, and this information may actually be included in the story to explain that reasoning to the public. Here we can see again the importance of being truthful while answering the media's questions and objections; misrepresenting the information about the extra features—e.g., saying they are hand-made when they are not—will likely be revealed by the reporter when she checks the quality of the new collection first-hand and realizes it is mass made. Then the printed story will most likely be an exposé focusing on the company's exorbitant prices and lies about the buttons being hand made—a public relations fiasco that is sure to cripple the launch of the new collection. The public relations director must resist all temptations to sugarcoat or manipulate the truth. Only answering questions honestly will maintain the company's reputation and credibility and that of its products. Still, it is important to keep a positive attitude while doing so. As mentioned, emphasizing the positive aspects of the news story is a must when answering questions in order to obtain the best possible coverage.

The successful public relations director looks for and recognizes certain negative reactions by reporters and learns how to effectively handle these. There are some standard objections that can be expected. For example, a reporter may indicate that he needs more information about your company. In this case of a very routine journalistic question, the director should already be prepared and have at hand a statement about the company, its history, and its business philosophy. Anticipating objections and answering them correctly starts the public relations director on the road to a successful pitch. Certain objections are frequently voiced at most pitches. Knowing this, a public relations director should gather the information to answer these common questions even before calling the reporter. This will counteract a situation where the public relations director would have to conduct more research and get back to the reporter with the information.

When the reporter's reply to the pitch is a simple "No," it's time to fish for more information. A simple approach can be simply to ask the question calmly and without confrontation, "May I ask why?" In many instances the reporter winds up explaining the objection at length and letting you in on their thinking process, which will help you refine the presentation and address the issues with which the reporter is most concerned. If the reporter feels the news story is too commercial, for example, then the public relations director can re-evaluate the release and perhaps present it differently or adjust the way the story is being implemented.

## Working with—Not against—the Media

The unsuccessful public relations director approaches the story pitch as a battle to be won at any cost. The editor is viewed as the opponent; questions and criticisms are overruled; an attempt is made to push and bully the editor into covering the story regardless of the contentious issues. This attitude may at times result in coverage, but over the long run it is sure to induce hostility, mistrust, and destruction of a harmonious working relationship. The key to successful pitching is **empathy**—that rare quality that enables the public relations director to understand the needs and behavior patterns of the editor, and deal with those realistically. Adapting to the moods of the editor or reporter is essential; in fact, in some instances and especially close to deadline, it may be necessary to forestall the pitch and wait for a more opportune moment. There is no way to prejudge his or her state of mind when first calling an editor or a reporter—he or she could be emotionally overwrought by personal or business problems. There is no point in fighting or resisting the agitated editor; instead, learn to listen before even attempting to pitch. It is much more important to listen than to simply talk during the pitch; give the editor or reporter a chance to ask questions and get involved, which will guide the pitch in the right direction.

## Getting a Coverage Commitment

After the story has been discussed and all the possible information is in front of the reporter, the next and most important area is to determine if the reporter is interested in doing the story. If you determine that in this activity you have answered their objections and they show an interest, in many cases the story has a chance and it is time to ask for commitment of coverage. This simple act of asking for a commitment, though, is sometimes the most difficult thing for the public relations person. But, after you have received a positive response, it is proper to say, "I can arrange for the interviews and photo op at

214

---

**Box 8.3   Real World Principle: The Media Does
Not Owe the Fashion Company Coverage**

The story could be the best in the world but if the editor does not like it, the story will not run. The public relations director must keep in mind that the editor's decision is influenced by many factors, most of which have nothing to do with the fashion company or its story. Breaking news, deadlines, space issues, pressure from the publisher to run certain stories, and demands from reporters to adjust the editorial schedule, are all considerations in the editor's coverage decision process.

Therefore, the public relations director should never become irritated or upset with the editor or reporter for not covering the story; besides being unprofessional, such a reaction can cause more harm in the long-term relationship between the fashion company and the media than the story is worth. Patience and empathy are important characteristics in the pitching process that will be remembered by the editor and will give you more coverage in the long run.

---

your convenience, and would Tuesday or Wednesday be more convenient for you," or you can say, "Would you prefer to do the interview in person or over the phone?" and then look to schedule the day.

### The Press Kit

The press kit is an essential tool for pitching. The press kit is a folder with several inserts that provide a general overview on the fashion company. It can be sent to the media to accompany a press release or it can be submitted alone as a means of introducing the company to the media or handling media interests. It provides needed information to the media and will give the story that extra dimension that will aid the journalist in the pursuit of information. The press kit typically contains:

- A press kit folder, preferably a standard 9-inch by 12-inch presentation folder with two inside flap pockets to hold the documents inside. At the very least, the folder should display the company's logo on a sticky label placed at the front of the folder. For a more professional look, the folder can be custom printed with the company's logo and the words "Press Kit" on the front, and the company's address and contact information on the back. Although such a printing job is typically expensive, it creates a more unique look that could better attract the media's attention.

- The press release and information in the right-side inside flap, if the press kit is sent out as part of a news release package that the company is pitching. The press release should be at the top of the stack, and under it should be supporting documents, research citations, attachments, photos and/or B-roll, as well as product information if applicable. Box 8.4 discusses how to create a B-roll fit for a press kit.

- Background information about the company. This should be included in the left-side inside flap pocket. At the top of this stack should be a background summary sheet which provides a general description of the company. This could include the company's legal name, the type of fashion business it specializes in, the address and contact of its headquarters, and whether it is a private or public company. If it's a public company, include its ticker name and which financial market it's traded on, how many employees are on staff, and so on.

▶ The fashion company's history and business philosophy, including when it was founded and by whom, important events in the company's evolution such as the introductions of new products, the release of special designs or collections, hiring of prominent designers, and mergers and acquisitions.

▶ Executive biographies for the top executives, typically the chief executive officer, the chief financial officer, the chief operating officer, and the director of design. Biographies should be short and summarized, highlighting the executive's education, professional experience, and participation in trade events and charitable activities. Each biography should be no longer than two paragraphs and include a mug shot of the person featured.

▶ A summary of the company's current product lines. This could be a typed document or a printed brochure if one already exists.

▶ The company's media clips, showcasing the most prominent and positive media coverage the company has had in the recent past. These clips should be copies of the original, and their formats are described in more detail in Chapter 9.

## Pitch Follow-Up

Merely calling with a pitch or sending a pitch letter and hoping for coverage is a job half-done. Today, with so many fashion companies vying for the media's attention, such a simplistic approach cannot be reliable. Follow-up procedures must be planned beforehand. The successes of most stories that are published or aired have one thing in common—a complete story, with back-up information, notable quotes, and accurate citations. However, such stories must be backed with proper pitching and thorough follow-up. Merely doing the pitch and then sending the release is just the start of the process of getting your story published or aired. There should be a set routine in place to find out if the release was received; it should also be part of the procedure to find out if there are any questions or if more information is needed. Public relations personnel should not be afraid to show an interest in the story by following up on the initial information sent to the media. A simple statement of asking the reporter to review the information may be just the thing that is needed. The decision to either call or send an email depends upon whom we are dealing with and the status of the relationship between the interested parties. But, if you don't ask or show an interest, the story may never make the news!

Therefore, the public relations director needs to follow up after the pitch to find out whether it was indeed received (in the case of a written pitch), what the reporter thought of the story, and if the reporter has any questions. Without this added task, the story may simply get lost in the shuffle or be ignored due to lack of information, no matter how good the story is. Keep in mind that the average fashion editor or reporter receives dozens of releases each day.

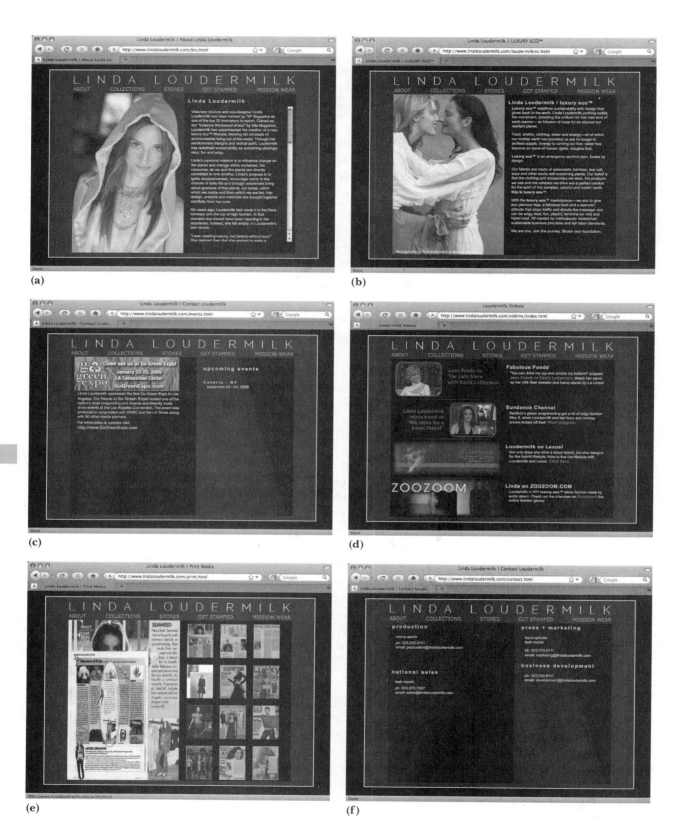

**FIGURE 8.2** Linda Loudermilk's Web site uses its About page to direct to the designer's press kit. From the About page, you can click to find out about (a) the designer, (b) her company, (c) her upcoming events, (d) her video media, (e) her press media, and (f) her contact information.

## Box 8.4 Creating B-Roll for the Press Kit

If the fashion company wants to get television and Internet coverage, it should invest in producing a B-roll. According to Business World News "90 percent of TV newsrooms now rely on **video news releases (VNR)** and B-roll provided by outside sources as a regular part of their newscasts." The B-roll is the television and the Internet's version of the press release. It provides the media with a scenario for a **video news story (VNS).** It also ensures that the message is delivered to the audience as planned. The shoot and voiceover makes the B-roll a vibrant public relations tool that helps the media save considerable time and money. The average time for a B-roll news item is usually about two minutes according to Garrett Appleton. A fashion photographer and video editor, Appleton received a BA in communications and photography from Lynn University, Boca Raton, Florida, where he graduated Magna Cum Laude as a member of the National Scholar Honors Society. He is the CEO of Garrett Appleton Production, Inc., based in Boca Raton (Garrett Appleton Production, Inc., 2009). Appleton says, "We can produce a two minute B-roll, fully scripted and edited, including the voiceover and a finished DVD for distribution to the media from $1,500.00 to $ 2,000.00. The variance in the price will depend on the location, time, and the amount of personnel needed for the shooting and completion of the B-roll."

The two minute B-roll is often the additional ammunition needed to get the story on the air. Sending the television media a visual story that contains interviews, headings, and a storyline to the **producer** will help move your story toward coverage. The B-roll will also help the **anchor** and reporter to set the story. Television stations welcome and encourage B-rolls, especially due to the increased costs in the production of television news. Anything that can reduce the costs of producing a news report will be looked upon as a plus. Any release that provides complete and accurate information, written and documented in a format that can be easily used by the media will stand a good chance to receive a positive reaction; however, in the television sector, that might not be enough to get the story accepted. The producer must evaluate the length of time the crew will be out shooting, how many locations it will have to visit, how far it must travel to the location, and so on, to determine if covering the story is worth it. When a producer receives a well-edited B-roll, it makes it much easier for him or her to give it the green light.

FIGURE BOX 8.4 Garrett Appleton, CEO of Garrett Appleton Production, Inc.

In addition, why not send a B-roll to the print media? Most newspapers have their own Web sites that feature video news. Here again, public relations companies are filling a need in packaging a news story.

The following is an example of a proposal for a three- to five-minute VNR including a two-minute B-Roll.

### TABLE BOX 8.4 One Location/VNR Shoot*

| Budget Item | Details | Cost |
| --- | --- | --- |
| Full day videotaping (up to 8 hours) | | $2,000 |
| Producer | | |
| Enhanced lighting gear | | |
| Videographer/digital broadcast quality camera | | |
| Raw video stock | | |
| Audio | | |
| Jib (large arm for camera for sweeping/high shots) | | $1,250 |
| Camera operator | | |
| Assistant | | |
| Editing $150/hour *estimated 10 hours | | $1,500 |
| Copy-right free music | | |
| Voice over | | |
| Graphics | | |
| Script Writing | Included in price | |
| Individual DVD | | $5.00 per each add'l copy |

*Please note this proposal is based on the times listed above. However, if there is a request for additional detailed, layered graphics, or special effects, there will be an additional charge for editing time.

## Box 8.5   Video News Release: Convenience or Influence?

For each of the facts and quotes, write down what is the fact/quote, whether it was attributed or researched, and whether you think it will make it easier or more difficult for the reporter to use the release. The following *Washington Times* article tackles the delicate issue of the thin line between providing VNRs for the media's convenience and providing them to influence the media's report. What are your thoughts?

### TV News Colored by Dose of PR, by Chris Baker

Chances are most TV viewers don't realize some of the news stories they see are produced not by journalists, but by public relations agents who work for big businesses and the government.

TV stations sometimes air video news releases (VNRs), prepackaged stories that look like real news reports, but are really designed to promote a corporate or government agenda.

In other cases, TV reporters incorporate video footage, or B-roll, from outside sources into their stories. Reports about the space shuttle, for example, sometimes include NASA-produced footage of the vessel blasting into orbit.

The apparent lack of disclosure when airing VNRs has helped compound questions about the integrity of broadcast journalism at a time when the line between advertising departments and TV newsrooms are increasingly blurred.

Federal regulators and lawmakers are trying to figure out if viewers should be told when they see material during a newscast that has been prepared by outsiders.

If you think it's an easy call, think again.

The Federal Communications Commission requires broadcasters to label VNRs only if the station has been paid to air it or if it deals with political or other contentious matters.

The agency collected public input on its regulations last week. It received only nine responses, primarily from executives and trade groups from the broadcasting and public relations industries, who said further regulation isn't needed.

The Radio-Television News Directors Association, a group that represents top newsroom managers, submitted a 13-page statement that said few TV stations air VNRs, and those that do almost always identify the source.

The association based its position on an informal survey of 100 members, according to Barbara Cochran, the group's president. Concrete data on VNR use is hard to come by, she said.

"It's kind of like the Loch Ness Monster. Everyone talks about it, but not many people have actually seen it," Ms. Cochran said.

The hardest data seem to come from the Project for Excellence in Journalism, a nonpartisan media research group that asked 103 TV news directors about VNRs in 2002.

Sixty-six percent said they never use them. Of the other 34 percent, 10 percent said they always label VNRs, but the remaining 24 percent said they labeled them either "occasionally," "rarely," or "never."

Sen. Ted Stevens, Alaska Republican, chairman of the Commerce, Science and Transportation Committee, has suggested the input the FCC receives will help him determine what to do with a bill that would require the agencies to label VNRs as government productions.

The Government Accountability Office, Congress' investigative arm, slapped the Bush administration in February for distributing VNRs that violated rules on covert propaganda.

The Center for Media and Democracy, a public relations watchdog group, was one of the organizations that wrote the FCC to call for tougher regulation of VNRs. Diane Farsetta, the group's senior researcher, rejected the idea that government shouldn't be telling TV newsrooms how to conduct their business.

"We're not saying VNRs should be banned. That would be a First Amendment violation. We're saying viewers should be told where they come from," she said. (Baker, 2005)

## Box 8.6   Keys to Success in Pitching

There are many different approaches in pitching the media and things you must know. Here are the top guidelines to a successful pitch:

1. Make sure you have a really good press release. If your story is weak or not newsy, it will not be picked up no matter how well your pitch is. Would it really serve the community and the media to cover your story? You must feel confident about the release before you pitch it. Put yourself in the editor's shoes and ask yourself, "Would I publish this story?" Of course, your answer should be positive; otherwise, the story needs to be reworked.

2. Be a girl/boy scout: always be prepared. Know your story thoroughly, have the facts and be able to cite them and back them up with reliable sources. Be an expert on the facts and have the facts and figures in front of you when you do the pitch.

3. Anticipate the answers to the questions and be able to research and get answers promptly if more answers are requested. Try to see the story from a journalist's point of view and look for the potential objections and negatives—don't wear blinders and ignore these issues as they will come back to haunt you during the pitch. Do your homework.

4. If you pitch the media with a phone call—make it fast (prepare a 30- to 45-second opening pitch) and be aware that time is of the essence with reporters. Talking too long or calling too many times is the "kiss of death."

5. Know to whom the pitch should be directed. Here again, before the pitch is set in motion make certain you know what the person covers and the type of stories they write. Read the different newspapers daily, review a variety of different television programs and spend time on the Internet—make this routine a part of your daily work. Get to know your target media.

6. Familiarize yourself with the personality of the media person to whom you are directing the pitch. Is he or she the type of person who seems open to conversation or are they usually not available when you call? When you reach them, do they curtly say, "I'm on deadline now," or do they listen patiently to the pitch? Either way, be careful not to become known as a nuisance. Decide on the best method to communicate to them.

7. Strategize how to deliver your message. Is it the type of release that must be communicated verbally at first or will sending the pitch letter work best? Is it time sensitive? Should you offer an exclusive or an embargo?

8. Determine the best time to do the pitch. Timing is something that is dictated by the media outlet you are pitching and the nature of the press release. What is the best day and best time?

9. The pitch must be accurate and the facts not exaggerated in order to get coverage. Integrity of the information is a vital aspect in gaining media attention. If you don't have an answer to a question, be honest and tell the reporter you will check it out and call them at a certain time and day. Make sure you make the call to the reporter as promised.

10. Whether you decide to pitch verbally followed by a release or to send the press release first and then pitch, don't over-pitch with either method and become a pest. Keep your messages spaced so as not to appear overly anxious or put pressure on the media.

11. Don't pitch a story that has already been published without mentioning it from the onset. If you don't, after this is discovered you may find the door at that particular publication will always be closed to you.

12. If you didn't get the story covered, don't do a number on yourself. Keep going! Maybe the story was not newsy enough, maybe it was more of an advertisement than a public relations story, or maybe you approached the wrong media outlet for this type of story. Do another read and determine what went wrong.

13. Always send a written thank-you if your pitch is picked up by the media. Be a relationship builder! (We will discuss this in more detail in the next chapter.)

To assume the pitch was received and read is not realistic; newsrooms are often very busy and chaotic places where the news stories deemed most important get the attention while the other releases are set on some stack for future perusal. To find out if the release was received and read requires finesse on the part of the sender. Many times a brief call or email inquiry asking whether there are any questions or a need for additional information regarding the release may initiate a response. But in the real world, most times the fashion company may not receive information on whether a story is set to go until the journalist sends an email or calls the company for more information. One of the best ways to follow up the pitch is to contact the reporter by phone or email within two to three days after the pitch is delivered. Simply state that this is a follow-up call to inquire whether there is a need for any further information. Here is an example of a short but sweet follow-up email:

> Hi ___[reporter's name]___, Kindly let me know if you are in need of any further information regarding the release about: ___[the news story]___ that I sent you on date ___[date of original pitch]___.
>
> Many thanks.
>
> [Signature]

If you do not receive an answer from the reporter after this follow-up email or call, then another reminder may be in vain. You will be called upon to use good judgment regarding another follow-up. Sometimes it may be best to send a brief note thanking the reporter for viewing the release. The follow-up is what separates the professionals from the amateurs. Following up on the pitch is like skating on thin ice. Dale King, the city editor of the *Boca Raton News,* whose views on follow-up calls are included in Box 8.7, said, "I don't mind a follow-up call or email regarding a press release, but, when I get constant calls and when the person starts calling and contacting our other journalists following up on the same story, that's when I get annoyed." The public relations person must be cautious not to upset the reporter or else the story could be killed!

## The Media Inquiry

The media inquiry is the journalist's method of obtaining and researching information for a story or prospective story. When a reporter contacts the public relations director with an inquiry, it means that the reporter is exploring the possibility of doing a story that might include the fashion company. Unless the story is a negative one, the public relations director should welcome the inquiry—this is the moment the company has been waiting for! It's time to act quickly and professionally, and work with the reporter to satisfy the inquiry as soon as possible. We will cover negative inquiries in Chapter 12. The inquiry could lead to a story, but not always; at times, the reporter may deem after researching the facts that the story is not newsworthy or not timely enough. In this case, the story will not appear in print, and the public relations director must not get frustrated with or upset at the reporter for not covering it. Remember that the media is free and cannot be controlled. Thus, it is foolish

## Box 8.7   Media's View on the Pitch: Interview with Dale King, City Editor, Boca Raton News, Florida

**Do you prefer a verbal pitch or a written one? Why?**

I prefer a written pitch. Often, phone call pitches interrupt reporters in the middle of working on something else. Clearly, the reporter can't switch from one to another and do the pitch justice. A written pitch—preferably emailed—should be sent telling the reporter exactly what the pitch is all about.

**What information do you look for in the pitch?**

The pitch should be adapted to the medium being pitched to. Obviously, larger newspapers with sections devoted to various subjects are the easiest to pitch to. For smaller, community newspapers, the pitch should be aimed at the local area, with a local focus that has a news hook. Even national public relations firms can pitch locally, but a national firm pitching a national story to a local paper is often pointless.

**What type of pitch turns you off to a story?**

Perhaps the worst turnoff is from people who try to make a story sound "local" when it isn't—and they talk on and on about why it is local, and won't take "no" for an answer. I call it my McDonald's Theory. When someone tries to pitch a story and I ask, "Is it local to Boca or Delray?" they say, "Well, you can get it (product, service, etc.) in Boca. I tell them, "Well, you can get a McDonald's hamburger in Boca, but that doesn't mean McDonald's is local." We define local as a person or group from Boca or Delray doing something locally (i.e., Heart Ball, Chamber of Commerce breakfast) or someone from Boca or Delray doing something outside

the area (i.e., helping with the tsunami, rescuing dogs left homeless by Katrina). Other turnoffs include constant calls asking when something is going to run or re-pitching stories in different formats (i.e., all right, if you won't talk to the doctor who does plastic surgery, will you interview a patient?). Blind public relations calls are also a turnoff (Hi, this is Michelle from the XYZ firm in New York, we'd like to talk to you).

**What type of pitch turns you on to a story?**

A pitch that's a turn-on comes from a person who will talk and not "command," from someone willing to provide background information, photos and set up interviews. The turn-on comes from a public relations person willing to meet you halfway—or more—and who understands if a particular story has no merit, and gracefully understands.

**Do you have any particular time or day that you wish to receive the pitch?**

Pitches are best after deadline—whatever that is for a particular medium.

**Have you any comments on the methods people use to follow up on their pitch?**

Emails and polite calls are best. Many public relations people get angry and frustrated if a story doesn't run by a certain date (I could name names). A good public relations person knows when he or she is dealing with a large, well-staffed paper, or a small one with few staffers.

to try to "flex your muscles" to influence the story. Calling the editor to complain that the story is not being covered, for example, typically only results in eliminating any chances of coverage the story did have and can destroy any rapport the public relations director might have already had with the reporter. So we can see that if the media inquiry is not answered effectively, the results can be disastrous. Integrity plays a very important role in responding to media inquiries. If the media is given information that is exaggerated or incorrect, it will ultimately end up as a negative story or no story at all. The best way to facilitate the inquiry turning into actual coverage is by promptly cooperating with the reporter and following up to ensure all questions are answered. There are two types of media inquiries: the solicited and unsolicited.

### The Solicited Media Inquiry

As its name suggests, the solicited inquiry is the result of the fashion company's solicitation for coverage for its news story using a press release or by other means. The media inquiry is what links the fashion company's release to the media coverage. In other words, when the media knocks on the fashion company's door for information in response to a press release, the fashion company better be prepared. It must have a strategy for immediately responding to the media inquiry. Essential for handling the request is the assignment of someone in the company the specific responsibility for answering the inquiry. Or, if the organization works with a public relations firm, make certain that the media inquiry is directed to the responsible person in the public relations firm. Also it is necessary to inform the internal staff of the organization as to the method that the media inquiry is to be handled. Media opportunities can be lost if the areas of communication and responsibilities are not clearly defined and outlined. In handling media inquiries within fashion public relations, planning is essential and it is important to have a structure in place. The success of communicating with the media will necessitate constant updates by the organization regarding areas of news that may attract the media. This can be accomplished at weekly meetings within the organization, and sending the internal staff copies of all press releases and written pitches that were sent to the media. Proper advance planning will lead to better results when the media calls.

### The Unsolicited Media Inquiry

The unsolicited media inquiry is rarer than the solicited inquiry and is not a response to a company's press release. Instead, it is the result of a source external to the fashion company, such as the reporter coming across the company's name while doing research, a verbal recommendation to the reporter, or even the Yellow Pages. As with the solicited inquiry, answering the inquiry quickly and honestly is extremely important. However, with the unsolicited inquiry, the public relations director cannot predict the inquiry and thus cannot prepare in advance for the questions. Therefore, it is often more difficult to answer the reporter's questions right away and further research is required. The public relations director then should inform the reporter he or she needs a little time, research the matter, and get back to the reporter as soon as possible. If the company has been experiencing financial or legal problems recently, there is a good chance the media inquiry is negative; we will cover this topic in Chapter 12.

## Media Coverage

After the initial inquiry has been answered, we move into the phase leading to media coverage—we have hit the jackpot! If information is not volunteered by the reporter, it is acceptable to inquire whether the reporter intends to cover the story. If the reporter feels it is not a story, the public relations director should cordially thank the reporter for the inquiry and work to strengthen the relationship with the reporter for future stories; we will cover appropriate relationship strategies in Chapter 9. If the story receives the green light, there are a series of steps that can be taken to facilitate a smooth and positive story:

## 1. Offer More Information

In some cases, the press release that has been submitted includes enough information for the reporter to complete the story without any further need to interact with the fashion company. However, most times, the reporter needs to conduct further interviews, receive more information on specific aspects of the story or verify information. If the story will be covered by television news, the video crew and the reporter will have to come out and shoot the segment, the products, and the interviews. Therefore, it is good practice to ask the reporter what additional information he or she will need for the story and whether to arrange for interviews. It is vital to find out what the reporter's deadline is so that these tasks are accomplished well before the story is due.

## 2. Be Prepared to Supply Additional Information

Whatever other information or facts the reporter might need, the fashion company must supply it as soon as possible to keep the story alive. Procrastination or delays are unacceptable and can easily kill the story if the reporter feels the company is not cooperating. The public relations director should strive to never find himself or herself answering a follow-up phone call from the reporter asking for the information again—that means the fashion company is way behind already and that the story is in jeopardy. Instead, he or she should be proactive and keep the reporter updated on the progress being made bearing in mind the reporter's deadline. If the information cannot be gathered before the deadline, the public relations director must inform the reporter as soon as possible to allow the reporter time to find an alternative source for the information or explore a way to re-write the story around this issue.

## 3. Prepare for Interviews

An important element to consider when an organization is expecting the media is whether or not to prepare a person in the company for the interview, and if so who that person should be. Naturally, the person being interviewed should be an expert or authority in the subject—e.g., the designer being interviewed about her new collection—or be intimately connected with the company's internal affairs, such as a high-level executive. However, we must keep in mind that essentially, the person being interviewed represents the company and anything he or she says stands for the company, so it pays to be cautious about the selection process. Briefing the individual to be interviewed is extremely important in order to deliver honest and accurate information. Role playing with the person or persons to be interviewed is a method that will prepare the interviewee for the media inquiry. A skilled public relations person can act as the reporter in the role-playing exercise preparing the person to be interviewed for the inquiry. In this activity it is important for the person to be interviewed not to appear to be rehearsed, but rather to be prepared and answer the questions

**FIGURE 8.3** Selecting the right person to be interviewed and photographed for a media story is important. Arranging for an interview by a model who is extremely tall and a designer who is really short, for example, could create a problem for photographers, and especially the video crew who are more restricted to a horizontal frame.

truthfully. The final comment in answering media inquiries is to never say, "No comment."

## 4. On-Site Coverage

Before the media arrives, make certain that the proper arrangements have been made for the interview. The staff must be apprised of the interview well in advance. The location of the interview must obviously be held in an area that is quiet and clean. No distractions. No telephone calls. Here, again, planning for the on-site coverage in advance will eliminate confusion and result in a productive session.

## 5. Arranging for Photos or Video

If the coverage will be on-site, then the fashion company must arrange for the appropriate accommodations for the media's photographers or video teams that will cover the story. A fashion show, for example, may necessitate special seating or placement arrangements for the photography or video team, which could at times have two or three different cameras at work simultaneously during the event. Each camera will need to be set up in a different location to provide shots from different angles and even varying heights. In addition,

FIGURE 8.4 When fashion shows are covered by the media, photographers and videographers typically need special arrangements to properly capture the event. In this photo, the media photographers are located strategically so as to get the best shots they can. The lighting for the catwalk must be adequate and sometimes be adjusted to allow proper capturing of video footage.

225

many video teams and even photography teams may require special electrical outlets for their lighting and cameras. The media team should be consulted before the event to see what their requirements will be.

### 6. Monitor Progress During Coverage

While the media is on-site covering the event, the public relations director must monitor the progress of the interviews and photo/video coverage, and remain alert for the needs of the reporter and photographer. He or she should also keep watch for possible glitches in the plan and work behind the scenes to correct these before they present a problem. It is up to the public relations director to ensure that all company employees are following the plan and are putting forth a positive image for themselves and the company.

## Coverage Wrap-Up

The wrap-up phase of the media coverage process is vital to getting the story completed and published or aired. As the reporter writes the story, more questions may arise and further research or interviews may be needed. Additionally, the story can be delayed or even killed if other important stories get slotted to take its place. Therefore, it is important to stay on top of the story until it is actually printed or aired. A few days after the reporter conducts the last interview (or in the case of a daily paper, that afternoon) it is recommended to make a quick call or drop a short email to check if the reporter has any more questions, problems, or needs additional information. If any questions

## Case Study 8.1   Obtaining and Handling Media Coverage

### IMG Fashion: Organizers of New York Fashion Week

IMG Fashion, a division of international sports, entertainment, and media company IMG, is the global leader in the management and production of fashion weeks and designer fashion events. Its portfolio of events includes Mercedes-Benz Fashion Weeks in New York, Los Angeles, Miami, and Berlin, as well as Fashion Fringe at Covent Garden in London, Lakme Fashion Week in Mumbai, Rosemount Australian Fashion Week in Sydney, Rosemount Sydney Fashion Festival, and MasterCard Luxury Week Hong Kong. IMG Fashion also represents the international commercial rights of Milan Fashion Week and Moscow Fashion Week.

Alison Levy is the public relations manager at IMG Fashion in New York. She has been instrumental in the publicity and media operations for IMG Fashion's premier fashion events in the United States. Before moving to New York, Levy worked as a freelance publicist in Milan organizing events for the fashion industry's top venues including Just Cavalli Café, Armani Prive, and Old Fashion Café, among others. Living in Italy, Levy had the opportunity to intern at one of the most prominent communication firms in fashion, Attila, while completing her Masters at the Scuola di Direzione Aziendale of Universita' Bocconi.

**What sort of media inquiries do you normally receive about the New York Fashion Week?**

We receive a variety of media inquiries about Mercedes-Benz Fashion Week in New York. Some questions that we get are from journalists looking to contact designers for interviews or looking to acquire specific information on the line that the designers are showing. A journalist may contact us with questions regarding current fashion trends (we refer those to IMG's Publishing Division). Other questions that we often receive are in regards to the actual event such as what will be taking place, how members of the press can register. We are also contacted when members of the press are looking for information on the event so they can write an article because they are unable to attend. On average we register about 4,000 press members from around the world each season.

**FIGURE CASE STUDY**

**8.1** Allison Levy, public relations manager, IMG Fashion, New York.

**What is the typical procedure that you follow when you receive an inquiry from the media? How vital is it to answer media inquiries quickly? What is the average turnaround time to answer a typical inquiry?**

The typical procedure we follow when we receive an inquiry from the media is to respond as quickly as possible. If the answer to their question is unknown often we will give them a resource that can assist them in finding an answer. It is very important for us to answer media inquiries quickly. It is so important because often the journalist contacting us is trying to make a deadline for a story, so we want to give them enough time to complete the story. Also, sometimes they are coming from another country and they are contacting us for information on dates in order to make arrangements to attend the event. You never know what kind of time crunch they may be under, so we try to accommodate them as best as possible. Some challenges that often occur is trying to figure out what is time sensitive and what is not. Unless we are contacted during an event (and we are onsite) we try to respond within 48 hours.

**Do you normally prepare information in advance of announcing the Fashion Week details, to make it easier and faster to answer media inquiries? If so, what does it include?**

We use a combination of talking points that all company spokespeople receive, and fact sheets that we share with the press. Some of the most important information we give them is the general information such as where the event is being held (Bryant Park), when it is taking place,

## Case Study 8.1   Obtaining and Handling Media Coverage *(continued)*

and how long the event lasts. Another important piece of information we include is event highlights, i.e., number of shows, general event information, sponsor information, number of attending press, special events taking place related to the event, expected celebrities, etc.

**When the media informs you that they would like to cover Fashion Week, what are the top concerns/items you need to square away to prepare for smooth coverage?**

At IMG Fashion, we employ a delicate registration process for Mercedes-Benz Fashion Week that helps manage the quality and quantity of press attained for our events. With this, all members of the press (national and international print publications, online media, national and international broadcast media, retail buyers, and stylists) who would like to cover our events must apply directly to IMG Fashion for their accreditation. This application process entails submitting coverage from previous seasons attended, assignment letters detailing their request to cover the coming season and tear sheets showcasing their published fashion/lifestyle work. Once received, the IMG Fashion Press Team reviews the application in anywhere from 7 to 10 days. Only upon approval are these persons admitted to cover our events. The approval process entails an in-depth review of materials submitted assuring that the caliber of coverage is on par with the caliber of our event.

**What sort of accommodations (e.g., space, electrical, lighting) do you typically have to offer to photojournalists who come to cover the Fashion Week events?**

We usually do not offer any accommodations for photojournalists who attend our events. However, there have been previous seasons where we have offered all members

of the press a press lounge. This lounge is helpful for photographers and editors who need to immediately work on their reporting post-show. As far as inside the venue (the actual runway), no special accommodations are made.

**What sort of accommodations (e.g., space, electrical, lighting) do you typically have to offer to TV crews who come to cover the Fashion Week events? Does each crew have different requirements?**

As far as television crews are concerned we do make accommodations for live truck parking so that these stations can park, lay cable, and conduct interviews to be immediately broadcasted on the local news. Most designers and sponsors will also work with TV crews to set up interviews in their lounges, backstage areas, and event lobby.

As far as access is concerned, all photographers and crews are permitted to shoot from the media riser located at the end of the runway. Additionally they have the option to work directly with the designers to get access to the front row and backstage area.

### Questions to Consider

1.  What are your thoughts about IMG Fashion's press accreditation process? What do you think are the pros and cons to screening applying journalists?

2.  How does IMG Fashion handle media inquiries? Do you feel it is consistent with what has been discussed in the chapter? Explain.

3.  If you were the organizer of a show at New York Fashion Week, would you have allowed photographers and video crews special accommodations? Explain why.

do exist, the fashion company should provide the answers as soon as possible, so as to get the story completed. If additional interviews are needed, these must be arranged as soon as possible as well. When the reporter has indicated that he or she has all the information and is done with the story, we need to know when it will print or air. The procedure for finding out when the piece will be published or aired is simply to ask! Most times public relations people are hesitant to ask the reporter as to the status of the story. They feel that by doing this they will irritate the media personnel and it may kill the story. Nothing can be further from the truth—remember the media needs product (news) and if your story will resonate with their target audience, they will look to get it published or aired. Media folks will gladly tell you if the story will make it or not. They will even tell you the date, time, and other information as to the status of the story. Although the scheduling of the story may be out of the reporter's hands, typically he or she knows when it will appear and will not mind if the public relations director calls once or at the most twice to check on the publication date. Do not abuse this wrap-up privilege, though—if you call more than two times, you are skirting the line with becoming a pest, endangering the entire relationship with that reporter. Space the two calls as far apart as you can so as not to appear as a nuisance. In addition, while you have the editor or reporter on the phone, you may as well talk to him or her about potential future stories in order to create a stronger relationship with the reporter.

## Chapter Summary

- ▶ Pitching a news story presents the story to the media in a favorable way that emphasizes why it should be covered.

- ▶ A proper pitch increases the chance of gaining coverage for the story; an improper pitch can not only kill the story, but also damage the company's reputation with the media.

- ▶ By pitching the right media outlet, and highlighting the newsworthy features of the story that apply to the needs of that media outlet and its audience, the fashion company can make the pitch more meaningful.

- ▶ The pitch is typically done verbally or in writing, and must be concise and to the point.

- ▶ The media's questions or objections are signs of potential interest in the story and must be addressed properly and professionally.

- ▶ Media inquiries can be solicited or unsolicited, and occur when the reporter calls and asks for more information about the company or its products.

- ▶ Media inquiries should be answered quickly and thoroughly for best coverage results.

- ▶ The fashion company should prepare its staff and premises for media visitation to ensure for smooth interaction with the media.

- ▶ The fashion company should carefully select and rehearse its employees for interviews, if needed.

## Key Terms

- ▶ anchor
- ▶ breaking news
- ▶ empathy
- ▶ needs
- ▶ objections

▶ pitch

▶ producer

▶ sale

▶ video news release (VNR)

▶ video news story (VNS)

## Chapter-End Questions and Exercises

1. What is the meaning of "pitching" in terms of public relations?

2. Why is pitching important? Do you think a good story would be published with or without proper pitching? Why?

3. Compare and contrast the different types of public relations news story pitches.

4. In your opinion, how is a news story pitch similar to a sales presentation, and how is it different?

5. Suppose you are the public relations director for a fictitious fashion manufacturer, launching a new collection.

   a. Set up the scenario and explain what the story is about.

   b. Determine the type of pitching you think is most suitable and explain why.

   c. List the media outlets you plan to target for this story and why.

   d. Outline your approach as to how you plan to pitch, and provide a sample text of what you intend to say or email to the press during the pitch.

6. Define "need." What are the media's, the fashion company's, and the consumer's needs within the context of the news story pitch? How does the news story fulfill these?

7. What are objections and are they a positive or negative element of the sales pitch? Explain.

8. How does one respond to objections during a pitch?

9. Is it proper to ask a reporter for a commitment to do a story? Explain.

10. *In-class role play:* Pair up with another student in the class and create a fictitious role-play news story verbal pitch scenario where one of you is the public relations director pitching the news story and the other is the editor answering the phone call. Write down a summary of what happened, the results, and your analysis of the conversation.

11. What is a press kit?

12. Name five items that are included in a press kit. Explain the importance of each.

13. What is a B-roll? How is it used?

14. What is VNR? How is it used?

15. Select an existing fashion company. Using available or fictitious information, create a sample press kit for the company with all of the recommended components.

16. Name five keys to success in pitching. Explain each.

17. What is a media inquiry?

18. Compare and contrast the solicited media inquiry with the unsolicited media inquiry.

19. *In-class role play:* Pair up with another student in the class and create a fictitious media inquiry scenario where one of you is the public relations director answering the phone call and the other is the editor calling with an inquiry. Write down a summary of what happened, the results, and your analysis of the conversation.

20. After the media accepts a story, list the series of steps that can be taken to facilitate the story.

# Media Relations

## Chapter Snapshot

To succeed over the long run in the field of fashion public relations, it is vital to develop strong, long-term business relationships with the target media that reaches out to the fashion company's public. Media relations focuses on creating and maintaining such relationships that can help the fashion company secure more coverage for its news stories as well as improve the results of the coverage. At the end of the day, the media consists of individuals who have personalities, opinions, and, unfortunately, even bias. It is up to the public relations staff to get to know the media as those individuals with whom they are in constant contact and upon whom they depend for positive exposure. Perhaps a maverick who is pitching his first press release knows best that the media principally never trusts a source unless the information offered by that source has been checked out; after that has been done and the source has been found reliable, the media is more likely to trust that source in the future. Being a respected source, operating in a professional manner, and developing meaningful news stories are all vital to developing long-term positive relations with the media. In this chapter, we will explore what media relations means and the various ways to create and improve such relations.

## Objectives

▶ Understand the concepts of media relations and the business relationship.

▶ Explore the dynamics of the business relationship with the media.

▶ Develop strategies to create a meaningful relationship with the media.

▶ Discuss the approaches that help create a rapport with media contacts.

▶ Comprehend why the public relations director must be "on the same team" as the media contact.

▶ Recognize the top strategies for developing and strengthening relationships with the media.

▶ Review the importance of ethics and performance in the fashion company-media relationship.

Through the practice of good **media relations,** the fashion company's public relations staff can develop good rapport with the editors, reporters, producers, online editors, and other members of the media. Within the field of fashion media, the media is constantly looking for news stories and opportunities to inform the public about new trends and styles; the fashion public relations director is looking for opportunities to get the fashion company's news stories covered. The two parties are essentially partners in creating and reporting on fashion news, and typically work closely to get the news out. However, the difference is that the public relations director's interests are ultimately to improve the fashion company's public image whereas the media's ultimate duty is to inform the public objectively about current affairs in the fashion industry. Conflicts arise when the two interests collide, or when one of the parties betrays the other's trust. The media and the fashion company are thus linked and interdependent. Building a meaningful business relationship with the media based on trust and truthful dissemination of information is a crucial part of creating a strong public image for the fashion company. In previous chapters, we've discussed the various initiatives that can be undertaken to bring about positive exposure for the fashion company and its products. Although media relations encompasses these initiatives, it is the actual verbal and written interaction with the media that define the effectiveness of media relations. At the focal point of such interaction is the creation and development of strong business relationships with the individual editors, reporters, newscasters, producers, and other representatives of the target media whose opinions and decisions affect whether and how a story is covered.

## What Is a Business Relationship?

We say that developing strong business relationships with the media is a vital element in successful fashion public relations—but what is a business relationship? The **business relationship** is an association between two people of different companies who reach a level of comfort, and who cooperate by sharing assistance, information, and logistics to achieve a common goal that benefits both parties (Sherman & Perlman, 2006). When forged, such a relationship strengthens over time as the two parties establish trust in each other and keep their promises on the delivery of assistance or information to the other party on time. Developing a personal rapport between the parties and an honest dialogue that facilitates the sharing is essential to the long-term survival of the relationship.

## The Business Relationship vs. Marriage

It was the former *Harvard Business Review* editor Theodore Levitt who said, "The relationship between seller and buyer seldom ends when a sale is made. The relationship intensifies after the sale is made" (Levitt, 1983). He goes on to say, "The sale starts a courtship to the point where a business marriage begins and the quality of this marriage determines whether there will be continued or an expanded business relationship, or troubles and divorce, how well the marriage is depends on how well the relationship is managed by the seller." We can apply the same principle to building business relationships with the media within the context of fashion public relations—the fashion company and the media work together to create a news story that delivers interesting and factual information to the consumer. The media benefits from the news story by delivering an important service to its readers, thus enhancing the publication's value to its audience; the fashion company benefits from the exposure and positive public image that result from the news story. If the fashion company lies to the media by publishing false statements in the press release, it betrays the media's trust; the media is not likely to believe the company in the future or cover its news

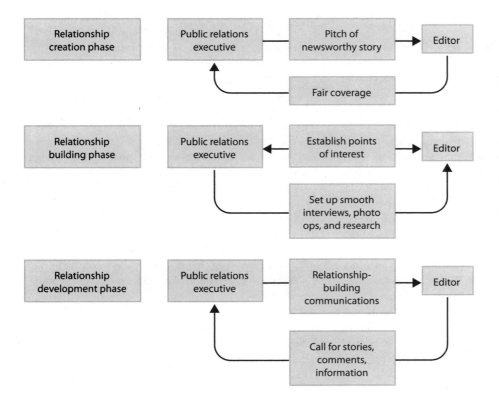

FIGURE 9.1 The business relationship within the fashion public relations field focuses on performance and continued cooperation between the fashion company and the media. This diagram shows the phases through which the relationship transforms until it reaches full and stable maturity.

## Box 9.1 Real World Profile: Theodore (Ted) Levitt

Harvard Business School Professor Emeritus Theodore (Ted) Levitt was a monumental and iconoclastic figure in the field of marketing and former editor of *Harvard Business Review*. Levitt influenced generations of both scholars and practitioners with his groundbreaking, carefully crafted, always provocative, and often controversial books and articles.

Levitt joined the Harvard Business School (HBS) faculty in 1959 and quickly gained an international reputation as an extraordinary scholar, writer, and teacher. His article "Marketing Myopia," which was first published in *Harvard Business Review* (*HBR*) in 1960 and argued that companies and entire industries declined because management defined its businesses too narrowly, immediately became a huge success, with requests for 35,000 reprints from 1,000 different companies soon after its publication. More than 40 years later, more than 850,000 reprints had been sold, making the article one of the best-selling *HBR* articles of all time.

The key question that all managers must be able to answer, he advised, is "What business are you in?" The railroads, for example, "let others take customers away from them because they assumed themselves to be in the railroad business instead of the transportation business," he wrote.

Nearly a quarter century later, Levitt created a still-raging controversy in the worldwide business community with his 1983 *HBR* article "The Globalization of Markets." Besides popularizing the word *globalization,* he asserted that new technologies had "proletarianized" communication, transportation, and travel, creating a new commercial reality—the emergence of global markets for standardized consumer products at lower prices, thanks to economies of scale—a sea change that was especially evident in companies such as Coca-Cola, Kellogg's, and McDonald's. He insisted that the future belonged not to the multinational corporation, but to the "global corporation" that did not cater to local differences in taste.

Levitt was the author or coauthor of seven other books, including *Marketing for Business Growth* (1974), *The Third Sector: New Tactics for a Responsive Society* (1973), *Marketing: A Contemporary Analysis* (1972), *The Marketing Mode* (1969), *Marketing* (1964), *Industrial Purchasing Behavior: A Study of Communication Effects* (1964), and *Innovation in Marketing* (1962).

FIGURE BOX 9.1 The iconic Theodore (Ted) Levitt passed away in 2006 at the age of 81.

The 26 articles he wrote for *HBR* (four of which won McKinsey Awards, an honor presented annually to the best and second-best articles of the year) made him and the late Peter Drucker the most published authors in the history of the magazine.

Levitt brought his legendary scholarship, vision, intensity, and dedication to good writing to his appointment by former HBS Dean John McArthur as editor of *HBR,* a position he held from 1985 to 1989. He is credited with transforming the magazine from an academic periodical into a more accessible publication that focused on important ideas and practices that influenced a readership composed of top business leaders.

Among his innovations were shorter articles covering a broader range of topics, a more reader-friendly design, and the introduction of *New Yorker*–style cartoons to provide an amusing perspective on the world of business. As an accomplished author, he was especially eager to attract more readers. "If people don't read what you write," he often said, "then what you write is a museum piece." Under Levitt's leadership, *HBR* solidified its position as the preeminent publication of its kind in the world. "He was arguably the best editor in *HBR*'s history," said current editor Thomas Stewart. "He helped bring the magazine to a new standard of readability while ensuring that its quality was never higher."

Although Levitt's many magazine articles and numerous books gained him a worldwide following outside of Harvard, within HBS he gained a reputation as a popular and demanding teacher and effective administrator, serving as head of the school's marketing unit from 1977 to 1983. He was appointed the

Box 9.1    Real World Profile: Theodore (Ted) Levitt *(continued)*

Edward W. Carter Professor of Business Administration in 1979. With a thick mustache and bushy black eyebrows, he favored a theatrical style in class, striding up and down the aisles and tossing chalk toward both blackboards and students. By the time he retired from the active faculty in 1990, Levitt was considered one of the school's living legends, a seminal scholar who had radically altered marketing both as a practice within corporations and industries and as a field of academic inquiry (Harvard Business School, 1983).

stories. Similarly, if the media distorts the story or uses the research provided by the fashion company to promote its competitors, it betrays the company's trust; the fashion company is not likely to provide information or press releases to that publication in the future.

Now let's examine how the public relations director can turn the coverage of one news story into a business relationship with that media, which yields multiple stories in the future. Within Levitt's marriage metaphor, the commitment to cover the story can be likened to the wedding ceremony vows. In essence, the public relations director is asked if the news story is accurate and if interviews and photo opportunities will be provided as promised before the deadline—and by accepting the commitment, the director answers "I do." The reporter is asked if he or she will cover the story in an unbiased manner, and by accepting the commitment, the reporter answers "I do." However, where a newlywed couple may leave the ceremony and drive into the sunset to begin their life together, our buyer and seller go to work on creating a healthy and mutually beneficial business relationship. The public relations director and reporter dive directly into the marriage phase; the director prepares for the interviews and gathers any additional information while the reporter begins the journalistic process of researching and writing the story.

What happens next often determines whether the ensuing business *marriage* will be short-lived or succeed in the long-term. The public relations person can simply schedule the interviews and email back the information, move onto the next story, and never call on the reporter again. In this case, the business marriage would dissolve following the publication of the story. On the other hand, the public relations person who remains involved in the coverage of the story can utilize this phase as a pretext for calling on the reporter to not only inform him or her of the story's status and make sure that that reporter is happy with it, but also to develop the relationship. By showing that he or she cares about informing the readers and by helping the reporter with the story, the public relations director develops a relationship with the media that will result in more published news stories in the future. The relationship cannot progress unless the director is able to be a problem solver and provide the reporter with newsworthy stories and research. The director can ensure a lasting relationship by making sure that each and every story will ultimately be mutually beneficial. Strange as it may seem, sometimes the best way for the public relations director to establish this trust and build a relationship is when a problem exists and the director solves the problem. Given a choice between running a story from an unknown company and a story from the public relations director who has proven as a reliable source, the reporter will tend to pick the latter especially when deadline is looming. A relationship can be developed to such an extent that in a pinch of a slow news day, the reporter initiates the call to the public relations director to see if he or she has any interesting stories for the reporter.

### The Right Side of the Fence

To maximize the business relationship with the media, the fashion company public relations staff must understand that they should work with the media, rather than against it or independent of it, to achieve the public relations campaign goals. Successful public relations personnel recognize they are "on the same side of the fence" as the media and that both parties rely on each other. If the media has no news to report or fails to report about the news properly, it will lose its audience and the fashion company will lose a vital outlet for reaching its consumer audience. In spite of the problems one may face in a relationship with the media, one must be able to solve the problem and maintain a level playing field. Maintaining a successful relationship requires a willingness to give as well as receive. Before the public relations director initiates a relationship with the editor or reporter, he or she must understand what the editor or reporter wants from the relationship. Editors and reporters want public relations staff to be team players and have a high degree of ethics and integrity. They want that comfort zone in the relationship; in other words, they want to be assured that the public relations personnel "will do what they say." The relationship strengthens only when the public relations director is able to provide the media with newsworthy and factual information, solve problems on the fly, and assist the media to cover the story properly.

## Creating the Relationship

The relationship with the media does not form overnight, nor does it form by itself. It requires diligence, ingenuity, and patience to create a meaningful relationship with an editor or reporter that will produce media exposure. The public relations director needs to understand the dynamics and factors that shape the decisions of the editor as well as the needs of the reporter who covers the story.

### Paper-People and People-People

Before we discuss creating a relationship we must first understand the reasons some of us are able to easily form a relationship and others find it difficult. Within the context of proactive media relations there is a nondiscriminatory classification of personnel that determines what functions a particular public relations person is best suited for. Any person who works in fashion public relations falls into one of two categories; he or she is either a *paper-person* or a *people-person*. This is not by any means a positive or negative comment on the person's personality or worth to the company. Instead, it simply guides us in the assignment of the duties to the person to best utilize his or her natural disposition for best performance results. The two categories are not necessarily cut-and-dry, meaning a person can have shades of each category. The person's placement within the categories may also be changeable—through education, training, coaching, and self-motivation, a person may have the potential to change from one category to the other.

Typically, paper-people prefer to work in areas that do not require an intense involvement of working directly with people. They prefer the areas of creativity such as writing, art, graphic art, animation, statistics, and other occupations that do not require too much interaction with people—they prefer to work with paper-oriented tasks. Although, they are able to maintain close and loyal friendships, they would rather work mostly with paper or computers than with people. On the other side, we have the people-people who love to talk and interact with others as the main part of their job. They do not enjoy working with paper-oriented tasks, computers, administration, office procedures, or working in an isolated environment. They need contact with other people to be happy. Their happiest and most productive moments are spent interacting with others. Professions such as sales, customer care, public relations, marketing, and such are where people-people are most comfortable. Therefore, people-people have an easier time forming relationships. This serves as a guideline in assigning personnel to the duties of media relations; it is helpful if these personnel lean toward being more people-people rather than paper-people. Giving paper-people the task of pitching and media relations often causes them to be unhappy with their job as well as reduces the rate of success in obtaining coverage commitments. In contrast, giving people-people the task of writing press releases and assembling press kits would have the same effect—they will likely become discontented and may have difficulties completing such tasks properly. Keep in mind that these guidelines are quite broad and should not be used as any sort of generic label without consideration to the person as an individual. The main point here is to utilize the company's human resources as wisely as possible to the end of maximizing results for the media relations efforts.

## Building a Common Ground

The old adage "birds of a feather flock together" points to an important factor in media relations. Fact is, that media relations is a relationship-based field within public relations, regardless of the type of company or product. How can we reach people if we are not willing to understand and respect them? Those who engage in media relations must first and foremost be empathetic to members of the media. That involves getting to know the media representative not only as an employee of that publication, but also as a person. One of the things that can help establish an ongoing relationship is to find a common denominator—things that are of interest to both the public relations person and the editor. There is no doubt that if the public relations person can establish one or more **points of interest** that are shared with the editor, it can lead to a development of that business relationship. How does one find such a point of interest? We have found that conversation, listening, and observation can create the potential for a future relationship. By chatting with the editor about subjects other than your news story, you may find that the editor shares your views or preferences on one or more topics. Paying close attention plays a key role in finding these points of interest. It is vital that the public relations director listens carefully to what the editor says over the phone or by email, and tries to pick up clues. For example, upon greeting the editor at the beginning of the phone conversation and asking how he or she is doing, the editor mentions having had a bad commute in the morning. Suppose that both the public relations director and the editor live in the same part of town—right there is a point of interest! Make sure you talk about these points of interest at an appropriate time when the editor is receptive to such conversation. In this case, it might be when you are about to complete the phone call, or perhaps at the start of the next phone call. Building a common ground develops a dialogue and trust, and leads to a better business relationship. Remember, the point of interest cannot be brought up at an inconvenient time; talking about yesterday's traffic jams while the editor is busy or on deadline is hardly the way to create a relationship. Avoid discussing religion or politics at all costs, especially with reporters, because these are loaded subjects that can backfire all too easily. By letting the editor know you share their interests and talking about this topic further, you can begin to build a relationship that is based on more than just business transactions. One caveat is that this cannot be faked. If you pretend to like what the editor likes, it will end in disaster because eventually the editor will somehow find out. So if your editor starts to quiz you about which team you favor for the NCAA Final Four basketball playoffs and you hate basketball, politely say that you do not follow basketball much and switch the subject.

Relationship building is based on trust and a deep understanding of the other person's moods, views, opinions, and his or her attitudes. Being able to adjust yours to another's is the first step to a harmonious relationship. It's called empathy! This must be an honest effort; not one based on taking advantage of the person, but a sincere desire to build a relationship. One of the things that the public relations director must be cautious of in building the relationship is not to overstep his or her bounds. By that we mean that it is best to keep the relationship from becoming too personal. It can be dangerous to mix business and personal affairs if you are not cautious. Actually, the director is walking on a thin line in deciding where the relationship is going. Keeping the relationship on a business level means there is less of a chance for the relationship to diminish due to personal issues. We all know that social relationships may often spur personal problems; these in turn can erode the objective perspective that both parties must maintain. This is not to say that the public relations director cannot ever go to lunch with the editor, or invite the editor to a barbecue. The occasional social interaction can be quite helpful in cementing a strong business relationship. It is when the business relationship becomes too much on a personal level that we often find trouble brewing. Although it is true that the points of interest can trigger the start of a relationship, they cannot be the only basis for the long term. Performance, satisfying the editor's needs, and solving problems are still the deciding factors on whether the relationship will last. Relationships are built on trust, but are tested by performance.

## Developing the Relationship

There is no mystery to being successful at fashion public relations. It takes a work ethic, creativity, positive attitude, and the ability to work with other people. One of the problems that many public relations personnel face is their own inability to understand how to develop a relationship with members of the media. We must first understand the stressful nature of working in the media; most reporters and journalists are almost always under some sort of deadline and are also under pressure to get the right story at the right time. As a result, reporters are naturally suspicious of any news that is sent to them from a company or a public relations firm; they want to check out the facts first before evaluating the story. Plus, reporters have to be careful with the type of relationship that they form so as not to create a bias. Most media companies have strict rules regarding their personnel fraternizing with public relations people. Many media establishments do not encourage lunch or dinner meetings with public relations people. However, if this type of meeting is necessary, usually the media organization's policy is that their employees pay their own way. This social arm's-length policy by the media makes it more difficult to establish a relationship. Knowing this and not trying to gain a relationship by buying lunch will keep the association on an equal level. Relationship building has to be based on mutual respect and a high degree of empathy. The best way to gain respect of the media is to maintain high integrity standards and do what you said you would; being honest and fulfilling one's promises is the best way to earn the right to a relationship. The old adage "My word is my bond" is an essential element in relationship building. If you tell the media that the story is an exclusive, you must adhere to the agreement. Soliciting another media source after you made the commitment is the quickest way to ruining the relationship and any chances for future media coverage. Going back on your word can result in irreparable damage. Build a reputation for telling it as it is! Being truthful to your media contacts is the start of building a relationship. Reporters say time and again that someone will never get a story from them because that someone lied to them. Ethical conduct on both sides will strengthen a relationship. It is short sighted to believe that embellishing a story and exaggerating the facts will lead to getting a story published. When ethics becomes part of your everyday work and you don't participate in spin or stretching the facts, you will find your media contacts will respond more readily to your future releases.

### Keeping Up with the Reporter's Current Work

As mentioned in the previous chapter, it is easier to create media interest when we contact reporters and editors who over time have shown by their coverage history that they are interested in our topic. It is important to isolate which publications are most likely to write about our type of news and then research their reporters and editors to find the ones whose article topics are closest to our topic. If our press release is about a new line of men's business shoes, there is no need to contact any sports magazines or women's fashion magazines. Publications that cater to professional males might be interested in the story because

## Box 9.2  Real World Profile: Nina Garcia

Nina Garcia is a prominent media personality in the world of fashion. As can be seen from her unofficial biography below, she has always been interested in the topics of women's cutting-edge styles as well as empowering women to create their own styles. Knowing her background and interests can help the fashion company create a more focused public relations pitch that will resonate with Garcia and likely lead to news coverage.

Garcia fits her fashion guru role on *Project Runway* around her full-time job of heading the fashion department of *Elle* magazine and writing her new fashion column in *Elle*, "Fashionina." She works closely with top designers and stylists and pinpoints the trends of the season in her monthly mission to develop the ultimate look book and shopping guide for stylish women around the globe. She also conceives the front-of-book Trends, Shops, and Accessories pages.

Garcia heads a staff of about 20 editors and assistants, with whom she works to develop stories and layouts featuring new trends in both fashion and accessories. Responsible for covering the designer fashion markets of New York, Milan, and Paris, she is relied upon as a fashion authority and has participated in numerous television interviews, most recently appearing on *The View* and the *Today* show as a trend expert.

Most recently, Garcia authored *The Little Black Book of Style* in which she breaks down the must-have pieces that every woman should have in her closet. *The Little Black Book of Style* shows women how to tap into themselves and the world around them to define their own signature look and personal style.

According to her bio on the *Project Runway* Web site, "Garcia got her start in the fashion industry in the early '90s, working in the public relations department for Perry Ellis and its then head designer, Marc Jacobs.

FIGURE BOX 9.2 *Project Runway* stars, from left, Heidi Klum, Tim Gunn, and Nina Garcia.

She then moved to *Mirabella* magazine as assistant stylist and market editor and ultimately found herself at *Elle*, moving up the ranks until she became fashion director in 2000. Born in Colombia, South America, Garcia attended college in the United States and traveled extensively with her family through Europe and Asia. She is fluent in Spanish and conversational in French" (Bravo, 2009).

it affects their readers. However, which editor should we contact? Just like we have to read the publication that we are targeting to become familiar with what they write about, we should read what the editors of our target publication are writing and identify who covers our topic, which in our example here would include business wear, men's wear, or men's shoes. Sometimes, research is not enough to reveal which editor to approach, and in this case we have to ask. Calling the publication's newsroom and asking who covers our type of news typically will yield the right person to contact. In general, the public relations director should work up a profile for each of the top reporters in the company's target media. This profile should include their full name, their title and contact information, as well as what type of reporting they are known for, the type of stories they specialize in, if any, and any notes about their news interests. Note all of that information in your Outlook address book or other contacts software, but double-check it to make sure the information is correct. Keep it updated and stay abreast of the news to see if the reporter has changed the type of stories they are writing.

## Relationship-Building Communications

The successful public relations director finds creative ways to stay in touch with his or her target media contacts and their support staff on a routine basis. Ideally, this contact would be over the phone, but at times it is wise to send a greeting card or an email. These communications, especially a birthday or anniversary card, can show you care enough about the editor or reporter to take the time to write out a card and mail it, and can help cement a business relationship. However, sending written cards or letters is not a substitute for actual relationship building through the development of newsworthy stories that appeal to the media and the delivery of these stories in a professional manner. Cards are meaningless unless there are some practical results to set the foundation of the relationship. In fact, such communications can be detrimental to the relationship if overused; remember that the media's attention is in short supply so do not waste it on a simple "how are you?"—have something important to say along with the greeting; otherwise, do not send the card or email out at all. Here are some examples of acceptable important messages for relationship-building communications:

▶ A thank-you for covering a story. This should be done within a few days of the story's publication. Also, it is only acceptable to give thanks once; beyond that, a second or third thank you can be interpreted as fake or an attempt to influence the editor toward favoring the fashion company. Printed thank-you cards are used occasionally but in reality, verbal thanks after the story has been published are more customary. Still, in this modern age of computerized communication, a thoughtful written thank-you always stands out.

▶ Congratulations for a well-written story about an important industry topic. If the public relations director is genuinely impressed with the reporter's piece on a specific issue within fashion, a quick note congratulating the reporter on a job well done is acceptable. This only applies to stories that cover a general industry subjects as opposed to a story about the fashion company or its products. Here, again, this message must be genuine and it cannot be overused—e.g., sending a congratulatory note every two or three months is already on the verge of being timeworn.

▶ Congratulations for a promotion. When a reporter or editor, with whom the public relations director has already been in contact, advances in the ranks of that publication or moves to a more prestigious publication, it is acceptable to send a greeting card.

241

▸ Tips on newsworthy information other than the fashion company's. If the public relations director hears of something newsworthy—that is not in competition with the fashion company, of course—he or she can forward the information to the editor or reporter in case they might want to cover it. In a way, it might seem the director helps the media do their job, but in fact editors and reporters depend on many sources to keep them up to date on the news. Although this may not help the public relations director immediately, it will develop the relationship and may help gain coverage in the future.

▸ **Fillers.** With some fillers, preparing and sending a full press release does not make sense. In this case, a quick email with a note that it's a filler in the subject line and a short synopsis of the story in the email text will suffice. There is no need to follow up on such an email with a pitch call other than to check that the email was received.

## Ethics and Relationships

Business and public relations ethics have significant bearing over the success of the relationship with the media. The public relations director can be smart, professional, show empathy, and know her or his news story inside out, but if he or she does not possess a sense of business ethics, he or she is destined to fail. Business ethics provides the public relations director and the editor with the guidelines that protect and preserve the business relationship. Just as a wedded couple vow not to cheat on each other, so do the public relations director and the editor agree not to mislead each other. Trust is one of the basic ingredients of the business relationship's foundation. Lying, deceiving, misrepresenting, not telling the whole truth, are all manifestations of an ethical problem. When a public relations person lacks ethics, his or her news stories are typically forged over lies, which eventually expose him or her for the fraud that he or she is, and destroy the media's trust and relationship. Ethics, therefore, is an extremely important factor in developing and maintaining a business relationship. As a public relations director you must ensure the editor gets what they were promised and find a remedy if there's a problem. Also, you must avoid promising something you can't possibly deliver. Assuring a television reporter he could bring his crew to interview the CEO without checking with the CEO first is quite risky. If the CEO is not available, the television crew will be out on the fashion company's doorstep expecting an interview. If the newscaster has to leave empty-handed, you can bet the farm that he is not coming back later to do the CEO interview, or any interview for that matter. The successful public relations director never lies to the media. The phrase "truth will out" is at the core of fashion public relations ethics. By telling it like it is to the editor, the public relations director will gain the respect and confidence from the media. Besides, beyond the pure ethical factor, 9 times out of 10 the editor will eventually find out about a lie or misrepresentation and will stay clear from covering news for the fashion company in the future. Finally, it is infinitely easier to tell the truth in all cases than it is to fabricate lies and then attempt to recall which lie was offered to which editor or reporter. In other words, telling the truth makes good business sense as well.

If a production-related problem arises that might affect the story—for example, if the new collection will not be ready on time for the press conference—the public relations director should first consult with the manager of the appropriate department within the fashion company to find an alternate solution. If there is no way to deliver the story as promised, the public relations director must face up to the problem and inform the media contacts who are involved as soon as possible. Some editors will not be bothered in the least bit about the news of a delay, whereas others who are under time constraints may hit the roof. It is crucial to remain calm at all costs, and try to avoid siding with either the editor or the fashion company. In this role, the director is essentially walking a tight rope and should speak with caution; he or she may need to remind the editor that the director called to inform the editor of the problem in the first place because he or she cares about the editor and the publication and that other public relations people might not have called at all. That said, if the fashion company is clearly at fault for the problem, an apology is in order. As long as the director did his or her part and made the arrangements with the editor in good faith according to the company's production schedule, the fault, should the editor decide to kill the story, does not at this stage lie with the public relations director. It may be helpful to point it out to the editor that the coverage was scheduled according to the production timetable, and that the editor was contacted as soon as the production problem became apparent. If the circumstances surrounding the schedule change are due to causes that are out of the fashion company's control, the editor cannot justifiably be upset with the director; in this case, honesty and care will likely win the director a solid relationship with the editor for future stories.

On the other side of the spectrum, the editor or reporter is also capable of destroying the relationship by acting unethically. Occasionally, the editor—unintentionally or purposely—allows his or her personal bias into the story, portraying the company in a negative light unjustifiably. Although the source of the negativity can range from a simple misunderstanding to a deep-seated childhood grudge against everything the company represents, negative exposure is damaging. The topic will be covered in more detail in Chapter 12; however, it is important to note that **slander** is illegal, and a public relations director cannot be afraid of that. Just because the media is a free press does not give it liberty to defame others wrongfully. The public relations director should research the topic of slander and become familiar with its legal definition and implications; this knowledge will assist the director to deal with the media fairly but without fear. Box 9.3 provides a sample of a typical journalist's code of ethics, and illustrates the reporter's duties in writing the story honestly.

## Availability for Comment

When the fashion company is easily accessible to the media, it facilitates coverage. Knowing that they can get in touch with the public relations director at any

243

## Box 9.3   Ethics and Media Relations

Ethics is vital to success in media relations. Being honest with editors, reporters, and other members of the media is an incredibly important part of fashion public relations. As the American Business Media's Editorial Code of Ethics below illustrates, there is tremendous stress in journalism on accuracy, balanced reporting, and honest representation, not only in consumer-oriented publications but also within the trade media. Founded in 1906, American Business Media is the association of business information providers, delivering business intelligence to industry, Madison Avenue, Wall Street, and the Beltway. Its 350-plus member companies reach an audience of more than 100 million professionals and represent nearly 6,000 print and online titles and 1,000 trade shows and well over $26 billion in annual revenues. The following is the American Business Media's Editorial Code of Ethics:

> Business-to-business editors have earned the highest level of trust among their readers. Many surveys have shown that executives and managers believe business-to-business publications provide the most accurate and credible information available. That trust is both a high compliment and a challenge for those who plan, write and edit publications. It sets a high standard they must maintain. American Business Media has always held its editors to such high standards. Indeed, the annual Jesse H. Neal Awards, named for the Association's first president, were established in the mid-1950s to encourage editorial excellence and have become the highest honors granted for business-to-business journalism. ABM's Code of Publishing Practice, a part of ABM's Constitution and By-Laws, has been in place for more than 33 years, and requires that ABM member companies maintain strict standards of journalistic ethics. The Editorial Committee works with its members to maintain editorial quality at member publications. As part of that mission, the Editorial Committee regularly reviews and updates this Editorial Code of Ethics and Guide to Preferred Practices, which has been approved by the American Business Media Executive Committee. This revision has two parts. The first part is a code of ethics primarily for print editions of publications, and the second covers online versions.

### I. General Editorial Code of Ethics

Editors, reporters, and writers employed by American Business Media publications adhere to the highest standards of journalistic practice. In doing so, they pledge to:

a.  Maintain honesty, integrity, accuracy, thoroughness and fairness in the reporting and editing of articles, headlines, and graphics.

b.  Avoid all conflicts of interest as well as any appearances of such conflicts.

c.  Maintain an appropriate professional distance from the direct preparation of special advertising sections or other advertisements.

d.  Show the distinction between news stories and editorials, columns, and other opinion pieces.

e.  Accept as their primary responsibility the selection of editorial content based on readers' needs and interests.

### II. American Business Media Guide to Preferred Practices

#### II-1. Conflicts of Interest

a.  Editors should not invest in companies and/or industries they personally cover (this does not preclude investments in mutual funds, pensions or 401(k) plans that hold shares in a manner not directly controlled by the editor). Their spouses and other immediate family members should also avoid personal investments that might reflect unfavorably upon the editor. Investing on the basis of "insider information" is, of course, a violation of securities laws.

b.  If a conflict arises in an investment held by an editor before his/her employment, or because of a merger or acquisition, he/she should immediately bring the conflict to the attention of his/her editorial management.

#### II-2 Gifts

a.  Editors should not accept any gifts or favors, except those of nominal value, from companies or associations they cover, their public relations representatives or any other person or

Box 9.3   Ethics and Media Relations *(continued)*

organization related to companies they cover. The editor's supervisor should determine what is of "nominal value."

b. Editors may accept occasional meals and refreshments in the course of business dealings.

**II-3 Outside Activities**

a. Editors should not accept freelance work from companies, associations, or any other entity they cover.

b. Because editors are expected to speak as authorities within their markets, they may accept invitations to appear on television, radio, and other electronic media, and may accept payment upon approval of editorial management.

c. Editors should not accept payment of any kind for making speeches, judging contests, or making appearances at functions held by companies or associations they cover.

d. Reimbursement of reasonable expenses incurred in connection with such speeches may be accepted.

e. Editors may also accept speaker gifts of nominal value for participating in such events.

**II-4. Travel**

a. Editors should not accept payment of travel and hotel expenses incurred in the course of performing editorial duties from any source other than their employers.

b. In cases of group press affairs, presentations, and other events involving representatives from several publications, editors should reimburse information sources for these expenses.

**II-5. Relationship with Advertisers**

a. Selection of editorial topics, treatment of issues, interpretation, and other editorial decisions must not be determined by advertisers, advertising agencies, or the advertising departments of publications.

b. Editors must never permit advertisers to review articles prior to publication.

c. Advertisers and potential advertisers must never receive favorable editorial treatment because

of their economic value to the publication. Similarly, non-advertisers should not receive unfavorable editorial treatment or be excluded from articles because they do not advertise. This provision applies not only to stories and articles but to all products of the editorial group, including lists, rankings, product or company of the year awards, and other such special features and events.

d. Editors must have the right to review, prior to publication, all sponsored content and other advertiser-supplied content.

**II-6. Separation of Advertising and Editorial**

a. Editors must make a clear distinction between editorial and advertising. Editors have an obligation to readers to make clear which content has been paid for, which is sponsored and which is independent editorial material. All paid content that may be confused with independent editorial material must be labeled as advertiser-sponsored.

b. With respect to special advertising supplements or advertorials: The words advertising, advertisement, special advertising supplement, or similar labeling must appear horizontally at or near the center of the top of every page of such sections containing text, in type at least equal in size and weight to the publication's standard body typeface [adapted from American Society of Magazine Editors Editorial Guidelines, Nov. 2004].

c. The layout, design, typeface, and style of special advertising sections or custom publishing products must be distinctly different from those of the publication [adapted from ASME, Nov. 2004].

d. Special advertising sections must not be slugged in the publication's cover (including stickers) nor included in the table of contents. In general, the publication's name or logo may not appear as any part of the headlines or text of such sections, except in connection with the magazine's own products or services [adapted from ASME Nov. 2004].

e. Editorial staff members and freelancers used by editorial should not participate in the preparation of custom publishing or advertising

**Box 9.3 Ethics and Media Relations** *(continued)*

sections, except that the chief editor may review contents of such sections before they appear.

### III. Editorial Code of Ethics and Guide to Preferred Practices for Electronic Media

Credibility is the key to the success of digital media offerings, just as it is for print publications; users must trust the advice and information presented. In order to build and maintain that trust, the distinction between independent editorial content and paid promotional information must remain clear. American Business Media believes it is possible to keep that clear distinction while still taking advantage of linking and other technologies that make digital media the unique and robust experience it has come to be for the user. With that goal in mind, ABM recommends the following standards, adapted from those of the American Society of Magazine Editors for the express needs of business media:

a. The publication's Web site should display the publication's name and logo prominently in order to clarify who controls the content of the site. All editorial content must be under the sole control of the editorial staff.

b. All online pages must clearly distinguish between editorial and advertising or sponsored content. Non-editorial must be clearly labeled. The publication's name or logo should not be used in any way that suggests editorial endorsement of an advertiser. The site's sponsorship policies must be clearly noted, either in text accompanying the article or on a disclosure page to clarify that the sponsor had no input regarding the content.

c. Hypertext links that appear within the editorial content of a site, including those within graphics, must be solely at the discretion of the editors. Links within editorial should never be paid for by advertisers.

d. Special advertising or "advertorial" features should conform to the same guidelines in section II that apply to print.

e. Special advertising sections or features must be displayed in such a way that users will not confuse them with editorial content.

f. To protect the brand, editors/producers should not permit their content to be used on an advertiser's site without an explanation of the relationship (e.g., "Reprinted with permission").

g. Advertisers or e-commerce partners must not receive preferential treatment in search engines, price comparisons, and other applications presented under the content provider's brand unless this is clearly disclosed. An editorial site should not vouch for others' tools that it may offer.

h. A Web site should respect the privacy of its users. If a site intends to collect information about its visitors—whether the data will be disseminated to third parties or not—it must offer users a chance to decline if they choose, through an "opt-out" option. As part of its privacy policy, the site should explain its use of cookies and other data collection methods and tell what it intends to do with the information it gleans. Potential benefits to the user—broader site access, better personalization features, etc.—should be presented as well.

i. Advertisements should not be intentionally placed next to editorial coverage of the specific product advertised. This does not preclude ads on search results pages, topic index pages, channel pages, and the like, as long as selection criteria for those pages are not weighted in favor of advertisers and are free of other commercial consideration. (American Business Media, 2008)

time is helpful in gaining coverage, especially when the deadline is looming large over the reporter's desk. It is vital for the director to have a cellular telephone number that can be given to media contacts for urgent matters. This way, the director can answer calls from the media even if he or she is in a meeting or away for the day after hours. If the reporter is still at the office at

## Box 9.4  Keys to Successful Relationship Building

1. Back up your story with facts, not spin. If the story has holes in it and all the facts are not presented honestly, it can mean the end of a relationship with the media.

2. Don't take a reporter's questioning personally. Reporters are trained to get the facts and their approach should not be interpreted as hostile. They are just doing their job of reporting the news, accurately.

3. Get to know the subjects that the media person covers and is responsible for. Try to understand and adapt to what would motivate them to publish your story.

4. Remember: media personnel are always on deadline. Respect their time. Don't waste it by sending too may emails or phone calls. Know when to fold.

5. When sending a release, make certain that all the necessary information is contained in the release.

6. Be an expert in your field and offer your services and information to your media friends. Not just to get a story, but also to help them when they are in need of information.

7. Send a personal letter or note of thanks (not an email). Keep your name in front of the media person in an unobtrusive way.

8. Tell it like it is and do what you said you would. A public relations person is judged by his or her deeds, not by his or her needs.

9. Do not ask for favors. If you need a favor, the story is not newsworthy enough to begin with and the coverage will not result in a meaningful positive influence on the company's public image.

7 p.m. trying to wrap the story up but has a question, the reporter needs to be able to talk with somebody from the fashion company before the deadline, which is likely to be 8 or 9 p.m. In such a circumstance, availability is extremely important. It is also good practice for the public relations director to keep handy—while the story is actively being worked on until it is published—the cellular telephone numbers of those employees or other people who were interviewed for the story, in case additional comment is needed.

Another facet of availability that can help build the relationship with the media is designating one of the company's employees as an expert whom the media can call upon for comment. Naturally, that employee must qualify as an expert in the field by virtue of his or her training and knowledge, by the number of years he or she has been involved in the fashion business, and through his or her work for any trade associations or organizations. If the company's CEO is also the vice-president of the trade association's export committee, for example, the CEO can be contacted by the media as an expert when a reporter is doing a story on fashion exports to Latin America. Even though the story may not be directly about the fashion company, the mention of its name in the CEO's title and the mention of it along with the trade organization can enhance a positive public image within the industry circles, and at times even among the consumer audience.

### Performance

As mentioned earlier in this chapter, the foundation of the business relationship is performance. Without results on both sides, the relationship will disintegrate as soon as one of the sides begins to feel that the relationship is no longer a two-way street. If the public relations director routinely falls short on his or

## Case Study 9.1  Media Relations

### Artistic Jeanius: Getting PR as a Small Business Owner

Daris Jasper is art director of Chicago-based Artistic Jeanius. He opened a unique fusion of an art gallery and clothing boutique to serve Chicago's new and emerging artist and fashion designers in September of 2007. The Champaign, Illinois native created the concept for the boutique while working in a retail fashion store. He did not enjoy having to constantly fold clothes and tidy up after customers, and this concern brought up the idea of owning his own boutique but with a more functional twist: the store is designed like a bedroom with a closet—a familiar and comfy layout for customers to shop in. Displaying the clothes on hangers in a closet or in dresser drawers allows the customers easy access to the items; employees have less need for folding and more time to establish relationships with the customers resulting in increased sales. Jasper holds a Bachelor's degree in Fashion Marketing and Management from the Illinois Institute of Art at Chicago, and serves as a secretary on the board of Osmosis, a nonprofit educational initiative that offers career advice by pairing a child with a mentor who is a professional in the child's desired design disciplines. Working with Osmosis is where Jasper's motivation for the success of Artistic Jeanius comes from, in hopes that he can use his dream of Artistic Jeanius to inspire others and have an impact on the world.

According to Jasper, developing relationships with the media was vital to the boutique's success:

As a small business owner with limited resources and being a new entrepreneur in a major metropolitan market, how does one get press and media attention needed to get the name out to the public? The answer is first find out who to contact and second get their attention.

In my experience, once I opened the doors to Artistic Jeanius I took the first step to getting in the press by gathering all the media that my target audience either read or reached by. I compiled a list of contacts consisting of key personnel to reach such as editors and producers at newspapers, magazines, radio stations, and television stations. It was important that I made sure that I was contacting

CASE STUDY 9.1.1  Daris Jasper in his boutique, Artistic Jeanius.

the right person or my press releases wouldn't be read by the person who would ultimately make the decision to feature me as a story. So, I called each media outlet to find out who that would be.

My next step was to grab their attention. Being a new business, I chose the approach offering the story of "New Openings." I know that newspapers often write articles about new businesses, so I wrote a press release about my grand opening and the artist that I was exhibiting. I made sure to let them know about how my space design was unique for a gallery/clothing boutique. I sent the releases out and called to make sure they had been received.

When I sent them out it was a little discouraging, but you have to be persistent. You have to call and talk with them and let them know that you sent a release out to them and pitch the story to them. I was fortunate that I made one initial contact to a newspaper/magazine called *Rolling Out*. The story interested him and he let me know that he wanted to come to Artistic Jeanius and interview me and the artist.

Sometimes it can be just on who you know. Before opening Artistic Jeanius, I worked full-time at a marketing company and one of my co-workers was a writer at the University of Illinois at Chicago. We were good friends and she wanted to help out so she being a guest writer at the time made a phone

248

**Case Study 9.1    Media Relations** *(continued)*

An Interview with **artistic Jeanius**

Artistic Jeanius Interior                                    Photos: Richard Peck

*This unique Art-House is where art lives! Known for featuring numerous art disciplines ranging from fashion, fine art, interior design, culinary, film, music, graphic design; Artistic Jeanius brings it all under one roof to give people an experience that stimulates all their senses.*

Artistic Jeanius owner Darius Jasper (left); Artistic Jeanius interior walk-in closet (right).        Photos: Nicolette Stanton, Alexandria Garcia

**How did the vision for Artistic Jeanius come about?**

Artistic Jeanius came about when I was working at a clothing store and realized that I liked the aspect of meeting and talking to new people as a sales associate, but I hated folding clothes. One day a light bulb turned on in my head and I asked myself where do people keep their clothes? - In the bedroom and closet. I figured if I designed a boutique like a bedroom and closet I could put all of the clothing on hangers; therefore eliminating the dreadful task of folding clothes. This would make things easier for the customer and give me the opportunity to focus on building relationships with customers. This would

**How significant is the Pilsen location to the vision and success of Artistic Jeanius?**

Choosing the right location was crucial for the success of my company. Pilsen is significant because it's Chicago's Arts District. There is so much creative energy giving me daily inspiration. It is a haven for artists and I feel blessed to have been given the opportunity to make my dreams come true.

**Has the community embraced your business?**

The community has given me very positive feedback. I can not express in words the feeling I get when new customers

the art house by pushing the limits with new concepts and ideas. I give the community members all of the credit for what Artistic Jeanius has already evolved into. They have made Artistic Jeanius a home for art. I cannot imagine where I would be without all of their contributions.

**Do you have expansion plans?**

In the past six months Artistic Jeanius has grown faster then I had anticipated which is amazing. I want to continue to grow by getting the word out about what Artistic Jeanius offers. Once the art house is fully established in Chicago I would eventually like to expand. If things continue to prosper I would like to expand abroad to Japan, Haiti, South Africa, and London.

**What were some of the most significant trials and tribulations you've experienced attempting to launch your business?**

The hardest and probably one of the scariest experiences of my life was launching Artistic Jeanius without my original partners. My best friend, my partner and I were in the process of getting financing to start our company when he was faced with a personal tragedy causing him to step down from his position. It was up to me to be strong for the both of us and continue working towards our goal. My second partner decided to step down just before we were ready to launch the company. With determination I took on all of the responsibilities myself. With a little help from my friends and other businesses I was able to open the doors of Artistic Jeanius.

**What advice would you offer to aspiring business owners?**

You have to ask yourself what you want in life. What are you willing to do to get it? The only genuine advice I can give to aspiring business owners is to follow your heart. It is important to stay focused and not give in to distraction. Anything is possible!

**Where would you like to see the AJ in the next 5 years?**

I want Artistic Jeanius to be a place where people come to get inspired. I want people to feel like they have a second

---

**CASE STUDY 9.1.2**  The result of Jasper's public relations efforts, the following article appeared in *Stoney Island* magazine's August/September 2008 issue.

call for me to the chief editor and told him about me and arrange for a writer to come out and interview me.

Another example of me getting more press was realizing that I had a friend who was a close friend of a writer for national publications and I decided to talk to her and get some advice about how to get more press and she told me that because my business was so unique they didn't understand what it was. So she told me to come up with a new term that would define what Artistic Jeanius is. Instead of calling it a gallery/clothing boutique, I call it an art-house; I couldn't call it a gallery because we sold clothing, and didn't want to call it a lifestyle boutique because Artistic Jeanius does much more than sell clothing and other goods. At the time Artistic Jeanius had expanded to include all arts from fashion, music, interior furnishing, home accessories, scented candles, fine art, and culinary. I planned to have it engage all the senses when a customer came in. She also advised me to post my

openings and events in the calendars of the local periodicals because writers often go out to different events to try and come across a story.

My biggest source of getting press I would say is just networking and hosting events that brings the media out. On four other occasions it was me just knowing someone who happened to have a friend in the media industry and having that person invited out.

I had an art opening the second month I was open, and one of the designers of a clothing collection I was selling invited her friend out who worked at a radio station. After she saw the place she asked me to come to her station and do an interview with her. Another time I let an associate of mine do a photo shoot. The photographer knew a radio host, the photographer told the host about me, and again I was invited to come in and do an interview and be a guest host. . . . Using social networking Web sites also worked when I made contact with the art director from *Image World Wide Magazine*. I told

## Case Study 9.1   Media Relations *(continued)*

**CASE STUDY 9.1.3**  The Ski Mask Way (artist Christophe Roberts). "It was a show where I played the role of a gallery owner who was snobbish and only showed landscapes and still life," Jasper described. "So the artist and friends came in with ski mask and took over the gallery, took everything off the walls, and put up his art instead. The Ski Mask Way represents: the artist getting rid of the ego by putting on the mask; making a statement aggressively through the way of art; and doing whatever it takes to be successful as an artist and designer. It takes all of us working together and helping one another out by sharing resources and information."

her that I was trying to get press about my business. She liked what I was doing in the arts and loved the concept of my art-house. She told her editor about Artistic Jeanius and they did an interview with me. I also had a new television program contact me after seeing Artistic Jeanius's MySpace page and they asked to come out during an art exhibition and interview not only me but the artist and designers that were being represented by me.

### Questions to Consider

1. How did Jasper get his first media coverage story? Do you think he should have done something different to gain this coverage?

2. Do you think Jasper's unique boutique design was key to gaining coverage? Explain.

3. How did Jasper use his personal contacts to gain access to the media? Would you say the introduction served as a point of interest for that particular media relationship? Why?

4. How does Jasper develop his relationships with the media? What sort of newsworthy stories does he create and supply to the media?

5. Does it seem like Jasper is delivering what he promised to the media? How does coverage about Jasper's boutique help the media fulfill its needs?

her duties of providing well-written and researched releases, arranging interviews, and setting up photo ops, the editor or reporter will soon despair of the director taking care of his or her part in the relationship and gradually start to ignore the director's releases, pitches, and communications. On the other hand, if the editor or reporter repeatedly promises to cover the story and asks the director to line up the interviews and photo ops only to not show up, or if the editor or reporter covers the story but barely mentions the fashion company's name, the director will soon despair of the editor or reporter taking care of his or her part in the relationship and gradually stop sending that editor or reporter press releases and relationship-building communications. After all, this is a business relationship and as part of it, both parties agree to accomplish certain tasks in return for the other party accomplishing their tasks. The public relations director must keep his or her end of the bargain, and encourage the same from his or her media contacts to develop and strengthen the relationship. To build and develop the relationship with the media, the public relations director should strive to be as organized, thorough, and effective as possible in order to increase performance. Well-written press releases that provide newsworthy stories with supported research as needed, well-organized and smooth interviews and photo ops that maximize the reporter's time, and persuasive yet considerate pitches are all elements upon which a strong and meaningful business relationship can be built and developed.

## Chapter Summary

▶ Media relations consists of various public relations initiatives that create a long-term positive business relationship with the media, resulting in better and more frequent media coverage.

▶ The business relationship provides a framework within which the public relations personnel can forge cooperative links with the members of the target media.

▶ The success of the business relationship depends on the needs of the fashion company and the media. The two sets of needs must complement each other so that both parties can benefit from the relationship.

▶ To implement media relations, it is helpful for the public relations person to be inclined to work with people as opposed to paperwork. Such an inclination lends itself to the creation of trust and cooperation between the two parties.

▶ Identifying and pursuing genuine points of interest can lead to the creation of a long-term business relationship that otherwise might have ended after the story was published.

▶ Staying abreast of the topics and types of stories the reporter has been covering helps to approach the right reporter for the story and strengthening the relationship with him or her.

▶ Members of the media are typically pressed for time, especially right before deadline; maximizing the media's time is thus a major influencing factor in relationship building.

▶ Communications that further develop the relationship with the media should be sent out periodically to keep the company's name in the forefront of the editor's mind.

▶ Ethics is extremely significant in the world of fashion public relations. When abused, it can lead to distrust from the media and even the utter destruction of the relationship.

## Key Terms

▶ business relationship
▶ filler
▶ media relations
▶ point of interest
▶ slander

251

## Chapter-End Questions and Exercises

1.  What does media relations mean? Give an example.

2.  Define "business relationship." Why is it so important in the world of fashion public relations?

3.  How is a business relationship similar to a marriage?

4.  Explain how and why the public relations staff should work with, as opposed to against or independent of, the media.

5.  What are the main characteristics that define a people-person and a paper-person? How should this classification help the public relations? Give an example illustrating both classifications.

6.  What is a point of interest and how can it be used to create a better relationship?

7.  Pair with another classmate for a simulated scenario in which one is the public relations director while the other is an editor at a target publication. Simulate a phone or personal conversation in which the director should identify and solidify one or more points of interest. Write down how the exercise went, the results, and your conclusions.

8.  What is empathy? How can it improve a business relationship? Why?

9.  Explain the concept "business relationships are built on trust, but are tested by performance."

10. Locate in the media a specific reporter or editor who writes regularly for the publication. Review some of that editor or reporter's recent articles, and write what topics he or she specializes in.

11. What constitutes relationship-building communications? How do these communications actually improve the relationship?

12. What is the role of ethics within the context of media relations? How does it improve/damage a business relationship?

13. What does the phrase "truth will out" mean? Do you agree with it? Why?

14. Write down a fictitious sample for each of the four relationship-building communications.

# Community Relations and Nonprofit Organizations

## TEN

## Chapter Snapshot

Besides fulfilling the moral obligation of giving back to the **community,** working with civic leaders and local **nonprofit organizations** on initiatives that benefit the community while reaching the target market with a positive-image message is an important part of any public relations campaign. In today's business world, partnering with community organizations is essential if a fashion company wants to stand out from the competition and raise the public's awareness of its brands. Such partnerships create a sense of recognition among the company's publics on an entirely different level than advertising or promotions. Community initiatives touch the members of the community on a personal and direct level. However, it is important that such initiatives are sincere and meaningful, and that they are carried through. Shallow initiatives that do not really help the community or that are promised but then not fulfilled can have the opposite effect of creating a negative public image. It is, therefore, important that a company carefully assess the nonprofit organization's goals, publics, and capabilities as well as the community initiative before embarking upon a partnership; it is also vital that the company properly manage the initiative to its completion.

## Objectives

▶ Define community relations.

▶ Understand the importance of giving back to the community.

▶ Discuss the various ways community involvement can be achieved.

▶ Explore common strategies to improve community relations.

▶ Define a nonprofit organization.

▶ Learn how to assess the goals, publics, and functions of a nonprofit organization.

▶ Explore methods to formulate and implement community initiatives.

▶ Discuss the moral and ethical implications of engaging in community relations.

The company's public is not some ambiguous group of faceless, nameless people. They are actual people with names and faces who live in the same city or town where the company or one of its stores is located. They have families, friends, jobs, and hobbies. They also have wants, needs, hopes, and dreams much like we do. It is vital for all of the employees of the fashion company to remember that the consumer of their products is a real person and not a mere "number" or mysterious entity far removed from life. In the hustle and bustle of the day-to-day business, it is possible to forget that the consumer can be a neighbor, a friend, or even a family member. Consumers are ultimately people, and the company ultimately exists to help these people live better by fulfilling their needs. Thus, it is in the best interest of the company to be involved in the community within which it operates, and support the people who through their loyalty make the company successful.

The objective of this chapter is to indicate the importance of linking the fashion organization with the community and nonprofit organizations in order to effectively reach the target market. We also will explore how to make an impact within the community by establishing relationships with the different entities. Each organization is unique and must be able to communicate its uniqueness in order to reach its goals. It is important for fashion companies to partner with or support one or more nonprofit organizations from the standpoint of gaining name recognition and creating a positive image for the company within the community.

## What Is Community Relations?

Community relations is an important and vital facet of public relations because the fashion company's involvement—both the degree and quality thereof—within the community can have a tremendous effect upon the company's public image. Thus constant positive involvement in community initiatives typically leads to favorable public opinion, and vice versa. The company's participation in a charitable cause that collects used clothes for the homeless, for example, creates **goodwill** within the community. Any town resident who sees the used clothes collection boxes in the company's stores is likely to view the company in a more positive light. They may realize that the company cares about the town and is doing its part to improve the quality of life in its community. In that resident's mind, when the town is doing better, that translates into a better life for him or her personally. If the resident has no existing opinion of the company, he or she will likely adopt a positive opinion about the company; if he or she already has an existing opinion of the company, the resident will likely modify that opinion for the better. The fashion company thus establishes a relationship with the community, which is made up of many individuals who live and work in that town. Therefore, the company's relationship with the community is in effect an aggregate of the relationships between the company and each of these individuals.

Fashion companies are discovering that they must be creative not only in product development but also in finding creative ways and means to become more involved with their publics. The ability to connect with their publics is vital in order to succeed. They must ask themselves how the organization can be more effective in getting the message across. We have discussed advertising, public relations, and special promotions and events as a means of reaching our target market. These tools cannot be effective unless the organization is able to reach their desired target market. More tools must be added to gain a better focus and reach the specific public. Being involved with the community, such as through a partnership with a nonprofit organization, raises the level of product recognition. Before embarking on a community initiative, it is essential to first find out the degree of recognition the organization has within the community. How does the community view the organization, positively or negatively? Understanding the current public opinion about the fashion company provides a perspective and context for any potential community project that is under consideration. It is also important to define the geographic extent of the organization's community. For example, a small retailer may only be concerned with a small area of a few miles whereas the department store may be concerned with several counties incorporating a 50-mile radius. Today, the community of a top fashion manufacturer can extend to all corners of the world. So we can say that the community is the extent in which the company would like recognition, and the geographic lines are drawn by the requirements and goals of the company. The ability to choose the right vehicle to make an impact on the community is the challenge; let's explore some of the common vehicles used to improve community relations.

## Community Events

A successfully implemented community event that appeals to a large segment of the community can generate tremendous goodwill and significantly improve brand awareness of the company overnight. The benefits of a well-run community-wide event are numerous and significant. Improved reputation for the company, increased visibility for its brands, better positioning in the market, and favorable media coverage are just some of the highly valuable outcomes of a successful

## Box 10.1    Real World Concept: Global Communities

Today, a community is no longer delimited by geographical boundaries. The world is now even smaller thanks to ease of travel, advances in telecommunications, and the Internet. A fashion company's community is no longer merely the city or state in which the company operates; in today's business world, that community can stretch across the nation and the world. Mail-order catalogs, readily available consumer media, and Web-based stores are some of the tools that allow a fashion company to expand its reach beyond its hometown.

FIGURE BOX 10.1  Over the years, 1.3 million hours have been given in community service nationwide, valued at $22.4 million. The simple, successful mission of Partners in Time, "Sharing Our Time To Make A Difference," has impacted nearly all segments of society. In 2006, 67,000 employees, families, and friends volunteered more than 130,000 hours of time, valued at $2.4 million, to nonprofit organizations.

community event. Often, the impact of such an event extends beyond the short-term exposure leading to and during the event; positive word-of-mouth about the event and the company can continue to spread weeks and months after the actual event had occurred.

However, not all community events are created equal. The scope of the event, its purpose, whether or not it is tied to a nonprofit organization, whether or not it seems commercial, how many people attend, as well as other factors all determine the event's prestige, contribution to the community, and effectiveness in terms of public relations. The Macy's Thanksgiving Day Parade is an example of a renowned community event. For more than 80 years, the annual celebration features pageantry, fun, and surprises that have made this annual New York City extravaganza a perennial favorite. In 2007, the parade featured more than 10,000 participants and was viewed by approximately 3.5 million live spectators, with another 50 million watching on television (NBC, 2008). Needless to say, it is a big production, but one with many public relations rewards for Macy's and its 800-plus stores nationwide.

There are a few caveats, though, when it comes to community events. As any event planner will attest, running any sort of public event is a test of one's nerves, patience, and resourcefulness. There are numerous variables to

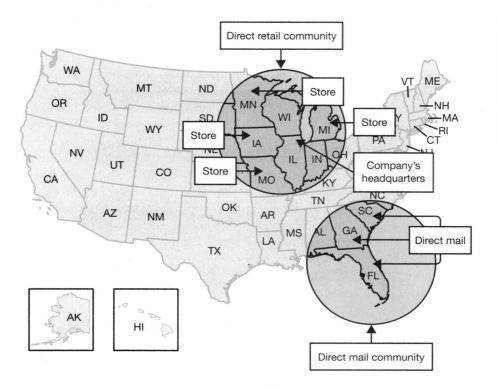

Direct retail community

Store

Store

Store

Store

Company's
headquarters

Direct mail

Direct mail community

FIGURE 10.1 By identifying
how and where a company
sells its products and
services, we can create an
approximate map of the
company's community to
better focus community
relations initiatives.

257

FIGURE 10.2 Watching
the colorful Macy's
Thanksgiving Day
Parade has become a
tradition for some 3.5
million Americans. The
retailer's spectacular
community event has been
successfully assimilated
into mainstream American
culture.

contend with: guest speakers, entertainers, caterers, vendors, attendees, and even staff may or may not show up; the weather, traffic, and electrical power may or may not cooperate; and the event itself may or may not be received well by the attendees and the media. Whenever the fashion company is considering a proposal for a community event, the ramifications of and remedies for the worst-case scenario should be considered: what will be the consequences if the event turns out to be a flop and how can disaster be averted? In the case of a wholly charitable event, such as a free neighborhood-friendly event organized by a fashion company to raise money for a local nonprofit organization, it may not be important whether the keynote speaker shows up or how much money is raised, as long as *some* money is raised; the community at large will likely still form a favorable opinion about the fashion company because the nonprofit organization received some funding it would not have otherwise. On the other hand, in the case of a community event that is commercial and not associated with a charity, getting results may be more crucial. Suppose a fashion manufacturer offers a free sales seminar to retail salespeople in New York City, and suppose the sales guru who is scheduled to deliver the seminar gets stranded at the Chicago airport en route to New York due to a snowstorm. Now, dozens of local salespeople who have arranged for time off work to attend the seminar show up at the venue only to be sent away; the resulting fallout can be devastating to the company's brands in that area. The salespeople will most likely form a negative opinion of the fashion manufacturer, even though it was not the manufacturer's fault directly. The salespeople reasonably expect the manufacturer to either get the guru to the seminar ahead of schedule, thus allowing for such mishaps as a snowstorm, or to provide a backup speaker. The salespeople's resentment as a result of the event's failure will now be extended to the manufacturer as well; they will feel that the manufacturer's business conduct is sloppy and unprofessional. Additionally, that resentment will likely transfer to the manufacturer's brands as well, and the salespeople may now think less of that manufacturer's products. That is not to say that charity events are not without risks either. Suppose that by accident the fashion company organizing the fundraising event transfers only a part of the funds raised to the nonprofit organization. The media gets wind of this and a news story breaks on television and in the local daily newspaper. The public may now view the company as unscrupulous and greedy.

As can be seen, a company about to undertake a community event must be cautious while formulating plans and vigilant while implementing the event, taking extra steps to ensure the event turns out a success no matter what. Use common sense precautions and arrange for backup speakers, entertainment, food, a power generator, and so on. Also, think of potential publicity disasters ahead of time, and come up with creative solutions. For example, it is beneficial to have the company commit a certain amount for the charity before the event begins; this way, even if event fundraising is dismal, at least the company's donation makes the event worthwhile. With safeguards against disaster in place, staging community events is a powerful public relations tool.

| Box 10.2   Real World Principle: Community Event |
|---|

What constitutes a community event can vary greatly. In simple terms, as long as the event has a time, a place, and a purpose, and as long as it invites at least one specific or broad segment of the community to attend, it can be considered a community event. It can be as simple as a small one-hour seminar for only a dozen people, or it can be an all-out art fair for thousands of people. The type of the event can also vary greatly according to the degree of creativity of the company's public relations executive. Events are not confined to boring lectures; an event can be as wild as a 1970s-themed costume dance ball or as unique as a full-scale fashion show featuring local teenagers and their pets. The important thing is that the event brings members of the community together, and that it does that for a specific positive purpose.

What sort of events are we talking about when we refer to community events? Essentially, any organized happening that benefits the community and is open to the community can constitute a legitimate community event. Some common community events in the fashion industry include: the charity fashion show, the charitable auction, and collaborative and fundraising events.

### The Charity Fashion Show

One of the more popular community events, the charity fashion show is an effective and proven public relations tool that is widely regarded by the fashion community as a positive community initiative. It combines the attractive features of a typical fashion show with the charitable elements of a fundraiser. This community event usually features a catwalk showcasing collections from one or several designers. If event organizers are able to draw big-name designers, then success in terms of attendance, fundraising, and media coverage is highly probable. Fundraising is typically achieved from the collection of attendance fees or from auction-type bids on the featured fashion items; either all or a portion of the proceeds are distributed to one or more nonprofit organizations or charity initiatives. The charity fashion show is a tested and true initiative that creates goodwill in the community and generates positive coverage in both the general interest and trade media.

**The Ebony Fashion Fair.**   In its 50th year, the Ebony Fashion Fair is a great example of a well-known charitable fashion show. The exciting traveling fashion show makes appearances in more than 175 cities during its annual tour of the United States, Canada, and the Caribbean. The show features more than 200 pieces from the fashion capitals of the world, including Paris, Milan, Rome, London, New York, and Los Angeles, giving exposure to both young Black designers and models. Many models have become successful actors upon leaving the show, such as Richard Roundtree of *Shaft* fame, and actress Judy Pace. Pat Cleveland has been a world-renowned model since her tour concluded with Ebony Fashion Fair, and professional model Sonia Cole went to Europe after her tour and is still modeling for most of the top European designers (Ebony Fashion Fair, 2009). According to the *Seattle Times,* the show is "a confluence

**FIGURE 10.3** Over its 50 years, the prominent Ebony Fashion Fair has made fashion news the world over and raised more than $52 million for various charities.

of popular culture, racial uplift, community pride, tantalizing entertainment and good business," which raises more than $52 million for local and national charities, especially those that focus on education (Givhan, 2006).

### The Charitable Auction

A fashion company can organize a sale of its last year's collection or clearance items and pledge all or a certain percentage of the proceeds to a nonprofit organization of its choice. Tax write-off is a possibility in this case because the company is donating the merchandise to the nonprofit organization, but this is something the company's accounting department or firm must evaluate according to the applicable state and federal laws.

***Project Runaway* Auctions.**   Here's an example of a fashion entity and a community working with a nonprofit organization on a charity auction. In mid-December 2007, New York City's mayor Michael R. Bloomberg launched an initiative to boost New York City's fashion hub. He teamed up with supermodel Heidi Klum, who pledged auction proceeds from her reality show, *Project Runway,* to support the Garment Industry Development Corporation (GIDC), a non-profit organization that serves the textile and apparel industry (Office of the Mayor of New York City, 2005). The mayor dedicated an additional $244,000 to educate 320 workers in nine factories on new production techniques. Getting involved with the community also involves developing a unique relationship with the leaders by getting them involved in the company's activities. The community is the place where everything starts and finishes. Profiling the community and understanding the needs and wants of its publics is essential in the ability to communicate with it. In the example of *Project Runway,* Mayor Bloomberg, and GIDC, there was a need to educate garment industry factory workers in order to improve productivity of American workers. Clearly, New York City must achieve more and better ways to compete with the world markets and the vehicle to disseminate this information is witnessed in the working relationship of the community a fashion entity and a nonprofit organization.

### Collaborated Fundraising Events

Another class of events that is gaining popularity in recent years is the collaborated fundraising event. Fashion companies partner with a nonprofit organization or community initiative and organize a community event to raise funds for that organization's or initiative's causes. Marathons and walkathons are examples of such an event, where people participate in the walkathon to raise the funds. Participants typically either pay an entry fee and/or invite friends to sponsor them, and the proceeds are then donated to the collaborating charity. This is an excellent tool for gaining exposure on the street level with the participants, their families, and friends, thus working to improve the company's public image directly.

FIGURE 10.4 *Project Runway,* the television reality show starring supermodel Heidi Klum, features aspiring designers in competition with each other. Proceeds from the show's auctions have been donated to the Garment Industry Development Corporation (GIDC), a nonprofit organization that serves the textile and apparel industry.

261

## Box 10.3 Walkathon Sample Family/Friend Letter

Dear [Enter friend/family member name here]:

I was hoping you could help me with a very special request. I recently made a commitment to the Cystic Fibrosis Foundation to help raise money to find a cure for cystic fibrosis (CF)—a life-threatening genetic disease. I made this commitment because [Add in personal story of why you are participating]. I am walking in honor of [Name of honoree].

On [Date], I will be participating in the [Name of event] and raising money and awareness for the CF Foundation. As a participant, I have committed to raise [Goal].

Here's where my special request comes in. I am asking you to help me meet this goal by making a generous contribution that will support the research and care programs of the CF Foundation and help find a cure for [Name of honoree]. He/she and 30,000 others like him/her need our help. It's important for you to know that the CF Foundation is a very efficient organization, and that nearly 90 percent of every dollar of revenue raised is available for investment in vital CF programs to support research, care, and education.

I have enclosed a self-addressed envelope for your convenience. Please consider making a donation of $200, $100, $50, or whatever you can afford. You may make your check payable to the Cystic Fibrosis Foundation. You can also donate online at http://greatstrides.cff.org. Just type my name under "Find a Walker"—it's simple!

I would like to raise the money by [Date]; however, I will gladly accept any donations after that date, as well. Any amount that you can donate will be greatly appreciated and all contributions are 100 percent tax deductible.

I am grateful for your support and generosity, and will keep you posted on my progress.

Warmest regards,

[Enter your name here]

[Insert photo of person you are walking in honor of here.]

**March of Dimes' March for Babies.** Shoe retailer Famous Footwear is a national sponsor of the March of Dimes' March for Babies walk that raises money to help fund the nonprofit charity's vital research to prevent birth defects, premature birth, and infant mortality. The retailer is giving back to the community by helping to fund March for Babies walks and at the same time gains exposure in the media and community for its charitable involvement.

### Education Initiatives

Knowledge and information are valuable commodities. Offering non-accredited education opportunities to both consumers and industry professionals is another proven community initiative a fashion company can utilize to generate goodwill. Education initiatives include seminars, classes, workshops, and lectures that are relatively short and are typically offered free of charge or at a minimal fee that covers costs. These educational initiatives are different from classes or workshops offered by a university or another educational facility whose main business and product is education. The fashion company is not in the business of educating, but rather offers to share the knowledge it has of the industry with the community in order to improve the industry. The educational initiative that is free of charge and open to the general public is of course considered more of a community-oriented program than the educational initiative that is expensive and open only to a select few, which essentially is a commercial endeavor. To qualify as a community initiative, the purpose of the class or workshop must be first and foremost to improve the community through education.

FIGURE 10.5 Because it is a prominent national sponsor, National Footwear receives recognition on the non-profit organization's Web site (see circled logo).

263

### Consumer Education Initiatives

This educational program is aimed to inform the consumer about certain aspects of the fashion industry to help the consumer improve his or her understanding of fashion, products, and style. When such a program covers technical topics, it typically gives consumers an overview of the topic in layman's terms. Topics can also cover subjects other than fashion: a seminar by a local certified public accountant (CPA) giving tax tips around tax time organized by the fashion company still constitutes an education initiative; if the seminar is effective and helpful, the consumer will have a better opinion of the fashion company which organized it. Today's consumers, especially within the U.S. market, are quite educated and keep up on latest styles and fashion products by reading magazines and Internet reviews; however, buyers appreciate any opportunities to expand their knowledge base, especially if it is free of charge. Even if the program only discusses the various garments and never mentions the company's brands, the mere offering of the program is perceived as a service to the community by consumers, and improves the public image of the company and its brands.

### Trade Education Initiatives

Certain fashion companies are in a position to offer educational programs to other members of the industry who are part of the business community as a symbol of their dedication to the industry's success. Manufacturers, designers, distributors, and suppliers can particularly benefit from offering such an initiative. It is in the manufacturer's best interest that retail store managers learn the latest techniques in inventory management, for example. Thus, the manufacturer that offers a seminar in this topic to managers within the manufacturer's area can be highly advantageous; the managers who attend the seminar will be grateful for the education and remember the manufacturer when they make buying decisions in the future.

### Topic and Speaker Selection

To provide meaningful initiatives, the seminar, workshop, class, or lecture should focus on a topic that is relevant and interesting, as well as feature one or more speakers who is considered an expert or an authority on that topic. The topic and the speaker's qualifications should be highlighted in any pamphlets or invitations for the program so that the audience is aware of who will be speaking and about what. It helps if the speaker is a good public speaker who knows how to keep an audience engaged and entertained.

## Community Improvement Initiatives

Adopting a highway, collecting gifts for children around Christmas, and serving food for the needy around Thanksgiving are all initiatives that help the community directly, and in turn improve the reputation of the fashion company that organizes them. In some cases, such a project can be run by the fashion company alone, without any partnerships in the community. For example, the company can collect canned foods in its stores and then donate them directly to the needy. However, in some cases it can be easier and more effective for the fashion company to partner with a nonprofit organization on an already existing food drive. The public relations director needs to evaluate which option would offer more community involvement and generate more goodwill. We will discuss the methods of conducting such an evaluation later in this chapter.

If the company chooses to implement the initiative independently, sufficient time, funds, and personnel must be allocated for the proper planning and running of the initiative. Even if the project is the simple collection of canned food, someone must promote the fact that the collection is happening, set up the collection stations, answer questions, periodically gather what had been collected, and finally distribute these in the community. In this example, it may suffice that the public relations director or one of the public relations staff is assigned to implement the project; however, in bigger projects, such as cleaning a stretch of highway, one person cannot be expected to do it all. Additional personnel from the company whose duties do not normally encompass public relations will likely be needed to assist. In this case, the company is wise to ask its staff for volunteers first before mandating participation of all, which in some case can cause conflicts. Costs for the project will be borne by the company and need to be budgeted for. In the case of the canned food collection, there are minimal costs for pamphlets and signs as well as for the distribution for the canned foods. There are hidden costs as well—the time spent by company personnel is also worth money, and the number of hours multiplied by the hourly rate for each staff provides a rough figure of these costs.

The success of the initiative is ultimately the responsibility of the public relations director, even if an outside company or employees from other departments are involved. The initiative is a community relations project and thus belongs directly on the public relations director's plate. The director therefore must be involved or at the very least stay abreast of the initiative's progress on a constant basis to ensure its success in a timely manner. With the company running the initiative independently, the director is also entrusted with soliciting media exposure. Drafting press releases, contacting members of the local media, handling inquiries, assisting reporters who report on the project, and other media relations activities should be implemented by the public relations director to maximize exposure.

Implementing the project independently often produces less media coverage than a partnership with a nonprofit organization; however, if media coverage does result, it will focus solely on the fashion company whereas in a partnership with a nonprofit organization, the fashion company must share the limelight with that nonprofit organization. No matter how well the project is run, though, it will never be as prestigious in the eye of the community as a partnership with a nonprofit organization. Because the nonprofit organization exists solely for the purpose of assisting the community, it ranks highest in community involvement. The fashion company, on the other hand, exists to serve its customers and make profits for its shareholders, and it will always rank lower than the nonprofit organization. This is another factor that must be considered as part of the public relations director's evaluation of the project.

## Sponsorship of Community Initiatives

Another common way to get involved in the community is direct financial support of a charitable initiative or nonprofit organization. This is an excellent way for a company to venture into community involvement for the first time. It requires only monetary commitment on behalf of the fashion company, so there is no need for the company to dedicate time or personnel to the project. The nonprofit organization or group responsible for the initiative is fully responsible for the implementation of the initiative. In this scenario, the fashion company receives the credit for funding the initiative and making it possible, but not for its implementation. Still, sponsorship is an effective method to support the community and improve public image. Typically the community organization implementing the initiative will credit the sponsoring company in press releases, advertisements, and brochures, thus generating goodwill for the company in the community. Take for instance Saks Fifth Avenue, which has been a sponsor of the St. Jude Children's Research Hospital since 2006. The high-end retailer is known for its fine designer collections for men and women, as well as accessories, cosmetics, and home furnishings, and the company regards the sponsorship as part of its social responsibility. (Saks Fifth Avenue, 2006). Saks Fifth Avenue has sponsored St. Jude—a not-for-profit, section 501(c)(3) organization—through open-ended requests for contributions from their customers, the donation of proceeds from the sale of children's books, employee giving, and proceeds from the sale of gifts. Saks

265

FIGURE 10.6 As a sponsor of St. Jude Children's Research Hospital since 2006, Saks Fifth Avenue has received several media pieces covering the company's involvement in the community. One opportunity for such media coverage occurred when actress Marcia Cross, most recently known for her role on ABC television's *Desperate Housewives,* read a holiday story to children at Saks's Beverly Hills store to raise funds and awareness for St. Jude.

also includes St. Jude in national and local newspaper advertising and dedicates two of its world-famous holiday windows on Fifth Avenue in New York to St. Jude. Together, Saks Fifth Avenue has raised more than $1 million for St. Jude. The sponsorship is an excellent opportunity for Saks Fifth Avenue to give back to the community as well as to improve its community image. The public relations value of the partnership is enormous; a 2007 fundraising initiative offered the sale of a children's book at Saks stores with proceeds benefiting St. Jude. That initiative was covered in both the consumer and the trade media.

Sponsoring an organization or a year-round initiative is an excellent way to maintain constant community involvement because the company's name is mentioned as a permanent sponsor in all of the organization's communications to the media.

### Other Initiatives

There are countless other initiatives that a fashion company can get involved in and consequently improve its relations with the community, and we cannot cover them all in this text. New and creative initiatives can sometimes create more community involvement and media coverage than traditional initiatives, and the public relations director should stay up to date on what competitors and other fashion companies are doing in the community to provide a point of reference to the company's own community involvement strategy.

## The Importance of Community Relations

There is a recent trend in business that a company should first start off with public relations rather than spend huge amounts of money for advertising. This is clearly stated in the book by Al and Laura Ries, *The Fall of Advertising and the*

Sponsoring a nonprofit organization or one of its initiatives carries less risk for a fashion company than partnering with the organization because under a sponsorship agreement the fashion company is not involved in the actual implementation of the initiative. Therefore, if the initiative fails or comes under scrutiny, the fashion company typically will not be brought out into the negative limelight. On the other hand, when the company is merely sponsoring the initiative, it generally has little say in how the initiative will be implemented; in this case, the company may also receive less publicity than if the company were involved in the implementation. The public relations executive needs to assess which venue would be more beneficial for the fashion company prior to formulating the strategy for getting involved in community relations.

*Rise of PR,* where the authors point out that today's major brands are born with publicity, not advertising (Ries, 2002). They indicate that the most successful modern brands show this to be true. In fact, as they point out in their book, an astonishing number of brands, including Zara, Starbucks, the Body Shop, Wal-Mart, and Red Bull have been built with public relations and little advertising. They point out that after the organization achieves its goal of recognition, the advertising element can come into play. According to this approach, the trend has clearly indicated that public relations is providing a greater **return on**

FIGURE 10.7 Community involvement helps build brands. Starbucks went from a single coffee shop in 1971 to become one of the most recognizable and respected global coffee brands today. Starbucks cafés can now be seen on virtually every corner around the country. It has used little advertising, but instead relies on public relations initiatives to gain recognition by the community. According to the company's 2008 Annual Stockholder report, Starbucks opened 2,199 new stores in fiscal 2006, bringing the worldwide total to 12,440 locations. As of October 2006, the company's long-term store target exceeded 30,000 locations worldwide.

267

investment (ROI) than advertising. This changing landscape has not occurred by accident. Why and how this has occurred? We do know that media-driven stories receive greater acceptance by the reader than advertising. But important to this issue is that public relations stories resonate primarily with the community, or shall we say they are community-relations driven. The effectiveness of public relations can be achieved best when all the elements of reaching the target market are implemented.

### Bridging the Gap Between Company and Market

To reach the community, the element of **PR marketing** must come into play. What is PR marketing? It is essentially taking the message of the organization and generating excitement about the goals and direction the organization is taking and having the media acknowledge this message. PR marketing creates creditability by contacting the media and motivating them to run the stories about the organization and its benefits to the community, which makes the community more aware of the organization. Community relations plays a major role in bridging the gap between the company and its publics and raising the market's awareness of its brands and products. How does one reach out to the community? It's called hard work and burning rubber and shoe leather. It requires one to get out there where the people are! Get to know the community leaders and build relationships with these individuals. Find out what they need and want, and the ways to satisfy these needs. This requires involvement—whether it means creating educational seminars, organizing events, or recruiting speakers that will meet the community needs. It requires research and marketing expertise to satisfy the needs of the community and be able to send the message via the use of the media.

### Building Community Trust

Community relations reinforce the company's relationship with its publics by establishing trust in the company for being an involved member of the community. This trust is a result of the company's monetary and time investments in the community to make it a better place for all of the people in that city or area. The initiatives that the company undertakes within the community makes the company's face a familiar one in the local community. After seeing the company's name repeatedly associated with local nonprofit organizations and other charitable causes, potential and existing customers grow to trust that company and its products. People tend to trust those with whom they share something in common rather than complete strangers. The same goes for companies. Consumers prefer a company that is recommended to them or whose name they recognize by association with positive feedback rather than a new company they know nothing about. This behavior is based on confidence and familiarity. When a trusted source recommends a company or product, the trust, which the consumer holds for the source, is then extended to that company or product. Community relations helps to establish confidence because the exposure in the media is positive and the public trusts the media. That trust is essential to creating a long-lasting relationship with the consumer and developing brand loyalty.

## Giving Back to the Community

Fashion companies are progressively becoming aware that in order to succeed in today's information-driven business climate, it is vital to give back to the community. The old adage "give and you will receive" applies here. It is important to give back to the community and support the people who make the company a success. When a company implements a strategy to organize, partner with, and sponsor community initiatives, it is taking the first step of making a positive reputation within the community, which comprises its market. Today, providing quality products and friendly service is no longer sufficient to survive in business; a company must support the community with community initiatives if it expects consumers to support it with their business. A company that lives up not only to its business responsibilities but also to its social and community responsibilities earns the respect of the community and cements a stronger relationship with its public. Giving back to the community works on a much wider sphere as well—it helps develop employee loyalty, improve relationships with suppliers and vendors, and create goodwill within the business community. Last but not least, giving back to the community fulfills a need that most of the company's executives and employees feel deep inside—the need to be part of something that is more than just a job and serves a higher purpose of helping the community.

## Nonprofit Organizations

Nonprofit organizations provide the community with a variety of vital social services to members of the community. Such social services may aim to help the needy members of a community, and in this case social services can complement existing government services or fill the void where government services do not exist. For instance, the London-based Breakthrough Breast Cancer, one of the United Kingdom's leading charities committed to fighting breast cancer, is such an organization; its efforts in research, campaigning, and education complement the efforts of England's Department of Health in treating and preventing cancer (Breakthrough Breast Cancer, 2008). Nonprofit organizations can also exist to serve segments of the community that are not in financial or welfare need. The Los Angeles-based California Fashion Association, for example, is a nonprofit organization established "to provide information for business expansion and growth to California's apparel and textile industries" (California Fashion Association, 2007). This nonprofit organization is considered a trade association, and its members consist of various professionals, companies and other nonprofit organizations from the fashion industry, including manufacturers, wholesalers, design companies, retailers, as well as suppliers such as contractors, financial institutions, educational institutions, and other businesses that service the fashion industry.

As the name implies, a nonprofit organization exists to serve the community rather than to make a profit, regardless of which segment of the community it serves. Nonprofit organizations are totally dependent on financial support, donations, and recruiting volunteers from its members and the community.

Due to financial restraints, reaching the community is primarily achieved through the use of public relations. Awareness is the goal to attract volunteers and donors; advertising is too expensive and most nonprofit organizations do not have the financial resources to implement major advertising campaigns in order to reach their communities. Nonprofit organizations depend on contributions and volunteers in order to exist. For example, the main fund-raising event for the aforementioned nonprofit organization Breakthrough Breast Cancer is the Fashion Targets Breast Cancer, a worldwide initiative inspired by Ralph Lauren, a partnership initiative we discussed in further detail in the Chapter 4 case study, "Fashion Targets Breast Cancer." Fashion Targets Breast Cancer is the flagship campaign of Breakthrough Breast Cancer and to date the campaign has raised over $16 million for the charity over the past 11 years. PR marketing is the means of forming a bridge for the community to be involved in the nonprofit organization. In essence, PR marketing requires the same set of procedures as marketing a product. Although advertising campaigns have included nonprofit organizations as part of their ads or have had the nonprofit organizations list their names as supporters, public relations becomes a more important player through co-opting with nonprofit organizations by virtue of the message being delivered in a non-commercial way. Working with nonprofit organizations alone will not reach the objectives fully without the participation of the community of the target market. Public relations lends itself more readily in establishing personal relations with the community, its leaders, and

**FIGURE 10.8** Through the fundraising efforts of the Fashion Targets Breast Cancer initiative, the U.K. non-profit organization Breakthrough Breast Cancer is able to conduct research projects to advance medical treatment and prevention of breast cancer. Here the fashion industry has come together to give back to the community by funding vital research that can help women across the world live healthier, happier, and cancer-free lives.

## Box 10.5   Real World Principle: Making the Message Matter

The media is interested in informing the public about issues and matters that affect the public at large. The fashion company's approach to the media must include information on how the initiative that the fashion company is organizing or sponsoring helps the public improve their lives.

its organizations. A more acceptable message is delivered when the media publishes a story about the fashion company and its relationship with the community or a nonprofit organization. Public relations delivers a stronger message to the community than any advertisement. Public relations is more adaptable to community activities due to its noncommercial approach. Getting active with the community and its resources gives the public relations message more acceptability, allowing the company to become part of the community itself. This public relations vehicle is a win-win-win for the community, the fashion company, and the nonprofit organization.

### What Is a Nonprofit Organization?

A nonprofit organization is a unique business entity whose goals and purposes are to serve its public. The public can vary from a small group with specific needs or characteristics, such as the dozen World War II veterans who may live in a town, to a large and general group, such as all Americans. Although a nonprofit organization may receive considerable revenues from donations, membership fees, and grants—for example, one of the largest nonprofit organizations, the American Red Cross, reported total revenues of $3,155,280,471 in 2006 (American Red Cross, 2006)—it cannot distribute profits to its shareholders or any private individual or entity. In fact, a U.S. nonprofit organization does not have shareholders, only board members and directors, because by law the American people own the organization; therefore, profits are not distributed to individuals, but are reinvested into running their programs, growing the organization and expanding its outreach.

### Checking the Nonprofit Organization's Legal Status

In the United States, nonprofit organizations are typically formed legally as a not-for-profit corporation or foundation. Their nonprofit status should be registered with the state where they are headquartered and their business licenses should be active for the current year. This status can be verified with the state's department of corporations or equivalent thereof, depending on the state. In addition, the nonprofit organization should also be recognized by the U.S. Internal Revenue Service (IRS) as a tax-exempt organization. There are several classifications for nonprofit organizations, such as charitable organization 501(c)(3), churches and religious organizations, political organizations, and private foundations. According to the IRS, charitable organizations under section 501(c)(3) of the Internal Revenue Code, "must be organized

FIGURE 10.9 The nonprofit American Red Cross relies on corporate sponsorships and the help of volunteers to carry out many of its programs.

and operated exclusively for exempt purposes set forth in section 501(c)(3), and none of its earnings may inure to any private shareholder or individual. In addition, it may not be an action organization, i.e., it may not attempt to influence legislation as a substantial part of its activities and it may not participate in any campaign activity for or against political candidates" (IRS, 2009). The organization must have an official certificate or document from the IRS affirming that it is recognized as a not-for-profit activity; in the case of newly formed organizations, the IRS sometimes grants a provisional status for several years before issuing its final determination and acceptance. The IRS also offers a searchable nonprofit organization database on its Web site (www.irs.gov) though it only lists the organization's name, city, and state. Another aspect of legality that should be checked is whether the organization is involved in any litigation or is in any business trouble. There are several sources for this information, such as Internet business sites, the Better Business Bureau, the local newspaper archives, and others.

The public relations director should thoroughly check all of the above prior to approaching a nonprofit organization to discuss sponsorship, partnership, or other collaboration. If that is not done from the outset, the fashion company leaves itself open to negative media. Suppose the nonprofit organization's director is under investigation for fraud and embezzlement. The saucy news involving the director will find its way into any media story involving that nonprofit organization, even if the story is merely covering the community event that the organization and the fashion company have partnered to implement. On the other hand, partnering with a legal and bona fide nonprofit organization is a foundation for a sound and long-lasting partnership that can focus on benefiting the community together.

As with all business agreements and partnerships, it is vital and highly advisable to thoroughly consult with the company's law firm regarding the organization's legal status and all of the project's details prior to initiating, implementing, and finalizing any partnerships, proposals, and initiatives with any entity or individual, nonprofit or not.

### Assessing the Nonprofit Organization's Goals, Publics, and Geographical Area

After the nonprofit organization is verified as legal and in good standing, it can be assessed as to the public it serves and how it serves them. It makes no sense for a New Jersey fashion retailer to partner with a nonprofit organization whose projects benefit solely the residents of Seattle. It is essential to partner with a nonprofit organization that operates in the community where the fashion organization's publics live and work. That is not to say that the publics of the nonprofit organization and of the fashion organization must be the same; only that the nonprofit organization's social services are rendered within the same community where the fashion company's publics are. We mentioned before the fundraising program that Saks Fifth Avenue launched to sponsor St. Jude Children's Research Hospital; to understand why the company is doing that, we can look at the company's statement about its social responsibility "to improve the communities that make our business possible." Saks Fifth Avenue regards the community as "not only where we work, this is where we live. Our company and Associates have a long tradition of caring for our communities." It is clear then that fashion companies recognize nonprofit organizations as a vehicle to help carry out their social responsibilities and implement community involvement initiatives. Now how does the nonprofit organization serve the community? What are its goals, services, and initiatives? The fashion company should evaluate whether these align with the fashion company's community relations strategies.

### Assessing the Nonprofit Organization's Success, Image, and Effectiveness

In the United States, a nonprofit organization must have its financial documents available for public viewing and be subject to review by the government to ensure no individuals or groups siphon money from the nonprofit organization for profit or personal use. Thus an individual or company that is considering donating money to a nonprofit organization can request to see its financials before making a donation; this way the potential donor can determine how the organization spends its revenues. In a successful nonprofit organization, the percentage of the revenues going toward administration and fundraising is very small compared to the revenues that go toward implementing the organization's programs. Another factor to consider is the nonprofit organization's image within the community. How is the organization regarded by community leaders, local politicians, and the public? The fashion company should ascertain the organization's image is favorable in the community because that organization's image will reflect upon the fashion company after a partnership is established.

## Community Partnerships

Before we discuss community partnerships, it is important that we analyze the structure of a partnership as it relates to business. What is a partnership? How stable are partnerships? What are the advantages and disadvantages of partnerships?

The Merriam-Webster dictionary defines a partnership as "a relationship resembling a legal partnership and usually involving close cooperation between parties having specified and joint rights and responsibilities" (Merriam-Webster, 2003). The top reason two or more parties enter such a relationship is the old adage that "two (or more) are better than one." In an ideal partnership, each of the parties offers something that the other parties lack but need. The parties join forces to achieve a common goal that benefits them all. In such a scenario, the parties complement each other and the partnership thus becomes a strong entity representing all of the parties, which together have much more to offer than each of the parties could offer individually.

From a business perspective, partnerships are advantageous because they allow each party to rely on the other party to deliver one aspect of the business without having to invest manpower, time, or experience. When a fashion company partners with a nonprofit organization on a specific charitable project, the fashion company typically relies on the nonprofit organization to fully take care of the logistics of running the project, whereas the fashion company takes a backseat role such as funding, advertising, promoting the project, and so on. Because the nonprofit organization is in the business of helping the community, it is already experienced in and equipped to handle community initiatives. It is thus typically most effective to have the nonprofit organization implement the initiative. The fashion company, on the other hand, has funds earmarked for marketing available that can make the initiative happen. It also has access to community and business connections that the nonprofit organization usually lacks. Such connections can help secure a venue for the initiative, provide vital resources, and attract volunteers. The fashion company's access to advertising and promotional resources can also help create additional and more prominent publicity for the initiative. The results of such a partnership are mutually beneficial to both parties. The nonprofit organization achieves its mission of helping its public, whereas the fashion company improves its public image and generates goodwill within the community. On the other hand, partnerships have some cons. They can be fragile and short-lived; according to the National Federation of Independent Business, statistics show that well over 50 percent of all business partnerships end in failure (National Federation of Independent Business, 2002). Although these statistics are related to the business community, we must understand that any partnership can be fragile and can have a short life if the entities are not compatible. The ability for a fashion company to develop a long-term partnership with the nonprofit organization is vital if the relationship is to succeed. Partnerships can also suffer from other obstacles such as friction and lack of coordination between the company and the nonprofit organization, especially during the planning and implementation of the first initiative. The employees of the nonprofit organization and the fashion company may not work well together, and conflicts may ensue as a result. Differences between the staff of the nonprofit organization and the fashion company in how the initiative should be planned or implemented can also create rifts that may at times threaten the viability of the project. Questions relating to specific responsibilities and duties—including which party is ultimately responsible for the success of the event—may also arise.

In a broad sense, however, these issues are common to all business partnerships and are not unique to just a partnership with a nonprofit organization. In that respect, the weight of these issues should not be exaggerated beyond the typical risk considerations inherent to any business undertaking. The benefits of partnering with a nonprofit organization are numerous and significant, and typically outweigh the risks as long as the nonprofit organization and the project have been approved from the legal and public relations standpoints.

## Identifying Nonprofit Organizations

One of the first rules is to ascertain the integrity of the organization, as mentioned previously in this chapter. The relationship depends on the commitment of both parties to perform the tasks assigned to them. It is imperative that prior to forming the relationship, the fashion company reaches out to the community leaders or **centers of influence** in the community and checks the background and track record of the nonprofit organization that the company wants to form this partnership with.

The second step in identifying a nonprofit organization is to define the fashion company's role in the partnership with the nonprofit organization. It is important to establish what the nonprofit organization expects from this relationship. The fashion company must be aware of the needs of the nonprofit partner and determine if their participation can satisfy these needs. The trend today in the nonprofit world is best described by changing the direction of the organization from solely a fundraising entity to an organization that also brings partners together to recognize and find solutions to community problems. The fashion company must first determine whether it wants to be involved in the nonprofit organization's activities by helping find the solutions to community problems, or whether it would prefer to just financially support the group without participation.

Nonprofit organizations are constantly looking for partnerships. However, before a fashion company even considers approaching or entertaining the idea to partner with a nonprofit organization, it must first do some homework. Determining whether it is a legitimate nonprofit organization is a basic requirement. But, after due diligence is performed, the fashion company must ask itself, is there a fit?

▶ Will this relationship enable the fashion company to resonate with its public?

▶ Is the nonprofit organization's mission parallel to the fashion company's thinking?

275

▶ Does the nonprofit serve a common good that the fashion company can relate to?

▶ Can this nonprofit organization and its other partners identify community problems, and are they able to solve them?

▶ Can the fashion company and the nonprofit work together?

▶ What will the fashion company's financial responsibilities be as a partner?

▶ Before approaching the nonprofit organization, has the fashion company identified and researched any other community partners?

▶ Does the fashion company want to be associated with these partners?

▶ What other nonprofit organizations have the same mission?

▶ How will the fashion company be mentioned in the nonprofit's press releases?

When these questions are answered, the fashion company must feel comfortable that it can contribute both financially and in an advisory capacity. Approaching the nonprofit organization is not a difficult task because it is always seeking partners and supporters; nonprofit organizations depend on donor participation and business partnerships that help bring more awareness and financial support. Finally, the approach should be that the fashion company should submit a written proposal listing its role as a participating partner—explaining its involvement as to support and participation. After this is accomplished it is important that there is a level of comfort with the people who manage the nonprofit organization. We have noted previously that the percentage of partnership failures is high. For the relationship to be successful, it is imperative that the prospective fashion company partner attend several board of directors' meetings of the nonprofit organization before making any commitments and observe the members' interaction and discussions. Also, getting to know the volunteers would be helpful before approaching the nonprofit organization. Volunteers provide insight into the workings of the organization. Because successful partnerships depend on relationships, it is suggested that the prospective fashion company partners also spend time with the nonprofit organization's executives and board of directors at their meetings and socially to determine their compatibility with these leaders.

Important to this relationship will be to determine if the community partners will recognize the social responsibility of the fashion company and its contributions. The partnership must be based on performance of both parties; this must be measured to determine its effectiveness. Develop a plan that involves the community and it becomes a "direct hit." Community organizations will welcome **guerrilla public relations** that will give them impact in the community. After a dialogue is created between the public relations and community leaders, the flow of information and delivery to the target market is relatively simple and measurable.

## Using Focus Groups to Evaluate Initiatives

The focus group is one of the best mechanisms to understanding the needs and wants of the community; it enables us to ascertain whether these needs and wants can be satisfied. Suppose the focus group determines that there is a need in the community for better education and recreational facilities for its children. The company must ask itself whether it has the financial and organizational resources to satisfy this need. The partnership can work only if the needs are understood and can be filled in a practical manner.

## Negotiating Partnership Agreements

In negotiating a partnership agreement it is necessary to put everything on the table as far as what each party in the negotiation can do and what it can't do. Also, it is imperative that the prospective partners relate their exact needs and determine if this relationship can satisfy those needs. Unless both parties are totally honest in relating what their objectives are, the partnership will fall into the 50 percent failure rate. Negotiations must be fair for both parties; both parties must benefit from the relationship. If later, one party thinks the other is not doing its share, then the partnership is headed for termination. The answer to a successful relationship lies in the ability of both entities to be in constant communication and to anticipate what each other needs to fulfill their end of the deal. Finally, at the conclusion of this exercise, both parties should walk away satisfied that they have made the right decision and feel positive as to the working relationship.

Public relations is an essential factor in the operation of a nonprofit organization so we must establish whether the nonprofit organization expects the fashion company partner to be active in this area. The fashion company must decide what it can do and what it can't do as it relates to the partnership. The role of the partner must be clearly discussed and agreed upon before the final decision to participate is made. Does the nonprofit organization want a passive partner who can donate funds, or do they want a partner who can play a proactive role both in fundraising and consultation regarding the direction the nonprofit organization should take? The fashion company must decide whether it has the resources, or wants to put in place the resources that the nonprofit organization needs. The commercial marketplace is in constant change, and so is the nonprofit environment.

## Working with the Nonprofit Organization to Gain Press Coverage

Before the public relations director can contact the media about the partnership, he or she must have full knowledge of the nonprofit organization and know the history of the organization and its future plans. Its performance in the community is a major factor. How is it serving the community? Who is it addressing? When armed with this knowledge, working to achieve press coverage is within reach. If the partnership is compatible, the synergy that it will create should help gain access to the media. It is much easier for the media to react to a nonprofit event or happening than a commercial one. But, like anything else, it takes planning and strategizing to gain press coverage. Commercial entities working with nonprofit organizations must assign a point person in its organization who will be responsible primarily for media coverage. The point person must be also acquainted with the goals, mission, and target audience of the nonprofit organization. This person must ride shotgun with the nonprofit partner on all the events and happenings. She or he must be at all the meetings conducted by their nonprofit partner and be a major player in public relations decision making. To maximize press coverage, it is important to find out who in the media is the community news person. If it is print media, read the various local newspapers and the reporters' articles to get a better sense of whom to contact. If it is TV coverage, make time to tune in to the local stations to get a fix on who covers the type of news you want to deliver. Spending time researching the media market pays dividends. Try to build a relationship with the community news media person by indicating your organization's involvement with the nonprofit organization and activity. Have the nonprofit organization attest to your involvement with their organization. For example, being associated with your local United Way will help reach the media and add another dimension to your participation.

## Measuring Effectiveness of Initiatives

Although we discuss the topic of measuring productivity in the next chapter, special attention should be given to how this relates to partnerships because here the fashion company is not the only party establishing the ground rules. How does one measure the effectiveness of joint community initiatives? This can be a subjective area. How we determine effectiveness really has to do with the end results, which in many cases is difficult unless proper research and planning is instituted. The first step in achieving an acceptable measurement is establishing goals and expectations that are agreed on by all parties involved. This should be accomplished early on when the parties enter into the agreement; when this is figured out in advance, effectiveness measurement procedures can be instituted. Analyzing the specific results of past events can serve as a reference point for measuring effectiveness of future events. Proper methods of tracking the results will ultimately give us an accurate measure of effectiveness.

Advertising effectiveness for television is measured by **cost per ratings point (CPRP), cost per 1,000 (CPM),** or **cost per 1,000-target market (CPM-TM).** These are measurable areas that are accepted by the advertising industry, and we will discuss them in further detail in the next chapter. Can we use the same values for community initiatives? Many public relations companies use these standards as a basis for their productivity reports to clients to measure the effectiveness of their public relations efforts. Others in the public relations industry measure effectiveness solely by the size of the print story or television news spot and compare it to the dollar value of a comparable paid advertisement. Although that sounds good, it does not necessarily tell the whole story. Of course, any company is ultimately interested in ROI, whether the company is buying a paid TV spot or paying for a public relations initiative; in both cases, the company needs accountability for what it is spending. But, the payout or the ROI is best determined and more accurately measured by the reaction to the public relations story. For example, if the press publishes an announcement of a fundraising event and that event draws a certain number of participants the effectiveness could be measured by the number of people attending, the amount of dollars donated, and whether that total reached the goals.

## Community Relations Ethics

As discussed earlier, before embarking upon any initiative to improve community relations, the fashion company should consider all facets of the initiative, including the planning, implementation, target publics, and as applicable a solid partnership with a bona fide nonprofit organization. As the foundation of the initiative, though, the company must really care about its community, and sincerely want to be involved in it. There are several ethical aspects that must be weighed as well prior to giving an initiative the green light.

### Final Goal Must Transcend Monetary Gain for the Fashion Company

When the main goal of the initiative is to generate more income for the fashion company as opposed to helping the community in earnest, the initiative becomes a public relations risk. The public is not dumb, and the media is certainly not dumb. When the objective is to make more money under the guise of philanthropy, there is a probable chance that word will get out resulting in significant damage to the company's public image.

### Diversity

Any community initiative must take into consideration the ever-increasing diversity in the United States. According to the Census Summary report 2000, African Americans and Latinos comprised 25 percent of the total U.S. population (or about 70 million people) and it's estimated that by the year 2050 the combined African American and Latino populations could reach about 40 percent of the total U.S. population (U.S. Census, 2000). These changing times necessitate a more empathic approach in diversity through understanding and respecting all cultures and creating an environment of harmony. Both nonprofit organizations and commercial enterprises must learn to communicate with this emerging population. They must understand their problems, needs, and wants to be able to engage in a successful relationship.

This change and shift in the makeup of our society creates a need to be able to communicate with people of different backgrounds, races, religions, cultures, and lifestyles, and levels of education, as reflected in the demographics of the community. Companies must understand this when they become involved in the community. They must address the needs of this diverse population and be involved in not only the social and cultural movements of the community, but must also be more conscious of other areas that are of happening besides its immediate concerns of better healthcare, financial needs, and educational opportunities.

## All Promises Must Be Fulfilled

In the field of public relations, the rule of always fulfilling one's promises applies even more strictly to community relations. People frown on being lied to and resent even more being lied to and taken advantage of at the same time. To promise a sponsorship of a charitable cause and then to take back that pledge, or worse—to pretend that the company is sponsoring the cause but in effect

## Case Study 10.1   Community Relations and Nonprofit Organizations

### Macy's Inc. Foundation

Retailers are concerned with community relations based on their demographics. Most organizations recognize that they must work within the communities with which they are involved. Nonprofit organizations are the best sources in order to connect with the community. Macy's Inc. Foundation contributed more than $36 million for nonprofit organizations in 2006. Gifts were directed in large part to Macy's core giving areas of arts and culture, education, HIV/AIDS awareness and research, minority issues, and women's issues. Here's the foundation's statement about its purpose and mission:

### Helping Our Communities

Macy's, Inc., its Foundation, employees and customers support thousands of nonprofit organizations annually, enriching the communities where we do business and where we live and work. We believe in 'giving back' because it's the right thing to do, and we are proud of our heritage as a community leader for worthwhile initiatives across the country.

Support for our communities comes through gifts from the company, the Macy's Foundation, and our employees. We've also made it possible for our customers to join us in "giving back" through our programs such as Thanks for Sharing, Shop for a Cause, and Go Red, the American Heart Association's women's heart health program.

Additionally, Macy's encourages its employees to be active volunteers through the company's award-winning Partners in Time program. Approximately 130,000 hours were volunteered through Partners in Time in 2006, which is valued as a $2.4 million contribution by the charities we benefit.

Through all of our efforts last year—company, Foundation, employees, and customers—more than $74 million was raised for nonprofit organizations across the nation (Macy's, 2008).

#### Questions to Consider

1.  What are the reasons Macy's gives back to the community?

2.  What do you think are the results from such community involvement?

3.  Do you think Macy's initiatives improve customer opinion of the company? Why?

not do it—invites a catastrophic public relations crisis. We are dealing here with initiatives that affect large numbers of people right in the company's back yard; the effects of these initiatives will shape the opinion of all of these people about the company in one broad move. Unethical conduct in community relations will likely be translated by the public as an indication that unethical conduct is taking place throughout the company's dealings with the community and its customers. The effect of such a failure can alienate thousands of existing and potential customers and turn them away from the fashion company.

## Chapter Summary

▶  The fashion organization should be proactive in its public relations activities with the community.

▶  Effective public relations is gained not only by newspaper articles and TV spots, but by reaching out to the community with events, fashion shows raising money for local nonprofits, and offering the community services that the specific community needs. Satisfying these needs is the answer to successful community relations.

▶ Community initiatives should focus on improving the community where the target publics of the company live and work.

▶ A company's involvement in the community typically creates a more positive public image for the company.

▶ Events, education initiatives, improvement projects, and sponsorship of initiatives are some of the common strategies for improving community relations.

▶ Community relations bridges the gap between the company and its publics, builds consumer trust in the company, and supports the community; this enhances the company's survival.

▶ A nonprofit organization is an entity that exists solely to serve the community. It is owned by the public at large, has no shareholders, and is recognized by the Internal Revenue Service as tax-exempt.

▶ Nonprofit organizations are an integral part of community involvement and are an ideal partner for community initiatives.

▶ A fashion company should assess the nonprofit organization's goals, publics, geographical area, public image, and effectiveness before plunging into a partnership with that nonprofit organization.

▶ A community initiative must be planned and implemented in an ethical manner, taking diversity into consideration and fulfilling all promises made, and its ultimate purpose must transcend monetary gain.

## Key Terms

▶ centers of influence

▶ community

▶ cost per 1,000 (CPM)

▶ cost per 1,000-target market (CPM-TM)

▶ cost per ratings point (CPRP)

▶ goodwill

▶ guerrilla public relations

▶ nonprofit organization

▶ PR marketing

▶ return on investment (ROI)

## Chapter-End Questions and Exercises

1. Define community relations.

2. What are the company's social responsibilities and moral obligations toward the community? Give an example.

3. What are the benefits of community relations?

4. How do community relations help the fashion company improve its public image?

5. Compare and contrast the charity fashion show, the charitable auction, and the collaborated fundraising events.

6. Find a community event not mentioned in this chapter that is sponsored or organized by a fashion company, and include a description of the event and its details, including:

   a. What is the fashion company's extent of involvement in the event's planning and implementation?

   b. What is the purpose of the event and did it achieve that?

   c. Who are the publics that the event is supposed to help? Are these publics part of the fashion company's community? If so, how?

   d. In your opinion, was the event a success? Explain.

7. Look up the event you researched in Question 4 in media archives and online for any media coverage that the event generated. For each coverage item include the following:

   a. Date of publication, the publication's name and type (newspaper, magazine, Web site, etc.).

   b. Summarize what was reported about the event.

   c. Was the coverage positive or negative? Was the company's name mentioned prominently?

   d. What in your opinion was the value of each media coverage piece in terms of image building for the company?

8. Define education initiative.

9. Why are education initiatives part of community relations? How does an education initiative help to improve the community?

10. Explain the difference between consumer and trade education initiatives and give an example for each.

11. Find a community improvement initiative not mentioned in this chapter that is sponsored or organized by a fashion company and include a description of the initiative and its details, including:

    a. What is the fashion company's extent of involvement in the initiative's planning and implementation?

    b. What is the purpose of the initiative and did it achieve that?

c. Was the initiative implemented where the fashion company's public live and work? Explain.

d. Look up the event you researched in Question 4 in media archives and online for any media coverage that the event generated. Include a brief synopsis of each coverage item. Then include your opinion about the initiative's success in terms of public image improvement for the fashion company.

12. Find a fashion company that financially sponsors a nonprofit organization.

a. Describe the nature of the sponsorship: is it strictly a monetary support or does the fashion company provide the nonprofit organization with other support?

b. What is the purpose of the nonprofit organization and does it help the fashion company's public?

c. Research media archives and the Internet for any media coverage that the sponsorship generated. Summarize the coverage and its public relations benefits for company.

d. What ROI do you think the company received from the sponsorship? Explain.

13. Find a nonprofit organization in your state, and find out whether that organization is legal. Is the organization recognized by the IRS as tax exempt? Is it registered with the state as a nonprofit organization? Describe the methodology you used to find the information.

14. What is meant by community relations ethics? Why should a company be concerned with such issues as diversity and fulfillment of promises? What do you think are some of the consequences of unethical community relations?

15. What is the section of the Internal Revenue Code called for an organization that operates for exempt purposes?

16. Scenario simulation—Create a fictitious fashion company that you own. Include the company's products or services, public, market, and any other business information you deem appropriate. Locate a real and existing nonprofit organization, and create a fictitious proposal that this organization offers your company; include the administrative and financial details of this proposal. Using the information outlined in this chapter, evaluate the nonprofit organization's legal status, goals, publics, geographical area, success, image, and effectiveness. Then evaluate the compatibility of the proposal with your fashion company. Conclude with a summary that explains why the proposal should be approved or disapproved.

17. What is PR marketing? Describe its function.

18. You are the public relation director for Dolce & Gabbana. Your management wants to partner with a nonprofit organization. Name an existing nonprofit that you would choose. Explain why. What kind of role would you suggest your company play? Passive or proactive? Explain why.

19. Name and explain the type of charitable event and nonprofit organization you would select if you were the event planner for:

   a.  Roberto Cavalli

   b.  Ed Hardy

   c.  Juicy Couture

20. What type of public relations opportunities would you expect from these charitable events? Name the type of media coverage that you feel will respond best to each of the events.

# Executive Functions and Duties

# PART IV

# Productivity, Budgeting, and Cost Accountability

## ELEVEN

## Chapter Snapshot

After the public relations campaign has been implemented, it is time to measure its effectiveness and return on investment (ROI). However, that is rarely an easy task; returns from public relations initiatives are difficult to quantify because the fashion company's public image is not a solid object or item. We cannot count the number of positive public opinions about the fashion company; neither can we put public opinion on an easel as if it were a painting, for example, and rate it on a scale from 1 to 10. Public opinion exists in the mental realm of the fashion company's audience and as such cannot be easily counted or measured. Therefore, measuring **productivity** within the fashion public relations field is a challenging task. In this chapter, we will discuss several traditional approaches for accomplishing this task. A similarly challenging topic that we will also cover in this chapter is budgeting for public relations. The annual funding a fashion company allocates for public relations depends on many factors, including the executive approach to business management, and thus the topic cannot be defined into a formula. We will discuss the various generally accepted methods for budgeting and the main factors that affect this process. Finally, we will touch upon the topic of cost management and how public relations personnel can keep expenses within budget.

## Objectives

▶ Understand the important role productivity monitoring and facilitation play in the achievement of public relations campaign goals.

▶ Explore the methods of measuring productivity within the fashion public relations field.

▶ Discuss approaches toward increasing productivity within the public relations department.

▶ Identify the steps management can take when productivity declines or falters.

▶ Grasp the guidelines for fashion public relations budgeting and the processes to calculate fund allocations.

▶ Discuss the top-down, bottom-up, and combination procedures for establishing public relations budgets.

▶ Compare and contrast the in-house budget with the outside public relations firm budget.

▶ Appreciate the importance of fiscal responsibility in the implementation of the budget through cost monitoring and accountability.

## Measuring Productivity

A fashion company that is not proactively improving its public image will become stagnant, and through routine attrition its name and brands will eventually fall irrevocably behind competing brands and wither away. The fashion company relies upon its public relations department to implement positive public relations initiatives that will generate enough goodwill and positive public awareness of the brands to keep the company ahead in the marketplace. But how much is enough? Should the public relations department of the small fashion manufacturer be expected to produce the same amount of positive press coverage as that of a famous leading designer? What about the type of coverage? Should the public relations staff be allowed to fall back on coverage in the same publications as long as they keep their overall coverage high? And, finally, how positive should the coverage be in order to count as adequate? Public relations directors face these questions and other similar issues on a daily basis, and have to make critical decisions based on their assessments of the situations and their understanding of the dynamics of the company's public relations arena.

### Measuring Results

Before we can measure productivity, we must be able to determine what constitutes public relations results. It must be noted that public relations efforts and results are difficult to measure directly and the methods to evaluate results vary from company to company. Measurements can range from assessing the space of the story that appeared in print media or the time it aired to the amount of sales in the target area. Typically, these measurements are not completely accurate because they do not relate to the actual accomplishment of public relations tasks, but rather the consequences of these tasks. It is a matter of business philosophy as to whether public relations efforts affect sales directly—some executives are strong proponents of the practical approach that all public relations actions should lead directly to improvement in sales; others believe that public relations must be a more broad and institutional field where initiatives should aim solely at improving public image without regard to sales. Thus it depends on the fashion company's business policy whether public relations must be measured against sales or other tangible audience interaction with the company. Additionally, because public opinion can take some time to translate into action by the consumer, there can be a delay from the time of initiative implementation to the materialization of the positive public opinions into sales. There are several traditionally accepted methods for determining ROI in the fashion public relations field. Keep in mind that none of these methods can be guaranteed to perfectly fit each and every public relations project; thus, remaining flexible is recommended—evaluating each initiative on an individual basis and determining which measurement method would fit it best. For example, the public relations director may have to use the *advertising value of media coverage* method to measure performance for a company news release, but the *public sentiment* method for a word-of-mouth campaign. Let's look at these methods and see how they would be implemented.

### Advertising Value of Media Coverage Method

The advertising value of media coverage method measures the comparable advertising dollar value for each editorial—that is, unpaid for—piece that is published as a result of the media campaign. Suppose a campaign to promote the fashion company's new collection has resulted in two published stories. A positive report on the collection appears during the local television channel's prime news and that the length of the report is two minutes, which according to the television station's advertising section is comparable to placing two 60-second spots during that same prime time—a cost of $10,000. The other published story appears in print in the local newspaper's Sunday edition and measures about a quarter of a page. The advertising value of a Sunday quarter page in that section would cost normally $8,000. Then the total advertising value of media coverage for this project would be $18,000.

### Impressions of Media Coverage Method

The **impressions** of media coverage method measures the number of people who are exposed to the media coverage stories that results from the public relations initiative. This measurement is accomplished by tallying the numbers of readership or viewership officially published by the media that covered the story. In the previous example, where the public relations campaign to publicize the fashion company's new collection resulted in two published stories, we would measure the coverage according to the numbers rather than the dollar value. In this case, suppose the television prime news program draws 250,000 viewers and the local newspaper's Sunday edition is read by 150,000 readers; then, the total impressions of media coverage for this campaign would be 400,000.

**FIGURE 11.1A** To illustrate how to measure productivity using the advertising value of media method, let's look at a real-life example. *Cosmopolitan*'s piece in its September 2008 "What To Wear Now" section featured Gucci's shirts, pants, belt, and boots (Cosmopolitan, 2008).

**FIGURE 11.1B** To measure the advertising value of this public relations piece, we consult the magazine's rate sheet. The piece was published in the "Style & Beauty" section and seems to be most close to 1/8 of a page, which according to the rate sheet costs $42,500. Thus we determine that the piece's advertising value is $42,500. If the piece had appeared in the main section of the magazine, its value would have been nearly double: $82,200 (Cosmo Media Kit, 2008).

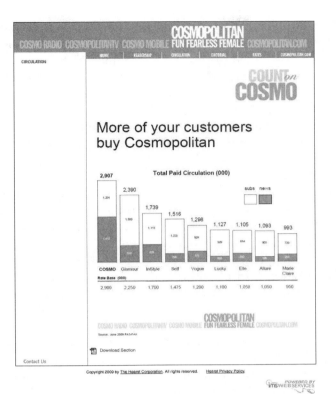

**FIGURE 11.2** Using the impressions of media coverage, method, the results from the *Cosmopolitan* piece discussed in Figures 11.1a and b could be measured by the number of readers that were exposed to the article. Virtually each media outlet offers advertisers its circulation numbers, and from this information sheet we can calculate that the piece was potentially viewed by 2.9 million readers. Because there is no way to measure how many of those people actually read the article, we must assume for the purpose of this measurement procedure that each person who received or bought the magazine at least had a cursory glance at the piece (Cosmo Media Kit, 2008).

### Public Opinion Method

Perhaps the best way to measure whether a story has resonated with the target audience is through the public opinion method using the questionnaire, survey, or the stand-by focus group. These tools, discussed in detail in Chapter 3, give us the grassroots opinion regarding product recognition. To measure results in the aforementioned new collection release campaign, the fashion company could conduct a focus group about the new collection before the campaign begins and, following the campaign's conclusion, compare the change in sentiment from each of the focus groups to determine the results of the campaign.

### Audience Response Method

The audience response method measures the direct audience response to the public relations campaign and can prove tricky and, at times, time consuming to implement. First, the fashion company must identify which audience action indicates a direct response to the campaign; also, the fashion company must identify how to measure which change in the selected audience action is the result of the campaign. In our example campaign releasing the new collection, for instance, the fashion company is likely to identify retail sales of new collection items as the yardstick. However, the company might have to institute a short survey at the cash register to discover whether the consumer has seen the published stories and determine which sales were made as a result of the media coverage and which would have taken place regardless.

### Departmental Staff Productivity

In a large fashion company, there might be several public relations employees who report to the public relations director. Productivity can and must be measured on an individual as well as a group level. The public relations director should formulate guidelines and statistics by which to evaluate not only the performance of each of the staff, but also of the overall success of the department as a whole. The task of measuring productivity can be daunting and stressful at times, but the director who shirks their responsibilities in this area will do their company and department a great disservice. So just what are the public relations director's responsibilities? Let's begin by taking a look at what is a realistic **public relations objective,** and how to set such an objective in a manner that invites participation and commitment from the staff.

### Setting Objectives

Creating public relations projections and realistic objectives, which are agreed upon by both the director and the staff, are the first steps to mastering productivity. Management must constantly monitor all public relations activities including increasing media coverage, establishing new media relationships, and retaining present ones. This necessitates implementing methods to improve productivity. Arranging and facilitating agreement between management and the departmental staff about the lesser objectives is extremely vital in reaching the fashion company's strategic public relations goals. Setting objectives can be a delicate affair, and having the departmental employee accept and commit to this objective or projection is vital to its success. Let's discuss how management arrives at public relations objectives, and what methods it uses to communicate these numbers to its team.

How does a fashion company arrive at and set up a realistic public relations objective? Developing the criteria for objectives is one of the most complex areas for both the public relations director and the departmental staff. It is vital that this objective be reasonable and attainable, projecting a definite and sensible number to be reached according to the measuring method employed. If this objective is unrealistic, it can be demoralizing for the employee and do more harm than the original intention of improving productivity. Objectives are typically set up and agreed upon prior to each launch of a new public relations initiative, as well as for the entire season or year. Each of the departmental staff should be given his or her objectives regardless of their ranking in the company—because productivity knows no exceptions. The top producers today could easily lose their position tomorrow if management neglects to be involved with their performance. Monitoring the activities of the departmental staff in an equal manner is a must for the public relations department to run well—otherwise, it would not be long before some

> **Box 11.1   Real World Principle: Unrealistic Objectives**
>
> Unrealistic objectives not only can demoralize, but may also distract a departmental employee, forcing him or her to focus time and effort on achieving something unattainable—often at the expense of accomplishing other important tasks.

accuse management of favoritism and bias. Guidelines must be established and updated with the times, but within that framework the public relations employee must always be involved in the setting and attaining of the objectives. The director's aim is it to measure the performance of all departmental personnel, regardless of their results or standing, so that every employee has a realistic objective he or she has agreed to. In establishing the final objective, the director must take into account media assignment, coverage history, and trends in each specific project. Some directors use coverage history for similar past projects as the benchmark for setting upcoming objectives, whereas others set objectives to fit the fashion company's overall public relations goals, i.e., if the company aims to increase coverage by 10 percent, then every departmental staff is expected to increase performance by 10 percent as well. Still others may use a combination of the two factors, or formulate a completely different method to set objectives.

To illustrate how objectives can be set, let's take our previous example of the fashion company that is launching a new collection. Remember that this is a flexible process that can and should be adjusted to fit the company's parameters. This particular fictitious campaign is planned to reach out to leading consumer publications in the local area with the release as well as photos and videos of the most unique items. The fashion company utilizes the advertising value of media coverage method to measure productivity on most projects, thus the public relations director and the project leader who will be responsible for implementing the campaign meet and agree on the objective of $30,000 for the campaign. Now the project leader can work on gaining coverage for the story with that objective in mind. Reaching such an objective will require coverage in one of the large daily papers as well as a local television station in the area, so the project leader is sure to focus on these outlets as a top priority while reaching out for smaller publications as well. A week into the campaign, let's say that one story has been published in the leading daily paper with a value of $12,000; the project leader is now a third of the way toward reaching the objective. If no coverage has been gotten two or three weeks into the campaign, it may be time to regroup and make some adjustments because there has been no progress toward meeting the objective. In this practical manner, the director and the departmental staff can effectively monitor their productivity toward reaching the objectives.

### Adjusting to Change

Nothing ever stays the same, especially in the field of fashion public relations. Changes in media personnel, reporting trends, and market conditions must be considered in developing public relations objectives. Market conditions that

293

should be taken into account include increases or decreases in unemployment, population, demographics, and consumer spending at a retail level within the geographical territory. The public relations director must ask several questions before finalizing the objective to ensure that it is realistic in the context of current and past media coverage. Here are a few of the issues that should be considered:

▶ Is the population in the area shrinking or expanding? By what percentage?

▶ Is the overall rate of coverage increasing or decreasing? Why?

▶ Is the public relations person neglecting his or her media base?

▶ Is the area in an economic rise or decline?

▶ Is competition spending more time and money to gain coverage in this territory?

▶ Are there any other changes in the territory?

▶ Is the public relations person calling on the wrong media contacts?

The director should remember that if negative changes are of no fault of the departmental employee, then the objective must be adjusted to a reasonable number so as not to demoralize the employee. Having attainable objectives can be a motivating force in itself when the person reaches these objectives. If the decline in the territory is not the employee's fault, then appropriate adjustments must be made in the objectives set.

### Productivity Facilitation

An important duty performed by the public relations director is that of being a productivity facilitator. It is all too easy to just give departmental staff their objectives, sit back, and evaluate them at the end of the season. However, over the long run this lazy practice will harm performance. The successful executive must be proactively involved during the course of the project, not just at the end. That is not to say that the executive must micro-manage projects, either; allowing staff to do their job is important, but it is also vital to know where things stand and take actions if matters seem headed for irreversible dire trouble. The actual action of setting objectives is by itself often overlooked as a performance facilitator. We must establish the objectives as discussed earlier in the chapter, and utilize the various managerial and corrective tools at our disposal to help the individual staff meet these objectives. The first and most important management tool of the public relations director is the employee's determination. When employees are involved and feel part of a project, their performance increases. When staff members are pushed into doing tasks that they have no motivation whatsoever to accomplish, they fight! Staff can even resist sound and constructive ideas simply because these ideas are thrown at them without their input or invitation for participation. Give the staff some input into a project, let their voices be heard, let them participate in the planning process, and then they will truly become part of the project and work hard for its success.

Improving productivity of the public relations department is vital to the success of any business. This can be done by conducting empowerment meetings, boosting morale, and providing the team with additional productivity tools such as training, seminars, research resources, and so on. But, let us assume the staff have these tools and know how to use them—now what do we have to do to improve their productivity? The following are some effective methods for dealing with productivity issues.

**Exploration.**   Drops in productivity can be traced to a host of reasons. Individual staff can be affected by a wide range of problems, from weakness or uncertainty in public relations procedures to a problem in their personal life that is distracting him or her from their work. But obstacles to productivity may be present on a company-wide level as well, producing a performance issue across the department. An example of that could be an installation of a new but malfunctioning computerized media clipping service, which makes it difficult to reproduce clips for press kits or as supporting documents for new releases. Regardless of the reason, it behooves the director to get to the bottom of declines in productivity and address the situation as quickly as possible to restore a normal flow of media coverage. In this capacity, the director must draw upon his or her knowledge in public relations methodology to spot and reinforce weaknesses; the director must also employ their people skills to initiate a dialogue with the staff that is meaningful enough for them to share their personal problems with her or him. By tackling these declines and solving the obstacles quickly, the department's overall productivity can be sustained in a healthy range, which in turn translates into improved public image for the fashion company.

**Formal Evaluations.**   An official meeting with the employee can be used as a tool to improve productivity; however, these should be used with caution because psychologically most people equate such meetings with the final warning before dismissal. Having a formal meeting with one of the staff can cause a ripple effect of anxiety across the department. If it is done improperly, other staff can learn about it and then wonder if they are next, with the likely result of a general productivity drop. However, used properly and at the right time, the formal meeting can help shake an employee out of a slump and stir them into action. And if it does not, then the director must evaluate whether dismissal is next.

**Shadowing.**   This can be an extremely helpful tool for the public relations director by providing first-hand insight into what the staff is actually doing. Before starting this exercise, it is imperative that the director discuss his or her role and relieve the employee of any anxiety or nervousness that one can experience having a boss observe their work. The director must assure the person this will not be a negative experience, but that of a learning one. In **shadowing,** the director follows the employee for the day, observing how they make phone pitches, how they compose their emails, how they converse with the media, and also evaluating their etiquette and communication. While accompanying the employee, the director should resist getting directly involved in doing any of the work itself. The director must remain a spectator and observer, making notes of what the person is doing well and where he or she is lacking. Shadowing offers the director a chance to directly observe the employee as well as a chance to see how he or she reacts to real-life situations, something that no simulation or training exercise can ever offer. Based on the day's analysis, the director can then create an accurate assessment of the employee's strengths and weaknesses. The director can even use this information to formulate a highly personalized training program for the employee that hones in on exactly what he or she needs to improve upon.

**Curbside Meetings.**   Another important tool for managing productivity is the **curbside meeting.** Termed *curbside* for its flexible nature, this casual and disarming one-on-one meeting with the project leader can be more productive than a dozen formal meetings. At the heart of the curbside meeting is informality, which allows the director and staff to talk freely and discuss matters in an open manner without fear of retribution or penalty. Suppose the employee is having trouble at home—it is unlikely the employee will talk about it in one of the departmental meetings in front of all of his or her peers. But this trouble may be such a distraction that the person cannot function at work. He or she needs to talk to somebody about this and vent. In such a case, this type of atmosphere is probably the only key that will bring the person's guard down enough to have a truly meaningful conversation that will shed light on the situation. An informal curbside meeting at the local coffee shop, for example, can do wonders for productivity. Because it is informal, the employee is not feeling like he or she is "in trouble" and is willing to talk about the problems he or she is encountering in the field. In addition, because it takes place away from the office, both director and staff will dedicate their undivided attention to the conversation, undisturbed by calls and other distractions. Barring personal problems, which company policy may prohibit the director from getting involved in, the director should aim to resolve the issue in the meeting, if possible, and offer potential solutions right there and then. If the employee recognizes an approach that he or she feels might resolve the situation, and which the director deems as reasonable, then it is agreed by the director and employee to try that approach and see if things improve. It is important for the director to follow up on this, and check back with the employee soon after to see whether the approach did indeed alleviate the problem. It is better to refrain from getting involved in employees' personal issues and offering advice; however, simply listening to the employee can sometimes do wonders.

## Public Relations Budgeting

Budgeting is an essential and vital business tool to control expenses and ensure profitability. The benefits of the budgeting process include its imposition for planning, its obligatory requirement for coordination of the communication efforts, and its allowance for management control over the direction in getting the word out to the company's target market. Budgets—whether annual, semi-annual, or quarterly—are part of the planning process that assures proper funding. Factually, budgets set up the ground rules of what can be achieved—without funding, no public relations initiatives will be implemented, no matter how important or minute they may be. These ground rules provide us with the information needed to make proper decisions. First, identify goals; then find a way to accomplish the goals.

Budgeting for public relations is one of the most nerve-racking tasks assigned to management whether it is for your internal public relations staff or for hiring a public relations company. Allocating the dollar amount for the public relations budget incorporates the same procedures that are used for the other internal departments and outsourcing entities. The questions must be asked as to the amounts of funding needed for personnel, the actual public relations activities and events, and for other expenditures. After this is decided upon, the budget can be administered and becomes part of the public relations program. The major problem is how much funding should a fashion company commit to for an area where there are no guarantees regarding the end results. Also, due to the nature of the public relations process, it is also difficult to accurately measure the results. At least the funding for an advertising budget will produce advertisements that will be published in the media of choice. Even in the case of hiring a top reputable public relations firm, there can never be a guarantee that a public relations story will be accepted by the media. However, knowing that, management realizes that with successful public relations exposure the results will far exceed any paid advertisement. So the budget must include all the management elements to give it an opportunity to succeed in giving the fashion company a return on their investment.

There are many different methods to establishing a public relations budget. However, we must understand that regardless of the fashion company's sales volume, the company's collective level of knowledge and marketing expertise is a deciding factor in organizing a public relations budget. It is important to define the public relations goals and then plan the strategy that will determine the costs. The result of this exercise is the creation of a strategy to implement the workings of the budget. The strategy is the action taken to accomplish the desired objectives of the budgeting process. Fashion companies utilize different methods for allocating the funding for their public relations department:

▶ Sales Percentage—One method is to set a public relations budget based on a percentage of sales for the previous year. The percentage will depend upon how the organization views the importance of public relations for its product. Advertising budgets typically range from 3 to 6 percent in many fashion companies, and upwards of 6 percent in some companies; however, the trend with some fashion companies is to put more emphasis into public relations than advertising because the fashion company executives feel it is more effective in getting the fashion company's message out to its audience. Based on a percentage of sales from the previous year or next year's projected sales, these percentages vary from company to company. The advantage of this method is that there is a fixed cost and once budgeted, it must be within the percentage as reflected in sales. The disadvantage is that when business is in a downturn, the need for more intensive media exposure is greater and additional funding will not be available. Also, because the funding is approved based on the sales figures rather than the need of projects, there may be surpluses that will be wasted; in this case there can be a tendency to overlook proper analysis to see whether the public relations program is meeting the objectives.

▶ Cash-Flow Percentage—Some fashion companies base their various budgeted items on the amount of profits for a period, such as quarterly— every three months—and then assign a dollar amount for the budgeting process. This, too, can present the same problems as a percentage based on sales.

▶ Competition Analysis—Determine through research the type of public relations exposure the fashion company's competitors are allocating and match or exceed it in the budget. Although this may be difficult to achieve, it is the good way to estimate the amount that competitors are spending. It is not difficult to find out how much a public relations company charges for its services. This can be determined by research with the target audience and engaging consultants who are able to get this information.

## Budgeting for Internal Public Relations Staff

Within the internal staff environment, where the fashion company's personnel implement the public relations initiative as opposed to an outside firm, public relations budget recommendations are arrived at in several ways. The **bottom-up budgeting** procedure dictates that the public relations director develops the public relations budget and proposes it to upper management for approval. The request for funding will include the public relations department's strategies, goals, and objectives, and the method in which the public relations activities will be carried out. The bottom-up procedure should list the target media sources including a timeline for the activities. The advantage of the bottom-up procedure is that the director can set up the plan for the allocation of funding in order to achieve the goals. The disadvantage is that when the plan is accepted by management, the entire outcome will rest on the shoulders of the director. In a small, independent company, usually one person makes the decision. Many public relations directors feel most comfortable with the bottom-up budgeting procedure. They would rather have the ability to direct and control the department's activities and submit it to top management for approval and allocation of funds.

The **top-down budgeting** procedure works as a corollary to the bottom-up procedure. It predicates that upper management decides on the public relations budget and hands it down to lower management with little to no flexibility allowed for the public relations director. The advantage to this method is that upper management retains control over the budget—and thus the direction of the department's activities—but the disadvantage of this procedure is that it does not include in the decision-making process the people who will have to carry out the functions, thus potentially diminishing motivation and results.

However, in the real world of fashion public relations, a third procedure—the **top-down/bottom-up budgeting,** which combines both of these budgeting procedures—is the preferred process. The procedure of budgeting for the company's public relations department is much the same as budgeting for all other company departments. The big advantage of this method is the total participation of all personnel involved with the outcome of the program. This combination of the bottom-up and top-down versions used in conjunction incorporates the total involvement of both top management and the individual managers in organizing the budget and making the decision together. The strictly top-down procedure is antiquated in this day and age; senior management has found that involving the junior executives, project managers, and even key individual staff in the joint budgeting decision creates the commitment necessary to yield better results while still allowing senior management sufficient direction over the department's overall activities. The public relations director feels more secure within this framework because he or she has assurance that top management is also in agreement with the budget, allowing him or her a level of comfort as well as some independent decision-making. Managers become more proactive in achieving their goals when the budget decision rests upon their shoulders as well as upon the shoulders of their top management. The final outcome of internal budgeting boils down to increasing productivity and returns on the investment while engaging the staff in the process.

### Budgeting for an Outside Public Relations Firm

Many of the fashion companies that choose to hire an outside public relations firm rely on that outside firm to provide a proposal regarding the budget. The fashion company then analyzes the recommendations and makes the final decision. The dollar amount of the budget is based on the fashion company's need for—and its perceived value of—public relations. Many fashion companies place a higher value on public relations than they do on advertising and other marketing areas. They feel it to be more effective when their target audience is exposed to a story in the press or seeing their product aired, than when they view a paid advertisement; they feel they get better results in reaching their consumer audience. The trend that public relations is much more effective than advertising for fashion collections is gaining in popularity with major design companies. Let's face it, major fashion shows like the New York Fashion Week and other shows around the country are really a vehicle for the public relations gurus to showcase their clients' collections. What better way of getting the new collection across than by having all the important media outlets covering at a celebrity-studded fashion show? These shows are a public relations director's dream come true.

Budgeting for a public relations firm is based on the type of firm that the fashion company is looking to engage and the fashion company's goals, as discussed in more detail in Box 4.5 in Chapter 4. The fees and arrangements vary from firm to firm. Most fashion companies look to their advertising budget and take a percentage from that budget for public relations. However, there are other companies that put most of their budget into public relations. Here again, the budgeting process is similar to the advertising budgeting process just mentioned and most often it is based on a percentage of last year's sales. This percentage will vary from 3 to 6 percent and up. The budget may also be based on the individual public relations firm's fees and not on sales or other areas in budgeting. The type of arrangement will vary. Most public relations firms prefer to work with a yearly contract. The contract will differ from firm to firm by virtue of the goals of the client and their budgetary allocation. One type of contract can be a set monthly amount for all public relations work deemed necessary by the client. Another type of contract is based on hourly performance and hourly payment for work performed. The public relations firm then renders a regular report detailing the total amount of hours performed for the client that week or month, depending upon the contractual agreement.

Before a public relations firm can generate a proposal, it is important to first find out from the client—the fashion company—what their goals and objectives are and enumerate the work load. Included in this information would be a discussion of the timeline and the client's expectations. Developing a realistic timeline to reach the fashion company's public relations goals is imperative; otherwise, the firm will lose focus and performance will suffer. The next step would be to know the dollar amount allotted for the public relations budget from the fashion company. Based on the fashion company's timeline, goals, and budget, the public relations firm can prepare a proposal stating the extent of its services. The proposal should include the public relations firm's responsibilities, functions, and duties to the client, and how it will be compensated. It is also important to note that the proposal should specify which expenses incurred by the public relations firm—e.g., telephone calls, couriered packages, and so on—will be billed to the client. The duties that the public relations company will be responsible for should be clearly outlined to include specific tasks, such as preparing press releases, creating and maintaining a press kit, submitting feature articles to the media, arranging and preparing the client for media interviews, and so forth. The proposal may also include non-traditional public relations initiatives such as customer newsletters, viral online public relations, and any other area that both parties agreed upon.

A typical contract is usually for a 12-month period. The contract can be based on a monthly retainer for all services as outlined in the proposal or billed by hourly performance. Either way, invoices are usually submitted at the end of the month and paid in 15, 30, or 60 days according to the terms in the contract. The greatest majority of public relations firms work by contract and are compensated by hourly rates, including a minimum of 24 hours per month. These rates can run from $50 per hour to $350 per hour and higher, depending upon the firm's experience, prestige, and talent. They also bill the client for all expenses including but not limited to postage, photographs, long-distance phone calls, UPS and Federal Express charges, and some firms even charge for telephone consulting time at the same hourly rate included in the contract. A project-based contract with a specific fee is not very popular with public relations firms. Established public relations firms are interested in building a relationship with their clients, and see this project-based relationship as too short-term. When a client wants to enter into a project-based contract, they should be prepared to pay a great deal more for the service. Although it may seem like a great vehicle for determining the performance of the public relations firm, it can also be a very expensive way of achieving the goal. The costs for work and services under such a contract will usually be above the market price and ultimately will not be cost-effective.

## Cost Accountability

Implementing the budget is vital to the bottom line of an organization. When the ground rules are not monitored properly and in a timely fashion, the results can be disastrous. The methods may vary, but an oversight procedure must be in place to keep the budget on target. This involves monitoring the expenses, setting spending limits for the activities, and properly reviewing these expenditures on a routine and frequent basis. Action must be taken as soon as a problem is detected or else it can mushroom into a major financial problem. Overspending is one of the most frequent problems that plague organizations today, and only by constant and careful monitoring can this situation be controlled. Managing the expenditures is only as good as the system that is used to implement and monitor the spending. The typical method used for the internal public relations department is to have the employees record their hourly activities, expenses, and results in a weekly report. These reports must be monitored weekly in order to stay within the guidelines of the budget. Some companies review the expenditures monthly; this really depends upon the dollar amount and company policy. The main point is to discover if there is overspending and take immediate action to find out the reasons, counter the deficit if possible, and control the spending in the future. The procedure for keeping tabs on the outside public relations firm's expenses is handled through the monthly invoice submitted by that public relations firm to the fashion company. Here again, monitoring the expenditures is vital to keeping the budget in line. It can happen that a public relations firm may include expenses that were not agreed upon in the original contract; the monthly invoice will alert the organization of the discrepancy and the situation can be corrected. The "nip it in the bud" action will save the organization lots of grief and make certain that the budget is being administered as originally planned and agreed upon.

## Evaluating the Budgeting Process

Although it is necessary to monitor the expenses and control the budget on a day-to-day basis, it is also essential to evaluate the overall results. How else can we tell if the budget is effective in reaching the goals and objectives? Evaluating the results of the budget will also give us a reading into the total costs as well as the ROI in order to determine if the budget is working. The evaluation process will help shape future budget planning. Is there a need for increased funding to accomplish the goals? If the goals are being reached, then we must ask ourselves if we should add more funding to maximize the public relations results.

## Case Study 11.1    Productivity, Budgeting, and Cost Accountability

### The Zimmerman Agency

The Zimmerman Agency is a solution-centric firm encompassing the disciplines of public relations, advertising, interactive, social marketing, and buzz. The agency boasts annual billings of $172 million and employs 164 full-time professionals all out of Tallahassee, Florida. According to Carrie Englert Zimmerman, the company's co-founder and "awesomeologist," she quips about her job title, energy is the heart and soul of the company, and the litmus test from which all creative ideas are spawn as well as the internal culture of the Z campus. All of the firm's clients are either national or global, including The Ritz-Carlton Destination Club, Club Med, Yachts of Seabourn, Aflac, Bertram Yacht, CitiBusiness, and others. Curtis and Carrie Zimmerman co-founded the agency in 1987 and are sought out worldwide for speaking engagements focused on creativity and WOW. Here are Carrie Zimmerman's comments:

**What are the top methods you use to measure results from a typical public relations project that aims to get media exposure (i.e., the value of the piece in advertising terms, the number of people who read the piece, etc.)? When do you use each method?**

From an analytics perspective, every client differs on the best matrix for measurement. The agency handles the majority of its business in the ultra-luxury arena; therefore, rarely is measurement quantity-based. For the ultra-luxury audience narrowcasting is essential, so aligning the client with others in the same "trusted brand neighborhood" equates to success. Geographic targets with a saturation goal are effective for less psychographically defined customers. Sometimes publication specific penetration objectives are identified. In the instance of the agency's work for Tobacco Free Florida, all measurement has been premised against the number of phone calls to the Quitline. The agency produced more smoke-free calls to the Quitline in five months than had been driven to the Quitline in nine years combined. That is success. The bottom line: Understanding the business objectives of a client and helping those objectives be met is the most effective method of measurement and a continued relationship.

Carrie Englert Zimmerman, co-founder of the Zimmerman Agency.

**What courses of action do you normally take in the case of sub-par performance on a project?**

A sub-par performance does not exist in The Zimmerman Agency. A clear program of checks and balances ensures success for every client. Internal goals are set against the strategies forecasted for each client. The internal platform portrays the path for supervisors and allows time for adjustments to be made should the execution appear to be questionable. If an individual is consistently not capable of producing the results expected, despite all of the team resources and balances in place, that person is fired.

**What are the guidelines you use to formulate a budget for a typical public relations project?**

The *correct* response is the typical public relations formula of slicing the program into portions and assigning the amount of hours per individual involved to execute each initiative. Each person's time is valued at the billing rate of that person—$250 per hour, etc. But, here is the REAL answer from a public relations agency owner who has experienced extreme success for her company: Your budget is often dictated by what the market will bear, how badly you want the client's name on the company portfolio list, how much money the client has, and the potential of the length of the relationship. The reality is, the client with the deeper pockets will get charged more than the fledgling company. The client with multiple opportunities for more business through different avenues in its company may have a more flexible budget. This is simply reality.

**What percentage of the company's revenues would you recommend to be dedicated to public relations?**

Anyone who is using the outdated methodology of a percentage-based budget is not monitoring the relevancy of the consumer offering. Whether the client is offering a product or service, public relations should not be drilled down to a percentage equation, but instead be premised upon the end objective.

**How do you control expenses and keep the implementation of the PR project within budget?**

The Zimmerman Agency creates an internal spreadsheet with every budgeted item accounted reflected. Each month, the actuals against budgeted are reviewed and revised as necessary. Specific to agency time and service, the firm does NOT keep 10 minute increments

of billable time. It is not the most profitable way to run the company, but instead, the team keeps clients for multiple years. Many clients of The Zimmerman Agency have been handled for more than 10 to 15 years. We don't keep time sheets, but we do keep clients.

### Questions to Consider

1. According to Carrie Zimmerman, what is the best method to determine the optimal productivity measurement system?

2. What are the factors that the agency uses to create a budget for her clients? Do you agree with these methods? Explain.

3. What do you think Carrie Zimmerman means by, "We don't keep time sheets, but we do keep clients"?

---

Conversely, we must also determine if we are allocating more funding than is necessary. Part and parcel of the budget review is the process of factoring in productivity. To render the budget analysis relevant, we must also evaluate the productivity of the individuals involved—are they performing their functions to our satisfaction? If performance is lacking while expenses are mounting well beyond the projected results timeline, then the state of affairs need urgent adjustment. The budget is only as good as the results that are realized. The evaluation process is the report card that will spell out whether the budgeting process is working according to the plan.

## Chapter Summary

▸ To ensure that it is proactively improving its public image, a fashion company should routinely measure the effectiveness of its public relations initiatives.

▸ In fashion public relations, measuring results is not an exact science because we are dealing with public opinion, which is something that is difficult to measure accurately; however, some methods exist to give management a rough idea of how a campaign or initiative is faring.

▸ The main productivity measurement methods in fashion public relations are the advertising value of media coverage, impressions of media coverage, public opinion, and audience response methods.

▸ It is vital to measure and monitor productivity both of the public relations department as a whole as well as of each of the employees within it.

▶ Setting realistic and feasible objectives that the involved employees agree with is the first step toward facilitating productivity in an organized manner.

▶ Beyond on-the-job training, drops in productivity can be dealt with using several approaches, the main ones being exploration, formal evaluations, shadowing, and curbside meetings.

▶ Creating a budget for public relations is both an essential and difficult task, with the main methods of budgeting being the sales percentage, the cash-flow percentage, and the competition analysis methods.

▶ There are three budgeting procedures for developing the internal public relations budget: the bottom up, the top down, and the combination top down/bottom up.

▶ When working with an outside public relations firm, the fashion company typically receives a budget proposal from the firm outlining the scope of the project, the firm's RFDs, and the costs.

▶ It is vital to not only develop a sound budget, but also to implement it correctly, control expenditures, and monitor returns on the investment.

## Key Terms

▶ bottom-up budgeting

▶ curbside meeting

▶ impressions

▶ productivity

▶ public relations objective

▶ shadowing

▶ top-down budgeting

▶ top-down/bottom-up budgeting

## Chapter-End Questions and Exercises

1. What is productivity in the context of fashion public relations? Give an example.

2. Is measuring results in public relations an exact science? Explain.

3. Describe the four methods to measure public relations productivity, and give a fictitious example for each.

4. Look through a popular fashion consumer magazine and locate a positive article about a specific designer or brand. Describe the story and its size in terms of pages. Then go to the magazine's Web site and look through its advertising rate card to establish the advertising value of the piece. Explain the calculation process and how you arrived at the final figure.

5. For the same example in Question 4, determine the number of impressions the piece received. Explain how you arrived at the final figure.

6. Do you think setting public relations objectives is beneficial to increasing productivity? Why?

7. Explain the four methods to dealing with productivity issues.

8. For each of these four methods used when dealing with productivity issues, give an example of a scenario illustrating how the method could help improve matters and why it would be appropriate to use over other methods.

9. Find a publicly traded fashion company on the Web site www.hoovers.com and find out the company's overall sales. Then figure out what would be its advertising/public relations budget based on the sales percentage budgeting method. Do you think that this is a workable budget for the company's advertising and public relations? Why or why not?

10. On that same Web site from Question 9, look for the company's cash flow statements under the financials tab. Find the company's net operating cash flow figure for the previous year, and use it to calculate the advertising/public relations budget based on the cash-flow budgeting method. Do you think that this is a workable budget for the company's advertising and public relations? Why or why not?

11. Which budgeting procedure do you think is best: bottom-up, top-down, or the combination of the two? Explain.

12. What are the various types of contracts that outside public relations firms normally offer? What is the difference between them?

13. What role does cost accountability play in the success of public relations?

# Crisis Management

## TWELVE

## Chapter Snapshot

**D**espite all of the hard work the fashion company puts into creating a positive public image, it is likely that at some point, somewhere in the media or other spheres, a negative story about the company will crop up. The source of the negative story can be the company's own doing—i.e., staff blunders—or an attempt by the competition to knock the company's reputation. The negative story can be a true depiction of events, or it can be a complete fabrication without any substantiation. The damage from such negative exposure can be disastrous; if the audience begins to view the fashion company and its products with suspicion, its retail sales could very well come to a screeching halt. Within the field of fashion public relations, crisis management is the function of identifying and countering such negative publicity. Crisis management can at times develop into quite a nasty affair, and the public relations staff should be prepared and ready to deal with it. In this chapter, we will define what a crisis is, and what the fashion company can do to respond to it, counter it, and ultimately use it to its advantage and improve its public image.

## Objectives

▶   Define the public relations crisis.

▶   Understand the anatomy of the crisis and the factors that shape it.

▶   Compare and contrast the self-inflicted crisis with the fabricated crisis.

▶   Discuss the consequences of the crisis upon the fashion company's consumers, business partners, staff, and the media.

▶   Explore the fundamental principles of crisis management.

▶   Understand the dynamics of crisis management and how the company can rectify the crisis to resolve negative exposure.

▶   Understand the four stages of crisis management.

▶   Discuss ethical issues in dealing with the crisis.

## The Public Relations Crisis

Establishing a positive reputation and building business relationships with clients, vendors, and the media is a long and arduous task in any business. In fashion, it is ever more so critical because the industry is driven by image and reputation. With all of the time, money, and effort that are invested in creating a positive public image, all it takes is just one crisis to put the organization in jeopardy. A crisis can quickly and swiftly wreck a solid positive public image. Such a turn of public opinion can send significant ripple effects through the company's marketing, production, and other departments, potentially rendering useless millions of dollars worth of advertising, causing devastating drops in sales, and even disrupting production. But what is a **public relations crisis?** Why do such crises occur, and how can we prevent them?

### The Anatomy of a Public Relations Crisis

There are many types of public relations crises. Crises differ in sphere, circumstances, scope, timing, source, and audience. However, they all share a common thread: Their end-result is a worse public image for the fashion company. As far as the public relations director is concerned, anything—regardless of its scope or severity—that actively subverts existing positive public image or creates negative public opinion is a crisis. Unchecked, the small and insignificant crisis of yesterday can easily develop into the shocking crisis of tomorrow. Public relations crises, therefore, should simply not be ignored. When a fashion company is accused of turning a blind eye to sweatshops with forced child and women laborers—a real-world crisis that we will discuss in this chapter's case study—its public image is liable to suffer significant damages. Customers who have been loyal to the brand might decide to switch to a competitor. Potential customers who had considered switching to the company's brand might shy away from its products. To pretend the crisis is not happening and just keep on with business as usual will not make the crisis go away. Carefully planned and implemented crisis management methods are key to turning a crisis around, and we will discuss these methods in the second half of this chapter. First, let's inspect the anatomy of the public relations crisis and the factors that shape it.

### The Crisis Sphere

To understand the public relations crisis itself, it is important to identify how the negative information is spreading. The **crisis sphere** is the environment in which the crisis is developing and where the audience is receiving the negative news. The crisis can exist in the following spheres:

▶ Media Sphere—When the crisis is published in the media (in print, broadcasting, or online), it is said to be occurring in the **media sphere.** Negative media exposure is typically the most detrimental because it reaches thousands, if not millions, of members of the audience at once and it is spread by a respected source—the media.

▶ Public Sphere—A crisis in the **public sphere** is spread through word of mouth among members of the audience. Friends and family are the source that spreads this crisis and thus they are believed even more than the media. Although this type of crisis is usually slow to develop, it is not easy to detect and combat because it is spread largely out of sight, on a grassroots, street level.

▶ Virtual Sphere—This sphere is a relatively recent development in the business world because here the crisis exists in the **virtual sphere** of the Internet. Within the Wild West of the Worldwide Web, rumors spread quickly through blogs, discussion forums, and emails without a sheriff to police them. Thus anyone can say anything online, and it can take quite some time to navigate the legal system and force the false postings offline. Because postings can often be made anonymously, it is easy for someone to post their negative opinion without much substantiation; however, such postings are the least credible in the eyes of the audience. Still, an e-rumor can inflict serious damage upon a company's reputation, especially if it is filled with emotionally charged inflammatory rhetoric, even if it is utterly false. Blogs are more credible because the blogger typically reveals his or her identity and, in a way, puts his or her name on the line. According to Public Relations Couture, an online resource for successful, emerging, and aspiring fashion publicists, designers, students, and educators to share tips, tricks, challenges, and commentary about the role of public relations in the fashion industry, the Internet has yet to be fully accepted by the mainstream public relations firms and fashion companies as the major public opinion-shaping force that it is. On its Web site, founder Crosby Noricks writes that:

> Fashion public relations rarely deals in crisis communication, but if there is one sore spot that continually emerges, it is negotiating the relationships and expectations between fashion PRs and fashion bloggers. Although many public relations agencies have begun to

value the voice of the fashion blogosphere, many still don't give out the kind of respect that fashion bloggers often feel is their due. Additionally, lingering bad blood from initial experiences, often due to poor decisions on the part of fashion public relations agencies, continues to impede any positive steps that are made. Blogs are appealing to fashion PRs for several reasons. Unlike traditional monthly fashion magazines, most fashion bloggers update daily, giving readers more immediate access to fresh news and content. Savvy consumers appreciate the insider tone and expert knowledge fashion bloggers share—as well as their independent affiliation. I think fashion blogs are gaining in importance within public relations because they provide a highly targeted audience, read by people who like to shop! Through comments given by readers about posts, it also gives insight into how people are reacting to a trend or product (Noricks, 2007).

Although blogs can prove a quick and targeted conduit to spread the fashion company's positive message, they can also spread negative exposure just as quickly.

▶ Media/Public/Virtual Spheres Combination—In today's high-paced world, news travel fast not only within any one of these spheres but also between one sphere and another. It is quite likely that a high-profile crisis will spread through all spheres simultaneously. Such a crisis may begin in the media sphere, but it can quickly spread into the virtual sphere as negative exposure starts popping up on blogs and forums. From there, it can be easily read and spread via word of mouth by individuals from one friend to another.

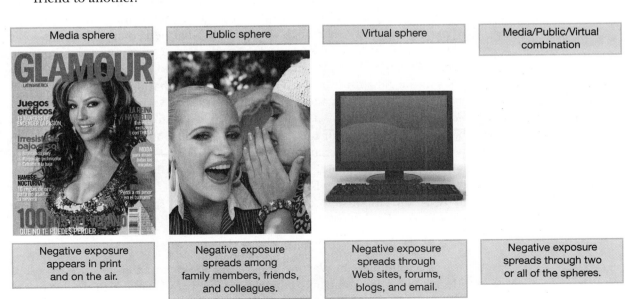

**FIGURE 12.1** The four crisis spheres.

### Crisis Circumstances

The content of the news surrounding the public relations crisis is probably the top factor that shapes crisis results. The **crisis circumstances** can be as trivial as a simple gaffe uttered by the company's CEO—such as mixing up names of important people or prominent dates—or as serious as a life-threatening production error—such as a highly toxic chemical somehow tainting the company's fabrics and causing violent sickness among infants. It does not take a genius to figure out that managing the latter crisis goes way beyond merely controlling public image; such a crisis could very well shut the company down, so every senior executive should be involved in responding properly to this debacle. A crisis of this magnitude could easily make prime-time national news, and mishandling it could seal the fate of the company. The CEO's gaffe, by contrast, would have little negative impact on the company and a response statement from the CEO joking about his memory could even produce a chuckle with the audience thus eliminating the whole negative aspect of the gaffe. Another element of the crisis circumstances—which is well known and well used by politicians around the world—is what else is on the news at the time. If the crisis breaks a week prior to the U.S. presidential election, it might prove to be a small bleep on a radar screen filled with election stories. On the other hand, a crisis breaking on a slow news day might get much more coverage than it deserves. Whereas politicians have enough access to the media to create another, more sensational story in order to divert attention from their own crisis, fashion companies typically do not have that luxury and must manage their crisis properly for it to be resolved.

### Crisis Scope

Beyond the sphere where it exists, a crisis is also identified by its scope. In practical terms, the **crisis scope** is essentially determined by the number of people exposed to the negative news and what percentage of these people are the fashion company's audience. A crisis that is spread to a few thousand people in a remote rural area cannot be equated to a crisis that reaches millions in the New York City area. This is not to say that the rural community is not important; on the contrary, the smaller crisis is very important and should not be ignored because it can easily mushroom into a national story. Still, if both crises were to occur simultaneously—considering which of the two should be attended to first in relation to the current status—the latter crisis is already large in scope and should be countered first. Also, the scope of the crisis management response should be somewhat comparable to the scope of the crisis itself; so the response to the former crisis will be smaller in scope than the response to the latter.

### Crisis Timing

**Crisis timing** can play an important role in how the negative exposure affects the fashion company. If the fashion company is already in trouble or has had other negative exposure in recent years, the current crisis is exacerbated. However, if the company is doing well and has been receiving positive exposure before the crisis emerged, the effects of the crisis on the company's public image might be softened. The duration of the crisis is also important in shaping the crisis—when negative coverage is brief, the exposure may not leave a long-lasting impression upon the audience, but if coverage repeats over a longer period of time, then negative exposure is more likely to worsen public opinion.

### The Self-Inflicted Crisis

When the source of the crisis is the fashion company's own actions—whether erroneous or intentional—the crisis can be said to be a **self-inflicted crisis.** In principle, such a crisis could have been averted had the company's management and employees been more careful or prudent. Because the company bears the responsibility for the crisis, it must also take a proactive approach to rectifying the damage the company caused those who were affected by the crisis. When faced with this type of a crisis, the company essentially should do whatever it takes to make things right with its customers, audience, and the community at large. We will cover the management methods for responding to such a crisis in more detail later in this chapter. The self-inflicted crisis can break through the company's own admission or through an investigation by the media or the authorities. The fashion company's admission of fault is usually the preferred way for a crisis to break from a crisis management perspective because it demonstrates that the fashion company is taking the first step toward resolving the crisis—taking responsibility for its blunders.

### The Fabricated Crisis

The **fabricated crisis** typically comes about through the efforts of external sources—such as dishonest competitors, disgruntled employees, or irresponsible reporters—who have a vested interest in seeing the fashion company experience negative exposure. This public relations crisis develops even though the fashion company has done nothing wrong. The **smear campaign** is a calculated campaign to hurt the fashion company's image, organized—typically anonymously—by an entity that is opposed to the fashion company. We find smear campaigns prevalent in political races where candidates sling false accusations and lies at each other hoping that one of these will hurt the other's image enough to allow them to be elected. In the business world, that usually translates into a competitor hoping that by running the smear campaign the fashion company will shrink in size and the competitor will capture its lost market.

**Media bias** is another form of the fabricated crisis, whereby the reporter doing the story for some reason has a negative agenda against the fashion company from the start. The reason for the bias could be a personal reason—i.e., the reporter dislikes the company or its brands—or perhaps could be a rumor that he or she has heard about the company that now taints his or her view of it. Such a biased report could constitute libel and is actionable in a court of law if it can be proven without a doubt, which is often the challenge. When outright lies begin to circulate in the public or virtual domains through word of mouth, then a **negative false rumor** is responsible for the fabricated crisis. Tracing back such a rumor to its source and bringing him or her to justice is

311

## Box 12.1   The Self-Inflicted Crisis

The Burlington, N.J.-based Burlington Coat Factory Warehouse Corporation has been haunted by controversy about its faux fur products for years. Undercover investigation by animal rights groups such as the Humane Society of the United States have forced the company on several occasions to apologize to the public for mislabeling the fur as faux and recall the faux fur coats they were selling. Here is one instance of negative publicity due to the crisis, dating back to 1998:

### Dog-fur coats recalled: Burlington Coat Factory says it was misled by garment supplier

NEW YORK (December 15, 1998: 5:58 p.m. ET)—Burlington Coat Factory is recalling an entire line of men's jackets after discovering they were lined with dog fur.

A company spokeswoman, Nancy Shrader, told CNN Tuesday that Burlington Coat Factory (BCF) believed the fur was from coyotes when it bought 400 coats from a vendor.

After learning from the Humane Society that the fur had come from dogs, Shrader said, the jackets were immediately pulled.

"It is not our policy to sell products with fur from domesticated animals," she said. "We find it repugnant."

Chinese Embassy spokesman Yu Suning said that while "it is natural for people to buy and sell cats and dogs in local markets. . . . The Chinese people do not have the tradition of using cats and dogs as materials for (the) fur industry."

The Embassy added that the Humane Society accusation "is not in conformity with the real situation."

One hundred of the jackets were sold in the chain's 250 nationwide stores, Shrader said. Burlington Coat Factory is offering a refund or credit for anyone who purchased the jacket.

Shrader did not identify the vendor, but an Associated Press report said the vendor was from Asia and that the dog fur came from animals slaughtered in China.

The Humane Society of the United States said its investigators bought a men's fur-trimmed coat labeled "Mongolia dog fur" from a Burlington Coat Factory outlet in New Jersey. A DNA test on the fur trim of the garment tested positive for domestic dog, the society said.

FIGURE BOX 12.1A  Anti-fur protests aim to tip public opinion against manufacturers that use fur in their fashions.

"American consumers are being tricked into purchasing garments made with dog and cat pelts because of misleading labeling practices," Patricia A. Forkan, the Humane Society's executive vice president, said in a statement.

The Humane Society said it conducted an 18-month investigation into the killing of dogs and cats for use in the international fur trade.

The society said at least 2 million dogs and cats are killed each year for their fur. Usually 10 to 12 dogs or 24 cats are killed to make one coat—more if puppies and kittens are used.

The Fur Information Council of America also condemned the alleged practice.

"The use of dog and cat fur is completely unacceptable and a practice we do not condone," council executive director Carol Wynne said.

"Consumers interested in buying fur should consult only with experienced and reputable furriers who know their product well and who carry properly labeled garments," Wynne added.

At the center of the controversy, shares in Burlington Coat Factory (BCF) closed down 13/16 at 13-1/8 (CNN Financial News, 1998).

The crisis seems self-inflicted because it appears that although the company has accepted responsibility for the errors, it has not taken sufficient steps to

## Box 12.1    The Self-Inflicted Crisis *(continued)*

**FIGURE BOX 12.1B** In response to an undercover investigation that found Burlington Coat Factory selling real fur advertised as fake, the company pulled advertisements from it stores nationwide among other steps to appease the public.

increase the monitoring of its suppliers so as to avoid a repeat of the mislabeling, and thus the public scandals continue. Here is another incident in 2006:

### Burlington Pulls Offending Fur Ads

*December 12, 2006*

In the wake of an undercover investigation announced Dec. 11 revealing that Burlington Coat Factory was selling real fur advertised as fake, Burlington has agreed to pull the offending advertisements from its stores nationwide and offered refunds to any consumers who may have inadvertently purchased the real fur garments. Burlington has also agreed to enter into discussions with The Humane Society of the United States about the company's policy on real fur.

The real fur jackets that were marketed by Burlington as "faux" contain internal labels stating that they are trimmed with "Racoon [sic] Fur of China Origin" or "Genuine Coyote Fur of China Origin."

Due to the lack of animal welfare laws and prevalence of garment factories, China currently ranks as one of the leading exporters of fur and supplies half of all of the fur products that enter the United States for sale.

Animals documented as raised and killed in China—often in barbaric ways—include dogs and cats

(read the report, watch the video), foxes, mink, and, of particular note, raccoon dogs (read the report, watch the video [warning: graphic images]), a species of canine whose fur resembles raccoon fur. The HSUS has commissioned DNA tests of the jackets, and expects to be able to determine within a week whether the coats are made of dog fur.

A loophole in the current Fur Products Labeling Act provides the fur industry an easy way to slip dog and cat fur onto garments, leaving American consumers, shopping off the rack in local department stores, uninformed and unprotected. The current labeling law, passed during the Eisenhower Administration, requires labeling of full-length fur coats, but excludes jackets and other products trimmed in fur if the value of the fur is less than $150. The HSUS is working to close this loophole through federal legislation, the Truth in Fur Labeling Act, introduced by Reps. Mike Ferguson, R-N.J. and Jim Moran, D-Va. Congress adjourned last week without taking action on this bill, but The HSUS intends to seek its reintroduction in 2007 (The Humane Society of the United States, 2006).

On the virtual sphere, Web sites such as burlington coatfactorylies.com have sprouted to provide negative exposure about the company on a constant basis, some going as far as posting online undercover video footage of the animals being skinned alive.

Finally, as public outrage continues, the crisis has escalated to reach Capitol Hill. At the time of writing, a Maryland bill has been introduced into legislation to close loopholes in existing legislation and make any such mislabeling illegal, as the following excerpt reports. We can see that negative publicity continues to dog the company since in the eyes of the public the company has not done enough to fully resolve the situation.

### Md. Bill Seeks to End Mislabeling of Fur Coats

*By Philip Rucker, Washington Post Staff Writer,*
*February 5, 2008*

Imagine discovering that the trim on your designer coat, labeled as faux fur, actually was rabbit. Or raccoon. Or even dog hair.

Some of the biggest names in retail—Bloomingdale's, Saks Fifth Avenue, and Burlington Coat Factory—have acknowledged that they sold coats made

313

**Box 12.1   The Self-Inflicted Crisis** (continued)

with rabbit or dog hair but labeled or advertised as different species or as artificial. They say they were misled by the coatmakers and have corrected the labels in recent months, after the Humane Society reported its findings from a two-year investigation.

The Humane Society said it had discovered those stores, and others, were selling coats that were trimmed with the hair of raccoon dog, a species of dog indigenous to China and other Asian countries that closely resembles raccoon.

Although U.S. law prohibits the importing of dog and cat fur, federal regulations don't require manufacturers to label the type of fur if the piece is valued at less than $150. So a lawmaker from Montgomery County plans to introduce legislation today that would change the rules in Maryland by requiring all manufacturers and retailers selling fur coats in the state to identify the species and country of origin on their labels, regardless of value (Rucker, 2008).

difficult; it is virtually impossible to prove guilt in a word of mouth campaign where typically it is one person's word against another's. However, there are people with vested interests behind such a rumor and the fashion company can project a list of suspected sources for the purpose of organizing a counter-rumor campaign. In such a case, the crisis might be too costly to fight in court, and other strategies can be employed that we will discuss later in the chapter.

### Consequences

What happens when the fashion company experiences a public relations crisis? In the initial stage of the crisis, it is virtually certain that some negative publicity about the company or its brands will take place. How the crisis is managed after the negative story is out will determine whether that negative exposure will remain firmly in the minds of the audience or be replaced by the company's positive crisis management message. The ultimate effects of the crisis can be mitigated and even turned around into positive coverage with proper crisis management in the right circumstances. However, crisis management aside, the consequences of the negative publicity—whether published for a short or long time—are real and serious. Negative publicity can damage the company's public image with consumers, vendors and buyers; such damage can linger for years and haunt the company's brands long after the publicity has come and gone. Additionally, as the crisis spreads from one sphere to another, the number of audience members exposed to the crisis can multiply exponentially. In the worst case scenario, millions of potential consumers can suddenly be aware of the company in a negative way, abruptly halting sales and orders. Still, the consequences stretch far beyond the retail front, and can affect the company's relationships with vendors, buyers, members of the media, and even with its own personnel.

#### *Effects on Consumers*

With the crisis in full bloom, the fashion company's consumers and potential consumers are likely to catch wind of the negative publicity. Reactions to the crisis are likely to be wide and varied, with some people taking the crisis to heart and adopting a solid stance against buying any of the fashion company's products ever again; on the other end of the spectrum, others might completely ignore the negative publicity and continue to purchase the company's products as if nothing had ever happened. In between the two extremes, other consumers are likely to adopt a vague position somewhere in the middle. The combined percentages of the consumers who form a wholly negative opinion and those who are vaguely in the middle are what will determine the degree of damage to the company's bottom line at the register.

### Effects on B2B Audiences

The negative effects of the crisis can potentially affect more than just retail sales. The company's B2B audiences are likely to get exposed to the crisis and might modify their relationship with the company. Vendors, buyers, representatives, wholesalers, and other members of the industry may choose to distance themselves from the fashion company while the crisis is in progress. Again, the degree of damage is determined by how many B2B audience members it affects and to what degree these members have adopted a negative opinion of the company.

### Effects on Advertising and Marketing Dollars

Besides influencing public opinion directly, the crisis will probably diminish the success of ongoing advertising and marketing efforts that are taking place at the time of the crisis. The dollars that had been invested in these ongoing efforts are then to some degree wasted. The advertising and marketing efforts will have to be changed dramatically in response to the crisis, and we will discuss that later in the chapter.

### Effects on Staff Morale

The effects of the crisis can also spill into the fashion company's own internal sphere. Negative coverage in the media can demoralize employee morale. When the administrative staff members see the newspaper article about the company's troubles, it is difficult to avoid chatting about it in the office with the employee at the next desk over. Not only can some office chats reduce productivity, but may actually prompt staff attrition. More importantly, though, the negative coverage may demoralize the staff in the sales and marketing departments and reduce their productivity at a time when a boost in sales and marketing is most crucial to keep the company afloat during the crisis.

## Managing the Crisis

Fashion public relations is not only concerned with gaining positive exposure; reducing and managing negative exposure is one of its most crucial functions. Often, it's not the nature or scope of the crisis, but the way it is handled by the fashion company that can dictate the outcome. To err is human, and people will often be willing to give a company the benefit of the doubt if it handles the crisis correctly. It's amazing that a number of well-known fashion companies do not have a crisis action plan in position to deal with when a negative incident occurs. Organizations should have a crisis plan in place that includes the message to the media and all concerned parties. Managing the media requests and press conferences should be a prime objective of the company by appointing qualified trained individuals to "meet the press." It's the course of action and process in preparing to limit any adverse events in order to avoid damaging the reputation of the company. This also includes managing any unfavorable events by communicating them with integrity to both the media, target audience, and company personnel in a timely manner.

We are living in a 24-hour communications age. With the advent of cable news, the Internet, and blogs, the news moves faster than a speeding bullet. Even Superman could not stop news of a crisis from reaching the vast audience it does. Knowing this, it would be foolish to think that a crisis could be shoved under the proverbial rug in order to avoid negative coverage. If it's news—it's out there! So what do we have to do when the crisis hits? Preparation and planning (the P&P) are our best friends. In fact the P&P should be part of all business plans. The plan should state how the company will react when a crisis appears. There should be a section in the plan devoted to appointing a crisis spokesperson and a crisis team as soon as the crisis is apparent. Then the managing process should be clearly spelled out—doing the research regarding the crisis at once and then managing the crisis. Contacting the media before they contact you is a must! Having all the facts, presenting them with integrity, letting the press know what happened, how it happened and what the company is doing about the crisis is crucial. Give the media the whole story!

## No "No Comment!"

"No comment!" This statement has been repeated time and time again by companies in crisis. However, when a crisis appears and the press corps starts calling, never say, "No comment!" This statement does nothing to counter the crisis or address the issues that brought the crisis into being, and in fact can make things appear worse than they are. For a reporter, the no-comment plea indicates the company does not have a grip on the crisis. Still we find that some executives when faced with a crisis, try to avoid the issue by saying, "We will get back to you," or "We will have a statement ready as soon as we investigate this matter," or "At this time we can't release any information." All lame excuses that could have been avoided, if they had a plan to deal with a crisis. This no-comment remark has a tremendous downside as far as the media outlets are concerned. It tends to spark their interest as to what the organization is hiding. The image of being guilty will be the first thing that a reporter will react to. Reporters love to play "hide and seek," and seek they will! If the fashion company is guilty and has caused the crisis, then admitting it and making amends may lessen the negative blow that will be delivered by the media. If the company can prove it is innocent and did not contribute to the crisis, then their story would have a good chance to be covered in a positive manner. Being up front with the media and telling them the story like it is will definitely prove to be beneficial in the long run. Remember, the public will be all eyes and ears when the crisis becomes news. The story that first appears in the media will have a lasting memory. That's why it is a definite "No" to "No comment!"

## The Court of Public Opinion

Public relations activities are very sensitive to public opinion. Just as the judicial court system has rules and regulations, so should a public relations crisis be judged by *the court of public opinion*. The objective of the public relations department or the outside public relations firm is to disseminate the information to the public with integrity and in a reasonable time. The public will be the jury and will not absolve a company that tries to deceive it. Just as the evidence is presented before the jury in a court of law to reach a verdict, so must all the information be presented to the public before rendering their decision of guilt, innocence, or forgiveness. Therefore, it is necessary for the fashion company to be prepared for the worst and hopefully, through proper management of the crisis with integrity, the company will be forgiven for its negative actions.

## Nip It in the Bud

By not letting the crisis escalate into a full-blown catastrophe, and by taking immediate action when the crisis occurs, time can become the fashion company's best friend; or, if the company does not react quickly, time can be its worst enemy. Knowing how to use time wisely can lessen the results of a negative event. Although many public relations firms would rather wait and get all the objections in place, it is advisable to act swiftly in getting the news out to the media. When the crisis occurs it would be wise to institute an immediate planning session that would include all the key people in the organization. During this session the management should finalize the plan on dealing with the crisis. When this is accomplished—which should be within 24 hours of the crisis taking place—the media should be contacted with a statement from the company's crisis spokesperson as to the details regarding the crisis. Taking appropriate action and communicating that clearly to the public are crucial to resolving the crisis problem.

## Honesty Is Paramount

What do we have to do after the crisis procedure is in place? What areas must be included in the presentation when dealing with the media? As we have mentioned in previous chapters, integrity is extremely important in fashion public relations, and there is no exception with crisis management. Being honest with the media and telling it the way it is is the best approach to handling any crisis situation. We have an expression in the fashion business, "The first markdown is the best markdown." In other words, if the company has erred and caused the crisis, it's best to take the hit at the beginning than to give false statements or to try and cover up the facts. Nowhere is stating the facts more important than when dealing with the media during a crisis. It takes only one incident to damage the goodwill of an organization if the crisis is not handled properly and immediately. Fashion celebrities routinely find themselves in crisis mode.

## Box 12.2 Stewart Convicted on All Charges: Jury Finds Style Maven, Ex-Broker Guilty of Obstructing Justice and Lying to Investigators

NEW YORK (March 10, 2004)—A jury found Martha Stewart guilty Friday on all four counts of obstructing justice and lying to investigators about a well-timed stock sale, and the former stockbroker turned style-setter could face years in jail.

On March 10, 2004 Martha Stewart was found guilty of lying to investigators about a stock sale! The Martha Steward crisis has left many people wondering if she could have avoided the prison sentence. We are not saying that public relations could have exonerated her, but maybe if she had a crisis plan prior to the problem that provided timely and upfront answers to inquiries, the outcome could have been different. We are not judging her guilt or innocence, but the verdict stated that she lied to investigators and that was the thing that resulted in the guilty verdict. It can also be said, if she wasn't the famous 'Martha Stewart,' she would have received a lesser sentence. Fame carries with it a burden of being the focus in the public's eye and being held to a higher standard than a Jane Doe! We are happy to note that Martha is back in town doing better than ever (CNN, 2004).

FIGURE BOX 12.2 Could Martha Stewart's jail time have been avoided if her publicists had been more cooperative with public inquiries? We will never know, but if nothing else it probably would have at least lessened the blemish upon her public image.

Some of them are innocent of the charges whereas others are guilty. The fact remains that when a crisis is managed professionally and with integrity, it can receive positive reaction by the public. The Martha Stewart crisis, discussed in Box 12.2, is but an example of how a public relations crisis can get out of hand with highly punitive consequences for the company's top executives.

Another example of a fashion public relations crisis was discussed in our first chapter. Tommy Hilfiger was subjected to negative false rumors and a smear campaign. It took several years for this malicious attack to be addressed and disproved. The amount of negative exposure was extraordinary and damaged the company's bottom line. Could this crisis have been managed better? Why wasn't more attention paid to the rumor by the company? Why didn't Hilfiger appear on *Oprah* at once and present his case to prove that it was a malicious rumor? Had the company acknowledged the rumor fully, perhaps the crisis would have been averted and the negative exposure, which spread like wildfire through email inboxes, would have been minimized. By managing the rumor expeditiously, it might have even resulted in some positive press. With proper management and planning, the crisis might have ended sooner than later. The moral of this example is that when a crisis is discovered, get the facts and prepare to deliver the story to the media in a timely manner with integrity. Just telling the truth is not enough; it must be communicated with an immediate response. The best approach is to get the word out to the media before the media knocks on the company's door. We must be aware that any crisis news will reach the media immediately, so when we recognize the threat of a crisis we must act to prepare all involved personnel in the company and inform them with what has happened, and then we must assign a spokesperson who can deliver the message to the media at once.

## Facing the Music

If the crisis is a result of its error or action, the fashion company must not only accept responsibility for the actions that led to the crisis but also accept the consequences of how it decides to manage the crisis. In most crises, there are several management avenues available to the fashion company, each with its own set of likely outcomes and potential consequences. The fashion company must be aware of the potential negative consequences of the course of action it decides to take in dealing with the crisis, and be able to face the music and suffer the penalties should any of these materialize.

Suppose a well-known fashion manufacturer mislabels its spring collection incorrectly with machine-washable instructions only to find later that the colors faded onto each other. The labeling was supposed to indicate "Dry Clean Only." The company discovers this error only after the merchandise had been shipped to its clients—the distributors, boutiques, and retail stores. Sales of the spring collection were extensive and thus the mislabeled merchandise ends up on the sales floor at prominent retail stores. Here, we have a crisis in action: what do we do? In an ideal world, the fashion company would react immediately and contact its customer base to tell them about the problem and what the company will do to rectify the problem. The company would inform all their customers to dry clean instead of wash, and to send back already spoiled merchandise for a full refund. The manufacturer would also send to any of the consumers who purchased the garments a 20 percent discount coupon toward any future purchases. The public relations department would assign a spokesperson who would contact the media and explain the problem. The crisis would be proactively managed by the fashion company, released to the media while retaining the company's relative control, and the solution would be in place.

Now suppose this well-known fashion company discovered the mislabeling problem but decided that they would wait and see what happens. In the real world, some companies would rather play a waiting game and see if they can avoid airing the crisis. After all, how many of their consumers would really wash this exclusive product? They would further rationalize that because their consumers are of a higher income bracket, they would have the clothing dry cleaned regardless of the labeling. Some of the company's executives would rather take a chance and play the percentages. But what if the merchandise is returned to the retail store in great numbers? And worse yet, what if the media somehow gets wind that the company knew about it but didn't act? It is quite evident that the fashion manufacturer will experience a crisis that they might not be prepared for. The media will jump on it while the retail stores

## Box 12.3   Consequences of Sweeping the Crisis Under the Rug

As can be gathered from the following *New York Post* article, the American public is not as forgiving as it used to be. Today, a fashion company—or any company for that matter—must really hone in on the meaningful actions it had better take in order to rectify the crisis. Corporations are beginning to realize that in the field of crisis management, actions speak at least as loud as words.

### Mea Culpas Don't Cut It for Faulty Firms

*By Holly M. Sanders, February 24, 2007*

Memo to corporate America: Sorry won't cut it.

That's the message some marketing experts said should be circulated after a spate of public relations fiascos involving fast-food purveyor Yum Brands, high-flier JetBlue Airlines, and the Cartoon Network.

The textbook response to a communications crisis—acknowledge the problem and apologize quickly—is a good start, but nothing more than a full explanation and a plan for fixing the problem will win back consumers.

"We're getting more apologies than we can possibly absorb right now," said Mark Stevens, author of the BusinessWeek bestseller, *Your Marketing Sucks.*

JetBlue chief David Neeleman issued a blizzard of apologies and took out full-page ads after a Valentine's Day storm canceled 1,100 flights, stranding passengers for days and creating one of the worst travel headaches in history.

"We are sorry and embarrassed," the ad began. "But most of all, we are deeply sorry."

Apologizing for the mistake is one thing; paying for it is another. JetBlue had to take other steps to placate angry passengers, namely penning a flier "Bill of Rights" that promised refunds for delayed flights.

Turner Broadcasting took a similar tack, apologizing for a Cartoon Network marketing stunt that caused a bomb scare in Boston. It also wrote a big check to the city for all the trouble and fired the head of the network.

"A lot of times companies will say sorry and the problem won't go away," said Dean Bender of PR firm Bender/Helper Impact. "You have to say, here's where we went wrong and here's how we will make sure that this never occurs again."

Yum Brands suffered a black eye last year after an E. coli outbreak sickened dozens of people who ate at its Taco Bell restaurants in the Northeast. The company moved quickly to stem the problem, switching food suppliers, but stopped short of apologizing.

So there was little goodwill left when a local TV station captured footage of rats scurrying around a Taco Bell/KFC restaurant in Greenwich Village. The video got national airtime and spread like wildfire on the Web, ensuring that the incident would become fodder for late-night television.

Yum called the situation "totally unacceptable" and vowed to shut down the restaurant—run by an unnamed franchisee—until it got a clean bill of health.

"They had a real problem to begin with," said Bender. "The rat situation is so visual and graphic it's hard for anyone to feel comfortable going back to that place."

Stevens said the company should shut down the franchise operator and fire the regional manager for starters. He also suggested a novel approach to reassuring customers that the food supply is safe.

"The CEO and his family should eat there for a week after the restaurant reopens," he said (Sanders, 2007).

and consumers will be angry with the manufacturer. Lawsuits could be filed. The fashion company will have to accept the merchandise for return and issue credit to its customers. But beyond that, the manufacturer's reputation will suffer. By not facing the problem after they discovered it, they are now faced with a major crisis. We call it the **Band-Aid effect**—instead of taking care of the crisis in earnest, the executives chose to put a Band-Aid over it and pretend that they "fixed" the problem; sometimes this approach might work, but when it doesn't work it can backfire terribly.

## The Four Levels of Crisis Management

According to Thierry C. Pauchant and Ian I. Mitroff in their book *Transforming the Crisis-Prone Organization: Preventing Individual, Organizational, and Environmental Tragedies,* there are four levels of crisis-related systems that must be addressed, in this order, so as to properly manage a crisis:

1. The character of the people in the organization—and their willingness to take responsibility and corrective action.

2. Culture existing in the organization—supports appropriate preparation and responsive actions.

3. Organizational structure—crisis management structure in which stakeholders are represented.

4. Plans and mechanisms for dealing with crises—crisis management team has fully prepared plans, disseminated them, and trained people in key roles (Pauchant & Mitroff, 1992).

As Pauchant and Mitroff have indicated in their book, the people in the organization should be willing to take responsibility and corrective action. This occurs when the organization has established a culture that encourages preparation and responsive action. The authors go on to say that the organization must include the stakeholders as part of the crisis management structure thus communicating their plan for dealing with the crisis. Finally, in dealing with the crisis, the planning process must come into play with trained personnel doing what they were trained to do—resolve the problem and provide proper information.

### Dealing with the Media

With the above-mentioned principles of Pauchant and Mitroff in mind, it is clear that an open-door policy in dealing with the media is essential during a crisis. The fashion company's employees must remain proactive, ethical, and calm. During each stage of the crisis the organization should never lose sight of the fact that dealing with the media in a well-timed manner is essential to survive the ordeal of a crisis. We must understand that the media will communicate the information as it sees it and it would be harmful to the company if the company tried to whitewash the problem. It would be better for the company to admit responsibility if the crisis was caused by the company and then offer their apologies. The company should then propose the actions they will take to rectify the situation. The true test of a stable organization is how they handle the media in a crisis. As Pauchant and Mitroff have indicated in their book, the people in the organization who are willing to participate in resolving the crisis problem and take the charge in meeting and satisfying the needs of the media are essential to crisis management. This can occur when the organization has established a culture that encourages proper action. To deal with the crisis successfully the company must ensure that the stakeholders are part of the crisis management team. Finally, in dealing with the crisis, the planning process must come into play with trained personnel doing what they were trained to do—resolve the problem.

## Long-Term Crisis Management

The keys to long-term crisis management are prevention, training, preparedness, and proactive immediate response. The fashion company's public relations director should stay routinely abreast of how the other departments in the company are doing and remain alert for potential development of crises. Instituting a plan for action in case of a public relations crisis and informing all company employees on what they should do when a crisis happens is essential. When a television crew appears on the fashion company's doorstep, the receptionist should know to remain calm, to immediately call the public relations director, and to act cordially with the television crew while they are in the company's facilities. The following are several vital principles to successful long-term crisis management:

1. Instill in company personnel a sense of balanced relationship between ethics and the crisis. In handling a crisis, an organization's culture regarding ethical standards impacts the way the crisis is managed. Ethical standards in each organization differ and this different culture can affect the resulting media coverage of the crisis.

2. Inform all company personnel of the crisis, and appoint a spokesperson and a crisis team to deal with the media. By taking immediate action and organizing the crisis team, the message to the media will unify. The media will acknowledge that the crisis is being dealt with by the organization. This will build a level of comfort with the media.

3. Insist on ethical behavior by management and all employees. The rules of ethical behavior must be understood and communicated to all employees. This will avoid any confusion that may arise during the media or official investigative process.

4. Review the fundamentals of what caused the crisis. A thorough review of the factors that led to the crisis will prevent this incident from occurring again. Identifying what went wrong may be a painstaking and nerve-racking process, but it is also a necessary process. Add to this process an analysis recommending how to avoid a similar crisis in the future.

5. Establish a strategy and plan on how to handle the crisis. Formulate a message that will resonate with the target audience and ease the effects of the crisis. After this has been accomplished the progress in reaching the objectives can be monitored to see if the crisis is being managed properly.

6. Finally, the role of public relations personnel in crisis management is to maintain a harmonious relationship with the media and customers during this stressful period.

## Box 12.4 "Loss of Innocence 101"

The following is an article that appeared in the University of Michigan's business school magazine *Dividends* about crisis management. Although the article offers a comprehensive overview on all types of business crises—public relations or otherwise—we have highlighted several important points in this article that crucially pertain to fashion-related crisis management.

### Guideposts through the Minefield

On the first day of his class in crisis management, Professor Gerald Meyers warned his students that they had enrolled in Loss of Innocence 101. "You've learned a lot about how to make things go right in an organization, to keep going, to spot opportunities and trends. But what the hell do you do when it all collapses?"

Meyers, who is former CEO of American Motors, is president of Gerald C. Meyers Associates Inc., a consulting firm that advises and assists senior management in crisis management and prevention. He is the author of *When It Hits the Fan: Managing the Nine Crises of Business* (Houghton-Mifflin, Boston), and *Managing Crisis: A Positive Approach* (with John Holusha).

The new class represents another example of how the seven-week option recently incorporated into the curriculum has made innovative courses available that would not have been possible in the more traditional 14-week format.

The course focuses on the stages of a crisis, how the "pain curve" develops, how to do a crisis audit, and the value of learning to manage a crisis (as opposed to simply letting it happen to you). Along with sharing his own experiences, Meyers gives students plenty of hands-on practice. He also recruits guest executives who exercised strong leadership during times of rapid change and can explain to the class how it felt to be within "the jaws-area of a crisis where the stakes are high and control is insufficient," as Meyers characterizes such situations.

His ability to convince some of the nation's top business leaders to fly into Ann Arbor just to talk to his class stems from his reputation as an executive who has weathered crises himself as well as an innovative and risk-taking teacher.

"As chairman and CEO at American Motors from 1978 to 1982, I had to ponder the impossible on a regular basis," says Meyers. "On the way through the mine field, I discovered what makes some corporations more vulnerable than others, and what a leader must do to ensure that his company benefits at critical turning points." During the seven weeks, the class considered the following types of crises, studied how particular companies handled them, and heard from the CEO (or former CEO) of the companies as follows: product failure—John R. Hall, chairman and CEO of Ashland Oil Company; management succession—Donald E. Petersen, former chairman and CEO of Ford Motor Company; industrial relations—Frederick G. Currey, former president and CEO of Greyhound Lines, Inc.; sudden market shift—Lloyd E. Reuss, former president of General Motors Corp.; hostile takeover—James W. Kinnear, former chairman and CEO of Texaco Inc.; public perception—Frederick Joseph, former chairman and CEO of Drexel Burnham Lambert Inc.

"I cast a wide net," Meyers says. "Every day I comb the New York Times and the Wall Street Journal to see who might be a good future prospect. Of course, sometimes, I have to wait awhile to get the person I want." About a year ago, Meyers, who also teaches at Carnegie Mellon, wrote to an executive who had been recently fired from a large manufacturing company. The executive understandably declined the invitation to talk to Meyers's students at that time. "He said, 'I'm being fired here—I have more pressing things to do,'" Meyers recalls. "I explained that he could help my students better understand crisis management and learn from his experiences. I suggested he reconsider in about nine months and he recently agreed to talk to one of my classes." Students in the class are organized into teams, each of which is given a crisis to manage, along with a telephone-book-sized book of clippings detailing the press coverage of their particular crisis. On handing them the clippings, Meyers says, "This isn't enough. I expect you to use this information as a base for further research." The team has a week to prepare its case in depth.

On the assigned day, team members sometimes have the opportunity to meet briefly with the visiting CEO for advice and questions before they go before the class to present the case, either in a press conference format or as if they are meeting with their company's board of directors. During the first part of the three-hour class, the presenting team makes the

**Box 12.4  "Loss of Innocence 101"** *(continued)*

corporate case and defends the company's actions, after which the remaining students challenge the advocates in assigned roles as adversaries. This "clash of the teams," as Meyers characterizes it, is being observed by the CEO or former CEO who had to handle the crisis. The CEO then speaks frankly to the students about the issues as he saw them, how he handled the actual crisis, which moves he later regretted, and what strategies were most effective. "Misfortune is manageable," says Meyers, "but there are rules for executives. Leaders must act decisively when trouble strikes because the credibility battle is won or lost in the first 72 hours. When credibility goes, the ball game is over."

On the day *Dividend* sat in on the class, the crisis under consideration was that of the Ashland Oil Company, one of whose fuel tanks had ruptured in 1988 in Jefferson, Pennsylvania, spilling more than a million gallons of diesel fuel into the Monongahela River and endangering water supplies in Pennsylvania, Ohio, and West Virginia. One community downstream was left without water entirely, schools closed in several areas, and hundreds of thousands of people had to take steps to conserve water. In addition, the spill killed 10,000 fish and several thousand waterfowl and mammals. To make matters worse, some of the welds on the ruptured tank turned out to be defective. Members of the corporate crisis team role-played by students included (besides the CEO): Charles Leullen, president and chief operating officer; Robert Yancey, senior vice president of the petroleum group; Dan Lacy, vice president of corporate communications; Robert McCowan, vice president of public affairs; Richard Thomas, general counsel; and Roger Shrumm, manager of media relations.

The adversaries, which consisted of the rest of the class, included the governor of Pennsylvania, Sam Donaldson of ABC News (played by Meyers), Tom Brokaw of NBC News, representatives of the New York Times, the Environmental Protection Agency, the American Red Cross, the Pittsburgh fire marshal, and several small business owners whose businesses had been adversely affected by the water shut-off, as well as lawyers, politicians, and representatives of various citizens' groups. Sitting in the back of the room was John R. Hall, CEO of Ashland Oil, who watched the proceedings attentively, occasionally breaking into a wry smile.

No matter how well-prepared the students were, they could not completely predict the direction of questioning and level of hostility they would face—just as in a real life situation. "I didn't realize how tough Sam Donaldson would be," says Dave Zoretic, who played the role of Hall. "He really challenged my capability as a CEO by demanding answers when there were none. At times, he seemed to be trying to start a fight. It helped me appreciate the difficulty of talking rationally at the peak of a crisis." Zoretic tried to remain faithful to his role and answer each question as candidly as Hall had done at the original press conference. Pressed to explain the decision to use 40-year old steel in the tank that ruptured, he admitted that it had been a "poor decision," although the practice of reconstructing oil tanks with used parts is a common one. "Come on, you did it to save a buck," retorted Donaldson. "Meyers admits that his Sam Donaldson-style character is in part a cartoon, devised "to illustrate just how irascible the adversaries may be. I expect students on the adversary team to go as far as I do at being persistent and tough—without being offensive. The first role-playing session usually is a shocker for some students, and some of the students playing adversarial roles wonder how far they should go, for fear of offending the visiting executive. "I tell them not to worry, that there's no way you can embarrass a chief executive who has been through a corporate crisis," says Meyers.

Similarly, he advises the advocacy teams not to hesitate about any question they want to ask of the executive whose experience they are reenacting. "You probably can't think of any question to ask that they haven't been asked before." The briefing sessions held before class between the advocacy team and the visiting executive may be among the most instructive parts of the course, according to some of the students. Rachel Freeman, who role-played Ashland's media relations manager, asked Hall why he waited several days after the tank explosion to go to the site of the accident and make the company's first public statements. "He said he simply had underestimated the magnitude of the problem and that he made the mistake of trying to learn everything he could about the tank before making any public comments," she said. "But overall, he managed the crisis well by being honest about

Box 12.4 "Loss of Innocence 101" *(continued)*

Ashland's oversights, and about what he did and didn't know at the time. He really seemed to want to teach us what he had learned from his experience."

During his time with students, Hall told them how he had made the decision to call the press conference, to apologize to the people of Pittsburgh, to inform them about cleanup efforts, and to explain all he knew at the time about the circumstances surrounding the tank rupture. "Honesty is the best policy always," said Hall. "Corporations live in a glass house. Lawyers tend to want to hold information back. But one document leads to another and things will come out." On dealing with the media, he said emphatically, "When the sharks are all around you and they're smelling blood—feed them."

Leaders who can thus rally their bravest instincts and focus exclusively on the crisis at hand are the ones who can pull a company through, maintains Meyers. "What drives managers in a crisis," he says, "is mostly human nature. The only thing that managers detest more than discovering mistakes is disclosing them publicly. Some companies are undone by their own fear, ignorance, or arrogance. Elements of a non-managed crisis are: chronic non-performance followed by denial, then anger and fear as the story unfolds before the public. And the sad aftermath of an unmanaged crisis is often that the organization is never the same." What qualities are needed in a business leader in a time of crisis? A leader must be creative enough to fathom the unthinkable, must have a deep knowledge of the business and know how it really works. In addition, a leader needs trusty sources of information within the industry, and within his own company, so he can size up the trouble and estimate his potential opportunity.

Many successful business managers don't possess all these leadership qualities, says Meyers, but they have another valuable skill: the ability to assemble a crisis team. Companies that can rally their most dedicated and courageous employees and mobilize them to address misfortune in an orderly fashion are way ahead of their competitors. "Companies that overcome a crisis should be copied with vigor," says Meyers, adding that the procedures are straightforward. "When trouble strikes, top officials should accept responsibility and admit the error, privately and publicly. They should tell the public the facts. If people or the environment will suffer, the company should say so and its officials

should get the information out quickly. The press will dig it up anyway, and there is little that is more painful than having your arm chopped off an inch at a time."

Next, Meyers says, management should cage its lawyers. "Learn from your legal counsel where the danger points are, and understand your exposure to litigation," he advises. "Develop a sense of limits on what can be said and done and what words or acts should be carefully avoided, but do not overreact to the legal concerns! Most public perception battles are lost by overzealous protection of legal positions. This stance produces the corporate stonewall, which makes even a sincere, concerned management look ignorant, indifferent, and probably guilty."

Each student's understanding of crisis management was well tested during the final exam. Meyers began with video footage of the wrecked Exxon Valdez oil tanker spilling oil into the water and of chaotic efforts to deal with the emergency at both the corporate and government levels. After about 45 minutes, he stopped the video, and told students that the president of Exxon had just called them for assessment of the situation. What would they advise? After the students had given their advice and assessments in their blue books, Meyers played the rest of the tape to show how the crisis actually unfolded. The final, like the case presentations, did not require lengthy analysis of all possible ramifications of the case, so much as the ability to size up the situation at hand and attend to immediate problem solving. "I discourage too much strategic thinking for the cases in this class because most MBA students spend a great deal of time on that and it just doesn't work for crisis management," says Meyers, who asks students to write brief papers on each crisis considering the following questions: Was there a crisis? Was it well managed? What type of crisis was it? What do you conclude about management's treatment of the crisis? "Typically, cases in other business courses haven't been as difficult as those we've had in Crisis Management," Dave Zoretic says. "The others have called for more strategy and hindsight and we had more time to assess team roles. In Meyers' class, you must be on top of all the facts, yet can't use the benefits of hindsight. The most exciting part is having to always stay within your role. There's no one there to bail you out if you get yourself in trouble—either as an advocate or adversary."

**Box 12.4  "Loss of Innocence 101"** *(continued)*

Meyers does believe in using some analytical tools to help students develop a general framework for recognizing and dealing with rapid change in business. An understanding of the dynamics and structure of a crisis can help executives shape its outcome, Meyers believes. He has devised a pain curve graph to show a pre-crisis period of nonperformance, denial, anger and fear, followed by the hot crisis period, in which pain can be expressed in dollars lost, jobs lost, reputation lost or, in the case of Union Carbide's chemical spill in Bhopal, lives lost. The curve then slowly declines to a post-crisis period of shock, uncertainty, and—for an unmanaged crisis—radical change such as bankruptcy, absorption by another company, sale of the company's best interests, or liquidation.

As a teacher, Meyers (when he's not Sam Donaldson) uses the Socratic method of leading students to their own solutions to case problems. He serves as a seasoned advisor, describing the experiences and techniques of crisis management with candor, vitality, and warmth, and being generous with his time. During the first class session, he gave students three phone numbers—including a "student-friendly 800 number"—where he could be reached "at 3 a.m. if necessary." (Several students did, in fact, call Meyers with questions at odd hours.)

"The art of crisis management is in its infancy," says Meyers, whose class will be offered again in 1995. "We are a long way from having a general theory or an established practice for dealing with rapid change in business situations. However, an awakening is at hand. American businesses in recent years have identified and used crisis teams, and some call regularly upon a handful of professional consultants who specialize in crisis management. The 1990s roared in with an uncommon array of historic misfortunes and opportunities. But crises can even be beneficial if they are properly managed because a crisis can shake up the established order and make rapid change possible."

**Seven Gains that May Result from a Business Crisis**

1. Heroes are born.

2. Change is accelerated.

3. Latent problems are faced.

4. People can be changed.

5. New strategies evolve.

6. Early warning systems develop.

7. New competitive edges appear (Dividend, 1994).

## Case Study 12.1 Crisis Management

### Nike's Sweatshops Public Relations Crisis

In the 1990s, Nike came under great scrutiny by the American public, alleging it produced its shoes in third world county sweatshops. As the largest American shoe brand, it stood at the pinnacle of the footwear hierarchy as the prime target for human rights groups and labor advocacy organizations. As can be seen by the progression of the negative media in Case Study Box 12.1, this public relations crisis haunted the company for years, with one story breaking after another to stoke the fire and keep the crisis going. With each new development, the company can be seen taking another step toward putting an end to the crisis. However, it wasn't until the company began to cooperate with the public groups and posted in 2005 on its Web site the locations of its sub-contractor factories as well as select audit reports from these factories that the crisis began to subside. This illustrates that even a multibillion dollar giant corporation such as Nike, with its army of lawyers and public relations experts, could not sweep the crisis under the rug; instead, the company bit by bit took responsibility, admitted fault, and began to make changes in its policies and production structures. While reading the following articles, pay close attention to what the civic groups allege about Nike, what Nike says in response, and what the media's verdict is, if any.

### Negative Media

#### Nike's Long, Drawn-Out Public Relations Crisis

As can be seen by the progression of the negative media in the chronological series of the following excerpts, this public relations crisis haunted the company for years, with one story breaking after another to stoke the fire and keep the crisis going.

#### Nike Shoe Plant in Vietnam Is Called Unsafe for Workers

*By Steven Greenhouse, November 8, 1997*
Undermining Nike's boast that it maintains model working conditions at its factories throughout the world, a prominent accounting firm has found many unsafe conditions at one of the shoe manufacturer's plants in Vietnam.

In an inspection report that was prepared in January for the company's internal use only, Ernst & Young wrote that workers at the factory near Ho Chi Minh City were exposed to carcinogens that exceeded local legal standards by 177 times in parts of the plant and that 77 percent of the employees suffered from respiratory problems.

The report also said that employees at the site, which is owned and operated by a Korean subcontractor, were forced to work 65 hours a week, far more than Vietnamese law allows, for $10 a week.

The inspection report offers an unusually detailed look into conditions at one of Nike's plants at a time when the world's largest athletic shoe company is facing criticism from human rights and labor groups that it treats workers poorly even as it lavishes millions of dollars on star athletes to endorse its products.

Though other American manufacturers also have problems in overseas plants, Nike has become a lightning rod in the debate because it is seen as able to do more since it earned about $800 million last year on sales of $9.2 billion (Greenhouse, 1997).

### A Nike Sneak

*By Eyal Press, April 5, 1999*
On January 11 Joseph Ha, a Nike vice president, sent what he thought was a confidential letter to Cu Thi Hau, Vietnam's highest-ranking labor official. In it, Ha blasted a number of human rights and labor groups that have been working to improve labor conditions in Nike's overseas factories and expressed admiration for Vietnam's authoritarian system. "A few U.S. human rights groups, as well as a Vietnamese refugee who is engaged in human rights activities, are not friends of Vietnam," wrote Ha to the Vietnamese official. The "ultimate goal" of these groups, Ha warned, is not to help Vietnamese apparel workers improve their living standards, but to turn Vietnam into "a so-called 'democratic' society, modeled after the U.S."—a charge that, as Nike knows, amounts to subversion in Vietnam.

## Case Study 12.1    Crisis Management Nike's Sweatshops Public Relations Crisis *(continued)*

Nike, Ha assured his correspondent, has no such intentions. "No nation needs to copy any other nation," he explained. "Each nation has its own internal political system. Nike firmly believes this."

So thrilled was the Vietnamese government by Ha's letter that, unbeknownst to him, it printed it in a state-owned newspaper. Word leaked to the BBC in London and shortly thereafter to the Financial Times, whereupon Nike began wiping the egg off its face. "Nike regrets that excerpts from private correspondence . . . were interpreted as our corporate attitude toward human rights groups," wrote Nike spokeswoman Hannah Jones in a letter to the *Financial Times*. As proof of Nike's enlightened labor practices, Jones cited the company's participation in "Bill Clinton's Apparel Industry Partnership" (Press 1999).

### Nike Identifies Plants Abroad Making Goods For Universities

*By Steven Greenhouse*

In a significant concession to the anti-sweatshop movement on college campuses, Nike Inc. became the first large apparel company yesterday to disclose the names and sites of dozens of its overseas factories—a move that the college groups said was vital to uncover unsatisfactory working conditions.

Student groups praised Nike for its disclosures about factories in Bangladesh, China, Guatemala, Thailand, and other countries, saying that having the names and addresses would make it far easier to verify whether Nike had made good on its promises to improve working conditions.

Last spring, students held demonstrations at Harvard, Yale, Princeton, and dozens of other colleges and universities, demanding that universities force companies making apparel with school logos to disclose the names and addresses of their factories. All told, manufacturers like Nike, Champion, Adidas, and Gear for Sports produce $2.5 billion worth of goods each year bearing the names of hundreds of colleges.

**CASE STUDY FIGURE 12.1A** Workers at an outsourced Nike shoe factory.

**CASE STUDY FIGURE 12.1B** Students make their voices heard during a United Students Against Sweatshops protest.

Nike, the giant footwear manufacturer, which has been a prime target of labor rights groups, disclosed the names of the 41 overseas factories it uses to make athletic gear for Duke, Georgetown, the University of Michigan, the University of North Carolina, and the University of Arizona. The 41 factories are in 11 countries and make sweatshirts, T-shirts, shorts, and other apparel carrying school names (Greenhouse, 1999).

**Case Study 12.1   Crisis Management Nike's Sweatshops Public Relations Crisis** (continued)

CASE STUDY FIGURE 12.6C  Nike is striving to provide more public transparency regarding its factory worker conditions.

## Nike Opens Its Books on Sweatshop Audits

*By Aaron Bernstein in Washington, D.C., April 27, 2000*
*Reports of factory conditions posted on its Web site will give critics info they've long been denied.*

Nike is about to hand a new weapon to its labor critics. In an April 24 letter, CEO and Chairman Philip Knight said that come May, the footwear colossus will post the results of all the company's factory audits on its Web site. The audits detail working conditions in some of the 500 factories worldwide where Nike makes its athletic wear.

Nike's move is likely to give critics an ongoing source of ammo in their war against sweatshops. It will also put pressure on other big garment makers, such as Reebok International and Liz Claiborne, to publicize audits of working conditions in their overseas plants.

For several years, Nike, like many other apparel and toy companies, has commissioned outside audits of its factories. The companies began doing so in response to the anti-sweatshop movement's exposure of poor working conditions in their factories around the globe. But critics such as the United Students Against Sweatshops (USAS) haven't been satisfied. They charge that such self-policing is a whitewash because Nike and other companies wouldn't make the audits public.

### "A Big Step"

Nike had countered that the results were confidential because its factories, which employ some 500,000 workers, are owned by subcontractors. "This is a big step," says USAS Executive Director Eric Brakken. "If Nike is willing to make its audits public, then the industry's arguments continue to break down, and other companies can't say they can't do it" (Bernstein, 2000).

## Nike's New Game Plan for Sweatshops: Unlike Giants such as Wal-Mart, It Now Has a System to Inspect—and Try to Improve—Working Conditions at Supplier Factories

*By Aaron Bernstein in Washington, September 20, 2004*
For many years, Nike (NKE) has been a lightning rod for criticism about sweatshop labor conditions in the low-wage countries that produce its sneakers. When Nike was getting pummeled on the subject in the 1990s, it typically responded with anger and panic. Executives would issue denials, lash out at critics, and rush someone to the offending supplier's factory to put out the fire before it spread.

Since then, Nike has constructed an elaborate program to deal with labor issues in the 900-odd supplier factories (none owned by Nike) that churn out its products in some 50 countries. Today, a staff of 97 inspects several hundred factories a year, grades them on labor standards, and works with managers to improve problems. Nike also allows random factory inspections by the Fair Labor Association (FLA), a monitoring outfit founded by human rights groups and companies such as Nike, Reebok (RBK), and Liz Claiborne (LIZ).

### "Drop in the Ocean"

As a result, when most human rights groups and even student protesters find a problem at a Nike factory, they now deal with the company directly instead of pounding it with public demonstrations. That's one reason why you don't see Nike getting hit with ugly sweatshop publicity so much these days. "You haven't heard about us recently because we've had our head down doing it the hard way. Now, we have a system to deal with the labor issue, not a crisis mentality," says Maria S. Eitel, Nike's vice-president for corporate responsibility.

None of this means that Nike or any other businesses have come close to solving the sweatshop problem. Far from it. The monitoring systems set up by a Nike and handful of other Western outfits such as Mattel (MAT) or Adidas have helped to address some of the more egregious problems at some factories, such as locked doors and unsafe chemicals, human rights experts say. But the inspections they do are limited and periodic and can't possibly catch all of even the most egregious problems (Benstein, 2004).

### Questions to Consider

1.  What do you think would have happened had Nike come out and revealed its factory list and instituted audits as soon as the crisis began in the early 1990s?

2.  Pick one of the reports above that includes a statement from Nike. Analyze the statement from a crisis management perspective. Include how you think the handling of the story could have been improved, and how it would have improved the story.

3.  Do you feel that Nike's crisis is still alive today? Why?

4.  What are your personal thoughts about the crisis? What source/s of information do you rely on?

## Chapter Summary

▶ Fashion public relations is not solely about a positive public image; it is also charged with preventing negative coverage.

▶ The public relations crisis can and often does result in negative publicity for the fashion company. If it is not addressed and managed properly, it can develop into a disastrous event that can decrease sales and even prompt the closing of the company.

▶ Each crisis has its own sphere, circumstances, scope, timing, source, and audience. It is important to identify these so as to properly understand how to rectify the crisis.

▶ The self-inflicted crisis emanates from actions or events that the fashion company or its employees are responsible for and that can generate negative publicity.

▶ The fabricated crisis is a negative false story created by a force external to the fashion company—typically the competition and disgruntled consumers or employees.

▶ The crisis can decrease consumer and vendor confidence in the company and result in drops in product sales.

▶ Advertising and promotional efforts during the crisis must be tailored to address the crisis; otherwise, they will be cancelled out by the negative publicity.

▶ It is essential to manage the crisis quickly and honestly. Hiding information from the media and the public has historically been shown to lead to intensified negative exposure and even legal trouble.

▶ Having a plan and preparing the staff for the event of a potential crisis can render response more effective and thus decrease negative exposure.

▶ The four stages of crisis management include: staff character, company culture, company structure, and crisis planning.

## Key Terms

▶ Band-Aid effect

▶ crisis circumstances

▶ crisis scope

▶ crisis sphere

▶ crisis timing

▶ fabricated crisis

▶ media bias

▶ media sphere

▶ negative false rumor

▶ public relations crisis

▶ public sphere

▶ self-inflicted crisis

▶ smear campaign

▶ virtual sphere

## Chapter-End Questions and Exercises

1. What is a public relations crisis? Give a fictitious example.

2. What are the factors that shape the crisis? Explain how each affects the example you gave in the previous questions.

3. Why should the fashion company address the public relations crisis? Wouldn't acknowledging it create more negative publicity? Explain your position.

331

4. Compare and contrast the four crisis spheres.

5. Do you think that in general the self-inflicted crisis can be prevented? How?

6. Who is normally behind the fabricated crisis and what are their interests in generating the crisis? Can you think of other sources for this crisis type that are not mentioned in the chapter?

7. Find a fashion company that has experienced a public relations crisis in the past. Research the facts that surround the crisis and answer the following:

   a. Was the crisis self-inflicted or fabricated?

   b. In which spheres was the crisis spread?

   c. What were its circumstances?

   d. How wide was the crisis scope?

   e. Did the timing of the crisis affect the degree of negative exposure? How long did the crisis last?

   f. What were the consequences of the crisis?

8. Explain the various effects that a crisis can have on a fashion company.

9. Why is planning and preparation so important in managing the crisis?

10. Do you agree with the text's approach to "No comment"? Explain.

11. How important is honesty to the process of crisis management? Why?

12. In the example you cited in Question 7, do you think the fashion company addressed the crisis successfully? What other strategies could the fashion company have adopted to address the crisis and what would the results have been?

# Administration

## THIRTEEN

## Chapter Snapshot

Although it may not be the most exciting facet of fashion public relations, proper administration and record keeping is an important component of a successful public relations department that not only allows for smooth implementation of the campaign, but also safeguards against misunderstandings, confusions, and even lawsuits. Additionally, correct administration provides historical information about past public relations initiatives, which can be used for reviewing performance and planning future initiatives. In this chapter, we will discuss the roles and benefits of collecting media clips—whether print, broadcast, or Web-based—and how these clips can be utilized within the fashion company—not only by the public relations department but also by other departments such as sales, marketing, and production. We will also discuss the online press center and how keeping it up-to-date can help gain more media exposure. Finally, we will talk about the preparation of reports for management and the proper documentation for interviews and correspondence with sources and the media.

## Objectives

▶ Understand the importance of proper administration in the field of fashion public relations.

▶ Discuss the need for obtaining media clips—in print, broadcast, and online—and establishing a media portfolio.

▶ Define the press center and its typical components.

▶ Compare and contrast the press kit and the press center.

▶ Explore the various reports that the public relations department should submit to management.

▶ Cover the type of records that should be kept as part of the preparation for press releases, photo ops, and other public relations initiatives.

Although *administration* is the topic of this final chapter in the text, it is by no means the least important activity regarding fashion public relations activities. Without proper administration methods, we find confusion and lack of control regarding the activities of the public relations department. Administration is the act or process of overseeing and managing activities in order to reach planned goals and objectives successfully. In the real world, companies that lack the ability to administer the workings of the organization are doomed to failure. Administration is the voice of the organization and its chief responsibility is functioning in the financial, marketing, and productive aspects of public relations. Proper administration is the ability to stay on top of the day-to-day activities, and also to monitor the short- and long-term plans, goals, and objectives of the company. In fashion public relations, it has to do with making certain that the happenings are reported to the proper channels; thus administration is the communication arm of the organization.

Successful public relations firms have one thing in common—the ability to make certain that all personnel are on the same page regarding the company's activities, policies, and any and all working relationships with clients. Administration is the act of carrying out these policies and deciding the activities that must be part of the company's operation. In larger fashion companies, the president, chief executive officer (CEO), or chief operating officer (COO) are relegated to the task of being the chief administrator with their assistants, VPs, and managers carrying out the day-to-day functions. In smaller companies, one person can be in charge of administration along with her or his other duties.

Fashion public relations relies heavily on proper administration. From monitoring media for published stories to keeping research notes, administration is a vital component of fashion public relations. When a fashion company's public relations staff pays attention to the small details and takes care of their administrative duties, the department functions more efficiently; this results in maximized exposure and improved public image. Administration in the fashion public relations field consists of media clips, the press kit/center, reports to management, and record keeping.

## Media Clips

In the administration of the fashion public relations department, the need to communicate the activities is paramount in order to establish the progress of the workload. Besides written activity reports and presentation meetings, how can a public relations firm indicate its activities to its clients and their management? The use of media clips plays a vital part in establishing public relations performance. The **media clip** can be developed as an audio, video, or print clip. Media clips are used for promotional activities and for a record of performance by a public relations firm as part of an activity report, which we will cover later on in this chapter. Making copies of published news clips, video clips, reprints, digital reprints, DVD clips, and Web-formatted online feeds help support a record of public relations performance as part of the activities. These clips are readily available for reproduction from many media clipping services and copies thereof should be sent to all concerned parties whenever a story about the company or its brands appears in the media.

### Media Clipping Services

**Clipping services** are on duty around the clock, recording media events as they happen. Their large monitoring networks of media around the globe produce more accurate results than any fashion company could ever achieve. No fashion company can afford to hire personnel to sit day in and day out to read and scan the media for published stories. Clipping services can inform the fashion company of published clips from remote and unlikely media outlets that the fashion company would otherwise never hear of. Some services specialize in print media while others specialize in broadcast or online media. There are also services that can monitor print, broadcast, and online media coverage both locally and globally. The use of media and clippings services enables us to monitor the media and obtain copies of published stories about the fashion company. These services are not costly compared to the results. The ability to have a print or video copy of the story is an invaluable tool for the public relations department. Box 13.1 lists a few major media clipping services.

### Media Portfolio

When the fashion company has copies of its media clips, the next step is to organize them as a record of its achievements into its own media portfolio. This clip book will be an ongoing record of any and all press coverage. It will have many purposes besides providing a history of the company's achievements. The clip book is easy to organize and maintain. The investment in the clip book is nominal, but the results can be enormous. It can be maintained in print format or online as part of the press center, which will be covered in the next section of this chapter.

For the print version, office or art supply stores have a great selection of binders in which to store media results. It is recommended to use a 12-inch by 14-inch binder that can store newspaper sheet-sized clips as well as magazine and other clips. When mounting the newspaper clips onto the binder page,

## Box 13.1    Major Media Clipping Services in the United States

1. Cyber-Alert, Inc. (www.cyberalert.com)—Located in Stratford, Connecticut, this company offers comprehensive media coverage, local to global. It monitors more than 25,000 news sources worldwide in more than 20 languages in 169 countries, and provides localized, customized service to fit to your needs. It covers local newspapers and trade journals, and provides round-the-clock monitoring of closed-caption text for all scheduled newscasts on more than 600 local television stations in the top 100 U.S. markets.

2. BurrellesLuce (www.BurrellesLuce.com)—This company reads each print edition of major publications, so they catch the large number of articles that appear in print that never make it online. They cover more than 50 million online and print sources, broadcasts from 210 U.S. markets, and full broadcast monitoring on the Internet, including Web logs. They cover Internet forums, blogs, social media, Web news sources, regional publications, daily and non-daily newspapers, consumer magazines, trade magazines, professional journals, news wires, and syndicated services.

3. Cision (www.cision.com)—Cision provides a service to view articles exactly as they appeared. Their in-house monitoring department monitors the printed editions of each publication and uses optical scanning to deliver all the clips as electronic images along with a thumbnail to illustrate the articles' placement within the publication. Coverage is easy to manage and share. Through Cision's search terms and tagging feature, managing, sorting, evaluating, and reporting the coverage client's and their competitors is easy. Clients also receive daily email alerts of the clips along with email and press report tools to easily share news across the client's organization.

always clip and mount the newspaper's banner name at the top of the page and then mount the actual story below it. This clip book will serve several purposes. Along with being a record of the company's accomplishments for its present clients, it also makes for a great marketing tool when presenting the company's record of performance to prospective clients. It can help entice other companies to work with the fashion company. In addition to maintaining a clip book, it is suggested to keep on file extra fresh copies of news releases and all other media clips in an organized filing system. These copies may be needed in the future, and having extra original copies for reproduction for presentation flyers and other presentation pieces will be in the company's best interest.

### Print Media Clips

Copies of published stories from the print media should be obtained immediately. This includes daily newspapers, weekly publications, consumer magazines, trade media, and newsletters. Delays in purchasing copies can prove troublesome later because the publication can easily sell out or, in the case of a daily newspaper, be replaced the next morning by tomorrow's edition. In this case, the public relations staff will have to contact the publication and arrange for back copies—which may or may not be available—to be sent to the fashion company at a much higher cost than purchasing the original issues. For print media clips, the public relations staff should aim to obtain:

▶ Several copies of the actual issue itself—This is the best clip because it is the most authentic and credible representation of the published clip.

▶ Reprints—Some print publications offer reprints at additional cost. Such reprints are designed by the publication's advertising staff normally and cost an additional fee. Reprints are typically reproduced on a glossy legal-size photo-quality sheet.

▶ Digital reprints—These are more difficult to obtain, but some publications offer digital images of the reprints that the fashion company can then post on its press center. If the story is published online as well, the public relations staff can log onto the publication's Web site and create a digital reprint from the Web page by saving it using special graphic programs. This is more tedious and technical. Plus, a do-it-yourself clip typically will have advertisements and other information that are not relevant to the clip, whereas the digital reprint provided by the publication is an organized and clean copy of the story.

## Broadcast Media Clips

Due to the nature of broadcast media, it is difficult to capture the broadcast as it happens; the television station may not know when the story will be broadcast until minutes before it is put on the air, and capturing a broadcast in a digital format is highly technical task. It is easier to use the clipping service's

**FIGURE 13.1** Designer Marc Jacobs's Web site includes media clips from various publications, listed by publication date.

clips instead. With the date and time of when the story was aired, the clipping service can then obtain a digital clip of the broadcast and reproduce it in DVD format for the fashion company. In some cases, the service may also offer Web-formatted digital clips of the broadcast in lower resolution so they can be posted online for live feeds and downloads.

## The Press Kit/Center

The press kit and **press center** are virtually the same, except the former is in print while the latter is online. The fashion company should develop both print and online versions and keep them updated, or at the very least maintain an online version. Establishing a press kit/center is an important part of fashion public relations administration. Besides serving as a pitching tool for the fashion company's news stories as described in Chapter 8, the press kit/center is also an archive of the company's releases for reference purposes. When a journalist needs to know when the company released a previous collection, all he or she has to do is leaf through the press kit or check out the press center's archives. The press kit/center also serves as a platform where artwork of the company's brands and collections can be obtained by the media.

### Press Kit

As covered in Chapter 8, the press kit is typically an information folder that is sent out to the media. It contains several inserts that provide meaningful information to journalists and editors. It can be submitted to the media to introduce a new press release, or it can be sent with general company information to introduce the company to the media and develop a relationship with the editor. The press kit typically consists of a presentation folder with inside flap pockets to hold the inserts. If the press kit is sent out as part of a news release package that the company is pitching, it includes the press release and information in the right-side inside flap along with supporting documents, research citations, attachments, photos and/or B-roll, as well as product information if applicable. If the kit is sent as an introductory package, a letter of introduction should be placed at the top of the right-hand stack instead. In the left-hand inside flap pocket, the kit should include background information about the company—such as an overview description, philosophy and history summary, executive biographies, and a summary of the company's current product lines—as well as the company's media clips, showcasing the most prominent and positive media coverage the company has had in the recent past. Some fashion companies transform their press kit into an online document and make it available on their Web site as a PDF document, as illustrated in Figure 13.2.

### The Press Center

The fashion company is wise to set up a press center in the corporate section of its Web site for it can assist tremendously in gaining positive coverage. Because the information posted in the press center is available around the clock and year round, it is a tool that can help a journalist on deadline gather basic information about the company quickly and without having to talk with any of

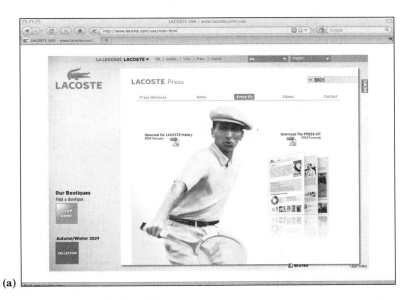

(a)

**FIGURE 13.2A–D** Lacoste makes its (a) press kit available online through its press center. It can be downloaded as a PDF file from the link on the center, right-hand side of the screen. Its virtual press kit pages include (b) basic company information and statistics, (c) historical facts, and (d) information about its advertising campaign.

(b)

(c)

(d)

**FIGURE 13.3** The Levi Strauss & Co. press center is a good example of a comprehensive media portal for the fashion company and its brands. The main page for the press center provides an orderly and user-friendly overview of available information at a glance. It offers a direct hyperlink for the two latest press releases, a main menu (the brown menu bar to the left) with press releases, story ideas, image gallery, and media contacts. To the left of that menu, it offers general information about the company—its history, workplace, and citizenship.

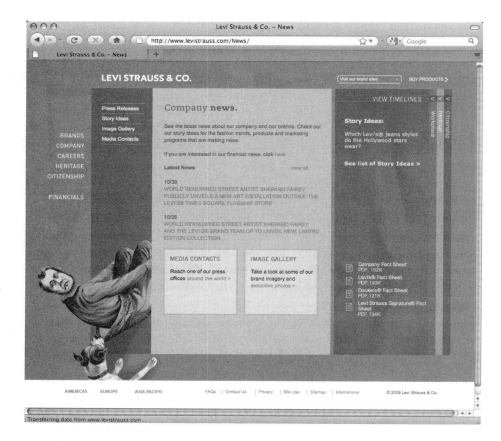

the company's representatives. In addition, because the information is posted online, it is available worldwide for anyone to view; therefore, journalists who are searching for a story might stumble across the fashion company's press center and decide to do a story about the company. Finally, because the press center content is text based—excluding the artwork, naturally—all documents and information can be copied and pasted by the journalist from the Web site right into the journalist's word processing document where he or she is writing the story; this saves the journalist time but also safeguards against misunderstanding errors, which are more common in verbal interviews. Let's look at some of the common components recommended for a fashion company press center.

### *Current Releases*

The most important part of the press center is the news page with the company's current press releases listed in chronological order with the most recent release at the top. The page can be organized with hyperlinks to each release, as can be seen in Figure 13.4, or as a long page with the text of the releases listed in line. Each release should be downloadable, printable, and its text should be set up so the journalist can copy and paste it with ease.

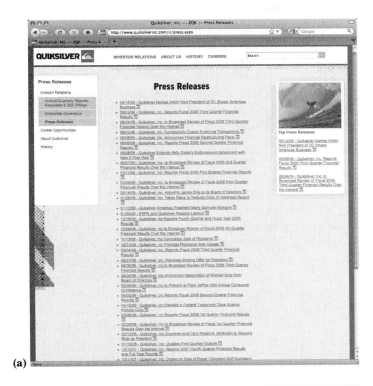

**(a)**

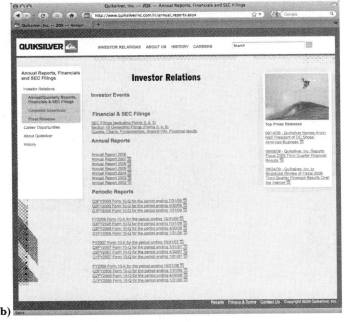

**(b)**

**FIGURE 13.4** Quiksilver, Inc.'s Web page for press releases uses the headline of each release as the hyperlink to the page displaying the individual release. The first screen shot (a) shows the main page, which lists the releases by date. When we click on the hyperlink "Quiksilver and Roxy Announce Exclusive American License Agreement for Children's Footwear," for example, we are led to another Web page (b) that displays the full release.

### Archived Releases

Many companies choose to archive news releases from previous years and list these in another Web page, as in Figure 13.5. This separation makes the distinction between today's news and yesterday's news and helps organize the data. Although it is recommended to keep past releases online for reference purposes, it is up to the company's preference whether to create a separate archive page, or simply to list all releases in date order.

### Story Ideas

Providing the media with story ideas is a helpful and beneficial feature of the press center (see Figure 13.6). This Web page offers journalists with general stories about the company that are not timely but can be covered as a feature during a slow news day. Having a list of such ideas available with one click of the mouse is attractive to the media, especially when crunch time comes around and there is an urgent need for filler stories.

### Photo Gallery

As seen in Figure 13.7, posting online the artwork that is available to accompany the press release makes it easier for the journalist to include the artwork with the story, and because artwork directs readers' attention to the story this is a vital feature of the press center. In addition to release-specific artwork, the press center can also offer general images of the company's brands and classic collections; when a journalist is writing about the company, he or

342

**FIGURE 13.5** Reebok's press releases for previous years are archived and can be browsed by the year they were published.

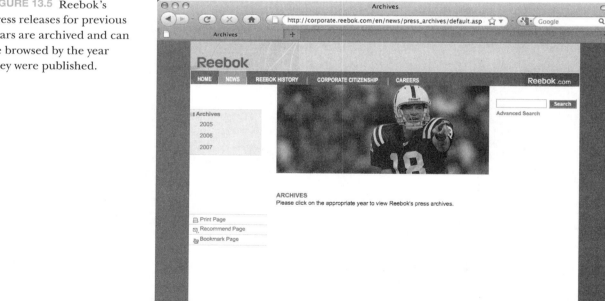

**FIGURE 13.6**
Levi Strauss & Co.'s story ideas Web page.

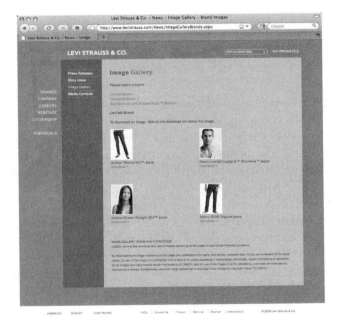

**FIGURE 13.7** Levi Strauss & Co.'s online image gallery is displayed by brand and collection.

she can simply pick a suitable photo from the gallery, download it, and use it with the story. The photo credit that the company wants used with each photo should be provided for the journalist.

### Company Information

The press center should include several documents detailing the fashion company's information. The data provided should be focused on answering potential media inquiries with accurate, well-researched information. To make access easier for the media, it is better to separate the documents rather than post one long document with all the information. The following are typical company information documents that could be posted on the press center.

▶ A company fact sheet that provides a general overview of the fashion company, including the company's legal name, the addresses and contacts of its headquarters and offices, a description of its business, whether it is a private or public company (if it's a public company, its ticker name and which financial market it's traded on should also be included), how many employees are on staff, and so on.

▶ The fashion company's history, including when it was founded and by whom, important events in the company's evolution such as the introductions of milestone new products, the release of special designs or collections, the hiring of prominent designers, and mergers and acquisitions.

▶ The fashion company's business philosophy, including what the company does to offer workplace diversity and employee satisfaction, the standards that the company uses to select its vendors, and if applicable information on work conditions in factories that supply the company.

▶ Brief executive biographies for the top executives, typically the chief executive officer, the chief financial officer, the chief operating officer, and the director of design.

### Community Involvement

It is important to include this information in a prominent location in the press center because community involvement is a catalyst for positive coverage. The company's social responsibilities should be explained in practical and simple terms rather than with broad and lofty notions. It should state plainly and simply what the company is actually doing in the community, including its views on community involvement, the community projects it is involved in, community projects it had successfully completed in the past, nonprofit organizations the company sponsors, and any charity events with which the company is involved.

### Press Contacts

When the media is interested but needs more information from the company, the press contacts page proves quite handy, especially on deadline. We don't want the journalist to have to comb through past press releases or through the staff directory to find out whom to call—it should be right there at the tip

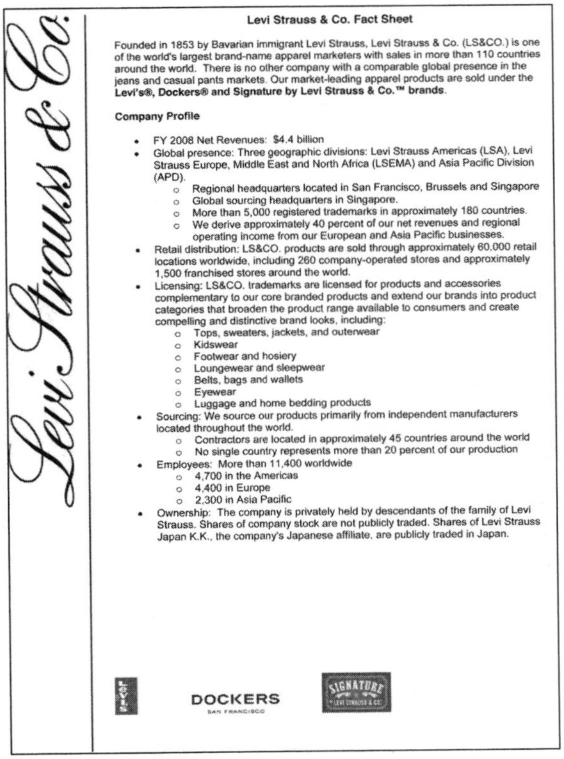

**FIGURE 13.8A** Levi Strauss & Co. has made its company fact sheet available for download from its press center in a PDF-formatted document.

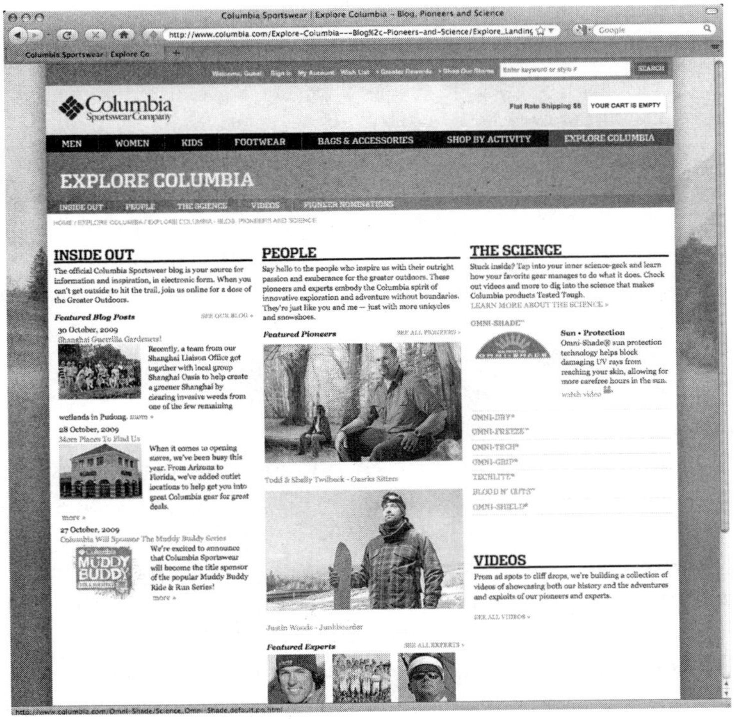

**FIGURE 13.8B** Columbia Sportswear Company, on the other hand, outlines its company history in the Web page itself, in narrative form, in-line, more or less by chronological order.

**FIGURE 13.9** Levi Strauss & Co.'s Web page on community relations is simple and easy to navigate, highlighting the main topics the media and visitors would be interested in. From the company's involvement in community improvement programs to the company's outsourcing practices, the information is well organized and easy to find.

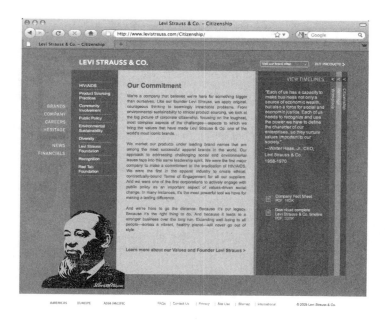

of the journalist's fingers, virtually speaking of course. It is vital to list the full contact information for all press contacts, including full name, title, telephone number, fax number, email address, emergency telephone numbers where they can be reached after hours, and mailing address. If there are more than two employees in the department, it is helpful to list which press contact is responsible for what duties for the media's convenience.

### *Format of the Press Center*

The press center's format should be simple and easy to navigate. It is preferred to present information in simple, text-based Web pages or in Adobe PDF format, which makes it easy for the journalist to copy and paste. Posting images with text as part of the image or posting information inside a Flash movie, for example, makes it impossible to copy and paste and may deter the journalist from doing the story or including that information because he or she would have to re-type the information.

## Management Reports

Activity reports and other systems of reporting on progress and productivity are essential to the management of the different departments within the company. The reporting system must be set into motion for in-house public relations personnel as well as any outsourced public relations firm. A proper reporting system creates and stores information in order to gather data over time and evaluate performance, results, and return on investment (ROI). This data is gathered and shared with the company's management, and is used to evaluate performance, monitor the goals and objectives, and help make major strategic decisions for the company's future.

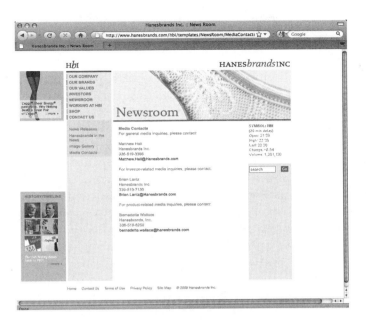

**FIGURE 13.10** Hanes' media contacts Web page categorizes its media contacts by general inquiries, investor-related inquiries, and product-related inquiries. Product-related inquiries are further sub-categorized by brand, with two different departmental personnel each handling a different set of brands. This makes it easier for the journalist to quickly determine who should be the best person to contact for the type of information the journalist requires.

In the real world of business, you are paid by deeds, not needs. Reporting to management by way of an **activity report** is an essential part of communicating to management what the department has accomplished over a specific time period. It is vital that you record the daily happenings and communicate the activities in a format that doesn't sidetrack you from your working schedule. Too many business managers become too involved with excessive meetings that prevent their employees and outsource firms from performing their job functions. The activity report is one way of preventing management from micromanaging and freeing up departmental employees or the outsourced public relations firm to spend more time being productive at their job assignment, thus eliminating unnecessary meetings. For perspective on this topic, we look to management experts such as Peter Drucker. In his book, *Managing for Results,* Drucker states, "The day-by-day method of management is inadequate even in the smallest and simplest business" (Drucker, 1964). Drucker goes on to say, "there is a need to do the few things right and do them with excellence." Doing the right thing is to spend the working hours in a productive capacity and not wasting time with unnecessary staff meetings that can be handled by a telephone call or a memo. When Drucker wrote the book more than four decades ago, he hadn't realized the job complexity and the tremendous demand of time that we would face in the twenty-first century. Although some may think that reporting to management verbally on a day-to-day level is adequate, giving the individual employee more freedom to explore the opportunities and concentrate on their job functions may result in greatly increased productivity.

We are all accountable for our work performance. Public relations practitioners, whether they are in-house personnel or an outsourced public relations firm, must be able to account for their performance. Just recording the hours worked is not sufficient in measuring performance. Listing the activities and the results related to the outcome is essential in order to measure the productivity of public relations personnel. The activity report is short and sweet, concisely conveying the department's activities and results in a straightforward manner. As such, it is a perfect vehicle to communicate one's activities to management and also chronicle the activities to ensure proper follow-through. It can be submitted on a weekly or monthly basis, according to management's needs. The weekly report is preferable for an in-house public relations department due to the very nature of the day-to-day interaction among personnel in the department and management. The monthly report is primarily submitted to the client by the outsourced public relations firm and is usually submitted with the monthly invoice for services. The information contained in both types of activity reports is essentially the same and requires standard performance information. Activity reports should include the actual workload, indicate the results of activity for a specific period, and list whether the objectives were accomplished or not. The report should include the basics: action item, activity, date, action and status, including all names and details involved, as illustrated in Box 13.2. The activity report can be viewed as a scorecard on productivity for public relations activities, and should be used as the effective management tool that it is.

## Keeping Records

It is difficult to question written communication; there is little arguing to be done with black ink on white paper that proves or disproves a claim. Keeping records eliminates the need to debate about who said what and when. In a field where a simple mistake can be amplified a thousand times if it reaches the media, record keeping becomes vitally important. Whether stored in digital format on the computer or in printed format in a filing cabinet, the records kept must be the originals or exact copies and, as a general rule, always should contain the date of the document. An organized public relations department is not only more productive, but also is able to answer media inquiries and management questions more quickly than the fly-by-the-seat-of-their-pants disorganized department. Record keeping provides a paper trail for each public relations campaign and initiative that can be analyzed later on for performance and responsibility. These records can be divided into internal communications and external correspondence.

### Internal Communications

There are many memos and emails that go back and forth between the public relations department and the other company's departments. The public relations staff routinely communicates with management, production, planning, sales, marketing, and even accounting. It is wise to file important memos for future reference; these include the following.

#### *Approvals from Management*

Whenever a specific campaign, budget, project, or initiative receives a green light from management, it is recommended to have the approval sent in writing to the public relations director and filed properly. Such a communication can be referred to in the future should questions come up later about whether the project was indeed approved.

## Box 13.2   Sample Activity Report

Here's a typical activity report with fictitious information. Note the clarity of the information and the details that must be included for each item.

**TABLE BOX 13.1   Public Relations Weekly Activity Report**

**Name:** John Smith
**Time Period:** January 3–10, 2008

| ACTION ITEM | ACTIVITY | DATE | ACTION | STATUS |
|---|---|---|---|---|
| Media placement Spring Collection Fashion Week | Press releases sent to: *W, WWD, Vogue, Glamour,* Style.com | Jan 3, 2008 | Story ran in all media listed under Activity | Published |
| Fashion Week | Created Cee Jay Fashion Week banners | Jan 4, 2008 | Banners displayed at Broadway & W.38th St. and 1411 Broadway | Completed |
| FashionWeek | Meeting reporters *W* and *WWD, Vogue, Glamour* | Jan 4, 2008 | | Completed |
| Fashion Week invitation/flyer | Created invitation/flyer | Jan 6, 2008 | Emailed/faxed to all companies | Completed |
| Press releases | Fashion week Cee Jay story | Jan 6, 2008 | Sent to all print, Internet & TV media contacts | Completed |
| Other activities | Developed press kits | Jan 7, 2008 | Distributed to all fashion media sources | Completed |
| Other activities | Media clips | Ongoing | Sent to Cee Jay | In Progress |

Additional tasks:

▶ Constantly calling and visiting our media contacts

▶ Created press releases as directed by Cee Jay, Spring collection

▶ Worked with fashion photographers—various functions on Fashion Week

▶ Worked with fashion photographers—pictures for future releases

Another way of reporting can be in memo form. One method can include a list of weekly/monthly activities in precise terms, stating the contacts, results, and future actions. The following is a sample memo-form report:

To: Vice President Marketing
From: John Smith
Re: Public Relations Weekly Activity Report
Time Period: Jan. 3–Jan. 10, 2008

ACTIVITIES:

1. Media placement Spring Collection Fashion Week; Press releases sent to: *W, WWD, Vogue, Glamour,* Style.com

2. Created Cee Jay Fashion Week banners

3. Meeting reporters *W* and *WWD, Vogue, Glamour*

RESULTS

1. Story about Spring Collection at Fashion Week ran in *W, WWD, Vogue, Glamour,* Style.com on Jan. 3, 2008

2. Created Fashion Week invitation/flyer

3. Developed press kits

SUMMARY

Productive week despite problematic issue with sending out the press releases due to a delay in receiving photographs.

Signed,

John Smith

### Media Releases

Anytime a company employee is interviewed or photographed for a press release or other media outreach, a media release must be signed by the employee first attesting that he or she is agreeable to the interview, and that he or she will have no claims against the company as a result of the media coverage that materializes. It is advisable to have the media release form drafted or at the very least approved by the company's legal department to protect the company from potential lawsuits. Such releases must be kept on file for as long as possible, preferably until the end of the statutory period is over, beyond which the company cannot be sued anymore in that state.

### Press Releases

Every press release, press kit, and media information sheet should be filed in a central place in chronological order or by topic. Each document should be filed with the research that was used to back up any statements made. Additionally, the notes made during any interviews with sources used in these releases should also be filed with the release. Having all supporting information in writing prevents the media from doubting the company's communication integrity, and avoids clashes with sources who later on claim that "they didn't say that." Although the written and research notes usually are admissible as evidence in legal disputes, record keeping compliance with legal requirements should be ultimately guided and approved by the company's legal council.

### Photo Information

Every photograph, illustration, or other piece of artwork that is used by the public relations department should be filed as well. For each photograph or other piece of artwork, the source and caption info should be included as well as the signed usage agreements from the artist granting the company the rights to use the artwork for promotional purpose. Again, the company's legal department should draft or at least approve the usage agreement.

## External Communications

Correspondence with individuals, companies, entities, organization, and media outside the fashion company are at least as important as—if not more important than—internal communications. The fashion company has less control over external entities than it does its own employees and departments; therefore, these external communications should be filed with care and attention so that they can be retrieved quickly to settle disputes or issues should they arise in the future. Again, the company's legal council should review and approve the record keeping procedures to ensure compliance with legal requirements.

### Media Correspondence

Keep all correspondence with the media on file for future reference. Besides helping to keep track of which media publication is interested in covering the company's story or has an outstanding inquiry, this will also help in reviewing past initiatives and analyzing which approaches to the media proved most fruitful.

## Case Study 13.1    Administration

### Online Press Center: Volcom, Inc.

As its About paragraph states, the Volcom brand is "athlete-driven, creative and forward thinking. Volcom has consistently followed its motto of "youth against establishment," and the brand is inspired by the energy of youth culture" (Volcom, Inc., 2008). This attitude of counter-culture, which is part of the company's core philosophy, extends to the company's press center as well. With its dissident graphic theme, Volcom's press center is anything but that of traditional design; it is set against a black background adorned with graffiti and stenciled messages of a borderline subversive nature. Against this background and the Web site's unorthodox page layout, members of the media can read the latest press releases and peruse the company's history. The company sticks to its skater style throughout the press center, illustrating that a press center does not have to be boring and can display some style.

#### *Questions to Consider*

1. Do you feel Volcom is justified in extending its rebel design theme onto its press center? Explain.

2. How would you improve Volcom's press center? What effects would your changes have on visitors to the press center?

3. Put yourself in the shoes of an editor or reporter viewing Volcom's press center for the first time. What do you think your reaction would be? Why?

351

(a)

**FIGURE CASE STUDY 13.1** Volcom's home Web page (a) outline the company's history. This links to the company's fact sheet (b) A sample press release (c) shows that the company's unique culture pervades even its most official communications to the external business world.

(b)

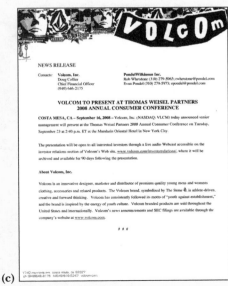

(c)

When a public relations campaign targets certain publications from which the company has successfully obtained coverage in the past, the correspondence on file can give clues as to what piqued these publications' interest, thus providing guidelines for the current campaign's implementation strategies.

### Correspondence with Partner Organizations

When the fashion company negotiates a partnership with a nonprofit organization or a charity drive to benefit a local community group, the details should be documented in writing and filed in that project's folder for the record. This serves several purposes: It eliminates potential confusions as to who is responsible for what tasks within the project; it delineates the project's scope and objectives, thus providing a direction for the individual tasks within the projects; and it serves as proof for the media that the company is indeed partnering with the nonprofit organization or community group. In the case of a question as to certain implementation details within the project, the correspondence that touched upon these details can be pulled out of the file and consulted.

### Interview Notes

Any interview with a source who is not a company employee that will be used as part of a public relations initiative should be well documented with notes or tape recording. Notes should be as detailed as possible and written in legible handwriting or in standard shorthand. These notes should be filed with the release that will utilize the statements from the interview and serve as supporting evidence for the release itself.

## Chapter Summary

▶ Administration is an important requirement for success in fashion public relations; without proper administration, the department will become less productive and begin to make mistakes that may eventually turn into a media fiasco.

▶ It is essential to collect media clips of published stories in a media portfolio, which can be used to obtain more coverage but can also be used by the sales and marketing departments.

▶ The clipping service is the ears of the fashion company in the media world, and it informs the company whenever a story is published about it.

▶ The press center is similar to the press kit, only it exists on the fashion company's Web site and has the potential to provide a lot more information to the media in the form of digital documents.

▶ The press center should include the fashion company's current press releases, archived releases, story ideas, a photo gallery, company overview, community involvement, and press contacts.

▶ The activity report provides management with a concise summary of the public relations activities and results for a specified period.

▸ Keeping records is vital for public relations success both for organizational purposes as well as to meet legal compliance for the company's protection.

▸ Internal record keeping includes filing approvals from management, media releases, press releases, and photo information.

▸ External record keeping includes correspondence with the media, correspondence with partner organizations, and notes from interviews.

## Key Terms

▸ activity report

▸ clipping services

▸ media clips

▸ press center

## Chapter-End Questions and Exercises

1. What is the importance of administration in the field of fashion public relations? What are the benefits of good administration?

2. What is a media clip and how is it used in fashion public relations?

3. Compare and contrast the print media clip with the broadcast media clip.

4. Find a media clipping service that is not mentioned in this chapter and answer the following:

    a. What type of media does the service specialize in?

    b. Does it offer 24-hour media monitoring?

    c. How does the service provide its clients with media clips?

    d. If you were a public relations director for a fashion company, would you use this particular clipping service? Explain.

5. Simulated scenario: You are the newly hired public relations director for a fashion company, and you are charged with preparing a press kit for the company:

    a. Create the company, its name, the type of fashion and styles that it deals with, and whether it is a public or privately held company.

    b. Create a press kit folder for the company.

    c. Write one or more press releases for the company's latest initiatives *or* write an introductory letter to the media.

    d. Include any research citations or attachments to press releases.

    e. Include artwork or photos to accompany releases, if you want.

    f. Write a company fact sheet.

    g. Write a community involvement sheet.

    h. Create an insert with the company's collections information.

6. Locate a well-known fashion company that has a press center online, and evaluate the press center along each of the components:

   a. Company's name and Web address of its press center.

   b. Is it easy to navigate and find information?

   c. Does it list current press releases?

   d. Are current press releases displayed on-line as text or as an attached PDF?

   e. Does the center offer archived releases?

   f. Does the center provide story ideas?

   g. Is there a photo gallery? Is it easy to navigate and download images? Are there photo credit instructions?

   h. Is company information included in the center?

   i. Is there information on the company's community involvement?

   j. Does the center provide specific press contacts information?

7. Simulated scenario: You are the public relations firm representative for a well-known fashion company (decide which and what project you are working on for that company). Create a fictitious activity report detailing your performance for the month.

8. Why is it important to keep records for public relations initiatives? How does it help safeguard the company against lawsuits or negative exposure?

9. Explain the concept of record keeping for internal communications. Give examples for each type of internal record-keeping category.

10. Explain the concept of record keeping for external communications. Give examples for each type of internal record keeping category.

# Glossary

**activity report**   A summary of the progress made on a public relations initiative during a specified time, detailing what was accomplished and when.

**anchor**   The journalist who presents the news segment from the news desk in the television studio. The anchor rarely goes out into the field; instead, he or she remains in the studio most of the time, presents the news stories that are part of the news segment, and mediates among the public, the network, and other news reporters. Typically, the anchor must approve which stories will be presented in the coming program.

**About paragraph**   A paragraph at the bottom of a press release providing the basic information about the company—its full legal name, a description of its business, where it is located, whether it is a publicly held or private company, a brief history, and its Web site address if one exists.

**action shot**   A photo of a fashion item in action (i.e., being worn) or an event happening in real time.

**advance time**   The approximate time prior to the deadline that allows an editor or reporter to comfortably cover a story so it can be included in the appropriate issue. Different reporters have different advance times, depending on the publication type and the reporter's preferences. If a magazine reporter's deadline is the end of the month for the following month's issue, for example, then he or she must have all their stories in by that time; if it takes him or her about one week to get the story approved by the editor and assigned and then two weeks to research and write the story, then the advance time is three weeks. Sending in a story too early can also be detrimental because by the time the deadline comes along, the story might be old news already.

**artwork**   Denotes a photograph, chart, illustration, sketch, video footage, or other graphic representation which runs next to the story to make it more interesting for the reader.

**astroturf**   "A new term has joined the jargon of the high-tech, media-smart political class: astroturf," notes the social scientist and author Walter Truett Anderson. "It refers not to fake grass but to fake grassroots—as in outpourings of public opinion made to look like spontaneous communications from the bottom but, in reality, engineered by spin doctors at the top" (Anderson, 1996).

**attribute**   To name the source of your information when using any quote or fact. In principle, all quotes and facts in a story (excluding editorial pieces) should be attributed to prevent a reporter's bias or opinion from entering the story.

**attended photo opportunity**   The type of photo op where a photojournalist or videographer attends the news story and captures it on camera or video camera.

**audience profile**   A guide for defining an audience based on a set of characteristics shared by members of that audience that sets them apart from other audiences; these characteristics include income level, gender, education, profession, and so on.

**audience segmentation**   Dividing the company's audience into smaller groups that allow for more customized, better targeted public relations strategies.

**B-roll, or B roll**   Supplemental footage that is added as a background to the main news segment or report. The name originated in the video editing room where the video track B contained the secondary footage that is played behind the main video on track A. Typical use of B-roll is when the television news report shows the anchor speaking, then continues her audio commentary while switching the video to file footage of what the anchor is talking about. B-roll has also come to mean the video footage provided free of charge by corporations and organizations as a means of gaining press coverage. For example, a tie manufacturer might shoot a video of its assembly line, hoping that segments will be used in stories about its new collection.

**B2B**   Acronym that stands for "business-to-business" and involves transactions that take place between fashion manufacturers and retailers or between any two business entities.

**B2C** Acronym that stands for "business-to-consumer" and denotes sales made by a business to an individual consumer, or the process of selling a product or service to the ultimate consumer, also known as the end user.

**Band-Aid effect** An approach to a public relations crisis that covers up the sign of a problem but does not resolve the problem.

**blog** See Web log.

**blogger** A person who publishes a Web log—or "blog," as they are commonly called—or personal diary on a Web page.

**bottom-up budgeting** An estimate by lower management of the operating costs needed to reach their goals. These estimates are communicated in proposal form to upper management for the final decision. Opposite of the top-down budgeting method.

**brand recognition** Existing and potential customers' awareness of the company's name, logo, products, and quality.

**breaking news** A story of strong public interest that has just been released and which the media could consider is in need of urgent coverage. An example of breaking news in the fashion industry would be a fashion designer announcing her retirement, or a fashion manufacturer announcing a recall of a certain product due to safety issues.

**business relationship** An association between two people of different companies who reach a level of comfort and cooperate by sharing assistance, information, and logistics to achieve a common goal that benefits both parties.

**buying criteria** A customer's perceptions of a product that determine whether or not the customer will purchase that product.

**buzz** Excitement, news coverage, and positive word-of-mouth about the company, its brand, and/or product.

**call-to-action advertisement** An advertisement that lead the audience toward a specific action that is a step in the direction of a sale. "Buy our brand!" "Come to our store today!" and "Log on to our Web site!" are all calls to action.

**cause-related activity** An activity or initiative in which an organization or corporation pledges a percentage of its proceeds toward a specific cause or nonprofit project.

**centers of influence** Individuals within the community who take an active role in improving and leading the community. Their opinions are held in high regard by the community at large and play a significant role in shaping public opinion.

**clipping service**   A firm that monitors the media around the clock and alerts the fashion company to a published story about that company or its products. Often, the firm also records media events as they happen or reproduces published media clips and submits them to the fashion company.

**community**   A group of people who share common interests or characteristics, such as geographic location, age, lifestyle, and so on. Specifically, within public relations, the community refers to the group of people—and their family and friends—who comprise the public in the geographical area where the company operates.

**community affairs**   In this age of guerilla marketing, community affairs is an integral part of public relations that handles the company's dealings with the community. It can range from sponsoring nonprofit organizations to developing community events with these organizations and local governmental service agencies, e.g., police, fire, and health departments. The objective of community affairs is to develop these relationships, which ultimately will benefit the company's public relations efforts.

**copy**   The main text in the press release; the material for the news story. It gives all the facts, quotes, and other information about the story. Copy can also refer to the main text of the published media story.

**cost per 1,000 (CPM where M stands for the Roman numeral for 1,000)**   The dollar cost of reaching 1,000 members of an audience using a particular medium.

**cost per 1,000-target market (CPM-TM)**   The dollar cost of reaching 1,000 members of a specific target market using a particular medium.

**cost per rating point (CPRP)**   A measurement used in planning a television advertising purchases. It is based on the ratio of the cost of a specific commercial time slot and the rating of the television program where the time slot will be shown.

**crisis circumstances**   The content of the news surrounding the public relations crisis.

**crisis scope**   The scope of the public relations crisis is essentially determined by the number of people exposed to the negative news and what percentage of these people are the fashion company's audience.

**crisis sphere**   The environment in which the public relations crisis is developing and where the audience is receiving the negative news.

**crisis timing**   The time, in relations to other events and news, when the public relations crisis develops and the duration of the negative exposure.

**curbside meeting**   A one-on-one meeting between a manager and subordinate in an informal setting.

**cutline**   The newsroom jargon for a photo caption. The cutline is a sentence or two placed directly underneath or next to a photo, describing what happened in the photo, which usually relates to the story and identifies the people in it.

**demographics**   A set of characteristics of a certain group that describes its members backgrounds, economic status, education, and other social factors.

**design**   Refers to the look and shape of the clothing item. This includes the selection and coordination of colors, patterns, themes, and other aesthetic elements.

**editorial**   An article written by, or on behalf of, the publication's editor or editorial board, typically giving an opinion on a well-known issue rather than reporting on facts. Editorials are printed either on their own page of a newspaper or in a clearly marked-off column, and are always labeled as editorials to avoid confusion with news coverage.

**editorial agenda**   The list of stories that will run in the next issue, their approximate hierarchy in terms of importance, which reporter will cover it, and in which section of the publication it will be published. This list is typically the result of an editorial meeting.

**editorial calendar**   Most weekly and monthly publications offer an editorial calendar for the year, which typically offers the main topics that will be reviewed in each issue throughout the year.

**editorial meeting**   A meeting with the editorial staff where the editors and reporters discuss the current news, agree upon which stories should be covered, and plan for future issues.

**fabricated crisis**   The result of smearing efforts by external sources—such as dishonest competitors, disgruntled employees, or irresponsible reporters—who have vested interest in seeing the fashion company experience negative exposure. This public relations crisis develops even though the fashion company has done nothing wrong.

**filler** News that is not timely, general information, or a public service message used to fill space in a publication or time in a radio or television presentation. A profile about the fashion company's head designer is an example of a filler.

**goodwill** Approval and support for the company, its brands, and personnel, typically as a result of the company's good reputation in the community.

**grassroots public relations** Initiatives that proactively improve the public image of the company, its brands, or products through informal, non-media, and interpersonal channels whereby members of the target audience themselves are encouraged to speak well of the company with other members of the target audience.

**grip-and-grin shot** A photo that features people receiving awards, cutting ribbons, or passing out fundraising checks. In such a photo, the person usually poses shaking hands with the person who presents them with the award and smiles at the camera.

**guerrilla public relations** Getting out there to the source of the target market with public relations strategies that work on the street level.

**image advertisement** An advertisement that creates brand awareness rather than achieves immediate buying reaction.

**impression** Each individual member of the audience that is exposed to a published story. In terms of fashion public relations, a story that is published in the media receives potentially the number of impressions that is equal to the total number of the media's audience for the specific issue, program, or Web page where the story was published. Virtually every media outlet—print, broadcast, or online—keeps track of its audience numbers—readers, viewers, listeners, or online visitors—for each of its programs and makes the data available for its advertisers.

**influencer** A person who is involved in public life to some degree and is well regarded by a large number of members of the community and the media. An influencer may be a local celebrity, a social activist, a politician, a journalist, or even the local football team's coach. When an influencer speaks, people listen and often follow.

**integrity** Adhering to an accepted set of ethical and moral standards. In business, integrity translates in the broadest terms to being honest and truthful with one's publics, keeping one's word, and delivering what one promises.

**intermediate audience** An audience of a company that has the power or responsibility to pass on messages from the company to other audiences. A newspaper is an example of an intermediate audience because it can disseminate the company's news to the public or industry professionals.

**kill a story**   When the editor or the reporter stops a story from being researched, written, or printed after it was already assigned and slated to be covered. A story is typically killed due to difficulties in researching or verifying facts, when the story is no longer timely, or when there is not enough space in the issue and other stories take precedence.

**lede**   or *lead* paragraph, is the first paragraph in a story and like the headline. It has to be a strong and informative paragraph that indicates the importance of the story and stresses its newsy nature.

**marketing public relations**   The marketing-oriented aspect of public relations.

**marketing triangle**   The combination and coordination of the three marketing elements—advertising, public relations, and promotion—to create the maximum consumer interest in the brand's products.

**media**   (plural of *medium*) Refers to the various channels of communication that are trusted to provide information to the mass public.

**media angle**   A specific aspect of the news item that is likely to be of interest to the media and result in coverage. A part of the media angle is also the actual approach that is being utilized to communicate this news item to the media.

**media bias**   Occurs when the reporter doing the story for some reason has a negative agenda against the fashion company from the start. The reason for the bias could be a personal reason—i.e., the reporter dislikes the company or its brands—or perhaps could be a rumor that he or she has heard about the company that now taints his or her view of it.

**media clip**   A sample issue or a reproduction of the issue containing a published news story about the fashion company. The media clip should include the logo or masthead of the publication, the date, the section (if possible), and the actual news story that was published.

**media compatibility**   The ability of a person to speak intelligently and professionally with the media.

**media relations**   Activities that implement initiatives that gain positive coverage by—and placement of positive stories in—the mass media without paying for it directly through advertising.

**media sphere**   When the public relations crisis is published in the media (in print, broadcasting, or online) it is said to be occurring in the media sphere.

**mug shot** or *head shot,* is a smaller photo of the person's face, typically a front portrait measuring from the chest or the bottom of the neck to the top of the head. The name is borrowed from police terminology, where the mug shot describes the front and side profile photos taken when someone is arrested.

**need** A problem the customer wants to solve, or something the customer feels he or she should have. In fashion public relations, we find that the audience's fashion needs are influenced by trends and styles.

**negative false rumor** Outright lies that circulate in the public or virtual spheres through word of mouth.

**news story** The main message about the news that the company is aiming to relay to the media and its audience. The story is essentially a description of the public relations method that the company is utilizing to implement the campaign. For example, if the fashion company selects the event method, then the story is an exciting description of the event that explains why it is news. To be effective, the story must be timely, newsy, unique, and worthy of publishing in the media.

**newsroom** The department of a newspaper, magazine, television, or other media organization that gathers and reports on the news.

**nonprofit organization** A corporation that exists to serve the community rather than to make a profit, regardless of which segment of the community it serves.

**objection** A reason the editor or reporter offers for not picking up the story. Objections are questions or statements that indicate the concerns that the editor or reporter has about a news story or product. These must be answered properly before the story is picked up.

**photo opportunity** The opportunity for the media to take photos or video footage, or to utilize already existing photos or footage that can be used as visual aids to the news story. Also called the *photo op.*

**pick up** When a media outlet expresses interest in the public relations story and then publishes it, it is said to have picked up the story.

**pitch** In fashion public relations, the talking points that are voiced or written to the media in order to solicit publicity about the news story.

**point of interest** Something that is of interest to both the public relations person and the media person, either within the business relationship's framework or personally.

**positivism**   The likelihood of the person to speak positively about the company and its products.

**preliminary budget report**   A report that estimates the overall cost of the campaign. Often, it also projects costs against a calendar, breaks the costs down according to categories of costs, and compares investment against the expected ROI to demonstrate whether the initiative is sensible from a business standpoint.

**press center**   The press center is essentially a virtual press kit—albeit more comprehensive and compact. It is that section of the fashion company's Web site that offers current and past press releases, artwork, and general company information to the media. The press center often displays a collection of the company's published media clips as well.

**press release**   An official company document that gives information about the company's news story to the media and the public. It typically follows a certain format that makes it easier for the media to use, and consists of the facts and quotes that the company would like to media to include in the story.

**proactive marketing public relations**   Acts as an anticipatory tool for product awareness that is used in concert with advertising, promotions, and selling.

**producer**   The newsroom employee in a television news station responsible for organizing television news programs. He or she decides which reports go on the air and which get left out. He or she puts together *running orders*—a list of the stories in what they decide is the right order.

**product shot**   A photo of a fashion item by itself or with other items. This shot does not include people, but rather solely objects and sceneries.

**productivity**   The ratio between the time spent by a fashion company employee on a particular task and the results received in return from that task. Productivity is typically measured against a range that is considered normal by the company. If time spent is higher than the norm but the return is low, then productivity is low and vice versa.

**promotion**   Non-media-based actions taken by the company to get the brand's products noticed by its publics, such as sales events, brochures, direct mail pieces, newsletters, community lectures, sponsorship of sporting events, and so on.

**proxy buyer**   A person who purchases a fashion item on behalf of the end user. The intermediate buyer purchases the item for the end user but does not use the item personally; for example, a husband buys a dress as a gift for his wife, or a mother buys a pair of shoes for her young daughter.

363

**public**   A distinct group of people who share a specific type of interaction with the company, and whose support—or lack thereof—affects the company's success. This is not limited to the consumer sphere only. Other publics include government regulators, board members, employees, stockholders, suppliers, and all members of the vast media. For example, one public of a clothing manufacturer is all of its garment suppliers. If relations with this public worsen considerably due to a poor financial report, scandals, or other negative news, the manufacturer may not get its garments, buttons, zippers, and so on, and production could stall leading to the company's closing. People who do not affect the company's success cannot be considered a public. For example, children are not a public for the manufacturer of business suits for adults.

**public opinion**   A highly complex topic, public opinion has been interpreted in a variety of manners and been the subject of several theories. For the purpose of this text and subject, public opinion can be defined as the aggregate attitudes or beliefs that are common to a large majority of a specific public. It is a viewpoint that one has adopted by either one's own experience or by exposure to influences that surround them in our society.

**public relations**   Refers to the act of building, improving, and enhancing relationships and communication with the company's various publics to create a favorable public image. Public relations' primary objective is to foster mutual goodwill between a company and its publics. Public relations increases brand awareness and creates favorable attitudes toward a company, its personnel, and its products or services.

**public relations objective**   A quantitative target for a public-relations-related initiative that the departmental person can achieve within the duration of a campaign, a season, or other specified time frame.

**public relations audience**   A group of individuals who have a business relationship—or the potential for one—with the fashion company, and who share some common characteristics that affect their perception of the company's corporate communications.

**public relations campaign**   A series of publicity actions that is actively pursued with the aim of achieving certain goals to improve the company's public image with its audiences.

**public relations campaign goal**   The result that the public relations campaign aims to achieve. As an example, a retailer that is opening up a new store in the neighborhood could set the campaign goal of making that new store known in the local community.

**public relations crisis**   A negative event, action, or statement that is spread or has the potential of being spread among the company's audience and that can damage the public image of the fashion company. The crisis can be based on factual reports, totally false allegations, or a combination of the two.

**public relations marketing**  A planned activity to communicate a positive understanding and acceptance between an organization and its public. It guides management in estimating changes in the marketplace by the response of public opinion.

**public relations message**  The public relations message is in essence a summary of what we want to communicate to a particular public relations audience. The message should be a concise, one to two sentence description of the main concept that we want the audience to retain from the initiative. For example, if a fashion company sponsors a local charity, its message could be, "Our company is an active member of the community and cares about its people."

**public relations method**  A set of public relations guidelines that outlines the process, formula, and practical steps for achieving a specific public relations result. Although there can be more than one method to achieve that specific result, each method delineates a unique set of actions that should be taken and serves as a map for those involved in the implementation of the campaign.

**publicity**  Refers to any favorable media exposure generated by public relations. Publicity includes any favorable news stories, television segments, radio time, and Internet exposure about the company's activities, products, and services. This could range from a brief mention of the company to the entire piece focusing on it. Notice that whereas some argue that "any publicity is good publicity," we argue that "any publicity is good publicity only if handled right." Negative publicity can only be good publicity if it's countered properly with positive public relations initiatives that address the source of the problem and spur favorable publicity later on.

**psychographics**  A set of characteristics of a certain group that describes its behavioral and psychological structure.

**quality**  The grade and relative excellence of the garments, materials, stitching, dying, and other fabrication processes used in the production of any clothing item.

**quote**  1. (verb) The act of printing a source's comment to a reporter. Usage: "The reporter quoted the manager as saying so and so." 2. (noun) A source's comment to a reporter. Usage: "He claimed that his quote was misinterpreted."

**ratings**  A method of measuring a TV program's popularity. Each rating point equals one percent of the total number of television households in the United States. Thus, a rating of 10 means the program was watched by 10 percent of the total number of potential viewers.

**reactive marketing public relations**   A response to negative situations that the organization may be confronted with and the attempts to act as a band-aid to reduce the amount of negative public opinion.

**responsibilities, functions, and duties (RFDs)**   Management's guidelines for job responsibilities and performance of its personnel.

**return on investment (ROI)**   The ratio between the revenues generated by a certain project and the costs for that project. High ROI means that the project was profitable whereas low ROI means that the company did not recoup its investments.

**sale**   An exchange of goods and services designed to deliver a mutual benefit for both buyer and seller, resulting in a continual and positive relationship.

**self-inflicted crisis**   When the source of the public relations crisis is the fashion company's own actions—whether erroneous or intentional.

**shadowing**   The process by which a manager, in agreement with the employee, follows her or him during the day, observing the manner in which the employee conducts herself or himself at the daily job function. The manager remains an observer and creates an assessment of the employee's strengths and weaknesses.

**slander**   A term used in both journalism and law, indicating a false, damaging, and defamatory statement or report that is printed or aired by the media about a company, individual, or a product. The media has a responsibility to fact-check everything prior to printing it, and that goes for negative information as well. When a media report contains slander, the company or individual who is the target of the slander can take the media outlet to court to demand a retraction and reparation.

**smear campaign**   A calculated campaign to hurt the fashion company's image, organized—typically anonymously—by an entity that is opposed to the fashion company.

**social media**   Sites based on user participation and user-generated content, i.e., social networking sites like LinkedIn, Facebook and Twitter.

**social networking**   The interaction between a group of people who share a common interest.

**source**   An organization, person, book, publication, or other source that gives information to the reporter for an article. Excluding a source that must remain anonymous for fear of retaliation, the reporter should cite the source for each fact used in the story.

**spin**   Presenting an event or action in such a way that will reflect most favorably upon the company. In conversational terms, spin typically implies that the presentation is not done in a truthful way, or that the facts presented are skewed so as to make the company look better than it deserves.

**supplied photo opportunity**   The type of photo op where the fashion company or its public relations firm provides the media with professionally taken photographs or video footage to accompany the story.

**supply chain**   The flow of goods through all the steps involved in getting the products to the end user.

**strengths, weaknesses, opportunities, and threats (SWOT) analysis**   A marketing term denoting an evaluation of these areas as it relates to the company, its brands, and products. A proper SWOT analysis is essential for strategic planning in any business.

**top-down budgeting**   Predicates that upper management decides on the public relations budget and hands it down to lower management with little to no flexibility allowed for the public relations director. A corollary to the bottom-up budgeting procedure.

**top-down/bottom-up budgeting**   Combines the top-down and bottom-up budgeting methods, and is the preferred process.

**video news release (VNR)**   The television version of the printed press release; it translates the printed word into the sound and pictures television newsrooms need.

**video news story (VNS)**   The video package containing a complete televised news report, which is ready to go on the air.

**video opportunity**   A relatively new category of photo op, where the news story is captured on digital video.

**viral/street public relations**   The improvement of public opinion as a result of the dissemination of positive information about the company through word of mouth by the average person.

**virtual sphere**   When the public relations crisis exists in the virtual sphere of the Internet.

**Web log (blog)**   A Web-based diary or log of personal thoughts. Typically, blog writers specialize in certain topics and express opinions and editorial commentary about these specific issues.

# References

## Chapter 1

About.com. *Urban legends.* Retrieved February 16, 2009, from http://urbanlegends
.about.com/od/tommyhilfiger/a/tommy_hilfiger.htm?terms=hilfiger

Blacks Retail Analysis (Eds.). (2006, February 10). Hilfiger's profit sinks
on slow U.S. orders. Retrieved on February 27, 2009, from http://www
.blacksretailanalysis.com/daily/archive/2006/02/hilfigers_profi.html

Morrison, P. (2007, June 30). Liz Claiborne, First internet urban legend victim?
*Los Angeles Times.*

Oprah.com. (2007, May 2) Oprah Winfrey interviews Tommy Hilfiger.
Retrieved February 16, 2009, from http://www2.oprah.com/tows/slide/
200705/20070502/slide_20070502_350_101.jhtml

*The Oprah Winfrey Show.* (1999, January 11). Transcript.

Snopes.com. (2002). The Tommy Hilfiger Internet rumor. Retrieved on February 16, 2009, from http://www.snopes.com/racial/business/hilfiger.asp

Theinsider.com. (2008). About Steven Cojocaru. Retrieved June 9, 2008 from
http://www.theinsideronline.com/about/stevencojocaru.html

Truthorfiction.com. (2009). The Liz Claiborne Internet rumors. Retrieved
on February 16, 2009, from http://www.truthorfiction.com/rumors/l/
lizclaiborne.htm

Walker, R. (2002, February 28). Consumer rumors. *Slate online.* Retrieved on
February 16, 2009, from http://www.slate.com/id/2062623

## Chapter 2

Gordon, M. (2001, August 5). Advantage Reebok. law.com. Retrieved on February 26, 2009, from http://www.calbaptist.edu/dskubik/reebok_nike.htm

Cantril, H., & Strunk, M. (Eds). (1951). *Public opinion*. Princeton, NJ: Princeton University Press.

C-SPAN Online. (2002, June 2). *American writers: Walter Lippmann*. Retrieved on February 17, 2009, from www.americanwriters.org/writers/Lippmannn.asp

Lippmann, W. (1922). *Public opinion*. (1997 reissue). New York: Free Press.

Maslow, A.H. (1943). A theory of human motivation. *Psychological Review, 50*, 370–96.

Montaigne, M. (1575). *Essays* (Cotton, C., Trans.). Retrieved on February 17, 2009, from Iowa State University's eserver.org: http://philosophy.eserver.org/montaigne-essays.txt

PR Newswire Release. (2003). Juicy Couture meets their match. Retrieved on March 20, 2003, from http://www.prnewswire.com

Society of Professional Journalists. (1996). Society of Professional Journalists' code of ethics. Retrieved on February 17, 2009, from http://www.spj.org/ethicscode.asp

## Chapter 3

ABC. (2006, June/December). Full year average 2006. Statement.

ABC. (2007, December 12). MRI Fall 2007 (Base: adults). Statement.

Apparel Search. (Eds.). (2009). Online fashion magazines and fashion news; fashion; apparel & textile industry. Retrieved on February 19, 2009, from www.apparelsearch.com/online_news_magazines.htm

Claritas Web site. (2009). Claritas customer profiling: Understand the characteristics of your customer. Retrieved on February 18, 2009, from http://www.claritas.com/claritas/customer-profiling.jsp

Hoovers Online. (2009). Recreational Equipment, Inc. information page. Retrieved on February 18, 2009, from www.hoovers.com/rei/—ID__54866—/free-co-factsheet.xhtml

Love My Shoes. (2009). Online press center. Retrieved on February 18, 2009, from www.lovemyshoes.com/content.cfm/section/press

March, L. (2008, April 24). High-end retailers banking on thanks. msnbc.com. Retrieved on February 18, 2009, from www.msnbc.msn.com/id/2363654

Mendelsohn. (2007). 2007 affluent head of household survey; HHI $85,000+. Statement.

New York Magazine (Eds.). (2009). Valentino. Retrieved on February 19, 2009, from nymag.com/fashion/fashionshows/designers/bios/valentino

O'Dwyer, J. (2005, June 29). Jack O'Dwyer's public relations newsletter. Retrieved on February 18, 2009, from www.odwyerpr.com/members/jack_odwyers_nl/2005/0629.htm

Recreational Equipment, Inc. (2009). About us. Retrieved on February 17, 2009, from www.rei.com/aboutus

Sherman, G. J., & Perlman, S. (2006). *The Real World Guide to Fashion Selling & Management.* New York: Fairchild Publications.

Sun-Sentinel (Eds.). (2008, March 20). Tribune puts WSFL-TV and Sun-Sentinel under one roof. *The Sun-Sentinel.*

Wilson, E. (2008, February 10). Marc Jacobs play it safe? Come on, now. *The New York Times.*

## Chapter 4

Breakthrough Breast Cancer. (2009). Retrieved February 19, 2009, from www.breakthrough.org.uk

Browning, A. (2005, September 28). The power of T-shirt slogans. BBC News. Retrieved February 19, 2009, from http://news.bbc.co.uk/2/hi/uk_news/4287446.stm

Drucker, P. *The Practice of Management.* (1954,1986). New York: Harpers Collins.

Fashion Targets Breast Cancer. (2009). Overview. Retrieved February 19, 2009, from www.fashiontargetsbreastcancer.com/index.php?cmd=overview&country_id=1

First Research, Inc. (2008, June 9). *Public relations industry report.* Retrieved on February 26, 2009, from www.firstresearch.com/industry-research/Public-Relations.html

Public Relations Society of America. (2000). Code of ethics. Retrieved on February 18, 2009, from www.prsa.org/aboutUs/ethics/preamble_en.html

## Chapter 5

Anderson, W. T. (1996, January 5). Astroturf—The big business of fake grass-roots politics. *Pacific News Service.*

Clark, C. (2007, October 31). Olsen twins focus on fashion career. *USA Today.*

Covert, J. (2008, May 22). Talbots in '08: Outlook's dim. *The New York Post.*

eNR Services, Inc. (n.d.). Case study: Lia Sophia. Share the love of jewelry. Press release.

The Gap. (2006). The Global Fund and (PRODUCT) RED. Retrieved July 5, 2008 from www.gapinc.com/red/progress_article_3.html

Hagwood, R. S. (2008, June 22). Timely help from celebs. *The Sun-Sentinel.*

Hein, K. (2008, July 17). Nike prepares global effort: Based around Beijing Olympics, the campaign includes a new worldwide spot and an event called 'Human Race.' *Adweek.* Online. Retrieved on February 19, 2009, from www.adweek.com/aw/content_display/creative/news/e3i50336777802bc299c1d9ae542bbbce8d

Nixon, R. (2008, February 6). Bottom line for (Red). *The New York Times.*

Shi, J. (2008, April 7). Going for the gold: Ralph Lauren to outfit U.S. team at Beijing Olympic games. *Fashion Week Daily.* Retrieved on February 19, 2009, from www.fashionweekdaily.com/news/fullstory.sps?inewsid=547827

The Talbots, Inc. (2008). Former Calvin Klein designer to lead design direction of the Talbots brand. Press Release. Retrieved on February 19, 2009, from www.thetalbotsinc.com/press/releases/2008/05202008.asp

Vitale, R. P., and Giglierano, J. J. (2002). *Business to business marketing, Analysis & practice in a dynamic environment.* Florence, KY: Thomson South-Western.

Warhol, A. (1977). *The philosophy of Andy Warhol, from a to b and back.* New York: Harvest Books.

## Chapter 6

Fashion Fights Poverty. (2008, April 29). Fashion fight's poverty's 2008 benefactor & presenting sponsor. Retrieved on February 19, 2009, from http://www.sinpr.com/ffp/media/FFPPressRelease_4.28.08.pdf

Associated Press. (2007, December 3). What's Victoria's Secret? Creating "lingerie fantasy."

Hoover's, Inc. (2009). MySpace.com. Company description. Retrieved on February 19, 2009, from hoovers.com/myspace/—ID__148345—/free-co-profile.xhtml

Hagwood, R. S. (2008, July 28). The hot new swimsuits are bright and luxe. *Sun-Sentinel.*

Merriam-Webster. (2003). *Collegiate Dictionary* (11th ed.). Springfield, MA: Merriam-Webster, Inc.

## Chapter 7

Barnett, L. (2008, June 4). Going for green. *Vogue.* Retrieved on February 19, 2009, from www.vogue.co.uk/news/daily/080604-hm-goes-organic.aspx

H & M. (2008, June 4). H&M continues to go organic. Press release. Retrieved on February 19, 2009, from www.hm.com/us/press/pressreleases/fashion/fashionpressrelease.ahtml?pressreleaseid=642&nodeid=334

Project for Excellence in Journalism. (2006). Principles of journalism. Retrieved on February 19, 2009, from www.journalism.org/resources/principles

## Chapter 8

Appleton, G. (2009). Garrett Appleton Production, Inc. Retrieved on February 20, 2009, from www.garrettappleton.com

Baker, C. (2005, June 29). TV news colored by dose of PR. *The Washington Times.* Retrieved on February 20, 2009, from http://washingtontimes.com/news/2005/jun/28/20050628-094856-8762r/

Business World News. (2001, February). Medialink Study.

Fortini, A. (2006, February 8). Fashion: The language of style. How the runway took off, a brief history of the fashion show. *Slate* magazine. Retrieved on February 20, 2009, from www.slate.com/id/2135561

Mercedes-Benz Fashion Week. (2008, August 11). Mercedes-Benz Fashion Week announces preliminary line-up for the spring 2009 collections in New York—September 5th–12th. Press release.

Sherman, G., & Perlman, S. (2006). *The real world guide to selling & management.* New York: Fairchild Publications.

## Chapter 9

American Business Media. (2005, March) Editorial code of ethics. Retrieved on February 20, 2009, from www.americanbusinessmedia.com/images/abm/pdfs/committees/EdEthics.pdf

Bravo TV. (2009). Bios: Nina Garcia. Retrieved on February 20, 2009, from www.bravotv.com/project-runway/bio/nina-garcia

Harvard Business School. (2006, June 29). Professor Theodore Levitt, legendary marketing scholar and former Harvard Business Review editor, dead at 81. Press release. Retrieved on February 20, 2009, from www.hbs.edu/news/releases/062906_levittobit.html

Levitt, T. (1983, September-October). After the sale is over. *Harvard Business Review*, pp. 87-93.

Sherman, G., & Perlman, S. (2006). *The Real World Guide of Selling & Management.* New York: Fairchild Publications.

## Chapter 10

The American Red Cross. (2008). 2006 IRS Form 990, return of organization exempt from income tax. Retrieved August 6, 2008 from www.redcross.org/static/file_cont7537_lang0_3150.pdf

Breakthrough Breast Cancer. (2008). Fashion targets breast cancer 2008. Retrieved August 6, 2008 from www.breakthrough.org.uk/who_we_are/media_centre/new_fashion_1.html

California Fashion Association. (2007). Official Web site. Retrieved on February 21, 2009, from www.calfashion.org

Ebony Fashion Fair. (2008). History. Retrieved on February 20, 2009, from http://www.ebonyfashionfair.com/assembled/history.html

Givhan, R. (2006, April 10). Meet me at the Ebony Fashion Fair. *The Seattle Times*, Living Section.

Internal Revenue Service. (2009, January 5). Exemption requirements. Retrieved on February 21, 2009, from http://www.irs.gov/charities/charitable/article/0,,id=96099,00.html

National Federation of Independent Business. (2002, April 1). What you should know before forming a partnership. Retrieved on February 21, 2009, from www.nfib.com/object/1583856.html

NBC. (2008). Macy's Parade. Retrieved October 7, 2008 from www.nbc.com/Macys_Parade

Office of the Mayor of New York City. (2005,1 December 2). Mayor Bloomberg and Heidi Klum announce measures to support city's garment and fashion sector. Press release.

Ries, A., & Ries. L. (2002). *The fall of advertising and the rise of PR*. New York: HarperCollins.

Saks Fifth Avenue. (2006). About us: Social responsibility. Retrieved on February 12, 2009, from www.saksincorporated.com/aboutus/social responsibility.asp

U.S. Census. (2000). Profile of general demographic characteristics. *Data set: Census 2000 Summary File 1.*

## Chapter 11

Cosmopolitan (Eds.). (2008, September). What to wear now. *Cosmopolitan* magazine. September 2008. Retrieved on February 21, 2009, from www .cosmopolitan.com/style/fashion/What-to-Wear-Now

Cosmopolitan Media Kit. (2009). 2008 display advertising rates. Media Kit. Retrieved in 2008 from www.cosmomediakit.com/r5/cob_page.asp ?category_code=rate

Cosmopolitan Media Kit. (2008). 2008 total paid circulation. Retrieved on February 21, 2009, from www.cosmomediakit.com/r5/showkiosk .asp?listing_id=360478&category_code=circ&category_id=27808

## Chapter 12

Bernstein, A. (2000, April 27). Nike opens its books on sweatshop audits. *Business Week*. Retrieved on February 21, 2009. from www.businessweek.com/bwdaily/dnflash/apr2000/nf00427b.htm

Bernstein, A. (2004, September 20). Nike's new game plan for sweatshops: Unlike giants such as Wal-Mart, it now has a system to inspect—and try to improve—working conditions at supplier factories. *Business Week*. www .businessweek.com/magazine/content/04_38/b3900011_mz001.htm

CNN. (2004, March 10). Stewart convicted on all charges: Jury finds style maven, ex-broker guilty of obstructing justice and lying to investigators.

CNN Financial News. (1998, December 15). Dog-fur coats recalled. Retrieved on February 21, 2009, from http://money.cnn.com/1998/12/15/companies/coats

Dividend (Eds.). (1994, Spring/Summer) Guideposts Through The Minefield. Dividend, University of Michigan Business School magazine. http://deep blue.lib.umich.edu/bitstream/2027.42/50766/2/1994-springsummer-dividend-text.pdf

Greenhouse, S. (1997, November 8). Nike shoe plant in Vietnam is called unsafe for workers. *The New York Times.* Retrieved on February 21, 2009, from http://query.nytimes.com/gst/fullpage.html?res=9A06EEDC1539F9 3BA35752C1A961958260&sec=&spon=&pagewanted=all

Greenhouse, S. (1999, October 8). Nike identifies plants abroad making goods for universities. *The New York Times.* Retrieved on February 21, 2009, from http://query.nytimes.com/gst/fullpage.html?res=9B04E1D71331F93BA35 753C1A96F958260

The Humane Society of the United States. (2006, December 12). Burlington pulls offending fur ads. Retrieved on February 21, 2009, from www.hsus .org/furfree/news/burlington_pulls_fur_ads.html

Noricks, C. (2007, March 27). Fashion public relations in crisis: The relationship between fashion public relations and fashion blogs. PR Couture Web site. Retrieved on February 20, 2009, from www.prcouture.com/2007/03/27/ fashion-pr-in-crisis-the-relationship-between-fashion-pr-and-fashion-blogs

Pauchant, T. C., & Mitroff, I. I. (1992). *Transforming the Crisis-Prone Organization: Preventing Individual, Organizational, and Environmental Tragedies.* San Francisco: Jossey-Bass.

Press, E. (1999, March 18). A Nike sneak. *The Nation.* Retrieved on February 21, 2009, from www.thenation.com/doc/19990405/press

Rucker, P. (2008, February 5). Md. bill seeks to end mislabeling of fur coats. *Washington Post*, p. B01. Retrieved on February 21, 2009, from www .washingtonpost.com/wp-dyn/content/article/2008/02/04/AR2008 020402979_pf.html

Sanders, H. M. (2007, February 24 ). Mea culpas don't cut it for faulty firms. *The New York Post.* Retrieved on February 21, 2009 from http://www.nypost .com/seven/02242007/business/mea_culpas_dont_cut_it_for_faulty_ firms_business_holly_m__sanders.htm

## Chapter 13

Drucker, Peter. *Managing for Results.* Harper & Row: New York, 1964.

Volcom, Inc. 2008, Sept 16. Volcom to present at Thomas Weisel Partners 2008 annual consumer conference. Online press release. Retrieved October 10, 2008.

# Suggested Readings

Advertising Age (Eds.). (2007, June 25). 100 leading national advertisers in 2007—Dollars in millions. *Advertising Age.*

Agee, D. L., Ault, W. K., & Wilcox, P. H. (2008). *Public relations writing and media techniques* (5th ed.). Boston: Allyn & Bacon.

Albrecht, S. (1996). *Crisis management for corporate self-defense: How to protect your organization in a crisis—how to stop a crisis before it starts.* New York: AMACOM.

Arens, W. F. (1999). *Contemporary advertising* (7th ed.). New York: McGraw Hill.

Cento, A. (1998, March 16). 7 habits for highly effective public relations. *Marketing News.*

Diamond, E., & Diamond, J. (1999). *Fashion advertising and promotion.* New York: Fairchild Publications.

Diamond, E. (1993). *Fashion retailing.* Albany, New York: Delmar Publications.

Dwyer, R. F., & Tanner Jr., J. F. (2006). *Business marketing, connecting strategy, relationships, and learning* (3rd ed.). New York: McGraw-Hill.

Hwang, S. (1993, September 21). Linking products to breast cancer fight helps firms bond with their customers. *Wall Street Journal,* B1.

Mitroff, I. I. (2005). *Why some companies emerge stronger and better from a crisis: 7 essential lessons for surviving disaster.* New York: AMACOM.

Laemer, R. (2004). *Full frontal PR: Building buzz about your business, your product, or you.* Princeton, NJ: Bloomberg Press.

Laermer, R. (2003). *Full frontal PR.* Princeton, NJ: Bloomberg Press.

Lefton, T. (2001 March 19). The great flameout. *The Industry Standard.* Retrieved September 27, 2008 from www.thestandard.com/article/0,1902,22685,00.html.

Lynch, J. E., & Hooley, G. J. (1990). Increasing sophistication in advertising budget setting. *Journal of Advertising Research,* Vol. 30 No.1, pp. 67–75.

Madura, J. (2004). *Introduction to business* (3rd ed.). Florence, KY: Thomson South-Western.

Mazur, G. (1997). Good PR Starts with good research. *Marketing News.*

O'Dwyers. Public Relations Newsletter. Industry news. www.odwyer.com

O'Guinn, T. C., Allen, C., & Semenik, R. J. (2000). *Advertising.* Florence, KY: Thompson South-Western.

Rath, P. M., Bay, S., Petrizzi, R., & Gill, P. (2008). *The why of the buy: Consumer behavior and fashion marketing.* New York: Fairchild Publications.

PR Newswire (1996–2009). For public relations companies, and in-house public relations departments. Media clips and photo service. Retrieved on February 21, 2009, from http://www.prnewswire.com

Promo (Eds.) (2002, March). History in the making: A look at 16 campaigns that helped redefine promotional marketing. *Promo,* p. 23.

Rugimbana, R., & Nwankwo, S. (2003). Chapter 1, *Cross-Cultural Marketing.* Florence, KY: Thompson South-Western.

Seitel, F. P. (2006). *The Practice of Public Relations.* New York: Prentice Hall.

Shrimp, T. A. (2003). *Advertising, promotion, and supplemental aspects of integrated marketing communications* (6th ed.). Mason, OH: Thomson South-Western.

Simon, L., & Pauchant, T. C. (2005, July 28). Developing the three levels of learning in crisis management: A case study of the Hagersville tire fire. *Review of Business.*

Stacks, D. W. (2002). *Primer of public relations research.* New York: Guilford Press.

Stone, E. (2008). *The Dynamics of fashion* (3rd ed.). New York: Fairchild Publications.

Swanson, K., & Everett, J. (2008). *Writing for the fashion business.* New York: Fairchild Publications.

Swanson, K., & Everett, J. (2000). *Promotions in the merchandising environment.* New York: Fairchild Publications.

Vocus. (2009). Web based, automated PR platform, for public relations companies and in-house PR departments and corporations. Retrieved on February 21, 2009 from http://www.vocus.com

Wilcox, D. L., & Cameron, G. T. (2006). *Public relations: Strategies and tactics, study edition* (8th ed.). Boston: Allyn & Bacon.

Winters, A., & Goodman, S. (1999). *Fashion advertising & promotion* (6th ed.). New York: Fairchild Publications.

# About the Authors

## Gerald J. Sherman

After serving in the U.S. Army, Gerald J. Sherman returned to college on the G.I. Bill. He received his AA from Brooklyn College and went on to receive his BA from Empire State College, State University of New York. Because he believed that education is the foundation that prepares one for future success, he went on to receive two post-graduate degrees—an MBA and a DBA.

Sherman has been active in the fashion industry for more than 25 years, and his accomplishments include positions as vice president of Sales and Marketing for major national fashion companies. He is an experienced public relations professional, marketing consultant, author, teacher, seminar organizer, and lecturer. His first book was *Womanpower in Textile & Apparel Sales* (Fairchild Books, New York, 1979, second printing 1980), which he co-authored with Eric Hertz. That book was written while he was teaching at the Fashion Institute of Technology (FIT), New York. Perhaps it was influenced by the fact that he had three daughters. He wanted women to have the same opportunities that their male counterparts had in carving out a career in the fashion industry. He said he wanted to raise the consciousness of fashion executives and open the door for women to play an important role in fashion sales and marketing. He believes the book served as a resource for women who wanted to advance in the fashion industry.

Sherman taught at FIT in New York for more than 10 years as an adjunct professor while active as an executive in the fashion industry. Sherman organized and lectured at more than 50 fashion industry seminars nationally and internationally. He conducted seminars in the Atlanta Apparel Mart and the Dallas Apparel Mart as part of FIT's out-of-state seminars program. Sherman also conducted fashion seminars at the Miami International Mart, Miami, Florida; the seminar "Fundamentals of Sales Management" for the American Management Association (AMA); and, under the sponsorship of FIT and Ashai Dow Chemical, seminars in Tokyo, Japan. Sherman also taught at Miami International University of Art and Design, Miami, Florida; Lynn University Boca Raton, Florida; and Johnson & Wales University, College of Business, North Miami, Florida.

He coauthored the book *The Real World Guide to Fashion Selling & Management* (Fairchild Books, New York, 2006, 2007) with his business partner, Sar S. Perlman, while they actively operated Sherman & Perlman LLC, a public relations, integrated marketing company, and consulting service.

## Sar S. Perlman

Sar S. Perlman is a published author and veteran journalist whose more than 150 articles have appeared in the South Florida *Sun-Sentinel, Art & Antiques* magazine, *Car & Driver* magazine, *Boca Raton Magazine, The Palm Beach Daily News, The Broward/Palm Beach New Times,* and other publications. Perlman received his BA from Florida Atlantic University. Following a five-year stint in journalism, Sar embarked upon a successful career in public relations. He has lectured at California State University at Berkeley and Stanislaus.

# Credits

## Chapter One

| | |
|---|---|
| 1.1 | Getty Images for Tommy Hilfiger |
| 1.2 | Courtesy of Fairchild Publications, Inc. |
| 1.3 | Getty Images |
| 1.5a | Getty Images/Uppercut RF |
| 1.5b | Flying Colours Ltd/Getty Images |
| 1.5c | Getty Images/Comstock Images |
| 1.5d | Getty Images/Tetra Images RF |
| 1.5e | Getty Images |
| 1.5f | Neil Beckerman/Getty Images |
| 1.5g | Getty Images |
| 1.6b | The Advertising Archives |
| 1.6c | Macy's |
| Box 1.4a | Time & Life Pictures/Getty Images |
| Box 1.4b | H. Armstrong Roberts/Classic Stock/Corbis |
| Box 1.4c | Getty Images |
| Box 1.6 | Jeff Vespa/WireImage |

## Chapter Two

| | |
|---|---|
| 2.1 | Time Magazine/Time Inc. |
| 2.3 | Photo © Etienne Boucher |
| 2.5 | Jose Luis Pelaez Inc./Getty Images |

| 2.7 | The Advertising Archives |
| Case Study 2.1 | Charles Sykes/Associated Press |

## Chapter Three

| 3.2a | Getty Images |
| 3.2b | Masterfile |
| Box 3.3 | Karl Prouse/Catwalking/Getty Images |
| Box 3.6 | Robert Harding/Picture Library Ltd/Alamy |
| Box 3.7 | Eric Ryan/Getty Images |
| Case Study 3.1 | Photo courtesy of Edy Eliza |

## Chapter Four

| 4.1 | Bill Pugliano/Getty Images |
| Case Study 4.1 | ShowBizIreland/Getty Images |

## Chapter Five

| Box 5.1 | Dave M. Benett/Getty Images |
| Box 5.4 | Walter McBride/Retna |
| Box 5.5 | Photo courtesy Shannon Nelson |
| Box 5.6 | Richard Drew/Associated Press |
| Box 5.12 | Nike |
| Case Study 5.1 | Photo courtesy of Brian Q. Smith |
| Case Study 5.2 | Photo courtesy Oscar Feldenkreis |

## Chapter Six

| Box 6.3 | Jim Ruymen/UPI/Newscom |
| Box 6.6 | Paul Fenton/Getty Images |
| Box 6.9 | Mark Mainz/Getty Images for Ashley Paige |
| Case Study 6.1 | Photo courtesy Rod Stafford Hagwood |

## Chapter Seven

| 7.2 | Getty Images |

## Chapter Eight

| 8.3 | Photo © Ido Rosenthal |
| 8.4 | Thomas Barwick/Getty Images |
| Box 8.4 | Courtesy of Garrett Appleton |
| Case Study 8.1 | Courtesy of Allison Levy |

## Chapter Nine

| Box 9.2 | Harvard Business School/photo by Richard Chase |
| Box 9.3 | Jennifer Graylock/Associated Press |

Case Study 9.1.1   Photo by Alejandro Garcia (Painting in background by
                   Paul Alexander)
Case Study 9.1.2   Photograph by Richard Pack and Alejandra Garcia,
                   courtesy of Daris Jasper
Case Study 9.1.3   Photo by Richard Pack (Art by Christophe Roberts)

## Chapter Ten

10.2        Julie Jacobson/Associated Press
10.3        Noah K. Murray/Star Ledger/Corbis
10.4        2009 LIFETIME ENTERTAINMENT SERVICES
10.6        WireImage
10.7        Getty Images
10.9        Talia Frenkel/American Red Cross
Box 10.1    Photo courtesy Macy's, Inc.

## Chapter Eleven

Case Study 11.1    Photo courtesy Carrie Englert Zimmerman

## Chapter Twelve

Box 12.1a          Getty Images
Box 12.1b          Pierre Grzybowski/The Humane Society of the United States
Box 12.2           Bebeto Matthews/Associated Press
Case Study 12.1a   Richard Vogel/Associated Press
Case Study 12.1b   Steve Liss/Time&Life Pictures/Getty Images

# Index

389